# *Oil Lamps 3*

*Victorian*

*Kerosene*

*Lighting*

*1860-1900*

## CATHERINE M.V. THURO

EPBM

ECHO POINT BOOKS & MEDIA, LLC
Brattleboro, Vermont

Published by Echo Point Books & Media
Brattleboro, Vermont
www.EchoPointBooks.com

Copyright © 2001, 2018 by Catherine M. V. Thuro

Oil Lamps 3
ISBN:  978-1-63561-069-7 (casebound)

Photography and interior design by Catherine M. V. Thuro
Title page illustration from a Bradley & Hubbard advertisement.

Cover design by Justine McFarland

# Contents

Dedication 4    Acknowledgments 5-6    Photography 7

Foreword 9

Preface
10

1/Introduction to Kerosene Lighting
12-35

2/The Early Years
36-64

3/Patented Lighting
65-78

4/Household Table Lamps
79-139

5/Banquet, Parlour, Student & Piano Lamps
140-165

6/Wall, Bracket, Hall & Hanging Lamps
166-207

7/Miniatures & Night Lamps
208-212

8/Lanterns & Heaters
213-226

9/Accessories & Novelties
227-234

10/Burners & Trimmings
235-248

11/Catalogues & Promotion
249-265

Appendix, Notes, Selected Reading, Index & Value Guide
266 to end

This book is dedicated to the memory

of my parents,

Ida Edna Thompson

and

James Macpherson Gripton.


They provided my brother and me with

an environment that nurtured observation,

education, love, and trust.

# Acknowledgments

The study of this subject continues to be exciting as more examples surface and more primary source information is uncovered. This combined with computer technology has made the potential to explore the kerosene era, to record it, to photograph examples, and to publish the results, both more challenging and rewarding. It makes the stride of the 25 year advance since OL-1 seem more like the leap of a century. In addition there has been an ever-growing number of collectors, dealers, researchers, family, and friends. They have provided the exchange of information and ideas, the examples to record and photograph, and most importantly, the encouragement to complete this work. I wish to express my appreciation to others whose friendship I have enjoyed, who have offered suggestions, and who have brought to my attention significant examples and information. Among them were:

Mary Alice Baier
Joan Bone
Phyllis Book
Dr. Chris Brooks
Mary Jane and David Broughton
Robin and the late Joyce Burne
Robert Calvin
James Claridge
Jack Cooper
E.B. Cox
Bob Culver
Lazlo Czer
David Denny
Jill and Keith Dill
Tom Diosy
Dorothy and John Dobson
Bret Farnham
Frank Fenton
Ralph Fierro
Joanne and Rick Fuerst
Dorothy Gooch
Carmen Gove
Peter Gregory
John Gray
Ron Hackl*
Wendy and Bill Hamilton
Carl Haussman
Jim Hayes
Bob Houle* and Nancy Main
Dennis Johnson
Tim Johnson
Wilma and Cam Kenny
Ken Kercheval
Joyce Lee*
Valerie and Eric Lister
Craig Littlewood*
Tim Martine
Wilbur Meyers
Craig Maue

Leon McCormack
George and Betty Michael
Peggy and Jim Mitchell
Tom Neale
Grant Oakes
Cliff Peterson
Jim Presgraves
Shirley Rope
Bette and Harry Rapp
Barbara and Cedric Ritchie
Joe Rocha
Arthur Ronat
Arthur Sanders
Dianne and John Sewell
Collins and Clarice Shaw
Bob Stahr
Ruth Stanley
Jeanne and John Wenrich
Roy Williamson
Alan Weathers
Evelyn Welz
Bob White

Their shared knowledge and enthusiasm have added depth and broadened the scope of my research.

It is a certainty that during the past few years, without the support and encouragement of my son Randy and friends Kimberly Brown, Joanne and Gerry Bloxam, and Ken and Alice Wilson, this book might never have been completed. They have my heartfelt gratitude.

Fellow authors and their spouses or partners have contributed by sharing their experiences and giving welcome advice. Some of these are mentioned elsewhere, and others include:

Peter Blundell and Marian
Neila and Tom Bredehoft
Dr. Bill Courter and Treva
Peter Cuffley
Thomas Dimitroff
Eason Eige
Regis and Mary Ferson
Hyla Fox
My brother Dr. James Gripton
    and his partner, Dr. Mary Valentich
William Heacock*
Lowell Innes*
Dr. Ann McDonald
George Michael
Dr. Arthur Peterson*
Dr. Loris Russell*
Jane Spillman
John and Elizabeth Welker
Kenneth M. Wilson and Alice
John Wolfe

*deceased

My thanks also to Larry DeCan, Gordon Cheney, Tom Childs, and Lisa Stroup who played important roles in the production of this book, and to Randy and Wesley Thuro for advice and set-up of my computer system. They helped to guide me through the new technology with diplomacy and patience. I am indebted to them.

Museums, institutions, organizations, and their personnel have made substantial contributions by showing me their collections and bringing to my attention, valuable related information. Over the past twenty years, in several instances, the individuals who assisted me have changed positions, moved on, retired or are now deceased. They are therefore listed in alphabetical order. This list includes past and present staff, also in alphabetical order.

The American Antiquarian Society, Worcester, MA. Georgia B. Barnhill.

The Bertrand Museum, De Soto National Wildlife Refuge, Iowa. Leslie Perry Peterson.

Black Creek Pioneer Village, Toronto ON Canada, Marty Brent, Russell K. Cooper, Jim Hansen, Jean Hughes, Lorraine O'Byrne.

The Chrysler Museum, Norfolk, VA, Gary Baker, Nancy Merrill.

The Corning Museum of Glass, Corning, NY, Gail P. Bardhan, Lori A. Fuller, Ernestine W. Kyles, Priscilla Price, Patricia J. Rogers, David B. Whitehouse, Nicholas L. Williams, Virginia Wright.

The National Archives, Washington, DC. Lee Johnson.

Oglebay Institute Museums. Holly H. McClusky.

Pennsylvania Historical & Museum Commission, Drake Well Museum Collection, Titusville, PA. James Mather Photographs. Sue Beates.

The Royal Ontario Museum. Toronto ON. Janet Holmes, Dr. Peter Kaellgren.

The Rushlight Club. *The Rushlight Bulletins*. Marianne Nolan, Editor. Daniel Mattausch, President.

The Sandwich Historical Society Glass Museum, Sandwich, MA. Kirk Nelson.

The Smithsonian Institution, National Museum of American History, Washington, D.C. Sheila Machlis Alexander, Anne Serio.

The Strong Museum, Rochester, NY. Carole Sandler.

Wellington County Museum & Archives, Susan Dunlop.

Whaling Museum, Old Dartmouth Historical Society, New Bedford, MA. Judith M. Downey.

Yarmouth County Museum & Archives. Yarmouth, Nova Scotia.

Permission to use photographs, illustrations, and ephemera has been granted by these public and private sources. On some occasions I was allowed to personally photograph collections.

Association for Preservation Technology. Published reprint from the *Russell & Erwin Catalogue of 1865*, First Facsimile Edition, 1980.

Pages from *Dodd, Werner & Co. and other Catalogues*. Jack Washka Collection.

Dover Publications Inc. Mineo, NY. Palmer Cox, *Brownies* and *The Meriden Britannia Silverplate Company*.

*Fostoria Glass Company, 1893 Lamp Catalogue,* courtesy David B. Dalzell Jr. and Hugh Buzzard.

*Crockery and Glass Journal 1874-1900*. Giftware Business. New York, NY. Sal Mateo, Publisher.

Pages from the reprint, *Hibbard, Spencer, Bartlett & Co. Catalogue*. Circa 1900. James Van Es Collection.

Pages from *Ives Patent Lamp Company Catalogues* from the collection of the late Vincent Ortello.

Pages from the retail *1888 Leonard Catalogue*. Julie Rich Collection.

Pages from *The 1880 Edward Miller & Co. Catalogue*. Alan Weathers.

*The Scientific American*. 1860-1890 issues. The Scientific American, New York, NY. Linda Hertz.

*Charles A. Starr 1861 Illustrated Catalogue*. McGurk Collection.

Photographs are from the collections of:

Kerry Bachler
Joanne and Gerry Bloxam
Francis Brown
Treva and Bill Courter
Larry De Can
Don Jewell
Jack Keiner
Dan and Nancy Mattausch
Ed and Abbie Meyers
Tom Mileham
Jim Miller
Brian Millsip
Brent Rowell
Darrell and Lela Sago
Jack and Emma Jo Washka
Janet and Jim Webber
Eileen and Herb White
and the author.

All have also contributed a wealth of information and expertise.

# Photography

Photography like research and collecting involves a little bit of luck and sometimes just being in the right place at the right time. Such was the case with the photograph of the kitties below. Neither I nor a computer had any part in the composition, or the arrangement. They have continued to be delightful subjects for snapshots and the only glass casualty has been a large prism, neatly snapped in two by a flick of the tail.

With the exception of the examples noted, I have taken all of the photographs. Many were taken under extremely difficult conditions. For those who share my curiosity about camera equipment that others use, I will note them here: My interest began just after high school with a course in photography offered by a noted Canadian nature photographer Victor Crich, F.R.P.S. Starting with a used 2¼" x 2¼" Korelle Reflex (the first to be made in that size) and a set of extension tubes, which served me well for over a decade, the camera is now a collectible.

The change to 35mm followed and in that size, the Asahi Pentax K2 DMD has been my favourite. This camera affords using a wide range of lenses from 50mm macro up to a 400mm telephoto used for a shuttle launch. For pleasure, including the photograph of the kitties below, but not for lamps, my choice is a Pentax 105 zoom with a metal body.

For home and occasional on-site use for lamps, etc., I use a Mamiya RB 6x7 with an 80mm lens. The interchangeable camera backs include Polaroid, black and white, and one for colour. The mirror-up feature, focusing grid and sturdy tripod on a dolly, all improve the final results.

My "studio" consisting of a 2' x 3' apparatus was custom made by the late Ron Hackl. My design, held together with bolts and wing nuts, rests on its own base in front of a north window. It can be disassembled in 15 minutes and used on a card table. Daylight fluorescent bulbs provide background light softened by Translum.

*Below: Senna and Tracy, at ease with fine quality early American lamps and pressed glass.*

# Foreword

Collectors and students of kerosene lighting will celebrate the arrival of the long-awaited *Oil Lamps 3: Victorian Kerosene Lighting 1860-1900* by Catherine M. V. Thuro. Her two previous books on kerosene lighting still in print are widely accepted as the definitive studies in the field. In her first book, *Oil Lamps: The Kerosene Era in North America* (1976), Ms. Thuro broadly examined the history, forms, and design of kerosene lamps. The second *Oil Lamps II* (1983), devoted entirely to glass lamps, was lavishly illustrated with hundreds of her color photographs.

Now in *Oil Lamps 3*, Ms. Thuro presents a broad selection of new examples and observations, again based on her painstaking research in primary sources such as manufacturers' catalogues, advertising, and patents. Added to this are observations she made from studying lamps in her own collection and those in many other public and private collections. In this third book she further elaborates on both the technical development of kerosene lamps, their burners and accessories, and also the design aspects. The book is richly illustrated with photographs that were mostly taken by herself. Ms. Thuro's study of kerosene lamps has been carried out over a period of some 25 years, obviously a labor of love for her subject.

Ms. Thuro gives special attention here to examples grouped by the major functional categories of kerosene lamps. Many of these are illustrated in color. After an overview of kerosene lighting, an introduction to the antecedents puts kerosene in perspective. Particularly fascinating is a large section on the glass lamps and lamp parts that were cargo on the steamboat "Bertrand" when it sank in 1865 on the upper Missouri River, en route to gold mining towns in Montana and Idaho. Ms. Thuro studied and photographed the recovered artifacts — essentially part of a time capsule of the tastes of their day — as part of her tireless pursuit of new information in her field.

Several other unusual topics discussed and illustrated are patent models and original wooden patterns for pressed and blown glass lamps. The final chapter consists of reproduced pages and illustrations from major period manufacturers' catalogues. As in all her books, a thorough index makes finding specific lamps, patterns, manufacturers, etc., easy in the encyclopaedic text.

Recognising the long period of time that Ms. Thuro has enthusiastically devoted herself to the study of kerosene lamps, one cannot help but wonder — and hope — will she soon be thinking of additional important material that she might include one day in an Oil Lamps 4? We would all be the better for that.

Marianne Nolan
Editor, *The Rushlight*

*HRH Queen Victoria.*

## Queen Victoria 1887

The Queen is shown here in a colorful, commemorative chromolithograph designed for distribution throughout her empire. In addition to display in government and public buildings, it was a popular feature of household furnishings. It was considered appropriate to have images of monarchs and much admired figures displayed in the home.

Representing the 50th golden anniversary of her accession to the throne, it includes four black and white vignettes in the corners. They bear the following titles and descriptions in clockwise order starting at the top right:

"THE CORONATION" TAKING THE OATH TO MAINTAIN THE PROTESTANT FAITH.

"AT HOME" PRINCE ALBERT PLAYING THE ORGAN BEFORE MENDELSSOHN.

"THE HEIRS" THE PRINCE AND PRINCESS OF WALES AND ALBERT VICTOR.

"THE MOTHER OF HER PEOPLE" THE CRIMEAN WOUNDED, 1850.

In the corners surrounding the vignettes, roses, thistles, maple leaves, and shamrocks represent England, Scotland, Canada, and Ireland. There is an indistinct signature in the lower right side of the oval.

Background information has graciously been provided by Barbara Rusch, President of the Ephemera Society of Canada.

## Preface

One of the objectives of this book is to present a blend of contemporary illustrations and representative examples extant that will serve as a guide for those who wish to select the appropriate kerosene lighting for American Victorian home restorations. It will also be useful for those who wish to choose kerosene lamps and fixtures to furnish their homes in the Victorian manner. Another objective is to provide collectors and researchers with additional examples and information to that published in *Oil Lamps: The Kerosene Era in North America*; and *Oil Lamps II: Glass Kerosene Lamps*. I will usually refer to the books as OL-1 and OL-2, although others often note them as T-l and T-ll.

Queen Victoria's reign (1837–1901) was characterised by the revival of several architectural styles and foreign influences, that produced an eclectic mixture of home design and furnishings. While these same influences were at work in North America, they usually resulted in different interpretations. This is very evident when one examines the lamps and lighting fixtures produced in North America, vis-a-vis those of England and continental Europe. These and other factors have combined to make the kerosene era the most significant period of lighting before the general usage of electric light.

The lamps made in America were shipped all over the world. It is possible that for decades, they may be discovered in remote areas of the globe. Some may still be in use. An 1860s lamp with perhaps a new burner, chimney, and wick, will function just as well as a lamp from the local hardware or general store. It is for this reason that there is such an amazing nineteenth century selection extant to study and collect.

In addition to the lamps and trimmings of this period, there is also an ever-growing supply of historic records available. These include catalogues, trade journals, books, newspapers, as well as genealogical and legal records. The potential for every sort of ephemera to play a valid role in research is now being recognised. There are so many facets to be explored and so many directions to take that the Victorian kerosene era will continue to capture our curiosity and fascination for decades, and perhaps centuries.

Kerosene lamps made in the nineteenth century were purchased for nineteenth century homes. This book will attempt to illustrate lamps that were suitable for homes of the wealthy, the middle class, and the lower class.

Until Y2K, we have perceived this period as the last century. It was regarded as the century before our time when our parents and perhaps grandparents lived. Now that it is one century removed, we may treasure its history more.

# Oil Lamps 3

CATHERINE M.V. THURO

# Introduction to Kerosene Lighting

CHIMNEY

SHADE

SHADE-HOLDER
BURNER
COLLAR
SHOULDER

THUMBWHEEL

WIDE PLATE
COLLAR

FONT OR FOUNT

CONNECTOR

Measurements given in the text
define the height to the top of
the collar unless otherwise noted.

STEM OR
COLUMN

BASE OR
PEDESTAL

BASE OR
PLINTH

*a. Drawing by Eason Eige.*

a. The composite lamp above, is almost the same as the one pictured in OL-2. Wide plate collar was the contemporary term used for the wide brass bands found on the shoulder. It is descriptive and easy to use. There were additional contemporary descriptions, however these are generally accepted today.

Not shown are the two commonly referred to parts of the font. The neck is the narrow opening under the collar, and the peg is the integral or attached extension at the bottom, that is cemented to the connector. Peg also described separate fonts.

*The Old Style.*

## Nomenclature

"THE OLD STYLE" Many owners of hanging lamps can relate to the situation pictured below, particularly if they own a very handsome, very heavy, and *very hard* cast iron example. It is surprising how seemingly intelligent beings can bump into the same lamp over and over again! Even with an extension device, it is easy to forget to adjust it properly.

Two of the hanging lamps opposite have incorporated methods of raising and lowering. The other two are fixed. All of them however, could be lowered with a separate extension or suspension device attached to the ceiling. Although "hanging lamp" was the generic name, the different variations became classified as shown.

Sometimes heavy cast brass or iron weights were used to counterbalance the lamps so that they could remain steady when lowered for lighting, filling, and cleaning. In other instances, parts of the lamp itself served as a counterbalance. There was a variety of combinations of complex methods employed. Springs, chains, weights, pulleys, and clutches allowed inventors to come up with many practical and patentable solutions. The successful ones allowed the lamp to be raised and lowered easily and to remain steady in a fixed position.

As in OL-2, a superior[ON] is included after original lamp or pattern names that were used by manufacturers, wholesalers or retailers. Other names have been bestowed by authors or dealers.

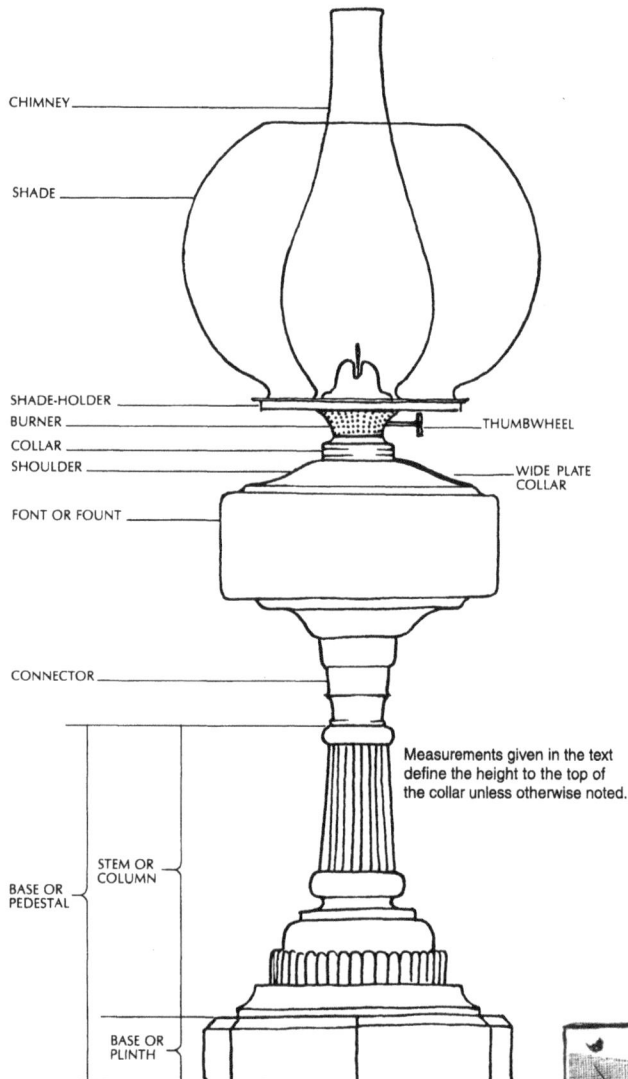

THE NEW AUTOMATIC LOWERED AND PUSHED UP

The Old Style

a.      b.      c.      d.      e.

For the table, all-glass lamps: a. Flat Hand Lamp. b. Footed Hand Lamp.
c. Stand Lamp. d. & e. Night or Miniature Lamps.

f.      g.      h.      i.

For the table: Composite lamps that included figural forms, combined different
materials as in lamp f. Vase or parlour lamps. g. & h. had detachable fonts. Student
lamps like i. had separate fuel reservoirs.

j.      k.      l.      m.

Fixed lamps fastened against the wall: j. & k. were called wall or side lamps.
Bracket lamps such as i. & m. ranged from fixed forms to examples with both horizontal and vertical positioning.

*r. Piano or floor lamp.*

*n. Harp lamp.*      *o. Hall lamp.*      *p. Hanging or library lamp.*

*q. Chandelier.*

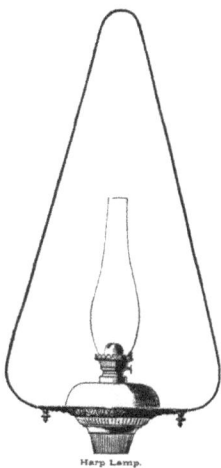

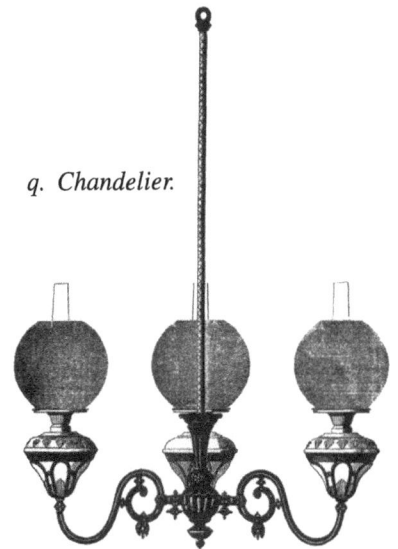

# Glass Lamps – Pressed or Blown?

These descriptions are often used very loosely when describing kerosene lamps. The little lamps shown above are typical of those made between 1840 and 1860. One was entirely free blown, and the rest were made using molds. Virtually all kerosene lamp bases were pressed after 1860. It is therefore not really necessary to use the word when describing bases. One of the challenges the lamps above present is determining the method of manufacture. It is the mold seams, or lack thereof, that tell the tale.

The glass bases were joined to the fonts by:

1. Glass wafers, fused to the font and base.
2. Fusing together while hot.
3. Using a metal connector.

Pressed glass fonts were usually made by forcing molten glass against a patterned mold with a smooth-surfaced plunger attached to a handle. This was rather like a mortar and large pestle. A gob (known as a gather) of molten glass was introduced into the bottom of a metal mold. The plunger was lowered into the mold, forcing the gather up between the mold and the plunger, until it reached the top of the mold. The patterns were made to conform to the lower portion of the font, and the plain upper portion was wider at the top to allow the plunger to be removed.

The next step was to reheat the wide top of the font in the furnace. When it was soft enough to be reshaped, it was drawn in to form a standard size neck opening.

Characteristics of pressed glass fonts.

1. If there are any bubbles on the shoulder, they will likely be oval or elongated, and usually pointing towards the collar.
2. Whether the font is lead glass or lime glass, it will have a shiny surface as a result of reheating when the neck was formed. This effect known as fire-polishing is sometimes used on other articles of glass. Here it is a beneficial by-product of the font pressing process. It is also the reason pressed lime glass fonts are often mistaken for the better quality lead or flint glass.
3. The interior will be smooth unless a patterned plunger was used.

Characteristics of mold-blown patterned glass fonts.

1. A pattern or mold seam on the shoulder close to the collar.
2. The interior will have an irregular surface that corresponds to the exterior pattern.
3. The patterns are less distinct and the glass is not as bright and shiny as may be found on pressed fonts.
4. There may be horizontal mold seams.

# Blown and Pressed, Uncommon and Common Lamp Fonts

The shape of the fonts, narrowing at the shoulder, establishes the fact that (a) and (b) are blown fonts. Both shoulder and horizontal mold seams confirm this. The interior of these lamps is irregular, another indication that the fonts were blown. Occasionally a pressed font has a slightly irregular interior. This could be the result of some uneven shrinking of the thick and the thin parts of the pattern.

Lamp (c) has often been considered a pre-kerosene lamp, however its appearance in catalogues throughout the 1860s make it an excellent choice for anyone wishing to select an all-glass lamp for that period. Most examples, like this one, are made of pressed lead glass and have well-defined patterns. The drawn-in shoulder of this lamp is quite flat. Others have medium to high shoulders, making it difficult to find a matching pair. The bases commonly have small scallops rather than the large ones shown here. The fonts were also combined with early composite bases.

Appropriate lip burners and chimneys are difficult to find and they may be more expensive than the lamps themselves.

Lamp (d) Ripple and Swirl has a softer pressed pattern, more like a blown design. The lack of mold seams above the pattern facilitates the application of engraving.

Pressed opal glass bases, especially round ones, used in combination with brass parts are relatively rare. Other examples are in OL-2 p. 27.

*a. Butterflies and Bows.*
*This rare blown font is combined with a base dated May 8, 1883, made by the La Belle Glass Co.*

*b. Heart base with Circle Band blown font.*
*Another lamp with a rare font combined with a familiar base pictured on the cover of OL-2.*

*c. Bullseye and Fleur-de-lis.*
*One of the most popular pressed, all-glass table lamp patterns of the 1860s.*

*d. Ripple and Swirl.*
*The pressed font is both rare and attractive. This lamp would date from 1860 to the early 1870s.*

*a. Wooden pattern for a pressed Triple Peg and Loop lamp.*

*b. Triple Peg and Loop pressed glass lamp. This would have been an inexpensive 1860s lamp suitable for the bedroom. Height 8¾".*

# Wooden Patterns

Wooden patterns are not to be confused with wooden molds. To experienced glassmen, they indicated how the final product would appear and how the required mold would be made.

This pattern for the Triple Peg and Loop lamp shows how the iron mold for the pressed font would have nearly straight sides above the pattern. It was this upper plain part that would be reheated and drawn in to form the neck. Sometimes the upper part of the design was softened or stretched during this part of the process.

The wooden patterns illustrated here are from the former Vincent Ortello collection. They are finely carved hardwood with a black finish.

*a. Wooden pattern for an 1860s Early Panelled Arches mold-blown lamp.*

The design continuing up the shoulder, and the narrow neck clearly indicate this wooden pattern was intended for a mold-blown font. The only examples of the font (b) that I have seen are ones in storage in museum collections. The one illustrated here is from the collection of the Royal Ontario Museum in Toronto, Canada. Another one I photographed in storage, in The Henry Ford Museum in Detroit, was unmounted, but appeared to be the same size

It was after seeing the unmounted font that I assumed the font on the lamp in OL-1 p. 168 (d), was of the same 1860s period. It was larger and more tapered than this example, but the pattern was the same. The clear glass font and black glass base looked convincing, however the replaced collar was suspect. Later when I saw the lamp in opaque turquoise with a white base and twentieth century collar, it confirmed the fact that these lamps were not of the 1860s.

*b. Early Panelled Arches.*
*Photograph courtesy of the Royal Ontario Museum, Toronto, Canada.*

# Mt. Washington Pressed Fonts

The Mt. Washington Howe[ON] pressed pattern on lamp (a) has been identified from a photograph. The Corning Museum Rakow Library has a collection of documents attributed by Ken Wilson to The Mount Washington Glass Company in New Bedford, Mass. They were acquired with other company records. I will generally refer to this company as MTW. Included with these documents are two photographs of lamp fonts and several of shades. The font photographs are signed Loomis Photo Boston, and the shade photographs are unsigned.

This lamp font was the only pressed example that has unusual straight sides. Like those opposite, it has a free-formed peg with a top that appears to be a wafer. Handwritten names or numbers identify the fonts. This font is marked 1 Howe and another pressed round shape is 1½ Howe. Some named fonts have numbers added to indicate different sizes or shapes of the same pattern.

Other named fonts include Law, an abbreviation for Lawrence that was also used by other glass companies, for what is commonly called Bullseye. There are Baker and Baker cut. Both are pressed patterns and the cut description refers to a wispy wheat style of engraving on the shoulder. An undecorated Baker font in OL-2 p 78 (f) is called Prisms and Diamond Point. Also on p78, MTW's Boston is called Bullseye and Comma. In OL-2 on p 28, the font that I called Prism was given the impressive name Zouave. One definition, according to *The World Book Encyclopedia Dictionary*, is that this was the name given to a member of a certain volunteer regiment in the Union Army during the Civil War.

Photographed against a black background, the frosted and engraved areas and the opal overlays define the shape and designs. Transparent overlays are difficult to distinguish from clear glass. One of these in OL-2 p 81 (d), can only be recognised by the shape and the cutting. The broad pear or turnip-shaped font seemed to be popular with MTW for plain blown fonts, or for glass with one or more layers that is known as overlay, cased or plated.

Lamp (a) with its bold and distinctive design has the depth and sharpness achieved by pressing, combined with the fire-polishing effect obtained while finishing the neck. The brass stem, in need of some restoration, and the double marble base suggest this lamp would be of the 1865–1875 period. Height to the top of the collar is 12".

The shade is pictured along with dozens of others intended for gas and kerosene lighting. Dimensions are not given, however the shades suitable for kerosene lamps appear to have four- or five-inch bases. They include Oregon, ball, and squat globe shapes and feature an impressive variety of engraved designs.

*a. Mt. Washington Howe*[ON].

*a. Courtesy of The Sandwich Historical Society Glass Museum.*

## Mt. Washington Blown Fonts

The lamp (a) and other MTW examples pictured in the
Loomis photographs, were also illustrated in the 1877–78
F. H. Lovell Company catalogue. Examples of these actual
lamp fonts reveal that they are seamless, blown, relatively
thin, and have faint horizontal ridges. Samuel Bowie
obtained a patent April 2nd 1872, that was classified as a
glass patent, but illustrated a lamp. The patent described a
mold for making blown hollow glass objects with a uniform
thickness and without mold seams. The mold was mounted
on a table that was rotated during the blowing process. Since
Bowie, primarily known as a glass decorator, was also from
New Bedford and was associated with the Mt. Washington
Glass Company, it is reasonable to assume these are
examples of this patent.

In the Loomis photograph, font (a) was No. 214 and font
(d) was No. 209. All including (b) and (c) were made by the
same method. The well-defined pressed opal glass base has
bright orange and gold bands. Height to the top of the collar
is 12½".

Oregon shades were also pictured with roughed bands
and this leaf band engraving. Similar designs were used by
other companies.

*d. Has a Mt. Washington # 209 font.*

# Frosted Glass

The word "frosted" is often used to describe a dull matte grey finish on clear glass. This was achieved in different ways that generally can be differentiated upon close examination. If not, the word "frosted" is perfectly acceptable. Lamps, fonts, chimneys, and shades are all found with this type of decoration. The methods are further described in OL-2.

Lamp (a) was acid etched. A hydrofluoric acid bath or fumes were used to produce a thin, light grey, soft texture. Before this treatment, a resist was applied to the areas that remained clear. It was commonly used to enhance the detail of animal and figural stems. There have been several different interesting examples found, however they are seldom seen at sales or shows.

The knobby leaf design with veins that resemble cat's whiskers (b) has been seen on other lamps and glassware. A vintage design is also included on the font and shade. Wedge-shaped rough stone wheels were used to create a relatively coarse textured, and sometimes sloppy, decoration. Copper wheels were used for fine quality and detail.

a. All-glass Owl lamp with a frosted finish and a wide plate collar.

b. Quad Loop lamp with a good quality stone-wheel engraved decoration and matching shade.

Most shades and some chimneys were frosted to soften the light and to provide a design or pattern. Few are found that match a font. Most Oregon shades and many in other shapes had frosted bands. These were accomplished by mounting the shades on a lathe and holding a pad with an abrasive, against the portion to be frosted. It was a fast and inexpensive way to create a single, or a series of bands, that were combined with other decoration.

It is not always easy to determine the techniques used to produce frosted designs and finishes. Shade (c) was first entirely roughed. A resist was applied and the shade was then acid etched to create the design. The etched areas can be clear or softly frosted like this example.

The acid etching process eats into the surface of the glass so that the design produced will be lower than the initial or first layer. The difference can be barely perceptible and often requires the use of a fingertip or fingernail to detect it.

Shade (d) is lightly frosted with roughed bands and a precise design consisting of sandblasted circles. These are loosely connected by stone-wheel engraved "squiggles." This is not a nineteenth century term, however it does describe the curved, wiggly lines that sometimes represent tendrils, and other times simply link designs or attempt to lightly fill in bare areas.

c. Roughed and acid-etched squat shade with a crown.

d. Squat shade with roughed bands, sandblasted circles, and stone-wheel squiggles.

# Sandblasted Glass

Precision is the most obvious characteristic of this technique used to give a frosted look to glass. It became popular in the 1870s and was widely used for chimneys and shades. Geometric designs like the star pattern shown here as well as foliage and scenes were favourite subjects.

To achieve this effect, compressed air was used to bombard the glass with sand. The process is still used today for glass as well as a multitude of other industrial applications. On kerosene chimneys and shades, the matte sandblasted finish produced is sometimes difficult to distinguish from that produced by an acid-etched process. In some instances, particularly at the lower edge of the frosted area, one can sometimes find the clear part lightly peppered from a few stray grains of sand.

Some companies illustrated their sandblasted designs in their advertisements.

The Star in Circle font with matching chimney is from the Centennial cast-iron hanging lamp made by Bradley & Hubbard (see page 192). Its recessed peg allowed it to also be placed on a gas jet.

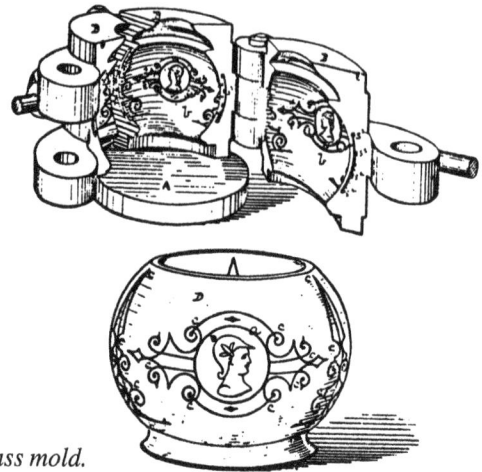

*a. Glass mold.*

# Fine Line Decoration

Creating impressed fine or bright line decoration against a frosted roughed background was the objective of two well-known glassmen. Both Washington Beck, who was head of his own independent moldmaking firm located in Pittsburgh, and Frederick S. Shirley, agent with the Mt. Washington Glass Company (MTW) in New Bedford, Mass., obtained patents for the manufacture of molds to be used for this purpose. Later they became involved in litigation regarding patents.

Beck's patent July 4, 1881 (a) was for the production of a mold made in the usual manner, with the exception of minute vent holes in the edges of the narrow ridges that created fine lines. This was to expel excess air and to allow the molten glass to adequately fill the mold.

The Shirley patent April 26, 1881, was for creating a mold using an electrolytic process. While not part of the patent specifications, Shirley mentioned in testimony at an earlier date that he burnished the fine raised edges of the design to enhance the effect of the fine lines. His mold could also be used to create fine raised or depressed lines. Both patent illustrations depicted globes with classical Greek motifs.

Beck's patent was applied for March 5, 1878 and Shirley's on April 6, 1878. Such a lengthy time for approval suggests problems with the original submissions. This was certainly the case here. Patent office and other records including trade papers and newspapers, provide information about the bright line decoration, and cone-shaped chimneys and shades. The many connections between glass companies make positive attributions difficult.

Washington Beck did not make glass. Chimneys and shades in cone shapes, with or without bright line decoration, were made by Mt. Washington and by Dithridge & Co., a company located in Pittsburgh and later Fort Pitt, Pa. Bradley & Hubbard (B&H), a major wholesale lamp manufacturer and distributor, bought glass from both Dithridge and Mt. Washington.

On July 14, 1868, Robert R. Crosby of Boston patented a cone-shaped chimney that had an "abrupt or nearly right angle" at the bottom of the cone. This was probably produced by Mt. Washington because Crosby assigned a reissue of this patent on May 8, 1877 to F. S. Shirley. The reissue was declared void in 1885. On Dec. 27, 1877, F. S. Shirley sent a letter to Beck requesting the price of molds " the same style of Dithridge but different patterns." The letter made it very clear that MTW intended to copy the Dithridge chimney.

Official documents have recorded the testimony of important witnesses including Beck and Shirley. Beck's descriptions of items made with his molds were consistent with the chimney and shade shown here. Beck also mentioned that Dithridge & Co. of Pittsburgh had manufactured about 200,000 of them. The flared top of this chimney is seen in Mt. Washington and in Dithridge advertisements. A similar one with a torn paper label has the following dates: JULY 14 68, JUNE 15 75, FEB. 13 77, MAY 8 77. The June 15, 75 date was for a patent issued to S. R. Kneeland for a "Conical shade with a reflective component."

The 7⅛" chimney and 5¼" shade shown here were probably made by Dithridge. The Deer, Dog, and Warrior fonts could have been made by any company, including Sandwich. See OL-2 p 26. Testimony by Shirley indicated that about 1876 or 1877, he had seen lamps made with fine lines, but could not identify the maker.

Bradley & Hubbard advertised the figural base of the lamp (a). Beck acknowledged that he made molds for B&H. An employee of Mt. Washington stated that they had been making glass with fine lines since 1875 and that they sold large quantities to B&H and others.

A pair of dated Crosby chimneys can be seen on page 101. The portion below the cone is more rounded than the patent illustration but less so than on the Dithridge cone chimney here, and on several other examples. The pair of chimneys on page 100 without fine line decoration, is marked Pat Feb. 1877 for the Feb. 13, F. S. Shirley patent for cone-shaped chimneys, with " a corrugated radiating surface" Dated examples are known, but not with the surface described.

*In his March 21, 1876 patent for a "Combined Lampstand and Match Box," E.R. Beach of New York, N.Y., claimed his pivoted receptacle was easier to use and cheaper to produce. He acknowledged the concept was not new and made reference to the drawer patented by Thomas Shanks of January 19, 1858.*

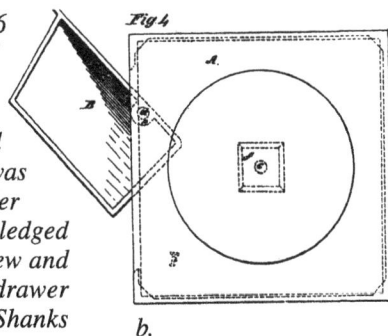

# The Best Pressed Late Lamps

It was a recognised fact even before the kerosene era that mold seams detracted from the appearance of glassware. With pressed one-piece lamps or fonts, the result of fire-polishing to finish the neck produced a seamless shoulder and the appearance of lead or flint glass. The complete font sometimes benefited from this effect. The role of the designer was significant in the visual success and quality of the final product.

The first step was to have the junction of the pattern and the plain shoulder, such that the final operation of finishing would minimize distortion. This was achieved in the examples (a) Westmoreland, and (b) Center Medallion. Some of the earlier designs for pressed lamps made it almost impossible to avoid distortion.

Westmoreland has many facets and lines that distract the eye from mold seams. It is suggestive of cut glass that was so popular in this same 1880 to 1900 period. The burner is one of several similar ones made from the mid-1870s on. Although often referred to as "Brooder burners." they were patented and advertised for "all sizes coal oil lamps." They

*b. Center medallion.*

*c. Base detail.*

were illustrated on glass table lamps and perform well as chimneyless burners.

From the shoulder to the well-detailed underside of the base, the mold seams of (b) Center Medallion follow the corners. Many of these later best pressed lamps were advertised as "Heavy One-Piece Pressed" and exhibit excellent qualities. They should not be confused with lamps made at the end of the century by a completely automated method. Without the hand finishing, the quality is obviously inferior.

To visually follow lamp (b) from the top to the base, one can observe what appears to be a change in quality near the base. Since it is a one-piece lamp, the difference has to be in the hand finishing of the font.

See Westmoreland OL-1 p. 317 and Center Medallion OL-1 p. 297 (i).

*a. Westmoreland.*

When Victoria became Queen in 1837, fluid lamps and candles provided most of the artificial light for the majority of homes in North America. The common fluids were whale oil, camphene (turpentine), or a mixture of redistilled turpentine and alcohol known as burning fluid. These were most often burned in glass lamps provided with a wick and a wick holder known as a burner. Capillary attraction brought the fluid to the top of the wick holder where it was ignited.

Over the next six decades and especially after kerosene was introduced, the search for a better burner inspired inventors to patent over two thousand burners. Gaslight was beginning to be installed in public buildings and the homes of the wealthy in cities and towns where artificial gas was manufactured and distributed. The gas fixtures also required special burners and encouraged patentees to beat a path to the patent office well into the twentieth century. By this time natural gas was also being used.

Lard oil was another popular lamp fuel that was readily available. It was however, more viscous than the other fluids, particularly when cold. This disadvantage motivated designers to devise lamps to overcome this problem. Their solutions produced many distinctive metal lamps.

In the 1850s, solar lamps burning lard oil  became very popular. These had tubular wick burners invented in the late eighteenth century by Ami Argand. The name Argand became a generic term for round tubular burners used for whale oil, kerosene, and gas lighting throughout the nineteenth and twentieth centuries. Illustrations of Solar lamps of domestic manufacture, as well as imported, that were advertised by wholesalers and retailers in the 1850s appeared in catalogues a decade or two later. It is difficult to say whether this was the result of an effort to dispose of surplus stock or if there still existed a demand for these lamps.

By the year 1860 the essential ingredients were in place for a remarkable four decades of kerosene lighting. The Kerosene Era coincided with and related to a remarkable and exciting period in American history and development.

Although Queen Victoria began her reign in 1837 at the age of 18, the current interest in and perception of what is described as Victoriana generally focuses on the later years of the century. Today "Victorian" is used to describe fashions and furnishings of the period, including American kerosene lamps and lighting fixtures. The design of the English and European lighting products had little influence upon the design of American lamps and fixtures.

American lamps reflect the surge of inventiveness and ingenuity that characterised the 1860-1900 period. Both in technology and design the products of this creativity were introduced to the public through advertising that was often amusing and occasionally bizarre. The term "planned obsolescence" may have not been part of their vocabulary, but it certainly was part of their marketing strategy!

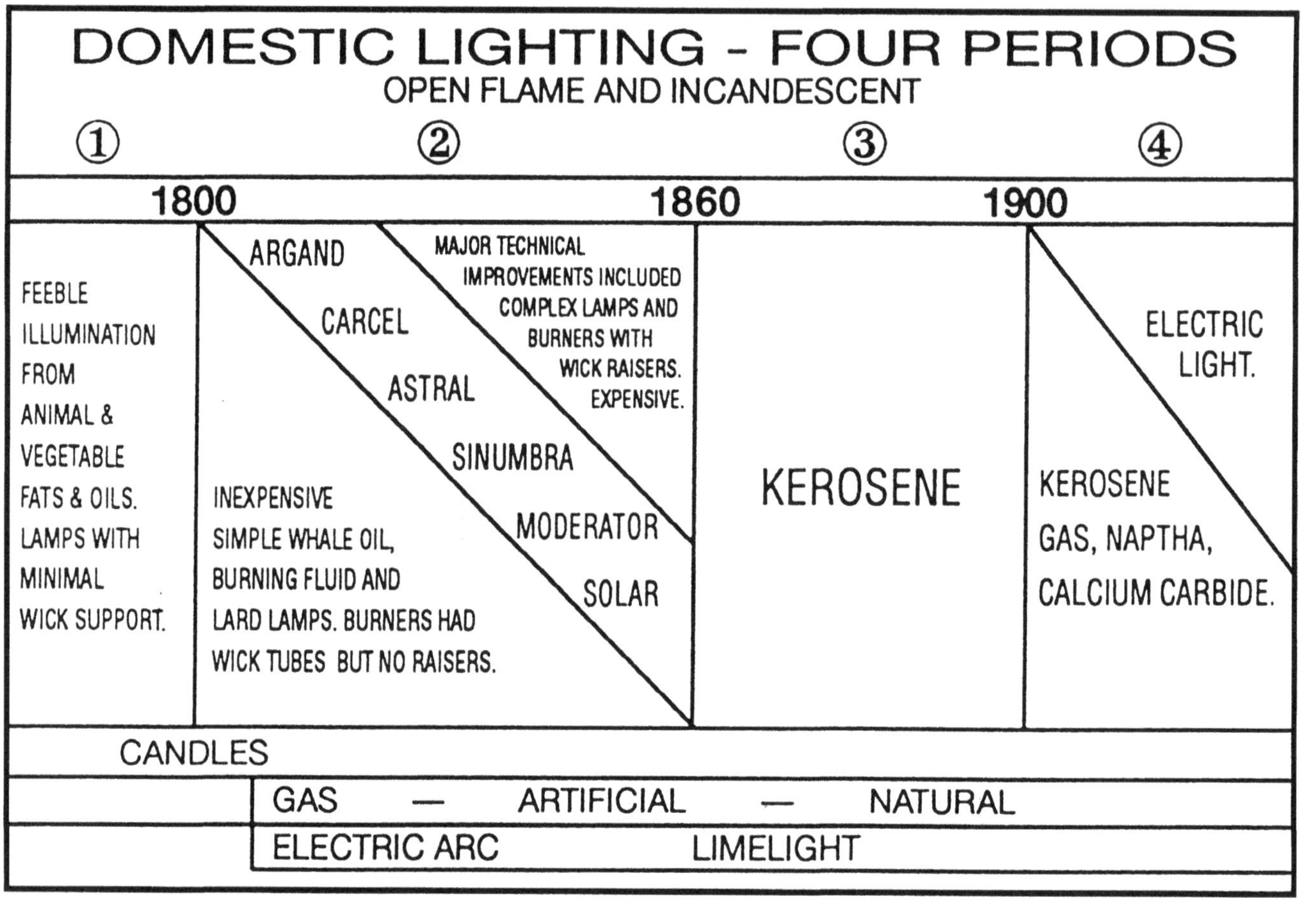

# DOMESTIC LIGHTING - FOUR PERIODS
## OPEN FLAME AND INCANDESCENT

①　　　　　　　②　　　　　　　③　　　　　④

| 1800 | 1860 | 1900 |
|---|---|---|

| FEEBLE ILLUMINATION FROM ANIMAL & VEGETABLE FATS & OILS. LAMPS WITH MINIMAL WICK SUPPORT. | ARGAND CARCEL ASTRAL SINUMBRA MODERATOR SOLAR / MAJOR TECHNICAL IMPROVEMENTS INCLUDED COMPLEX LAMPS AND BURNERS WITH WICK RAISERS. EXPENSIVE. / INEXPENSIVE SIMPLE WHALE OIL, BURNING FLUID AND LARD LAMPS. BURNERS HAD WICK TUBES BUT NO RAISERS. | KEROSENE | ELECTRIC LIGHT. KEROSENE GAS, NAPTHA, CALCIUM CARBIDE. |

CANDLES

GAS　—　ARTIFICIAL　—　NATURAL

ELECTRIC ARC　　　LIMELIGHT

*a.*

The Lighting Chart (a) above must be viewed as a generalisation, intended to place into perspective the 1860-1900 kerosene era. This was the most significant period of domestic lighting and lamp manufacture, before the advent of the electric lamp. As a subject to study, it is particularly fascinating due to the vast numbers of examples extant and the burgeoning supply of primary source material. This new supply adds to, and sometimes reshapes, previously published information.

A remarkable variety of lamps was developed in the 1860s. This was in recognition of the need for brighter, safer, cleaner, and more efficient home lighting. Those listed in the diagonal slash above were generally purchased by the upper class. Complete original examples are considered rare today. Museums and some restored homes have some outstanding examples of nineteenth century lamps — and some embarrassing ones.

Once an abundant and inexpensive source of petroleum was found, kerosene lamps became an instant success.

Illustration (b) is an example of a primitive wrought iron lard oil or grease lamp, known generally as a Double Crusie. They are thought to have been imported in the eighteenth and nineteenth century. There is significant wear at the point of contact between the holder and the lamp, indicating considerable use.

*b. Iron Double Crusie.*

**Genuine Improved Patent Chemical Burners, Lamps and Chandeliers.**

This remarkable 1844 illustration served as the frontispiece of Vol. 1 of *The New York Farmer and Mechanic*. It is unusual not only because of its exaggerated proportions and perspective, but also because of the variety of lamps and fixtures illustrated. There are also reflectors, shades, and prisms. Two of the tall lamps have bases that resemble an English lamp illustrated in OL-2 p. 144.

Volume 1 contains January to June issues of the weekly publication that includes state, national, and world information as well as poetry, patent information, and recipes. It is "EMBELLISHED WITH ENGRAVINGS" and today offers researchers an exceptional resource. There is a reference to the welcome disappearance of St. Johns Wort from the clover fields and pastures in New Jersey and Pennsylvania, although it was conceded that tincture of the flowers and leaves was sometimes used with "good effect in some complaints of the stomach and bowels." Instructions are given on how to observe the growth of an oak tree from an acorn in a glass, and a recipe for ox head soup.

A smaller and better known Wm. H. Starr advertisement with seven different lamps in a show window is repeated several times. The advertising copy below the illustration varies. The first in January proclaimed:

ECONOMY AND BEAUTY!

*In announcing to the public his newly improved Chemical Lamps and Burners, the undersigned would tender his grateful acknowledgements to his former patrons and friends, for their very liberal patronage, and unsolicited but flattering testimonials in their favor, and begs leave to introduce his latest improvements in supplying Churches, Halls, Hotels, Libraries, Stores and Parlors, with his Improved Chandeliers, Lamps, and Chemical Compounds and Vegetable Oils and Fluids challenging competition in the cleanliness, clearness, brilliancy, beauty, safety and economy, of the light thus produced, and which is adapted to every possible variety of use.*

In March, another advertisement described,
*STARRS' PATENT LAMPS, WARRANTED,
OR THE MONEY REFUNDED.*

*A saving of more than fifty per cent, to all who make a trial of Porter's Fluid, and genuine Chemical Oil, and the Patent Safety Burner Lamp, unequalled for beauty and brilliancy, each burner emitting a light equal to 15 sperm candles at the trifling expense of eight mills per hour — every burner warranted.*

WHOLESALE CASH PRICES OF GREENOUGH'S PATENT LAMPS AND CHEMICAL OIL.

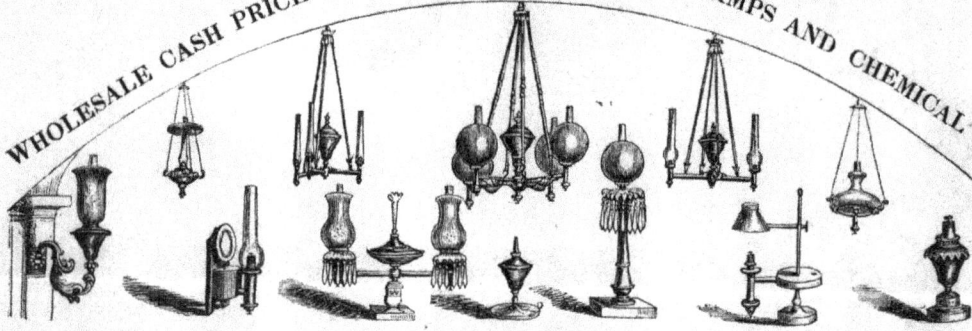

SOLD WHOLESALE ONLY BY STANLY, REED & CO., COMMERCIAL STREET, BOSTON—F. W. PEARSON, AGENT, 81 JOHN STREET, N. Y.—H. CLEVE-LAND, AGENT, 188 CHESTNUT STREET, PHILADELPHIA.

Mr J. S. Blair

New York, April 28th 1845

**Bought of DIETZ, BROTHER & CO.**

No. 13 JOHN STREET, New York, and 62 FULTON STREET, Brooklyn.

Manufacturers & dealers in improved Camphene Lamps, Solar Lamps, Girandoles, Hall Lamps & Lanterns, Lamp Wick, Lamp Shades & Glasses of all kinds, Wholesale & Retail.

| PURE SPERM OIL, REFINED WHALE OIL, CAMPHENE, CHEMICAL OIL. BURNING FLUID. | | | |
|---|---|---|---|
| 3 Pat Solar Sand Lamps wh Cut Globes | 108 ? | 6 00 | 19.50 |
| 3 Paper Shades & frames | | 50 | 1.50 |
| 3 Extra Chimneis | | 1/6 | 56 |
| | | | 21.56 |

Mr J. R. Blair

New York, Nov 13 1846

China, Glass, and Lamp Manufactory, All Articles Matched to Patterns; Lamps Altered and re-finished, and made to order; Glass Made and Cut to any style; Goods Loaned for Parties.

**FACTORY 29 GOLD STREET.**

**Bought of J. STOUVENEL & Co.**

Depot No. 3 John Street,
(NEAR BROADWAY.)

NOTICE. All barrels sold by me are received again at charged prices, (if returned in good order) within four months from purchase; but a deduction will be made for any unnecessary holes bored in them or other damage.

Boston, Jany 18th 1853

Mr Jeremiah Clowes & Co

**Bought of R. H. SPALDING,**
SUCCESSOR TO J. PORTER,
Nos. 8 & 9 Tremont Row, opp. head of Hanover Street,

Sole Manufacturer of H. Porter's Patent Burning Fluid; also, genuine Camphene and Alcohol; Manufacturer and Dealer in Fluid, Chandeliers, Brackets, Astral, Mantel, Hanging & Side Lamps: Portable Lamps of every description. Solar and Camphene Lamps, Lanterns, Chimnies, Glass Drops, Wicks, &c. &c.

28   Pre-kerosene ephemera

*a. Free-blown night lamp with drop whale-oil burner.*

*b. Alabaster glass hand lamp.*

*c. Waisted-loop hand lamp.*

# Pre-kerosene Lamps

Ephemera and examples of pre-kerosene domestic lighting demonstrate the look of lamps that preceded kerosene. Sometimes it was only the burner, as in (b) and (c), that was required to change the lamp from whale oil to burning fluid, or to kerosene. These two pressed one-piece

*d. Houghton & Wallace lard lamp.*

*e. Wick holder detail.*

lamps were finished at the bottom, rather than at the neck.

The metal lamps burned lard oil. The significant feature of the Houghton & Wallace 1843 patent lard lamp (d) & (e) was its heat-conducting wick holder. Both this lamp and the 1851 Kinnear patent lamp (f) were intended, among other claims, to maintain adequate viscosity of the lard oil with heat generated by the flame.

The Kinnear lamp, rarely found this complete and with much of the original gilt finish remaining, was made by S.N. & H.C. Ufford in Boston.

The example (g) of the 1835 Samuel Rust patent is stamped on the bottom: S. RUSTS PATENT / NEW YORK. As with most known examples, the thin silver plating is almost completely worn off, except on the underside of the base. The burner, a forerunner of the kerosene burner, included a toothed wick-raising mechanism, shaft, and thumbwheel.

*f. Kinnear lard lamp.*

*g. Samuel Rust lard lamp.*

*a, b, c, d.*

# Pre-kerosene Glass Lamps

These lamps are distinctly different from kerosene lamp styles. The two center ones can be dated by their use in burner patent drawings. They are flanked by two similar related examples that have been attributed to the Union Glass Company of Philadelphia in the 1830s.

Several variations of lamps (a) and (d) are known and we can expect current research to reveal more. They combine heavy blown fonts with blown hollow stems and elaborately detailed pressed bases. The parts are joined with wafers. Many different cut designs have also been used. The neck of (a) has been crudely ground and is still really too high to accommodate the high collar used here.

When patent illustrations were submitted at an early date, they were in the form of large colored renderings, not the line drawings currently available with patent specifications. The close resemblance of lamp (b) to the Rust patent rendering (e) dated Dec. 16, 1835, is much more apparent than it is in the line drawings. This lamp therefore can be dated as an example of the 1830s design. The stone-wheel engraving has a coarse texture.

The patent model for the September 25, 1837 Samuel Rust burner was submitted on a glass lamp with the same pressed foot and ribbed knop. The blown font was an elongated bulb shape with a similar, engraved design. This and many other Rust patent models are in the collection of the National Museum of American History.

The Star and Punty lamp (c) is also illustrated in OL1 on p. 79, and on p. 7 in this book. Both the font and base are pressed and they are joined with a wafer. The patent for R. W. Sargent's vapor lamp dated March 17, 1857, is illustrated with a drawing of a brass stem and marble base lamp, with a slight variation of this font. Examples of these lamps have been seen in clear and colored glass.

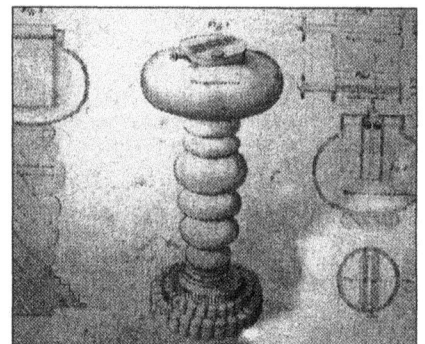

*e. Samuel Rust patent illustration from a colored rendering. Photo courtesy The National Archives, Washington, DC.*

# Pillar-molded
# Pre-kerosene Lamp

This fine example of an American glass lamp is unlike any other that I have seen. The pewter burner with brass wick tubes appears to have had the left wick tube replaced with a more tapered one. The right one has an extension sleeve that might have served to adjust the amount of wick exposed. There are a few remaining chain links that would have been attached to caps for the wick tubes.

Few American Pillar-molded lamps have survived and this one with thick opal threads accentuating each rib makes it outstanding from the standpoint of both early American glass and lamps.

The lamp does not appear to ever have been taken apart in the past although it must be considered a possibility.

The placement of the inverted lead-glass bobeche to form a skirt below the font gives a sense of balance and completion to the lamp. A bobeche was usually placed above a candle socket to catch the melted wax. They were used on everything from single candlesticks to chandeliers and are available today for this purpose. An example of this design was used in the January 9, 1877 patent illustration for a glass gas chandelier by John H. Hobbs. There they were described as "ornaments."

The design is again shown in the illustration above, from an 1890s United States Glass Co. catalogue page titled "BOBACHES." It could have originally been used during a much earlier period.

It is likely that the plain brass stem originally had a damascened or damask finish, popular during the pre-kerosene period. The lamp is 14½" to the top of the burner tubes.

# Gaslighting: A 150 Year Romance

Dan and Nancy Mattausch, owners of the lamp pictured opposite, have provided this photograph taken by David Gentry. In addition, Dan has offered the following description of the lamp and an insight into the nineteenth century role of gaslight in America.

This very early portable gas lamp dates from 1845-1855 and is complete with a gas Argand burner and scarce paper shade. It was probably manufactured in Boston by either the H. N. Hooper or Wm. Carlton Company. The leather hose (itself a rare survivor; later hoses were usually rubber with a cloth covering) conveyed gas to the lamp from an overhead gasolier or wall mounted bracket. ("Sconce" is always an inappropriate term for gas bracket and was not used in the period.) Gas lamps were commonly called "portables" and they allowed gas lights to be positioned on table tops for reading or for the illumination of handiwork.

Gas lighting in various forms existed much earlier and much later than most people realize. The first American gas light patent was issued in 1810, and as late as the 1960s some rural homes were lit with acetylene (a.k.a. carbide) gas lights, an entirely different system developed in the 1890s. (See "David Melville and the First American Gas Light Patents," in *The Rushlight*, December 1998 for an account of early gas lighting at, www.gaslights.org>.) Gas for illumination can be derived from a variety of sources, but the traditional process involved "cooking" coal at a central plant, which released coal gas that was purified and then distributed throughout the city. While natural gas was used for illumination on a sporadic basis in some regions, "gas" lighting in the nineteenth century almost always means "coal gas."

One of the defining features of coal gas lighting is a centralized distribution system (much like water and electricity) with piping throughout the house. In contrast with kerosene and other liquid fuel lamps, a lit gas lamp could not be moved from room to room. This lack of portability was offset by convenience. Users of liquid fuel lamps were obliged to do maintenance such as trimming wicks, filling fonts, and cleaning chimneys. In contrast, residents of homes piped and fitted for gas lights were only required to turn a valve, light the burner, and occasionally clean the tip with a hairpin or the edge of a sheet of paper.

By the mid-nineteenth century gas was available in cities large and small, and it became the third largest industry in the United States. The introduction of electric light in the 1880s was a wake-up call to the gas companies, and the price of gas lighting soon dropped dramatically due to the cheaper gas production and more efficient burners. The most significant invention was the "Welsbach" incandescent burner which achieved popular acceptance in 1893. Welsbach burners heated a mantle that gave off a brilliant light and for nearly two decades were actually much brighter than the best electric light bulbs. Twentieth century Coleman and Aladdin lamps use incandescent mantles that are a direct descendent of the original Welsbach gas light.

The last phase of gas lighting had its origins early in the nineteenth century when it was discovered that carbide, when combined with water, released acetylene, a gas that burned with an intense white light. Unfortunately, producing carbide required extreme temperatures, and it was available only in minute quantities. With Thomas Willson's invention of the electric arc furnace in 1893 and the availability of inexpensive hydroelectric power at Niagara in 1895, carbide could be economically manufactured for the first time. While the use of coal gas was almost exclusively urban, acetylene was very popular in rural areas that had not been electrified. Unlike coal gas retorts, individual acetylene plants located in the backyard or basement were affordable and easy to operate. While coal gas lighting was a non-factor by 1930, acetylene lights remained in use in many areas until rural electrification was completed in the early 1960s. This late use accounts for the relative availability of acetylene burners and fixtures which are commonly confused with much earlier gas lights.

Finally, a word about terminology. The term "gas light" is often used inaccurately to describe liquid fuel "gasoline" lamps and sometimes even burning fluid lamps! Although they employ incandescent mantles, gasoline lamps that use liquid fuel in a reservoir or central source should not be referred to as "gas lights." (The issue of correct nomenclature is more complicated in acetylene lighting because there are self-generating lamps such as bicycle lights and miner's lamps that hold both water and carbide.) Nevertheless, despite the confusion introduced by marketing claims, the general rule is that traditional gas lights receive their fuel in a gaseous form via pipes from a central source. Thus, coal gas, natural gas, or acetylene gas lights are properly termed "gas lights," and gasoline lamps, a distant cousin even when centrally supplied with fluid, are not.

*Portable gas table lamp ca. 1850.* >

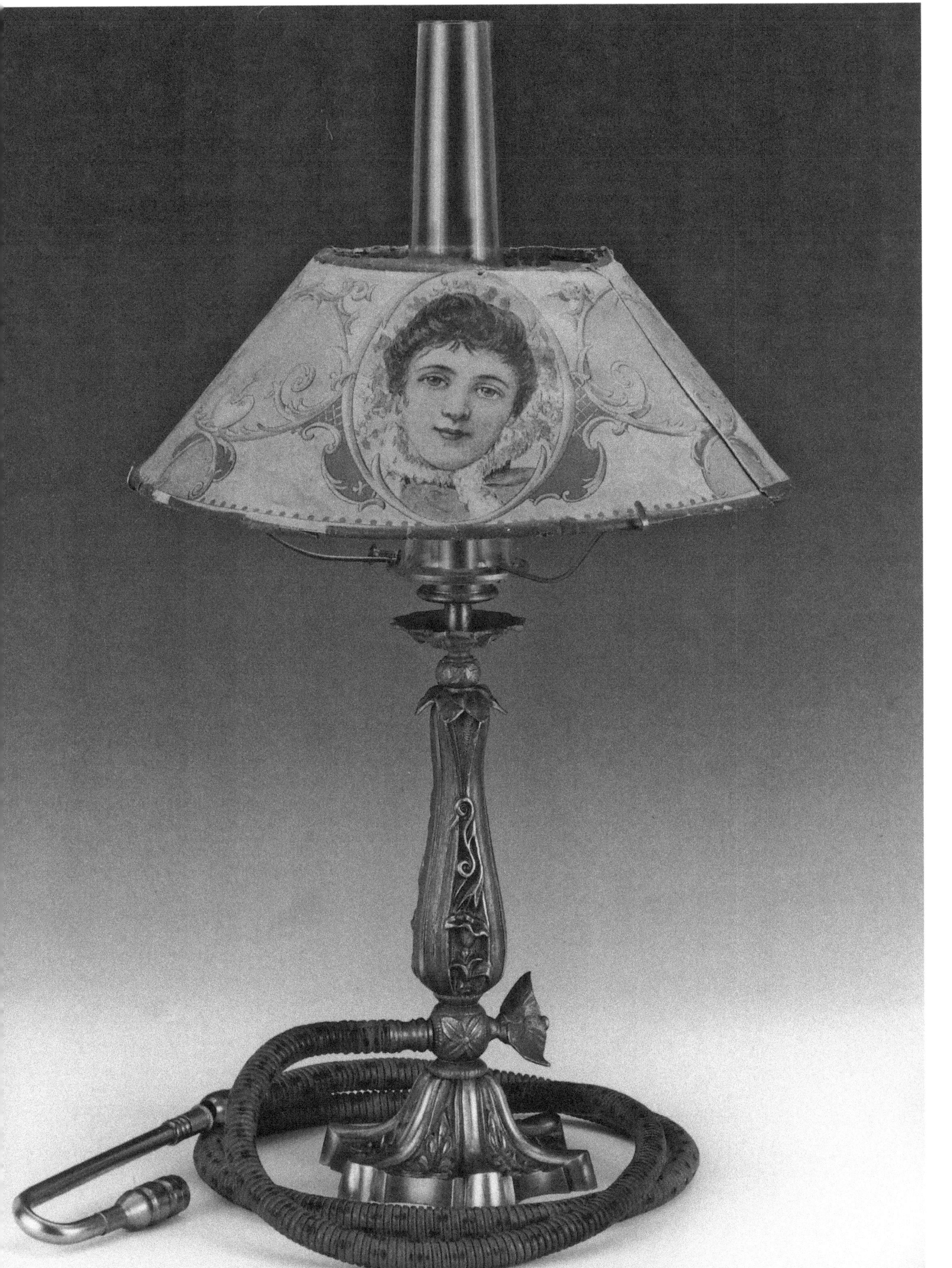

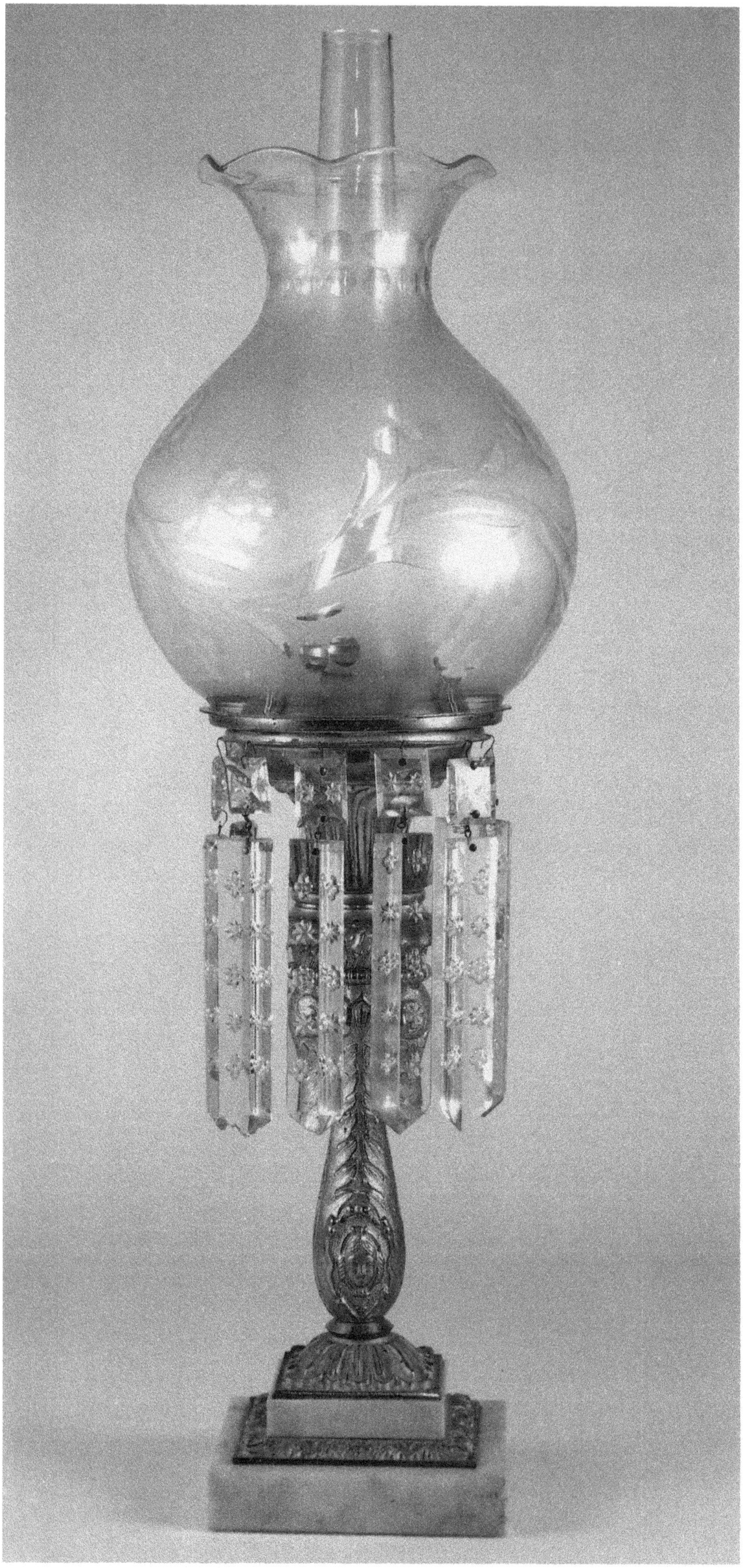

## Solar Lamps

Before the 1860s and to some extent continuing into the kerosene period, portable solar table and banquet lamps with Argand burners would have been the choice of the wealthy. The number of solar lamps that appeared in catalogues or are now extant attest to that. Not only were the lamps spectacular, with tall brass or overlay stems, but also many of the shades eclipsed the early kerosene ones in size and shape.

These lard-oil lamps were clean burning and efficient. They were probably the primary option for elegant lighting where gas was not available. Because they would have been considered part of fine furnishings, many were later converted to kerosene and some later still to electricity. Factory conversions consisted of removing the Argand burners and replacing the shoulder of the font with a metal plate and common kerosene collar. Many other conversions simply used the base with a glass font.

The example pictured here and also illustrated on plate 32 of the 1860s Dietz & Company catalogue was located in a barn in New England. It still retains most of its original finish and contains lard from its last days of use. The chimney is original and a Pyrex duplicate has been made for experimental use. The old shade is a replacement. These lamps had a direct influence upon the design of the earliest kerosene lamps.

The height of this solar table lamp is 22½" to the top of the shade. Taller examples are included in Chapter five.

a.

b.

c.

d.

e.

Elaborate candle holders like a, b, and c known as girandoles, were converted to lamps when fonts and burners were added. Some were set in plaster of Paris and others could accommodate a font with a large peg like (d), without plaster. These pegs, as they were known, are rare and can be recognised by their larger size (too large to fit into brass connectors) and the lack of the usual indentations intended to make a more secure set with plaster.

They were most popular in the 1850s and 1860s. In addition to candles, some held matching fonts that could be used for burning any fluid including kerosene. Example (e) has old ruby, blue, and green overlay fonts set in plaster.

Overlay fonts were made in North America and in Europe. Some twentieth century ones have been found with Czechoslovakia impressed in the glass on the neck, under the shoulder.

# The Early Years

As the transition from the use of earlier fuels evolved, a number of pre-kerosene bases were combined with distinctive and related fonts. Those with the No. 1 collars could also be used with whale oil and burning fluid, but those with the larger collars would have been intended for kerosene. The fonts have a connection to solar lamps in that solar lamp prism or shade rings can be mounted on a step or ring at the shoulder of the font. Another connection is that with the exception of the ones marked with the Dietz name and No. 3 collars, the style of engraving is very similar. It consists of circles, berries, and leaves, often with traces of black and gold in the deeply incised parts.

Some of the fonts like (a), (d), and (e) are unmarked, while (b) and (c) are marked on the shoulder: J, F. DODGE MAKER BOSTON. See billhead below. Others like (f), opposite, are marked E. P. DODGE 8 TREMONT ST. BOSTON. Combining these fonts with old bases would have been an easy way to get rid of old stock.

The bottom of the font (c) bears no indication that it ever had a peg. As a font to be supported in a ring holder, it would have required one about 4¼" in diameter. I have not seen this size in a kerosene fixture.

These fonts are heavy. The glass is thick and not particularly good quality. Much of the surface of this font has a fine dimpled texture, unlike the chill marks occasionally found on some other early fonts.

Heights are: (a) about 11", (b) 10½", and (c) 5".

a.                                           b.                                           c.

Example (d) has been fitted to resemble number 132 in the Fellows, Hoffman & Co. Coal Oil Lamps catalogue of the late 1850s. This is shown in OL-2 on page 146, and the lamp is also pictured without a shade, in OL-1 on page 161. It is 18" to the top of the shade.

Lamp (e) has had an old collar attached to the original one, increasing its height to 12¼". Both black and gold accentuate the leaves in the engraved design. Example (f) has the original cast brass shade ring and prisms it had when found in Maine in the 1970s. An engraved shade, just over 5", completes this graceful table lamp of the late 1850s or early 1860s. Height to the top of the shade is 18¼".

The most interesting base is probably (a) opposite with silvered stem and a patented connector that I referred to as a cup connector in OL-2 p. 35. Other examples are pictured there with both brass and pewter connectors. Since that time I have come across and have been notified of examples dated Nov. 2, 1858. This refers to a patent issued to Samuel Slocomb, of Cambridge, Mass., listed as Candlesticks, &c. It appears to have been more successful as a lamp base.

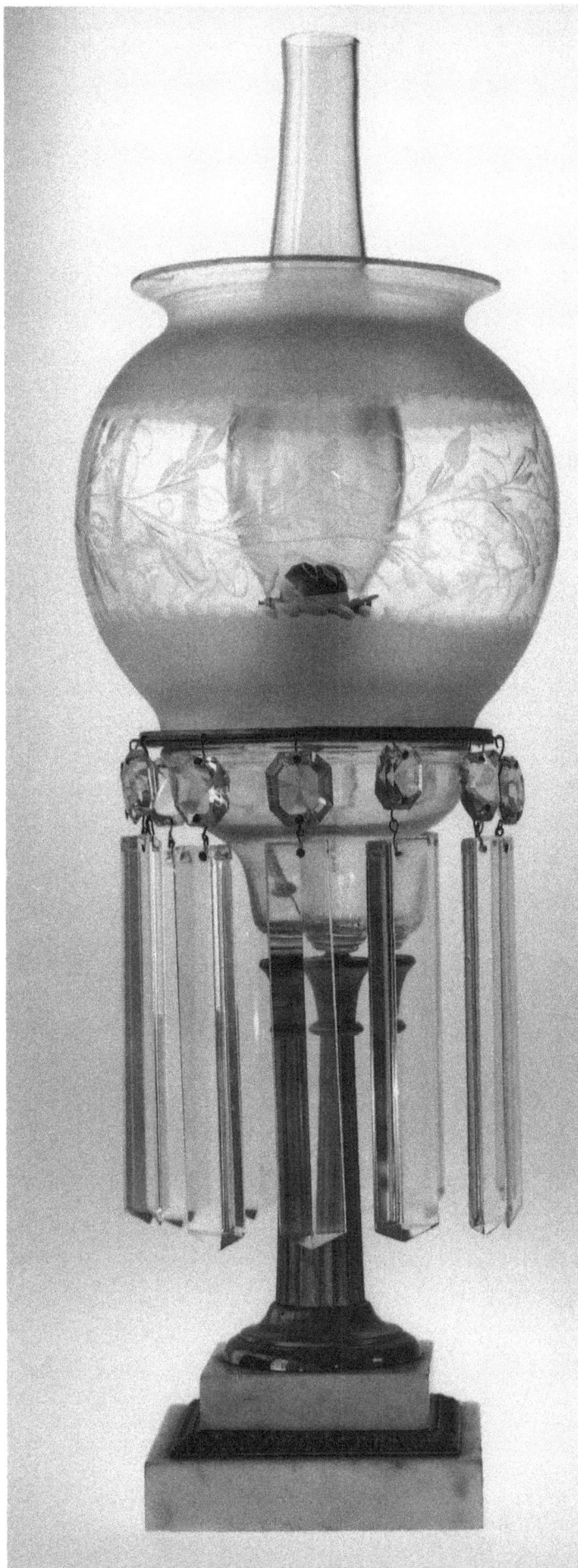

d.

e.

f.

# Dodge and Similar

This unmarked Dodge-type font has the same characteristics as the ones on the previous pages. It has been seen combined with another base of this design with a one-piece blue stem and black glass base. Other bases with this type font have included a brass solar lamp base, a beautiful blue and white decorated stem with marble base and one with a spectacular Bennington base. The quality of the bases chosen far exceeded the quality of the fonts. In most instances, the prisms and early shades compensated for the mediocre fonts. The shade and prisms on this lamp are reputed to be original. Height to the top of the shade is approximately 20".

When I first photographed this lamp against a window, the bottom half inch of the green stem had what appeared to be a dark band. The top line of this band started swinging from side to side. Obviously there was a liquid inside the hollow blown stem. When the stem was disassembled, inside the cemented lower portion of the connector, there was a threaded hollow tube. It was sealed with extremely hard wax that required a very small drill to penetrate the wax, in order to remove a sample of the liquid. Chemical engineer John Gray had it tested. It proved to be petroleum based rather than one of the other pre-kerosene based fuels. Why it was there and why it was sealed so tightly is a mystery.

I have seen another base with a blue stem and white base. The font was a variation of the Macklin kerosene font with a No. 2 collar. These bases, possibly made at Sandwich in the 1850s, have a blown hollow stem fused to a pressed-glass base. The base imitates a double marble base with stamped or cast brass separating the marble layers.

# Kerosene and Other Oils

Although 1860 to 1900 has been chosen as the period for this book, it should be kept in mind that kerosene or coal oil began its history well before, and continues to be used today. Rights to the name kerosene, chosen by Abraham Gesner who was issued a patent for it, were sold to The New-York Kerosene Oil Company. Later Samuel Downer obtained permission to use it. An 1861 New-York Kerosene Oil Company letterhead stated "KEROSENE" was their trademark, and cautioned against its use for other oils. Both in patents and in general use, kerosene and coal oil became generic names.

In *The Boston Almanac* for the year 1861, published by Brown & Taggard, in a Downer Kerosene Oil Company advertisement, the president Samuel Downer stated that he made his oil from Albert Coal. In 1862 Downer started building a refinery in Corry, Pennsylvania, in the oil region north of Titusville. It was said to have the capacity to refine approximately a million gallons a year.

When Julius Ives published his lamp catalogue circa 1868, he included pages of testimonials submitted by prominent citizens who offered both praise and poetry in support of Ives' Lamps. There were presidents of related companies, publishers and professionals. The contribution of Samuel Downer was the following informative and reassuring letter:

Letter from SAMUEL DOWNER, Esq., Boston.

## FACTS ABOUT PETROLEUM
### NEW U.S. REVENUE LAW—PENALTY FOR ADULTERATION

GENTLEMEN: I am in receipt of your favor requesting for publication such information, regarding the qualities and safety of Petroleum, as may have come under my experience or observation. I am very glad to reply, hoping that its circulation will induce the public generally to a more thorough investigation concerning the nature of the oil they use. It is a subject that has deeply interested me, from the fact that myself and those connected with me were the first in this country who extensively pursued its manufacture, and, I may say, the first in any country that brought the process of refining to such perfection that it came into general use as an illuminator.

I feel that, in a measure, we are also interested in the business in which you are engaged, and take pleasure saying to you, what we often do to others, that since the introduction of Petroleum, we have used no lamps with the pleasure and satisfaction we have enjoyed with yours. If as much care and discretion were used in the selection of fixtures for the use of oil as of gas, the value of our productions would be doubly appreciated, and the comfort of the people enhanced.

Crude Petroleum is composed of a variety of liquids — some are volatile at very low, others at higher temperatures. By distillation these substances are separated, and by peculiar and scientific processes, depending in their excellence upon the education and experience of the refiner, the different products are brought into use for various purposes.

Gasoline, being the most volatile, passes off first, and is the most inflammable and dangerous of its substances.

Naphtha, the next in volatility, passes off after the gasoline. It has a strong, peculiar odor, is very inflammable, and the more of it that is allowed to remain, by unprincipled distillers, or afterward mixed with good oil, by nefarious speculators, the more inferior and objectionable the article for use in lamps, on account of its inflammability.

Refined Petroleum is that which next passes off, and is of such a nature that, when properly prepared, will not ignite at a temperature less than 110° Fahrenheit, which is, of course much higher than is ever attained in ordinary lamps. This is the illuminating oil so universally used and known as kerosene, and after proper treatment in the refining processes, is as safe for use as sperm or other oils.

The remainder is a heavy oil with other substances, and usually called Lubricating Oil.

The test which at present is almost universal is an igniting point of 110° Fahrenheit, obtained by oil being put into a glass cup, about three inches wide and three inches deep, which is immersed in a tin vessel filled with water, under which is applied an alcohol lamp, the oil heated at the rate of about 15 minutes from 90° to 110°, or about one degree per minute, and when heated faster than that, the lamp is temporarily withdrawn. Into this oil the bulb of a thermometer is permanently suspended, so that the oil will just cover it. The oil is not stirred nor touched. When the oil has arrived within some 5° or 10° of the point desired, the lamp is withdrawn, and the oil comes up to the desired temperature by the heat of the water, or still more where the flame is applied direct, that portion of the oil in immediate contact gets warmer, and the flashing point can be obtained at almost any point, and even igniting at some degrees less.

In regard to the safety of oils standing 110° or even 100° igniting point tried by this test, my experience is worth something. While we manufactured Coal Oil and Petroleum of Oil Creek and Virginia, whose specific gravity was heavy, out of the many millions of lamps used we have never heard of an explosion, and up to that time many thousand gallons of other oil were imported and mixed with it, and must again have gone into millions of lamps, and still our attention had never been called to what is called an explosion, although the article was easily ignited.

In the country, Petroleum is the universal light; in villages, the principal ones, and in large cities, very largely used, for even with the wealthy, there the kerosene lamp, for the beauty of its light, is the favorite for the study. I do not recommend any one to use any oil than that of the full fire test, and that from the best manufacturers, for the way it is *manufactured* has more to do with safety than $100°$, or $110°$, or $120°$ lighting test and poorly manufactured. Our market is supplied with the following oils: first, the best quality of the best manufacturers; next the oil bought for foreign orders, and rejected for fire test and other qualities not coming up to the warranty; third, we are obliged to fling away vast amounts of naphtha; the heavier proportion of these are bought very cheap, and used to adulterate oils. Let any expert go into our households, and he will find the oils which left the hands of honest the refiners with a fire test of $110°$ so depreciated by adulteration, that they will ignite, not flash, at $75°$ to $80°$, $90°$, and so on up to $110°$, and the quantity of these oils is very large. Now, considering the population say of New England, New York, Pennsylvania, and New Jersey, some eight or nine millions of inhabitants who must burn several millions of lamps each night, yet the papers do not chronicle — and the reporters are famous for picking them up — on an average, two accidents per day, with all the amount of poorly manufactured and badly adulterated oil; and these few, I doubt not, could be shown to be the results of inexcusable carelessness of ignorant persons, perhaps in filling the lamps with poor oil, when lighted, or trying to kindle the stove-fire with the same inferior article.

Refined oil in moderate quantities is stored with the general merchandise of a merchant's stock and has ceased to be a bugbear with our insurance companies.

In this connection, I would like to call attention to the recent enactment by Congress; its value and importance can not be too highly appreciated. In the amendment to the U. S. Revenue Laws, passed March 2d, the following tests and penalties, in regard to the quality and adulteration of oil, were established:

**"Section 29 And be it further enacted, That no person shall mix for sale, Naphtha and illuminating oils, or shall knowingly sell or keep for sale or offer for sale such mixture, or shall sell or offer for sale oil made from petroleum for illuminating purposes, inflammable at less temperature of fire test than 110° Fahrenheit, and any person so doing shall be held to be guilty of a misdemeanor, and on conviction thereof, having competent jurisdiction, shall be punished by a**

**fine of not less than $100, nor more than $500, and by imprisonment of not less than six months, nor more than three years."**

I regret that it was not enacted long ago, but now hope for great public benefits by its speedy enforcement.

Yours, with much regard,
SAMUEL DOWNER
*Boston, March 9th, 1867.*        *President.*

This verbatim reprint of Downer's letter provides information about the manufacture of kerosene, the quality control and the reporting of accidents. The safety factor was of great concern to manufacturers and consumers alike. These concerns developed into major marketing strategies between gas lighting and kerosene lighting with each side eagerly reporting news of their opponent's fresh disasters.

a. Downer Mineral Sperm Lamp, also marked, Mch 8, MY31, June 21, 1870. Height, 8 5/8".

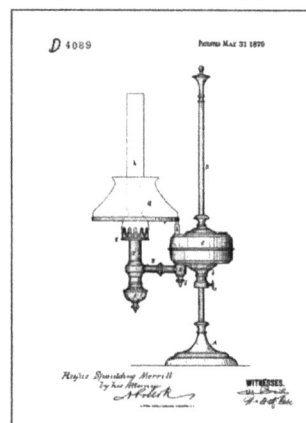

b. Design patent issued to Rufus Spaulding Merrill, of Hyde Park, Mass. on May 31, 1870.

In the absence of any reference to Downer and his oxymoron mineral sperm oil in patent records; the above patent and several invention patents issued to R. S. Merrill, appear to relate to Downer's lamps. These include:

March 8, 1870, for a lamp burner.
March 15, 1870, for an improvement in burning heavy hydrocarbon oils for illumination. Merrill obtained two reissues for this on March 2, 1876.
June 21, 1870 related to student lamps. The patent drawing relates to the one above.
Sept. 13, 1870. This illustrates the glass lamp above with an argand burner and chimney.

Reports in 1875 *Crockery & Glass Journal* issues mentioned that Union Glass Company in Boston was sole U.S. agent for the "Moehring Mineral Sperm Lamp" manufactured by The Downer Oil Company. Downer metal lamps have also been reported and may play an important role in documenting Downer's or Merrill's lamps.

# Disasters

In detailing the cause of Ellen Shannon's tragic death on her tombstone, one of the best-known and most publicised grave sites in America was created. In an old cemetary in Girard, Pennsylvania, near the south shore of Lake Erie, this stone relates the following sad story.

IN MEMORY OF

**ELLEN SHANNON**

AGE 26 YEARS

WHO WAS FATALLY

BURNED MAR. 21 1870

BY THE EXPLOSION

OF A LAMP FILLED

WITH R. E. DANFORTHS

NON-EXPLOSIVE

BURNING FLUID

Was this the result of careless handling? In his patent of Dec. 12, 1882, for a blast lamp, patentee Robert Reach of Washington, DC, made the following comment "In this connection I would state that I deem Danforth's patented non-explosive oil the only reliable non-explosive burning-fluid, and that I use it exclusively for my blast-lamp."

It would appear that the negative publicity had little effect upon the sale and use of the product. Perhaps the frequency with which such accidents occurred drew little attention.

The following report was printed in the February 24, 1881 issue of the *Crockery and Glass Journal.* One of the city dailies, in speaking of a recent gas explosion which shattered a large building, says:

"An event like this naturally reminds us once again, as the kerosene lamps so often do, that in the happy electric days to come — when they do come — such catastrophes will be heard of no more. It should likewise remind carpenters that they cannot be too cautious when working near gas pipes, since it shows that so tiny an error as that described may easily prove the cause of a terrible disaster."

The writer is evidently a gas burner, and, as such has no use for kerosene; therefore knows nothing of its pleasures as an illuminator. If he were to study the subject he would find that the danger in the use of kerosene lies in the quality of the lamp — a cheap and ill-constructed lamp being worse in comparison than a tin gun-barrel. It has taken a great many years for the majority of people to regard the cheap lamp and a flimsy gun-barrel as parallel engines of destruction; and in the meantime many good souls have gone on their upward flight. There is, however, no excuse today for anyone to be without a safe and inexpensive lamp for the use of kerosene, for while Edison and his competitors have been at work to bring those happy electric days nearer to us, other men with just as much and just as good gray matter in their skulls have expended their skill in the perfection of the kerosene lamp.

We predict that the careless handling of electrified wires in the average household will kill just as many if not more people than kerosene has ever done, for it will leave no possible chance to recover a burning body in a half-roasted condition. The solitary advantage of electricity as a servant-girl annihilator lies in the fact that it leaves a more presentable corpse, which may be consolation enough for those who would die early.

New York, June 13 1860.

Mess W. B. Glover &Co

To **CHAS. WATERMAN, Dr.**

MANUFACTURERS' AGENT FOR THE SALE OF

# IMPROVED LAMPS, FOR BURNING ANY KIND OF COAL OR KEROSENE OIL.

Also, the New Excelsior Improved Burners, Lamp Fixtures, &c.   Coal, Kerosene and Carbon Oils,

AT MANUFACTURERS' PRICES,

No allowance on Breakage and Leakage.
No claims allowed unless made within ten days after receipt of the Goods.
**TERMS.**—Nett Cash on delivery of the Goods in current funds in New York.

**43 JOHN ST.,** (UP STAIRS.)

| | | | | | |
|---|---|---|---|---|---|
| ✓ | 1/2 | Dz | No 1 White Stand Coblipey Lamps Dz | | 4 50 |
| ✓ | 1/2 | " | 2 Do " " " 10.00 | | 5 00 |
| ✓ | 1/2 | " | 1 Globes & Holder 4.50 | | 2 25 |
| ✓ | 1/12 | " | 2 Fount Burner & Chimy | | 75 |
| ✓ | 1/6 | " | 3 Chimy Harps 3.00 | | 3 17 |
| ✓ | 1/6 | " | 2 Plain Do 12.00 | | 2 00 |
| ✓ | 1 | " | 2 Life Chimnies | | 1 13 |
| ✓ | 3 | " | 1 Do Do Ground 1.00 | | 3 00 |
| ✓ | 1/4 | " | Gold & Grape Shade 2.25 | | 56 |
| ✓ | 1/3 | " | Cramp Black Do 3.00 | | 1 00 |
| ✓ | 1/6 | " | Do Green " 3.00 | | 50 |
| ✓ | 1/2 | " | Crown Do 3.00 | | 1 50 |
| ✓ | 1 | " | 104 Lamps | | 6 50 |
| ✓ | 3 | Barels of Culls 4/ | | | 1 12 $ 31.9 |

**METAL SPINNER.**

JOHN F. IDEN,

METAL SPINNER.

137 ELM STREET,

NEW YORK.

The invoice above and the John F. Iden advertisement in an 1860 New York city directory serve to introduce this period of kerosene lighting. A little artist's licence may have been taken with the illustrations; and the information on the invoice may not be entirely understood today, but there is little available on that particular date.

The prices noted may useful for comparison and the Iden information relates to the description of John F. Iden and his lamps in OL-2 pp. 38 and 39.

## The Charles A. Starr Catalogue

This catalogue from the collection of the late Charles McGurk, along with two other catalogues of the late 1850s, constitute the best known records of the first kerosene lamps. The other two are the late 1850s Fellows, Hoffman & Co. catalogue pages illustrated in OL-2 pp. 146-147, and the 1859 Southland's Catalogue and Wholesale Price List pages, illustrated in OL-1, pp. 18-19.

Ideally all of these illustrations should be laid out for comparison. Simple harp hanging lamps with or without smoke bells, that were basic forms sold until the end of the century, are featured in all catalogues. It is difficult to determine the age of a particular example, and because a relatively good supply is available today, it is a potential choice for appropriate locations in restorations. This would be largely determined by trimmings and by the original prices.

Other hanging lamps appear to have separate reservoirs and seem also to be closely related to gas fixtures. They are rarely seen today. Only ring font holders are shown in any of the hanging or bracket lamps illustrated. The basket and other type holders emerged later. Both brass and glass fonts were used. Side lamps had a Japanned finish, however neither the metal nor the finish of the hanging or bracket lamps was mentioned.

It is the table lamps that are of greatest interest. Most can be identified, or closely relate to known examples. There is even a Brittannia [sic] Handle lamp, mentioned in the Southland's catalogue. An example is pictured in OL-1 p. 17. Four examples of the Ring Punty series are shown and both the round and the turnip overlay fonts that are often seen with gold accents but very poor workmanship are included. For those particularly interested in glass lamps, the most welcome surprise is the appearance of the Triple Dolphin base with the plain round font. Table lamp No. 687 Triple Diamond Medallion, also in the Russell and Erwin 1865 catalogue and the Dietz catalogue of about the same time, pictured here, establishes an even earlier date for the pattern. It is pictured in OL-2, p. 84 (d).

Shades are described as either Oregon or Ground and Engraved. The latter would refer to the globe shades with a small lateral projection at the top. Most, but not all of the Oregon shades have roughed bands. An excellent variety is offered for study, comparison, and dating.

In the past a full size reprint of this Starr catalogue was made available to members of the Rushlight Club.

ILLUSTRATED CATALOGUE OF LAMPS, Chandeliers, Brackets, &c.,

MANUFACTURED AND FOR SALE BY

CHARLES A. STARR,
No. 117 FULTON STREET,
NEW YORK CITY.

JOHN W. ORR,
ENGRAVER ON WOOD AND PRINTER,
No. 75 NASSAU STREET NEW YORK
1861.

Allow me to bring to your notice the accompanying Plates, representing about Seventy different styles of

Chandeliers, Stand-Lamps, Brackets, &c.,

for burning Kerosene or Coal Oil. In addition to these, I have a large number of other styles, to which are added, from time to time, such desirable patterns as present themselves.

Also, the separate parts of Lamps, and all kinds of Lamp Trimmings connected with the trade.

Trusting that the reputation and long experience of the house (having been established about 17 years) will be a sufficient guaranty for the prompt and faithful execution of all orders entrusted to me.

I remain, respectfully yours,

CHARLES A. STARR.

NEW YORK, AUGUST 1ST, 1861.

Kerosene and Coal Oils, Fluid, Camphene, Alcohol, &c., constantly on hand, and for sale at lowest market prices.

J. W. ORR, PRINTER, 75 NASSAU ST., N. Y.

No. 101.

No. 200.

No. 806.

No. 4.    4 Light.

No. 3.    2 Light.

No. 80.    4 Light.

No. 60.    3 Light.

No. 3.    4 Light.

No. 3.    8 Light.

No. 4.    2 Light.

No. 4.    3 Light.

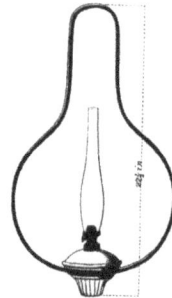

No. 51.

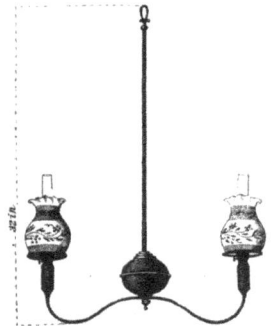

SALOON PENDANT.

No. 687.

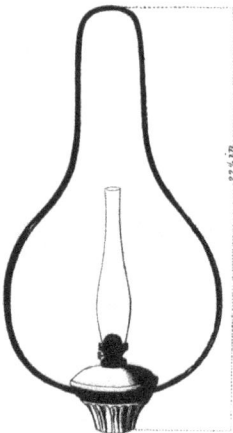

No. 50.

No. 428.

No. 157.

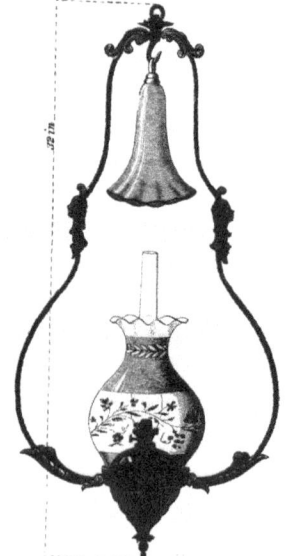

No. 400.

44    Charles A. Starr, 1861 illustrated catalogue

No. 487.  No. 350.  No. 301.  No. 2. Side.  No. 390.

No. 50. Bracket.  No. 1. Side.  No. 696.

No. 1102.  No. 600.  No. 760.  No. 750.

No. 1025.  No. 723.  No. 690.  No. 1026.  No. 1050.

No. 60. Bracket.  No. 1. Bracket.

No. 10. Bracket.  No. 20. Bracket.  No. 50. Bracket.

No. 110  No. 4.  No. 25.  No. 10.  No. 30.  No. 100

No. 500.  No. 375.  No. 325.  No. 521  No. 221  C & B.

No. 901.  No. 800.  No. 1100.  No. 1101.

No. 675  No. 621.  No. 421.  No. 321.  No. 330.  No. 622.

No. 850.  No. 801.  No. 807.  No. 820.  No. 900.

# PRICE LIST.

| No. | STYLE OF BASE. | STYLE OF FOUNT. | STYLE OF SHADE. | PRICE. |
|---|---|---|---|---|
| 800 | Double Marble, Brass Column, | Rich Cut and Gilt, | 4 in. Oregon, | $ 3.87 ea. |
| 723 | Marble, Brass Damask Column, | " " " | 4 " " | 3.62 " |
| 850 | Double Marble, Rich and Heavy Brass Column, | Brass, | 4 " " | 4.75 " |
| 760 | Marble, Brass Column, | " | 4 " " | 2.62 " |
| 600 | " " " | Assorted Colors, Glass | 4 " " | 2.62 " |
| 820 | " " " | Clear Pressed, " | 4 " " | 2.75 " |
| 801 | Glass and Glass " | " " | 4 " " | 2.00 " |
| 900 | Double Marble, Brass Column, | Assorted Colors, " | 4 " " | 2.75 " |
| 807 | " " " " | Cut and Gilt, " | 4 " " | 3.50 " |
| 901 | Marble, Brass " | Brass, " | 4 " " | 4.00 " |
| 690 | " Cut Glass " | Rich Cut & Engraved, Assorted Colors, | 3 " " | 3.25 " |
| 750 | Glass and Glass " | White Glass, | 3 " " | 15.00 dz. |
| 621 | Marble, Brass " | Rich Plated, Cut and Gilt, Colored, | 3 " " | 25.00 " |
| 675 | " " " | " " " " " | 3 " " | 25.00 " |
| 696 | " " " | " " Cut and Colored, | 3 " " | 20.00 " |
| 1026 | Full Gilt, Glass Stand, | Full Gilt, Glass, | 6 " Porcelain, | 22.50 " |
| 1100 | Bronze, | Bronze, | 4 "Gr'd & Eng. | 5.25 ea. |
| 1101 | " | " | 4 " " " | 4.00 " |
| 1102 | " | " | 4 " " " | 3.75 " |
| 1025 | Full Gilt Glass, | Full Gilt Glass, | ........ | 16.00 dz. |

| NAME AND NO. | NUMBER OF BURNERS. | STYLE OF SHADE. | PRICE. |
|---|---|---|---|
| Chandelier No. 3, | 8 Burners | 4 in. Oregon Shade | $30.00 ea. |
| " " 3, | 6 " | 4 " " " | 24.00 " |
| " " 3, | 4 " | 4 " " " | 16.00 " |
| " " 3, | 3 " | 4 " " " | 14.00 " |
| " " 3, | 2 " | 4 " " " | 9.00 " |
| " " 4, | 4 " | 4 " " " | 10.00 " |
| " " 4, | 3 " | 4 " " " | 8.00 " |
| " " 4, | 2 " | 4 " " " | 6.00 " |
| " " 80, | 4 " | 4 " " " | 20.00 " |
| " " 60, | 3 " | 4 " Gr'd & Eng.Gl'b | 15.00 " |
| Saloon Pendant, | 2 " | 4 " Oregon Shade, | 4.50 " |

| NAME AND NO. | STYLE OF FOUNT. | STYLE OF SHADE. | PRICE. |
|---|---|---|---|
| Harp Lamp, No. 157, | Brass, | 4 in. Oregon Shade and Smoke Bell, | $ 8.50 ea. |
| " " " 300, | Glass, Mov.Bot. | 6 in. Oregon Shade and Smoke Bell, | 5.00 " |
| " " " 400, | Brass, | 4 in. Oregon Shade and Smoke Bell. | 4.50 " |
| " " " 806, | Glass, | 3 in. Oregon Shade and Smoke Bell. | 24.00 dz. |
| " " " 101, | " | ........ | 18.00 " |
| " " " 50, | " | ........ | 10.00 " |
| " " " 51, | " | ........ | 7.00 " |
| Hanging, " 301, | " | ........ | 13.50 " |

| NAME & NO. | STYLE OF FOUNT. | STYLE OF SHADE. | WIDTH OF WICK. | PRICE. |
|---|---|---|---|---|
| No. 1, Bracket, | Brass, | 4 in. Or. Shade, | 1 inch, | $ 6.50 ea. |
| " 10, " | Glass, | ........ | 1 " | 20.00 dz. |
| " 5, " | " | ........ | 1 " | 15.00 " |
| " 20, " | " | ........ | ¾ " | 10.00 " |
| " 50, " | " | ........ | 1 " | 26.50 " |
| " 60, " | " | 4 in. Or. Shade, | 1 " | 36.00 " |
| " 1, Jap. Side | " | ........ | 1 " | 12.00 " |
| " 2, " " | " | ........ | ¾ " | 8.00 " |

| No. | STYLE OF LAMP. | PRICE. |
|---|---|---|
| 100 | Clear Pressed Glass, | $ 4.00 doz. |
| 110 | " " " | 5.50 " |
| 30 | " " " | 5.50 " |
| 25 | " " " | 4.50 " |
| 10 | " " " | 3.50 " |
| 20 | Blue " " | 4.00 " |
| 4 | Brittannia Handle, | 7.50 " |

| No. | STYLE OF BASE. | STYLE OF FOUNT. | PRICE. |
|---|---|---|---|
| 428 | Marble, Bronze or Gilt Column, | Clear Pressed Glass, | $ 9.00 doz. |
| 350 | " " , " " | " " " | 7.00 " |
| 687 | " " " " | " " " | 9.50 " |
| 321 | " " " " | " " " | 7.25 " |
| 375 | " " " " | " " " | 7.25 " |
| 521 | " Gilt Column, | Engraved " | 7.50 " |
| 421 | " Bronze and Gilt " | " " | 8.50 " |
| 500 | " Gilt " | Clear Pressed " | 7.50 " |
| 325 | " Bronze or Gilt " | Engraved " | 8.00 " |
| 221 | " Gilt " | Clear Pressed " | 5.50 " |
| 330 | " Bronze or Gilt " | Engraved " | 7.25 " |
| 487 | " " " " | Full Gilt, Colored Glass, | 12.00 " |
| 1050 | Gilt Glass Stand, | " " " | 13.50 " |
| 390 | Marble, Bronze or Gilt Column, | Clear Pressed " | 7.00 " |

## TERMS: NETT CASH.

This price list will be very valuable when used with others of the same and of other periods of time. It will also be useful to compare it with the prices of other products of the same time. When undertaking a study, it should be kept in mind that wholesale or retail prices should be factored in, as well as wages and earnings for the period.

Edwin Drake, wearing a top hat,
was photographed in 1861 at the site
of his oil well in Titusville, Pennsylvania.
Today it is the site of the Drake Museum
where historical records of the early days
of oil are preserved and displayed.

Once it was established that kerosene
represented a lighting breakthrough and that
petroleum would provide an abundant supply
(if not limitless as was supposed), the rush to stake
claims was as frenzied as that of the gold rush!

DRAKE

*John A Mather photograph from
Pennsylvania Historical & Museum
Commission
Drake Well Museum Collection,
Titusville Pennsylvania*

# The Early Years of the Pennsylvania Oil Fields

By the late 1850s it was understood that an abundant source of petroleum could provide the country with an inexpensive and safe source of lighting. It was also well known that this could translate into instant wealth. At that time the country had very limited communication. The South was on the brink of the Civil War, and settlement in the West would see decades of conflicts and hardships. Nevertheless industrial production seemed to flourish in the Northeast.

The rush to stake oil claims has been likened to the gold rush. There are indeed similarities, in that to some it brought instant wealth by the simple act of discovery. The gold rush lasted over five decades in the west, whereas the frenzy to establish oil sources in Pennsylvania was concentrated in the 1860s, and the initial location involved a relatively small area.

Far more tales have been told about the Gold Rush than the rush to discover oil. They were similar in some respects, and very different in others, but both were significant events in American history. The appeal of gold is easy to understand, but the initial interest in oil is often misunderstood. An abundant source of oil *was not* sought after for fuel to drive engines. The 1860s rush to discover oil was a rush for power — the power that money can buy. It was the prospect of all the money that could be made by supplying homes with an abundant cheap source of light — not supplying horsepower. Travel and transportation in those days required real horsepower — the kind with ears!

The history of the oil regions of Pennsylvania is preserved in primary source documents at the Drake Well Museum in Titusville, Pennsylvania, in contemporary publications such as *The Scientific American*, and perhaps most importantly, in the photographs of John A. Mather.

Mather emigrated from England in the first part of the century as a musician. Shortly after his arrival in America his interests turned to photography. Upon learning of the oil strikes in Pennsylvania, he decided to try to set up a business in Oil City. There he started and there he stayed, taking photographs for nearly four decades. In those days, glass plate negatives were used and the film had to be developed on site. In addition to his studio in a store in town, he devised a mobile darkroom on a wagon, and another on a barge for water travel. By the time his career was over he had produced *over 19.000 glass plate negatives!* Tragically most of them were lost in a fire in 1892. However of the remaining over 3,000 plates that survived, more than 2,000 have been identified and are housed at the Drake Well Museum. The photographs shown here are were printed from original glass plate negatives. They offer a remarkable visual history.

In addition to oil fields, the photographs show homes, commercial buildings, citizens, and modes of travel, as well as fires and floods. Muddy roads, and wagons with iron tires remind us of the difficulties encountered in not only transporting people and goods, but in transporting the oil itself.

Most of the oil was transported to refineries in Pittsburgh. It was transferred from large vats shown in (a) to barrels that were taken to Oil Creek and placed on barges, to be floated or drawn by horses, down to Oil City. Water levels were very low at that time. In the October 18, 1862 issue of *The Scientific American,* it was reported that above Wheeling, "The Ohio river is so low in most places that it can be crossed on foot by man and beast for a distance of nearly a hundred miles." Oil Creek flowed into the Allegheny River above Pittsburgh, where it met the Monongahela and became the Ohio River.

a.     THE OIL REGIONS OF PENNSYLVANIA—PIT HOLE CITY, VENANGO COUNTY, PENNSYLVANIA.—[Sketched by Theodore R. Davis.]

The illustration (b) from *The London Illustrated News*, February 27, 1875, and (c) and (d) photographs by John A. Mather, are from the Pennsylvania Historical & Museum Commission Drake Well Museum Collection, Titusville, Pennsylvania.

Teamsters like those pictured could never have imagined that a century later, teamsters would, among other things, be driving trucks powered by another product of the same petroleum they were hauling for lighting.

Pithole Creek ran into the Allegheny River a few miles east of Oil Creek. According to Paul H. Giddens in his book *Early Days of Oil*, a successful well was drilled on January 7, 1865. This started a stampede to Pithole Creek that resulted in the town of Pithole being created in May, in the wilderness on Holmden farm. In September the town had grown to include: "Two banks, two telegraph offices, a daily newspaper, a waterworks system, two churches, a theatre, over fifty hotels, the third largest post office in Pennsylvania, and about 15,000 inhabitants."

Sadly in the fall this oil source dried up. The spectators and speculators left the area. With no reason for its continued existence, Pithole became a deserted village by January 1866, and the town soon reverted to grasslands. It was boom to bust in merely a year!

During the summer months, the Drake Well Museum in Titusville, operates the Visitors Center on the deserted site of the former town of Pithole.

Clearly, the roads were hardly fit for man or beast. At times it was said that if large animals became mired in the mud and if there was no means to extricate them, they would have to be shot! The common varieties of wagon jacks available at the time would have been quite useless here. One can only wonder at the outcome of this seemingly hopeless predicament!

b. *Transporting barrels on Oil Creek.*

c. *First Street, Pithole.*

d. *Bad Roads, Sherman Well, Oil Creek, 1863.*

*John A. Mather photograph from Pennsylvania Historical Museum & Commission, Drake Well Museum Collection, Titusville, Pennsylvania.*

## A Women's Tea Party

The dramatic documentation of female pioneers is just one aspect of pioneer life revealed in this John Mather photograph. The women's plight described in an account written in 1844, would apply to most nineteenth century situations as the West was opened up. The following excerpts from *The New York Farmer and Mechanic* are from a work identified only as a "beautiful extract" from a "recent work by S. Margaret Fuller."

"The great drawback upon the lives of these settlers, at present, is the unfitness of the women for their new lot. It has generally been the choice of men and the women to follow, as women will, doing their best for affection's sake, but too often in heart-sickness and weariness. Besides, it frequently not being a choice or conviction of their own minds that it is best to be here, their part is the hardest, and they are the least fitted for it. The men can find assistance in field labor, and recreation with the gun and fishing rod. Their bodily strength

is greater, and enables them to bear and enjoy both of these forms of life.

The women can rarely find any aid in domestic labor. All its various and careful tasks must often be performed, sick or well, by the mother and daughters, to whom a city education has imparted neither the strength nor the skill now demanded.

The wives of the poorer settlers, having more hard work than before, very frequently become slatterns; but the ladies accustomed to neatness feel they cannot degrade themselves by its absence, and struggle under every disadvantage to keep up the necessary routine of small arrangements.

With all these disadvantages for work, their resources for pleasure are fewer. When they can leave the housework, they have not learnt to ride, to drive, to row alone. Their culture has too generally been to make them "the ornaments of society." Accustomed to the pavement of Broadway, they dare not tread the wildwood paths for fear of rattle-snakes!"

## The Bertrand

With the discovery of gold in 1862 at Alder Gulch in Montana Territory, towns like Virginia City, Deer Lodge, and Hell Gate sprang to life overnight. Supplies for these towns were shipped by boat from St. Louis to Fort Benton. From there, goods were hauled overland to the mining communities. The entire trip covered over 2,000 miles and took as long as three months. Yet, without the vital lifeline of steamboats and their supplies, few of these frontier towns would have survived.

The Missouri River, or "Big Muddy" as it was sometimes called, was a dangerous and unpredictable river that challenged the best of the riverboat pilots. The ship *Bertrand* was one of its casualties and included in its cargo was a supply of lighting destined for western stores.

*This poster, the information about the Bertrand and the illustrations on pages 53 and 64 were provided by the*
De Soto National Wildlife Refuge
Department of Interior
U.S. Fish and Wildlife Service

# 1865, 1865!
# HO! FOR THE GOLD MINES!

## THROUGH
# BILLS LADING

### GIVEN BY THE
## MONTANA & IDAHO TRANSPORTATION LINE
### TO
## Virginia City, Bannock City, Deer Lodge
### AND
## ALL POINTS IN THE MINING DISTRICTS.

The Steamers of this Line leave St. Louis as follows:

DEER LODGE, Saturday, March 4th.
BERTRAND, Thursday, March 16th.
BENTON, Saturday, March 11th.
YELLOW STONE, Saturday, March 18th.
FANNY OGDEN, Saturday, April 15th.

The New Steamer DEER LODGE, built expressly for the Fort Benton trade, will remain between Fort Union and Fort Benton, until the cargoes of all the boats of this line are delivered at Fort Benton.
We are also prepared to furnish Land Transportation to all of above points, and, having Trains of our own, Shippers can depend upon their goods being delivered according to contract.

*For FREIGHT or PASSAGE, apply to*

JOHN G. COPELIN at OFFICE OF UNITED STATES INSURANCE CO.,
south-east corner Main and Olive Streets, or

JOHN J. ROE & CO., Convent Street, between 2d and 3d Streets, or

ST. LOUIS

JON. McENTIRE, 72 Commercial Street.

## J. EAGER,
## 41 Broad Street, N. Y.

# The Ship *Bertrand*

We hear of sunken treasure and of buried treasure. The tale of the *Bertrand* is one of both sunken *and* buried treasure. It is a tale of a ship discovered and a ship uncovered. The peculiar circumstances of this strange combination have created a window that opens onto scenes of life, on a particular date, and at a precise time: April 1st 1865. It is indeed "**A Moment Frozen in Time.**"

The *Bertrand* was a supply ship destined for the western gold fields. It was among the first ships of the season to take advantage of the swollen Missouri River. Everything from goods to restock the general stores, to mining supplies and personal belongings was aboard.

The ship, built in Wheeling, West Virginia, in 1864, left St. Louis March 1865, and stopped at Omaha, Nebraska, to pick up some passengers. On April 15th about 25 miles upstream, it struck a snag and sank. Fortunately all the passengers got ashore quickly and safely. The Missouri River flowed through flat sandy soil. Snags and trees could cause the banks to become undercut and the river to change course very quickly. Shipwrecks were not uncommon. During the 1800s over 400 riverboats sank on the Missouri. In the case of the *Bertrand*, both the ship and the river were lost!

When salvers arrived to rescue the *Bertrand*'s cargo, they were instructed to proceed upstream to the ship *Cora* with a more valuable cargo. Upon returning to the *Bertrand* site, both the ship and the river had disappeared! Presumably the river had quickly changed course and silt had covered the ship. Over the years the value of the cargo grew in men's minds, and the enthusiasm for the search was kept alive. Using sophisticated detection equipment, the ship was located in 1968 by salvers Jesse Pursell and Sam Corbino from Nebraska. The luck for posterity was that the location was on the DeSoto Wildlife Preserve in the southwestern corner of Iowa. The result of this was the careful and costly operation to reclaim and preserve the treasure.

There was not the anticipated gold or mercury or whiskey, but a treasure trove of artifacts that present a true picture of that time and circumstance. It was Marianne Nolan, editor of *The Rushlight*, who suggested to me that there might have been examples of lighting on board. I had only heard of the *Bertrand* bottles. A call to my neighbour Joyce Lee, and we were on our way the following week.

Expecting to find a storage facility, it was a delightful surprise to discover the De Soto Visitor Center was an architectural gem. The visitor's center caters to the wildlife interests and houses both the records and the artifacts from the Bertrand. It is the scope of the treasure and the state of preservation that makes this collection such an exceptionally valuable research resource. No matter where one's area of interest may lie, many more will be aroused when one views the collection.

The kerosene lighting artifacts discovered were catalogued before there was much interest and information available on the subject. While not really inaccurate, the nomenclature was at times inconsistent and different from that generally used today. The fact that some identical examples were classified at different times in different ways, by different people and in different categories, makes it difficult to come up with accurate totals of each item and condition.

Considering the fragile nature of some of the objects, and the circumstances of their recovery, it is virtually impossible to reconstruct the numbers involved in the original shipment. Quantities recovered represent from one to over a hundred examples, and the condition ranged from fragmentary to excellent.

Some of the glass and marble was subject to deterioration. The brass burners range from excellent to almost complete disintegration. Little of the original finish remains. This may not have been recognised, and it may have been removed during the cleaning processes, or the original finishes may not have survived. Attention given to original metal finishes is fairly recent.

The most exciting and significant information from the ships cargo is contained in the selection chosen for use in remote Western mining towns. This was at a time before railroads penetrated the west. Water was the main supply route and the discovery of the *Bertrand* gives an accurate representation of what was available and desirable at that particular time.

The burners, chimneys, and shade holders selected are not too surprising, but the choice of lamp fonts (or pegs as they would have been listed at the time), is particularly interesting. Remarkably, they include mold blown, free blown, common pressed, and plunger-pressed designs *and* pillar molded! Perhaps the greatest surprise was the pillar molded small fonts. This technique was rarely used for *any* lamps made in the United States after 1850! Will other examples be recognised in the future?

Hobbs, Brockunier & Company in Wheeling, West Virginia, used the same plunger-pressed designs found on the *Bertrand*, with their patented September 20, 1870 clinch connectors. See OL-1 pages 24 and 151 for examples. These fonts made without the patented indentations and mounted on other bases were considered to have been made prior to 1870. Now we know that they could have been made as early as 1865, and possibly earlier. This is important information to have when furnishing restored homes.

For this subject and time period, no other source of information can compare with this discovery in terms of identification and dating. Very little can compare with the excitement and the story of the recovery.

a.

b.

c.

## April 1, 1865:
## A Moment Frozen in Time.

The visitor's center display reinforces the moment, while taking the visitor through the experiences of those involved in the recovery of the artifacts that had been buried for over a hundred years. Cool temperatures and reduced light levels serve not only to protect and preserve the considerable numbers and wide variety of items on view, but also provide an appropriate ambience.

Only wide open spaces shown in (b) present both a "before" and an "after" picture of the site of the buried ship *Bertrand*. Photograph (c) taken during the recovery gives only a slight indication of the enormity of the project. The ship, approximately 178 feet in length, was not only buried 28 feet below the surface, but also *below the water table!*

Heavy equipment was used to strip away the top layers of cover. When water was encountered at a depth of 10 feet, it was necessary to surround the ship with 210 well points. Water was pumped continuously for the duration of the recovery to keep the area dry. Over 200,000 objects were recovered during the operation which lasted about a year and a half. Stabilising and recording the collection however lasted over a decade.

The soil that made cleaning a tedious task was blue clay. On the other hand it excluded air and was a major factor in the preservation of the artifacts. To view foodstuffs such as pickles and brandied cherries still packed in their original containers is truly astonishing! It is also an indication that there were some customers waiting for treats beyond the bare necessities.

Photograph (d) shows the initial separation and cleaning of lighting artifacts. This would have been relatively easy compared with cleaning fragile objects such as fabrics and leather. There were however some lighting objects of a less durable nature that survived remarkably well. These included a mica chimney, candles, and paper labels.

Lamps in (e) are laid out for cataloguing, and in (f) representative or actual numbers are displayed behind glass walls in a climate controlled situation that is unaffected by visitors.

It is not entirely accurate to claim that the ship had remained undisturbed from the moment it sank. Missing vital parts of the ship was clear evidence of removal, and the almost complete absence of the most sought after cargo, namely whiskey and mercury, is suspect.

d.

e.

f.

# Pressed Fonts From the *Bertrand*

To use the 1860s contemporary nomenclature, these fonts would have been ordered as pegs. Today they are referred to as fonts and the bottom appendage required to cement it to the base is called a peg. Obviously for discussion it is easier to describe them as font and peg. The fact that they were shipped as separate parts allows us to examine them more closely and to make comparisons. In this instance it is by comparing photographs.

It was through assistance of Leslie Perry Peterson, museum curator and cooperation of the staff at the Visitor's Center that I was able to photograph and study the Bertrand artifacts. In the absence of a studio, it was necessary to improvise. Two 75-watt reflector bulbs provided the light. White cards and mirrors were used to reflect and direct light. To give definition to the edges of the clear glass, pop cans were wrapped with black felt. This created a movable cylinder that could be positioned easily. There was one heart-stopping moment that glass collectors can relate to. It was the sound of a loud sharp crack! With a sickening feeling, the lamp being photographed was slowly approached and carefully examined. Amazingly there was no damage visible. Further examination revealed that it was a dent in the pop can that had suddenly expanded with the heat from the lights.

Another circumstance that I found impossible to overcome was the fact that the fonts could not be balanced on their pegs and therefore had to be inverted to balance on their broader based necks. This resulted in shadows at the top of the pictures and surrounding the necks, and an absence of shadows at the bottom of the pictures around the pegs.

All of these fonts are pressed glass. Both (a) and (b) are

*a. Double Bullseye.*

*b. Bullseye and Fleur-de-lis.*

*c. Peg indentation detail.*

shown in OL-1 p. 92. One of these is combined with an opaque white glass base; the other is an all-glass lamp with a scalloped base. The three fonts (d), (e), and (f) are plunger-pressed designs with the patterns pressed on the inside. It has been established that these were made by Hobbs, Brockunier & Company in OL-1 p. 151.

The fact that all of these fonts considered here were pressed with their pegs formed in one operation, and the fact that the indentations in the pegs are of the same design makes it highly probable that they were all made by Hobbs. Each of the two octagonal indentations per peg has four long and four short sides. Other pressed pegs with distinct designs may be attributable to specific lamp manufacturers or they may have been designed by a mold maker who supplied several manufacturers.

It is known that Hobbs provided different pegs with fonts (d) and (e) to adapt them to their May 24, 1870 clinch connector patent. See examples on page 110 where another feature of plunger pressed designs is discussed. Font (e) that I named Bethesda in OL-1 p. 148 has had nothing but the pressing technique to associate it with Hobbs. Now with the same peg design it is safe to assume that it is a Hobbs lamp manufactured before 1870. The design is most unusual with a distinct division between curved rhythmical forms and strong geometric lines.

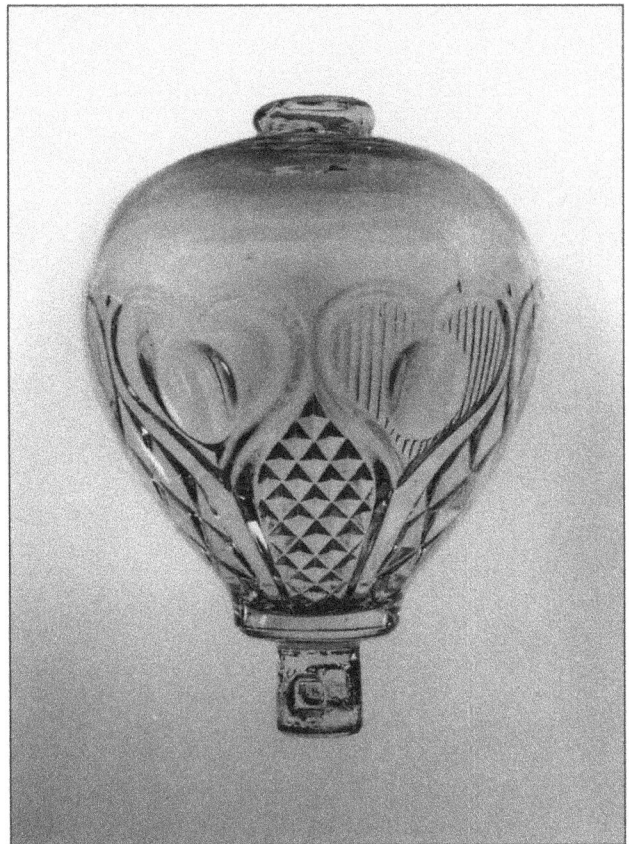

*e. Hearts under glass.*

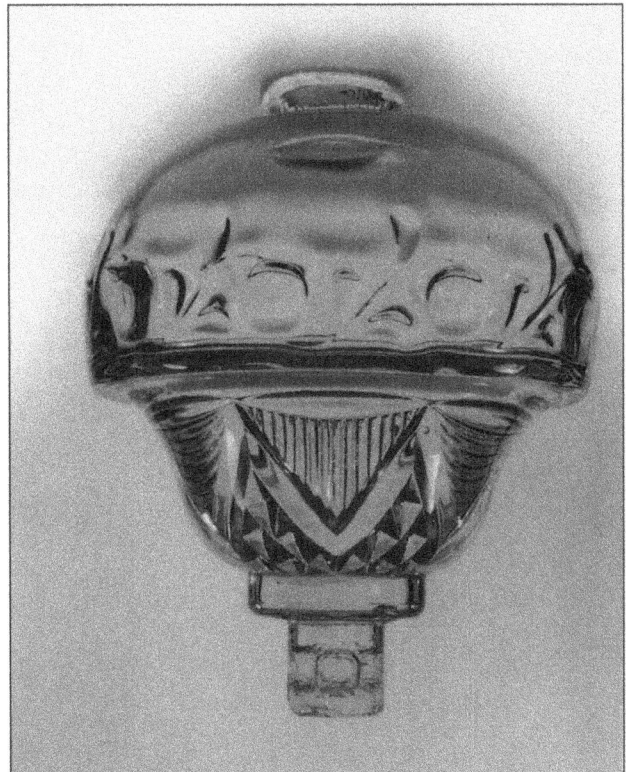

*d. Veronica.*

*f. Bethesda.*

*a.*

*b.*

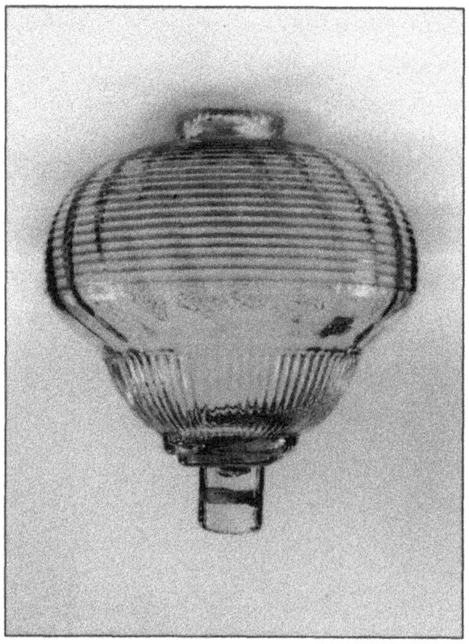

*c.*

*d.*

*e.*

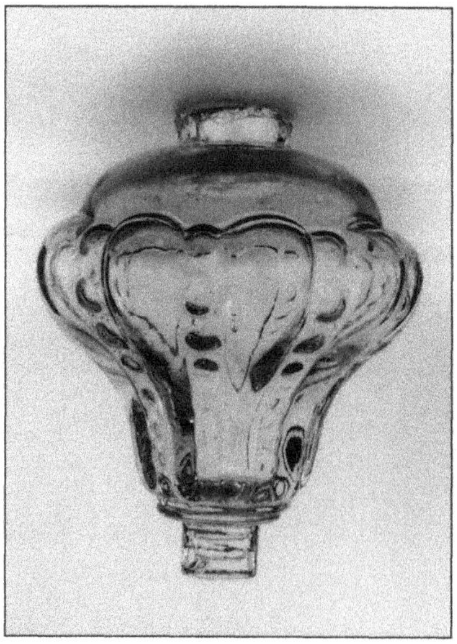

*f.*

The remainder of the Bertrand fonts have pegs that differ from the Hobbs pegs. Heart and Stars (a) has a peg with two mold seams and a molded flat rectangular indentation. Font (b) has a seamless peg with two ground indentations. Some pegs are free-formed and others are rather indistinct with the exception of (f) which has a wide rectangular indentation. Fonts (d) and (e) are optic molded. This required blowing the gather successively in two different molds to achieve an undulating effect. It was often used with opalescent glass. Although the peg (e) does not have the octagonal indentation of those on the previous page, it is shown on page 114 (c) with a Hobbs clinch connector.

It appears that one-piece glass stand lamps were not included. They would have been more difficult to package and ship. This serves to emphasize the fact that there is no substance to the theory that font and base combinations of composite lamps indicate that both parts came from the same source. The combinations are worth noting because they may be a factor in combination with other data.

The Heart and Stars pattern was made by Atterbury & Company and others. Variations are shown in OL-2. Font (f) has a distinctive shape that is rarely seen. It was also made in a larger size. It is good to have confirmation of the fact that all of the unmarked glass lamps were actually made as early as 1865. Perhaps some examples remain in the western states today.

g.

As mentioned previously, the appearance of the pillar-molded font (g) was unexpected. There were several of them on display and yet I have never seen a similar example in any collection. The thick vertical undulations give these fonts a fluid appearance. They have seamless free-formed pegs with a ground indentation.

The seldom seen free-blown font (h) also has a free-formed peg. A well-detailed engraved design encircles the font. It consists of five berries and a spray of six leaves repeated three times. Additional examples of the ten panelled hand lamp (i) had the same trail detailing on the applied handle. All of the glass, fonts and hand lamps have necks that would have been fitted with No. 1 collars. Based on the style, thickness of glass and techniques used to manufacture both (h) and (i), they would likely be judged to have been made at an earlier date.

The diminutive flat hand lamp (j) has a dimpled font that is the result of what is known as mold-chill. It would be called a night lamp today. Old glass is often found with imperfections that add to its appeal and make it an excellent choice to display early chimneyless burners. There is a daisy-like design on the base, consisting of a raised button and rayed flutes.

A substantial, bold, applied handle with a fancy detailed trail has been attached to (k), a mold-blown ribbed footed hand lamp. This is another distinctive lamp to look for in the western states.

Lamp (l) is an example of an Atterbury patented hand lamp that combines pressing and blowing techniques to create a design between the inner and outer walls of the font. It is marked on the base with raised letters: PATENTED FEB 11 & JUNE 4 surrounding the date 1862.

h.

i.

j.

k.

l.

*a.*

*b.*

*c.*

*d.*

*e.*

*f.*

# Bertrand Fonts for Bracket and Hanging Lamps

Most of the fonts pictured are commonly found today. They would have been listed as founts. One exception is (a) with a 32 rib wide base that is quite stable when used alone. It is surprising that more fonts were not made for this dual role. The neck of this font has four distinct external ribs.

Supplying goods to those remote mountain towns must have been an enormous challenge. Depending upon that one source of supply would have also been stressful. Fragile, heavy, and necessary items such as these fonts, would vie for space with other household items.

Following the route that Lewis and Clark discovered just 60 years earlier meant that the trip was all upstream. This was in sharp contrast to floating the barrels of unrefined petroleum down Oil Creek, or down the Allegheny River to Pittsburgh. Transporting barrels of kerosene must have made that commodity valuable and expensive.

# Bertrand Bases and Connectors

With the exception of the pressed fonts, the glass quality ranged from fair to poor, The bases should have been considered unacceptable but there was no likelihood of them being returned! They were found in black, a watery pale green, and a translucent medium blue that was attractive. Although the connector (k) is attached to an opal or milk glass portion of a base, there were no complete ones listed. The definition of the stems was poor and the bottoms were quite wobbly. They were not completely flat but had chamfered or bevelled edges.

Brass stems were found in two styles (i) and (j). These will be an asset when dating lamps. The marble or marble-like bases however, had a problem and presented difficulties for those who attempted to explain the obvious deterioration and disintegration of the stone. One of these was catalogued as "fused sand" and further described as "Base: buff to brown. Particles fine and well sorted. Remnants of brown surface layer: thin, smooth, hard, and in some places shiny. About ¼ of base has surfaces uneven and apparently distorted by heat or erosion." I have been advised that some types of stone or marble may exhibit this kind of deterioration due to weather, or chemicals such as acid rain. The description continued, "Nut and bolt in concavity on bottom."

The connectors pictured in (k) and (l) are like those commonly found on lamps today.

g.

j.

h.

k.

i.

l.

a.

## Atterbury Lanterns

There were sufficient numbers of lantern parts recovered to indicate the example (a) pictured was part of the cargo and not one used by the crew. Few, if any, of these survived intact, but many parts were reclaimed. The following patent information is marked on the glass in raised letters spaced around the globe circular indentation for the reflector: PATENTED MAY 12 1863 / AND NOV 17.

The dates refer to patents 38,457 and 40,594, issued to brothers James S. and Thomas B. Atterbury. These patents described methods of applying metal reflectors to glass lanterns. Atterbury & Co. of Pittsburgh would have made the glass globes, but there is no indication of the metal manufacturer. The metal was catalogued as "brass, steel or iron." The museum catalogue information describes the burner (b). Impressed on the wick sleeve of burner with some of the information missing or incomplete: "VAN KIRK & FULTON / PAT. / JANY. 5. / 1864." Impressed on the thumbwheel is "VAN KIRK & Co / PATENT / JULY 17 / 1860." The 1860 date refers to No. 29,221 granted to J. T. Van Kirk of Philadelphia, and assigned to C. A. VAN KIRK & CO, also of Philadelphia. This was for a spring clip to hold a chimney and didn't apply here, but does apply to p. 63 (l). The 1864 patent No. 41,172 was granted to M. B. Wright of West Meriden, Conn. It covered the chimneyless lantern burner (b) pictured.

The shade holder (c) is marked "WEDEKINDS PAT. / FEB. 4. 1862." It is an example of one patented by Christian Reichman February 4, 1862. No. 34,332. This was assigned to Gustav Wedekind. These men were well-known lighting patentees from Philadelphia. The paper shade holder (d) is stamped "WEDEKIND'S PATENT / March 24TH 1863." This patent No. 37,990 was for an improvement in the placement of the clasps. Example (e) is unmarked but corresponds with the W. F. Shaw patent No. 22,311 of Dec. 14, 1858.

These patented paper shade holders, or clasps as they were also called, suggest paper shades were very popular. They could be shipped flat and fastened together later. Some styles were circular while others were originally made in flat strips. Any that were on the ship may not have been recognised as lamp shades or they may not have survived. Very few have survived under much more favorable circumstances. This also explains the absence of glass shades.

Some of the lighting was catalogued with household articles and sometimes other intriguing items were included, particularly: "Fur lined boots with colored designs on the exteriors and one pair of fur pants with the feet attached-leather soles." These were from "J. F. SCHIEFER & CO / SADDELERY / 90 N MAIN ST / ST. LOUIS." They were destined for "P. DORRIS / Virginia City / Montana."

b.

c.

d.

e.

# Bracket and Hanging Lamps

The cast iron wall bracket (f) was found with what was described as traces of a "Shiny black finish." Perhaps these bracket lamps would be more accurately restored this way than with the currently popular flat black finishes. This example with a reflector pin has a basket font holder with a 5½" ring supported by delicate iron loops. The cast decoration has also appeared on hanging lamps.

A separate wall mount is shown in (g) along with the one used with the bracket (h). This smaller bracket with the cast upright ivy decoration was illustrated in the Bradley & Hubbard 1873 catalogue and the 1865 Russell & Erwin catalogue. In addition to the smooth polished reflector, it has been found with a fluted tin reflector patented in 1862. The measurement of the ring is not given, but the outside diameter of one in a private collection is 4⅜".

The hanging or harp lamps were the most basic and inexpensive offered at that time. They continued to be offered for decades. The heavy wire one on the left (i) has no provision for a smoke bell. Perhaps it was intended to be hung from a high ceiling by a wire or chain. The second one (j) has a rope twist brass frame with a cast smoke-bell hook and the ubiquitous hand held wreath that served as a hook. Both harps had plain brass ring font holders.

These lamps could have been made more attractive with a paper shade added, but they would not compare with the attractive ball or Oregon shades with frosted designs available at that time in the East. Clearly, their fragile nature and the weight of more ornate frames ruled out such lamps as part of the cargo.

f.

g.

h.

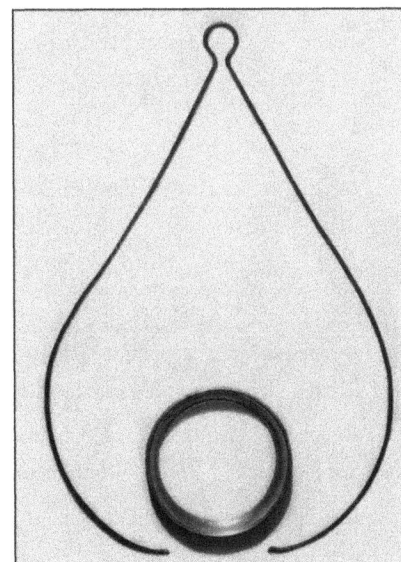

i.

j.

*a. Photograph courtesy the Bertrand Museum.*

b.

c.

d.

# Chimneys

Chimney information noted here is derived from catalogue listings from the Bertrand Museum. These listings comprise 38 lots ranging from one to 140 per lot for a total of about 450 glass chimneys, plus 10 mica chimneys. Presumably the chimneys were intended to be used with the burners pictured opposite. It should be noted that this was the period before the popularity of slip burners and chimneys.

In photograph (a), a frosted chimney is illustrated. This was described as their number 681. The records included the following information: "Transparent colorless glass. Band of frosted glass $2\frac{3}{8}$ inch wide located $\frac{1}{2}$ inch above base and fading out along the edges, especially the lower. Flared rim $\frac{3}{16}$ inch wide (inside measurement) around lower opening which is $1\frac{1}{4}$ inches in diameter. Maximum diameter is $2\frac{11}{16}$ inches. Upper edge rounded and irregular: measures (from outside) approximately $\frac{7}{8}$ inch by 1 inch. Height $7\frac{3}{4}$ inches." The description implies a brushed finish rather than an acid finish.

There were minor variations in the sizes described. They have been averaged for this account. Four heights: 4 inches, 6, 8, and 10 inches were found. The most common size was 8 inches with bases of $1\frac{5}{8}$ inches. These numbered about 120, and the other three sizes about 55 each. If the tallest chimney in the photograph (a) is $7\frac{3}{4}$ inches, then the other two would be the 6 inch and 4 inch size. The slim 4 inch sizes were likely for the NE PLUS ULTRA burners.

The two short chimneys (b) fit the description of seven catalogued in lot 1647 and also 43 in lot 1638. They are $4\frac{1}{4}$ inches high and have a maximum diameter of $2\frac{7}{8}$ inches. The top outside diameter is $1\frac{5}{16}$ inches and the bottom outside diameter is $1\frac{5}{8}$ inches. There are slight variations to these measurements noted. By a strange coincidence, I have examined a chimney with these exact measurements and with two vertical mold seams as noted in the description. This one however was marked PAT AUG 7 1866! Could the Bertrand examples have been a prototype for this invention? It was No. 56,952 patented by Anson Judson of Brooklyn, New York, as a form "To prevent the fracture of the chimney by the unequal exposure to heat to which other forms are subject." Judson referenced the January 5th 1864 patent No. 41093 of Joseph Ridge of Indiana, for a short chimney in combination with a special burner. Neither patent provided dimensions and several other burner patents illustrated short, wide chimneys.

The four chimneys in (c) and (d) in very good condition were selected at random. Many of those recovered showed evidence of deterioration.

# Bertrand Burners

There were approximately 300 burners catalogued in 24 lots ranging from 1 to 107 burners per lot. It was impossible to relate the descriptions to the random selection of burners photographed without knowledge of how or if they were marked. They can however be separated into categories.

The first category involved the majority of burners. These were manufactured by Holmes Booth and Haydens (H. B. & H.) and are pictured from (e) to (k). The patents associated with the first six burners were: January 11, 1859, January 24, 1860 and September 16, 1862. The first of these was for the reissue No. 648, of the Edward F. Jones patent spring clip shown on (e). The January 24, 1860 date was for a patent issued to George Neilson and assigned to Holmes, Booth and Hayden [sic.]. This was for the corrugated lip of the cone found on Jones and other burners made by H. B. & H.

The third Sept. 16, 1864 patent date, that is frequently found around the base of burners stamped on the wick case, was for patent No. 36493. This was issued to L. J. Atwood for a wick tube that had several features including a flared base to make threading the wick easier.

There were several burners marked NE PLUS ULTRA as shown in (k). These small round-wick burners, marketed for many years, are found with one-inch seamless or molded chimneys. They are marked on the thumbwheel wheel with the Holmes, Booth and Haydens name and Neilson 1860 patent date.

Over 25 Van Kirk burners were recovered. They included examples like (l) with the tabs that form the gallery to hold the chimney, having small side projections. There were also examples with the side projections connected forming a lattice effect. Both these styles are found today. This was the burner referred to on page 60 where patent statistics are given.

Not pictured here are the Cornelius & Baker burners. Two are listed. They are described as having "CORNELIUS & BAKER / PHILA" on the wick screw (thumbwheel) and "PATENTED / DEC 9 1862" on the exterior of the burner plate, enclosed in an oval, with an oval sunburst between the 2 lines. I am not sure what that refers to. The patent was granted to Robert Cornelius of Philadelphia. It was described as a method of securing the shade (chimney) to the dome (cone) and the dome to the lamp (burner) by means of a spring clip. Also included was an improved wick tube design described as "auxiliary vertical end guide pieces for directing the air at the ends of the flame and preventing it from expanding or burning irregularly."

Today the Cornelius and Baker are the most sought after burners of those on the Bertrand cargo list.

e.

f.

g.

h.

i.

j.

k.

l.

# Bertrand Accessories and Parts

The choice of the rather special match safes (a) appears relatively sophisticated for such a rugged destination. They were catalogued as brass match safes with segmented roll-top covers, approximately 2¾" in length and 1⁵⁄₁₆" high.

Square wooden matches found on the site were described as being approximately 2½" long. Matchbox fragments and an empty case had the following information: 6 BOXES / SUPERIOR / 2 DOZEN / TELEGRAPH / MATCHES / MANUFACTURED BY / A. EICHLE / ST. LOUIS MO. They were destined for VIVIAN & SIMPSON / Virginia / CITY. M.T.

Green on white three cent Internal Revenue stamps were on the match boxes.

Patent dates embossed on the thin brass base of the mica chimney (b) refer to patent No. 29,172 issued to James Y. Humphrey, July 17, 1860 for a mica chimney and patent No. 35,239 issued to Timothy T. Jacobs for an improved method of securing chimneys to lamps. Remnants of a paper label with instructions adhere to the example illustrated.

b. Patented mica chimney.

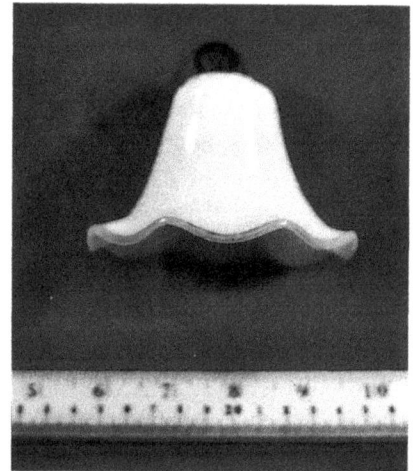

a. Brass roll-top match safe.

The smoke bells were likely intended for use with the frames illustrated on page 61. The one pictured (c) has a transparent bright red edge. The majority of these opal glass bells found today with colored edges are trimmed with red or different shades of blue. Green and black are uncommon.

c. Smoke bell.
Photograph courtesy the Bertrand Museum.

d. Smoke bell.

I do not have the catalogued information related to this example, however the dimensions are apparent from the photograph.

Some of the plain white smoke bells are described as having eight scallops and some with ten. They measure from 3" to 3½" high. It will be very useful to compare these artifacts with catalogues and extant examples.

# Patented Lighting

Patents for profit.

Patents for protection.

Patents for promotion.

No matter in which order you place their importance, patents were the magic of the kerosene era! Over five thousand kerosene related patents provide a framework for research. In addition to the basic invention patent records there were design patents, trademarks, reissues and extensions recorded. There are also application files and litigation records available. The people, places, and companies noted in the patent records suggest relationships to be explored.

From the time *Scientific American* was founded in 1845, the editors took a strong interest in patents. The publishers, Munn & Company, even offered readers a complete patent soliciting service, arranging for clients all the details required to obtain a patent. For an additional fee they would publish an illustrated description. In their annual *Scientific American Reference Book*, a "How to Get Rich" section offered the prospect of fame and fortune to inventors, no doubt encouraging thousands of minor and trivial inventions. Through the balance of the century Munn & Company were the No 1 patent solicitors and promoters in the United States.

The *Scientific American* publications give life, meaning, and sometimes humour to the official patent information. While trends are noticeable in the *Patent Gazettes* or *Patent Office Reports,* they are much more obvious in the *Scientific American.* The impact of current political and economic conditions on invention also is quite evident. The development of ideas can sometimes be traced from a casual suggestion through to a successful patent. After kerosene was established as an illuminant and petroleum

*Is there a genie in the lamp smiling down at the boldly marked Atterbury patent date on the base?*

successfully drilled for, transported, and marketed, the interest of inventors turned to ballooning and the feasibility of flying.

The public was caught up in the aura that surrounded inventors, and the magic created by the word patented. If there was a patent remotely connected with their product, manufacturers prominently displayed the fact. The claims of the patentee were seldom explained. If it involved a manufacturing improvement the public generally didn't know or care. While for most of

this period it was a legal requirement to mark products with applicable patent dates, it was not necessary to do it in such a prominent manner as was done in the example here. It is described in OL-1 p. 132.

Credit given for an original idea is often hotly debated. All subsequent relative patents are improvements. Success can be measured in terms of novelty or of success in the marketplace. It is really the latter that is of greatest interest to the inventor and the manufacturer.

## COAL OIL BURNERS, SHADES, CLASPS, ETC.

(Continued.)

*E. F. Jones burners from the Russell & Erwin 1865 Hardware Catalogue.*
Courtesy the Association for Preservation Technology.

These burners are generally conceded as the most successful burners of the early 1860s. The measure of success being popularity and profit. Patented first in the late 1850s by Edward F. Jones of Boston, it featured the readily recognisable spring clip to hold the chimney and cone in place. If a manufacturer's name is included on the thumbwheel, it is Holmes, Booth & Haydens. They were located in Waterbury, Connecticut.

A news item reported in the *American Gas-Light Journal* dated February 1, stated "A VALUABLE PATENT.— The small, flat brass spring used on some kerosene lamps, to secure the chimney, is the invention of E. F. Jones of Massachusetts. This patent has proved a very valuable one to its inventor, as from one burner factory in Connecticut alone, where 200 dozen burners per day are made, he is paid $300.00 per month." With a patent fee of $15.00 at that time and a skilled workman's wage around $2.00 per day, this would have been a great incentive for creative minds.

Changes were introduced to the U.S. patent law in 1861. The term for invention patents was increased to 17 years. The fee for design patents was set at $10.00 for 3½ years, $15.00 for 7 years and $30.00 for 14 years protection. The application fee for inventions was reduced from $30.00 to $15.00.

The fee for foreign patentees was made the same as for United States citizens — except Canadian inventors. They were charged $500.00! This was in retaliation for the Canadian law allowing only their own citizens and British subjects to obtain patent protection in Canada. The refusal of reciprocity was a contentious issue that took over a decade to resolve. During that period Canadians could scan the weekly United States patent reports, select a promising invention, and rush to the Canadian patent office to apply for a similar patent that would protect them for the production of the device in Canada.

A cursory investigation suggests that this seldom happened and, in fact, the enormous fee of $500.00 for Canadians to secure a United States patent really placed them at a great disadvantage. Few could afford to enter the American market. This situation led one Canadian to give away his idea for a burner. His letter, published in *Scientific American,* offered the invention to anyone who wished to patent it. The letter was signed "A Poor Canadian Burner."

In 1873 reciprocity between the United States and Canada was finally achieved. The *Official Gazette* stated that Canada had "expunged that unfriendly condition." Canadian patent protection became available to United States citizens and Canadians were no longer assessed the prohibitively high fee for a U.S. patent.

The following is a verbatim account included for its information and perspective of the time.

### BOSTON TRADE NOTES

(Regular Correspondence Crockery and Glass Journal.) Boston, August 10th, 1875.

#### The Patent Office

A Correspondent, in an account descriptive of a visit to the Patent Office at Washington, says:

Since the organization of the Patent Office one hundred and ten thousand patents have been granted. Between five and six hundred of these were to citizens of foreign countries; the remainder to American citizens. The acting Commissioner, General Duncan, in an exceedingly able and interesting lecture, delivered before the American Social Science Association last March, makes the following distribution of patents: "To New England, about twenty per cent, Massachusetts having as her share ten per cent, and Connecticut five; to the Middle States, thirty-six per cent, New York alone receiving twenty-three per cent; to Ohio and Illinois, seven per cent each; to California, two per cent; and to the eleven States that engaged in the rebellion, but four and one-half per cent." In evidence of the impulse given to the southern mind by the removal of the institutions which produced such complete mental and physical stagnation may have taken the fact that while, before the war, the agricultural inventions of the South were barely two per cent of the whole, they have, since the close of the war, reached seven per cent.

Inventions are most numerous in agricultural implements and household conveniences. Of agricultural inventions, the greatest number is from the West; of inventions in manufactures, from New England and New York. The applications for patents form a curious index to the mind of the country. There are what may be called epidemics of inventions. Whatever interest is dominant for the time being is almost unerringly indicated by the business of the Patent Office.

It is like laying the finger on the pulse of the nation and counting its heart beats. During the rebellion, invention and improvements in everything that could in any way be used in war, completely overwhelmed the examiners. During the velocipede mania four hundred and thirty-two applications were made for patents in four months' time. Never a great fire but brings out some improvement in fire escapes or heating apparatus. Never a great burglary but is almost immediately followed by one or more inventions and locks. Scarcely a kerosene accident but brings an improved burner. In this one article over four hundred patents have already been granted. Last spring when so many banks were deceived by cheques altered from small to large amounts, there were filed in less than a week, over forty applications for patents for an invention by which such alteration could be at once detected. Each one of forty applicants expected, no doubt, to make his fortune from so exceedingly useful an important invention. They all embodied the same idea; and an examination showed that a patent had been issued for the very same thing thirty years ago. When planchette was all the rage, a dozen inventions of that kind were before the examiner at one time. To all of them patents were refused on the grounds that it was not a useful invention; but, on the contrary, decidedly pernicious and mischievous, many persons having thereby been rendered insane.

Before granting a patent, various questions besides the novelty of the invention are considered. This is of course the primary question; "Is it new with the applicant?" The decision of this question involves an immense amount of labor and research, an examination of all of the reports and countries, and numerous scientific works. Legal questions are also involved which must be carefully decided. The question of novelty being settled, that of utility arises. Is the invention useful; or is it trivial, inoperative, or positively injurious and hurtful? In either case a patent is refused. A

notable case of refusal of a patent on account of the msichiveous [sic] tendency of the invention occurred under the administration of Hon. Joseph Holt. The applicant desired a patent for "a policeman's club, so constructed that, upon releasing a spring, a triple row of keen-edged lancets would leap from hidden recesses and mangle the hand of an adversary." The applicant's professed object was to provide a weapon which should obviate the necessity of the carrying of firearms by policeman, and yet to furnish them with full means of protection. The Commissioner refused the patent on the ground that while the professed object was laudable one, "the transforming of the implement to a weapon of offence in the hands of desperadoes, as would inevitably be done, would be a great evil." In his decision occurs the forcible sentence: "An invention, to be patentable, must not be useful to the few with a chance of it becoming hurtful to the many; but it must clearly appear that in view of the interest of the whole community, the good would decidedly preponderate over the evil."

In almost all classes of invention, the names of women appear as patentees. In articles of wearing apparel they are largely represented. For several improvements in cooking stoves there are female names. An Indiana lady has invented the fluting machine; another, within a few months, has taken out several patents for different improvements in the construction of axles; and women's names are attached to some valuable improvements in surgical apparatus, this last forming a strong argument in favor of the idea by some eminent physicians that women are peculiarly fitted by nature for the study and practice of medicine.

Leaving the "model hall," we descend to the lower floor, and passing the examiners' rooms; the library, with its twenty thousand volumes; draughtsman's room, where are preserved drawings of every invention for which

a patent has been sought since the organization of the office; the record room, where are the printed reports of patents granted, the issue of each week in a separate volume, we come to the sunny southeast corner, where, in a pleasant room brightened by the most cheerful of inanimate things, a blazing wood fire, the Commissioner "improves each shining hour." We will go in here.

The stream of business is at flood tide, and we sit quietly and watch and listen. One o'clock is set for the hearing of a "case of interference." An interference is a proceeding to determine which of two or more persons has the right to an invention, each claiming to be first inventor. The principals are not present. There respective attorneys argue the case — outwardly calm, inwardly raging. "Their words were smoother than butter, but war in their hearts." The decision is made, and they retire; one jubilant, the other in an unmistabable [sic] fit of the sulks. "Will the General see a gentleman?" inquires the magnificence at the door. The General will; and a quiet-looking elderly man enters, evidently under great excitement, that kind of excitement so intense that it produces a calm almost like death. He lays a model on the table. "This does not represent my case," he says. "I find that the model is made wrong. This," holding out a little piece of machinery, "should have been put in instead of that. Can I substitute it now?" "How is your drawing?" the Commissioner asks; "Does it correspond with this model, or with what you intended?" "It is like this." "Then all you can do is withdraw this and file a new application." "I have spent months upon this;" his hand trembles and there is a quiver in his voice. The General's keen eye takes in all, and very gently he says: "I wish I could do otherwise; but in these matters the office has no jurisdiction. we [sic] have to go according to law."

# Design Patents

*a. Design No. 9,724 patented January 30, 1877.*

*b.*

This patent design for a "lamp-holder" was granted to Joseph Kintz of West Meriden, Conn. It was used on the Bradley & Hubbard bracket lamp shown on p. 183. That font holder is marked with the Kintz date and another for an invention patent date, Jan. 31, 1870, granted to N. L. Bradley of Bradley & Hubbard.

There were more than ten times as many kerosene lighting related invention patents as design patents. They are interesting to study and compare. As with invention patents, the patent copies can offer information and specifications about invention or design that can lead to further research. In addition to the name or names of the patentees and their addresses, the patent may have been assigned to other individuals, manufacturers or even wholesale distributors. Occasionally the name of a witness may be recognised as a familiar one in the lighting field.

Most of the patent illustrations are line drawings, however sometimes photographs were submitted. This may be an indication that the patent was commercially produced. Many design patents listed under glass also apply to lamps. Sometimes manufacturers or lamp dealers used a line illustration with letters or numbers in their advertisements or on their letterheads. These can be useful for identification.

With a fee as low as ten dollars for three and a half years protection, it is particularly interesting to note how much protection manufacturers would pay for. Since they could well afford the thirty dollars for 14 years protection, they would likely only pay that amount if they expected to produce the design for a long time.

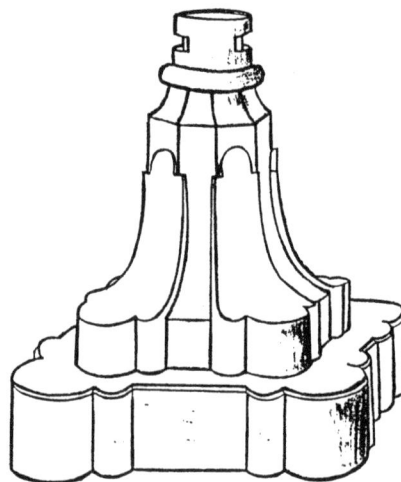

*c.*

Lamp design patents (b) and (c) were granted to Henry Whitney of The New England Glass Company. They are No. 4021 May 10, 1870, for the font and No. 3068, June 2, 1868, for the base. For further information about the font, see page 113, and for an example of the base, see page 105 (c). Examples extant of this patented lamp base have been found with gilt designs in remarkably good condition. It is difficult to say whether this is due to the quality of the manufacture or to the care taken by the owners.

The font patent appears to be the same as the one that appeared a year earlier in an advertisement. See page 113. Other patented articles were known to have been manufactured before the patent was granted. The description of the peg was given as a "central pin or projection." One would expect that it would have had a generic name by that time.

# Patent Models

The patent office required a model to be submitted with each application. They had to be no larger than 12x12x12 inches. Occasionally this was exceeded, particularly if a production model was submitted. The most appealing models were miniature replicas of much larger inventions, such as furniture. Unfortunately in this regard most lighting patent models are actual size. Many inventors adapted currently available production models to demonstrate their invention.

In 1870 the model requirement was repealed, however the Patent Commissioner overruled this, and the requirement continued until 1880. After that, models were only required for two categories, perpetual motion machines and flying machines, or by special request.

There was no tag for this brass and copper model, and in fact it was inverted in a tin container when I purchased it from O. Rundle Gilbert after one of his famous auction sales. The clue to its identity was the script engraving that read Platt & Rosecrans/ Cin^ti O. This referred to patent No. 33,402 granted October 12, 1861. A British patent No. 985 was granted on April 7, 1862 for the same invention. There was no reference to the occupations of the patentees, however an article in the September 6, 1862 issue of *Scientific American* mentioned another patent for index scales by these two gentlemen who they described as Dr. A. H. Platt and Gen. W. S. Rosecrans!

A prominent Civil War general may now be also recognised as an early kerosene Argand burner patentee. The burner which had a short chimney was for "Burning Lard, Whale, Cotton-Seed and Coal-Oils." The advantage of this burner over an Argand lamp which required an expensive custom-made font with a "metallic tube extending entirely down through the lamp open at the lower end" was that it could be adapted to ordinary lamps and brought "within the reach of all classes." Six wicks were intended to be adjusted by the six-toothed wheels to form a circular wick. I have not heard of a production example, however if there was one, it may have had a different appearance from the patent model. Height of the model is 7½".

Argand lamps and burners continued to be popular during the 1860-1900 period. Student and parlour lamps, were the most popular type of Argand kerosene lamps but they were also complex and costly to construct. A less expensive solution was a separate burner that could provide air to the inside and outside of a circular flame. Strong demand produced intense competition not only to provide Argand burners with the basic air-flow and circular flame requirements but also to incorporate unique designs for special features. Patents abounded and almost every major manufacturer advertised a special variety. Many of these variations can be found today.

*Anson H. Platt and General William S. Rosecrans Argand burner patent model. October 12, 1861.*

*a. Brass and glass patent model inscribed:*

**E. S. Blake's
Perpetual
Lamp Chimney**

*The*

*Red White & Blue*

*forever*

## E.S. Blake's Perpetual Lamp Chimney

Perhaps the most interesting part of this model is the script engraving on the lower brass band inscribed in upper and lower case italics.

This model was submitted for the second of three similar patents obtained by E. S. Blake of Pittsburgh. From the patriotic inscription and the Civil War period, as well as the basic concept, it can be assumed that it was really intended for practical rather than decorative use. Perhaps it was intended to be used on military sites.

The sheet-brass frame that would fit over a burner held small flat pieces of glass. Easy replacement and ease of shipping were stated advantages. Ease of cleaning was not mentioned!

The patent information has been marked with a steel stamp in an arc around the cylindrical chimney as follows: E. S. BLAKE. PATENTED JULY. 18. 1862. & FEB. 9. 1864. Although it is very clearly marked July 18, the date was actually July 15. Invention patents were granted on Tuesdays, a fact that is often used when researching patents.

Blake's first 1862 patent, and the one that most closely resembled the model, was No. 35,866. The second one was No. 41,473 and a later third one, No. 44,508, was patented Oct. 4, 1864.

The curved steel stamp with the patent dates that was used to mark the model would have been custom made and expensive. Such stamps were usually used to mark products that were mass produced. This indicates **Blake** was confident that his patent would be granted or perhaps that this model was submitted later.

## Perkins and House Shade-Holders for Lamps

*b & c. Brass shade-holders patented by O.N. Perkins Dec. 10, 1872, and M. W. House July 29,1873.*

At first glance one would expect these shade-holders patented by O.N. Perkins and M.W. House to be among the patents to be associated with the well-known Perkins & House Safety Lamp. These lamps were manufactured by and extensively promoted by the Cleveland Non-Explosive Lamp Co. Actually it was only the House patent that had a direct link.

John M. Perkins of the lamp company was from Cleveland, and Orson N. Perkins was from Meriden Connecticut. Orson N. Perkins assigned his patent to Edward Miller & Co. of the same place.

The two Perkins had an association with Edward Miller & Co. in that Miller made burners for the Perkins & House lamps. The patent records reveal many potential connections.

The claim for the shade-holder (b) describes a method of manufacturing a shade-holder that is attached to a burner, however the specifications describe it as being attached to the lamp top which seems more likely.

Shade-holder (c) consists of brass wires attached to a cast brass ring. It is fastened to a Perkins & House burner with a thumbwheel dated Jul. 21. 63 and Dec. 10. 67. Both awkward in function and appearance, it probably had little if any success. Height is approximately 3¾".

This article was published in the January 2, 1868 issue of *The Mining and Petroleum Standard and American Gas-Light Journal.*

## Collins' Patent Lamp

Among the multitude of improvements in coal-oil lamps which have been brought out since the discovery of petroleum and its application for illumination purposes, none perhaps have met with as much success with the public as the "COLLINS' PATENT SUN BURNER" as it is called. This lamp is clearly illustrated herewith. It will be observed that the body, or lamp receptacle, is of the usual form: the burner and chimney being the novel feature of the invention. The chimney is broad at the bottom, and slips over the diaphragm or flat cone and rests upon the perforated disc below. The space between the disc and the cone, or diaphragm, being open to give free passage to the light through the base of the chimney, the cone or diaphragm being supported by standards rising from the wick-tube, and has its seat against the side of the chimney, while the slots allow air to pass above the cone, sufficient to support combustion, and the perforated disc below gives free ventilation to the base of the flame.

In this manner a simply constructed burner is obtained, and the draft is so arranged, together with the non-conductability of the glass at the base, as to prevent the heating of the top of the lamp, and the generation of gas, making it practically non-explosive. The glass chimney can be easily removed by hand without burning the fingers, as the lower part is always cool. It is said to save one-third of the oil, as no light is hidden below the metallic cone or diaphragm, consequently all the light is obtained due to the combustion, making a clear, white, and cheerful illumination.

This really useful and valuable invention seems to meet with remarkable favor, and we understand the patentee, M. H. Collins, is receiving a royalty amounting to $130.00 a day, which gives some idea of the value of a good improvement in the simple article of a lamp.

Messrs. Fernald & Darrow, No. 69 William Street, are general agents for this burner, of whom further information may be obtained.

The article referred to Collins' first burner patent of September 19, 1865. The princely sum of $130.00 per day makes the Jones royalty of $10.00 per day pale by comparison. Either amount, however, would have provided a great incentive to come up with the proverbial "better mousetrap."

This burner probably initiated the popularity of the cylindrical "Sun" chimney, although it was not illustrated on his 1865 patent drawing. It was shown on his next burner patent of February 4, 1868, just after this article appeared. The early Collins burners are characterised by two supports rising from the wick tube, and with a knurled edge. Later burners have four supports attached to the cone and tabs below the edge as in example (b).

*a.*

*b.*

M.H. Collins patent model chimney and burner No.126,184 dated April 30, 1872.

This brass burner with a dull silver finish has the feature of the 1868 patent that allows the chimney and cone to be lifted off the base plate together, for ease of trimming the wick and for lighting. The novel feature is the addition of two small projections on the outer edge of the cone. The constricted part of the chimney has had two vertical grooves filed on opposite sides. This combination created a secure bayonet fastening.

# Chimney-top Heaters

The patent chimney-top heater model (a) was submitted by J. B. Greene of Providence, Rhode Island, for patent No. 36,584 dated September 30, 1862. The overall height and width is 3⅛" and it holds ¾ cup of liquid when filled to the top. It is made of tin and has a flat bottom just above the band of holes that allow the heat to escape.

Photograph (b) shows a heavy rod below the bottom of the container that allows a space to prevent the air from the chimney from being blocked off.

Three brass springs hold the cup securely on a 1¾" chimney.

*a.*

*a. & b.  J. B. Greene Patent Model.*

*c.  W. L. Fish Lamp Chimney Heater Patent Model.*

W. L. Fish obtained his patent No. 35,598 for the chimney heater above on June 17, 1862. Fish, of Newark, New Jersey, obtained a reissue of this patent April 17, 1876, No.7069. This was assigned to The Kerosene Lamp Heater Company.

This patent model is exceptionally well made and lacks only the cover which was provided with a hole to fit over the chimney top. Height to the top of the chimney is 8". It is basically a heavy copper chimney with a handled cone attached. Included is an approximately ½" mica window.

An illustrated article that appeared in *Scientific American* July 26, 1862 included illustration (d) opposite.

They have used detailed renderings of different views rather than the patent drawings that are elevations resembling the patent model. The article is repeated here.

### Improved Lamp Heating Attachment

Ever since the discovery of the inexhaustible oil wells of Pennsylvania, petroleum has been produced in such quantities so large as to cause it to be offered at such very low prices that extraordinary efforts have been made to use it for heating as well as for illuminating purposes. Were it not for

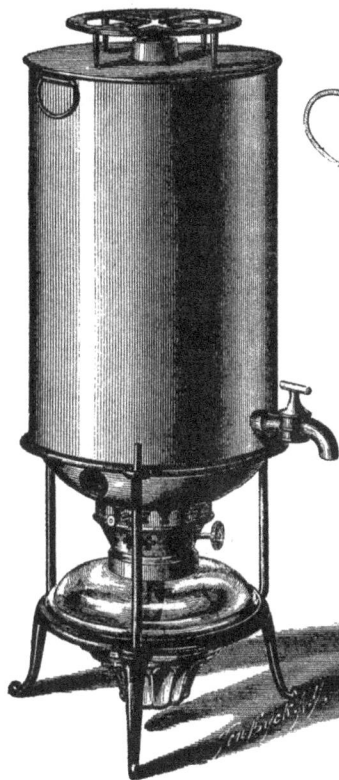

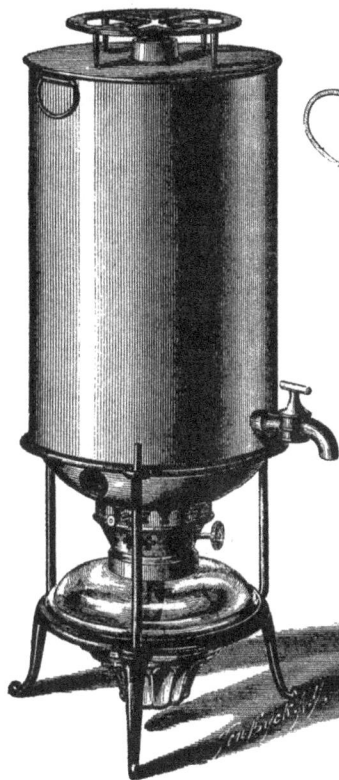
Fig. 1
Fig. 3
Fig. 4
Fig. 2

FISH'S LAMP HEATING ATTACHMENT.

d.

the disagreeable odor and the smoke which result from its combustion, it would afford a cheap substitute for the spirit lamp in chemical laboratories, and for gas in culinary operation; indeed its very low cost would probably cause it to be used to a large extent for cooking in summer, in place of wood and coal. Many plans have been suggested for producing so perfect combustion of rock oil that no smoke would be emitted, but, so far as we are aware, none of these has been entirely successful — at all events, in its application to heating purposes. By the plan which we here illustrate, the inventor claims the combustion to be absolutely perfect, so that not a particle of unconsumed smoke is left.

It consists simply in placing a metal chimney over the flame; to avoid a great waste of heat which would occur by radiation from the walls of the chimney, the chimney is carried

through the vessel to be heated. The engravings represent the plan as to be applied to a tea and coffee boiler, Fig. 1, and to a nursery lamp, Fig. 2; a section of the latter being shown in Fig 3. A is the lamp, B the chimney, and C the vessel of water surrounding the chimney. A hole made in the side of the chimney on a level with the flame, and filled with a plate of mica, through which the flame may be observed in adjusting its height to give just the amount of heat required. As a considerable portion of the heat passes up through the chimney, arrangements are made to utilize this heat which would otherwise be lost. Accordingly, a light iron stand, Fig. 4, is constructed to support a vessel of water or any other cooking dish directly over the top of the chimney. The inventor says that he has fried meat in the nicest manner, by placing a frying pan on this stand.

The utility of this invention, if all that is claimed for it by the inventor is sustained, is very great, and the variety of uses to which it can be applied is almost exhaustless. The boiler Fig. 1 is intended for making tea or coffee in warm weather, though it is well suited for use as a table urn, or for a restaurant heater, or for heating water in barbers' shops, or, in short for any similar purpose where a large fire is not required.

The nursery lamp, after this plan, is claimed to be superior to all others. The chimney passing through the water causes a constant evaporation, which moistens the air of the room, while the light issuing from only one side of the lamp, permits it to be directed wherever needed, or to be obscured entirely. Either of the vessels may be used with gas as well as with oil, and for the nursery lamp, the ordinary kerosene lamp is sufficient. The patent for this invention was granted through the Scientific American Patent agency, June 17, 1862, and further information may be obtained by addressing the inventor, W. L. Fish, at 252 Broad Street, Newark, N. J.

In the same issue, Fish advertised for agents in the United States and Canada.

**Fish's Patent Lamp-Heating Apparatus.**

From one to fourteen quarts of water boiled with an ordinary Kerosene Lamp, or Gas.
*Summer fires dispensed with.*
Send for illustrated Pamphlet which will be sent by mail free. Agents wanted.
WM. D. RUSSELL, Agt.
206 Pearl Street,
New York.

e. Advertisement in Harpers Weekly, July 25, 1863.

a. Lamp chimney patent model for J. A. Greenfield and C. H. Fry Jr. patent No. 219,716, September 16, 1879.

c. Bartholomew lamp chimney patent model.

The patentees from Bellaire, Ohio, filed the application for this patent six months earlier. There may have been a problem having it approved. They described the purpose of the unusual shape and combination of seamless glass and metal. "This construction, while it prevents the impingement of the flame upon the sides of the chimney, gives a symmetrical form, and, in connection with a metallic cap having a base-rim with an upwardly-tapering flue termination and a narrow draft-throat, gives an increased surface of white light in the flame, with a direct center draft. The chimney flaring outward and the flue of the cap flaring downward to the base gives a direct central draft, with the effect of rounding the edges of the flame without elongating it. Height is 6½".

b. Patent illustration for C. L. and C. Bartholomew chimney.

Charles L. and Cassius Bartholomew of Newark, Ohio, patented this chimney No. 215,785, March 27, 1879. Their claim could be summarised as follows:

A lamp chimney provided at its lower end with an annular indentation, the flange of which does not project beyond the periphery of the cylindrical base, to permit its use with either a slip or lip burner. They describe these burners as that class of burners which are provided with upwardly projecting flat springs or "fingers" to hold the chimney, or that class of burners in which small clamps and a set-screw are used for securing it in position. The patent illustration (b) shows the chimney with both types of burners.

Loris Russell had one of these in his collection so that confirms they were produced commercially. They are so practical, functional, and attractive that one would expect this patent to be very successful. The glass is of good quality with two vertical side seams. Height is 7".

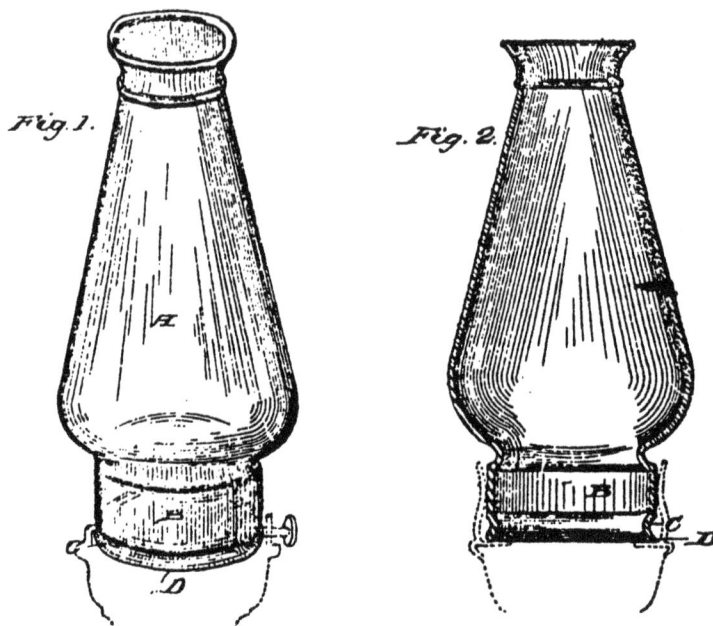

# Lantern Patent Model

This was not the first lantern to substitute a chimney for a globe, and perhaps there were more. A patent model also exists for a lantern patented by Arnold Withmar of St. Louis, Missouri. The patent No. 100,578 dated March 8, 1870, had the same objective but mounted the chimney in the usual manner with the truncated end at the top.

Withmar described his improvement as substituting "an ordinary so-called coal-oil-lamp chimney. This is purchasable at every country or town store, whilst the "globes" are not such stock in ordinary trade."

Seymour Hughes of Jersey City Heights, New Jersey, obtained his patent No. 135,711, February 11, 1873. He also stated the advantage of easy replacement. Part of his claim included "The crown or dome slitted at the lower edge to form the spring-holding jaws, and made open or provided with a removable cover at its upper end." And also that, "The globe may be inserted or removed through said crown, and adjusted and supported therein."

The model appears exactly as the patent drawing. Examples vary to some extent. This model is 11" to the top of the dome. Each of these lanterns is clearly custom made. Until an example or an advertisement is discovered, it will not be known if they were commercially made.

*Hughes lantern patent model.*

# SOMETHING NEW!

### MORSE'S PATENT

# Self Extinguishing Street Lamp

#### MANUFACTURED BY

## SAVAGE & MORSE,

### PLANTSVILLE, CONN.

*c.*

*a.*

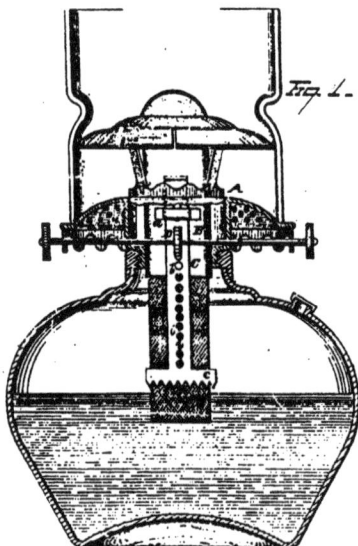

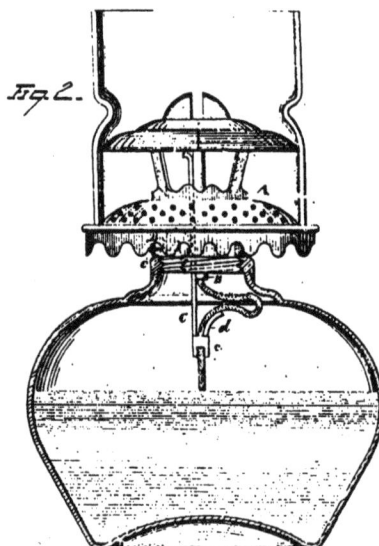

*b.*

## Auxiliary Wick-Raiser Patent Model

Edward F. Morse of Plantsville, Conn., obtained his patent No. 203,063 April 30, 1878 for an improvement in lanterns and street lamps. One-half his right was assigned to J.B. Savage of Southington, Conn. He described it as follows:

"The object of my invention is to provide the burner of a street-lamp with an auxiliary wick-adjusting attachment, whereby the amount of oil consumed in any given length of time having been determined, the light may be automatically extinguished at any desired time by regulating the amount of wick immersed in the oil of the lamp."

A Collins No. 2 burner (c), has been modified to incorporate the Morse patent. It has a felt wick. These were very popular, but few have survived. The construction was rather elementary, and its operation is clearly shown in drawing (b).

Morse suggests other forms of construction may be used. He further suggests that a time indicating dial might also be incorporated. This was actually done on other advertised models. A domestic version was also made, not necessarily by Morse. The advertising claimed the homeowner with the device would no longer have to stay up late at night to extinguish the hall light!

The manufacturer claimed, "Your lamp filled once a week will give a clear light for about six hours each night. About one-half pint of good oil will run the lamp for twelve hours at a cost of a mere trifle." Price quoted for the Lamp, Lantern, and Post complete was $8.00.

# Marks Samuels
# Patent Model

It would appear that the patent model was the model for the patent drawing. The base is almost identical. Marks Samuels of San Francisco, California, obtained his patent No. 115,528 for an improvement in lamps on May 30, 1871. There are sufficient numbers extant to establish they were commercially produced.

M. SAMUELS.
Improvement in Lamps.
No. 115,528.                    Patented May 30, 1871.

This very distinctive font is Samuels' solution to separating the reservoir, in the form of an outer ring, from the font which he described as a vertical oil tube. According to Samuels, "By no possibility can the tube which contains the oil become heated, thus avoiding any possibility of exploding the lamp."

*Samuels patent model.*

## Kleeman Student Lamp Patent Model

Shown here with its original patent model tags, this lamp is probably the best-known basic student lamp. It was No. 37,867 patented by Carl A. Kleeman of Erfurt, Prussia, March 10, 1863. There were reissues on Aug. 4, 1868, No. 3068 on March 29, 1870, No. 3900 and another on December 10, 1873. The latter was issued to Charles F. A. Hinrichs of Brooklyn, N. Y., assignee of Katharina Kleeman, executrix of Carl A. Kleeman, deceased. Later this patent was the subject of litigation that was reported in *The Crockery and Glass Journal* trade paper.

Most of the patent models here have their original tags that are held together with red cloth tape. Models that became parted from their tags were sometimes identified by markings on the models or by comparison with patent drawings. The initial patent model sales by O. Rundle Gilbert at Garrison, New York, saw the majority of models selling between two to ten dollars apiece. Many were damaged and there were were no catalogues or patent copies available. Later when that changed, prices went up substantially. This lamp sold at one of Gilbert's sales.

*Photograph courtesy Smithsonian Institution.*

# Household Lamps

This chapter includes lamps up to about 13" to the top of the collar that would have been considered everyday, functional lamps. With only a burner and chimney, they were easily carried about. Trimmed with shades, they were upgraded for use in bedrooms and parlours. They were advertised both ways and were also sold without trimmings.

This example, just under 13" high, is almost identical with the Atterbury 1881 catalogue illustration shown in OL-1 on page 186. The fonts have the same engraved design, and the stems were shown in both cylindrical and tapered forms. Both the font and shade have roughed bands and similar engraving. The stem and base are of black glass, and there is minimal enamel decoration on the stem.

The lamp also serves to illustrate the occasional use of inaccurate patent dates. The underside of the base is marked, PATD NOV, 23RD 1875. There doesn't appear to be another Atterbury patent on that date, so presumably the reference is to the Thomas Atterbury patent below.

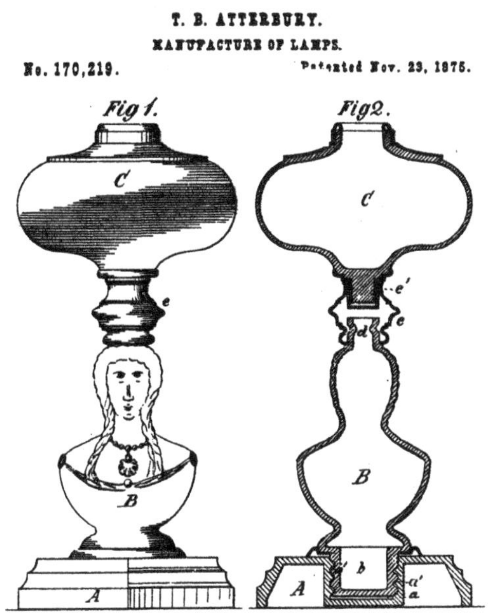

T. B. ATTERBURY.

MANUFACTURE OF LAMPS.

No. 170,219.                    Patented Nov. 23, 1875.

Fig 1.                    Fig 2.

The single patent claim states, "As a new article of manufacture a lamp having a pressed-glass base, A, and a hollow blown-glass pedestal, B, substantially as described." This patent clearly describes the lamp on page 102 that happens to be marked in the same manner and *not* this lamp pictured! The outward appearance of the hexagonal bases is the same, however this lamp has a hole for a threaded rod and nut most commonly used with similar composite lamps. With the exception of the Vine pattern font and threaded connector, the lamp on page 102 conforms to this patent illustration and description.

*Atterbury composite stand lamp.*

# Ripley & Co.

Atterbury and Ripley made many similar patented lamps. They both favoured incorporating iron handles.

*a. Patent model for a wall or bracket lamp. Ripley patent No. 101,512 April 5, 1870.*

*b. Original patent model tags. One is for the receipt of the model when it was first submitted. The larger tag was attached to the model when the patent was granted.*

Daniel C. Ripley Jr. submitted the model (a) to the Patent Office when he was only twenty years old. The base has a bead and circle within an eight-point star. See OL-1 p.198 for a similar lamp with an applied handle. Height: 2 ¾"

This is not really a glass patent but one for a means of attaching a metal handle to a glass lamp by securing it with cement between the bowl of the lamp and the collar, and adapting it for use as a wall or bracket lamp.

The patents of Daniel C. Ripley and the one issued to his son Daniel C. Ripley Jr. provide most of the documentation regarding lamps made by Ripley & Co. The following list includes many important Ripley dates and facts noted in the *Encyclopedia of Pressed Glass* by John and Elizabeth Welker.

1865 Ripley & Co. established.
1865-7 About this time George A. Duncan joined the firm as a partner.
1870 Daniel C. Ripley died.
1872 Daniel C. Ripley Jr. became president.
1874 Ripley sold his interest in the company to George A. Duncan who changed the name to George Duncan & Sons and continued business at the same location.
1875 Ripley built a new factory and again operated as Ripley & Co.
1891 The company joined the U.S. Glass Co. combine and Ripley became the first president of that new merger of eighteen glass manufacturers.
1910 Ripley with his son D.A. and F. Freese founded the third Ripley & Co. The company is no longer in business.

Between their January 7, 1868 and November 15, 1881 patents, the Ripleys were granted eight other patents for lamps and one for a baptismal font and candle holder.

No. 73,112.  Jan. 7, 1868.
Reissue No. 3,035 July 14, 1868 and No. 3078 Aug. 11, 1868.
Lamps with one, two or more handles.

No. 87,367.  Mar. 2, 1869.
Glass pedestal for a handled or low lamp.

No. 3,834.  Feb.1, 1870.
Design patent for stems of articles of glassware.

No. 3,842.  February 8, 1870.
Design patent for a baptismal font with candle holders.

No. 101,512. April 5, 1870.
Metal handle for lamp.

No. 104,205. June 14, 1870.
Known today as the Wedding or marriage lamp.

No. 107,544. September 20, 1870.
Another Wedding lamp.

No. 151,435. May 26, 1874
Attaching metal handles to lamps.

No. 177,425. May 16,1876.
Metal socket used to connect glassware and lamps.

No. 230,340. July 20,1880.
Hollow stem composite lamp.

No. 249,676. November 15, 1881.
Hollow stem one-piece lamp.

No. 257,389. May 2, 1882.
Lamp shades and globes.

At the present time it appears that all Ripley & Co. patented lamps and shades made after 1876 used only paper labels as identification. Such labels and decoration are very important to the documentation of all lamps. Thus far no examples of the last Ripley patented shades have been identified. Examples or drawings of each of the other patents is included in OL-1 or this book. On the following pages, some of the relationships between Ripley & Co., George Duncan & Sons, and Adams & Company, all of Pittsburgh, are explored. I will generally refer to them as Ripley, Duncan, or Adams.

*a. Ripley patent pending hand lamp. Height: 2⁷/₈".*

*b. Ripley patent hand lamp. Height 3".*

*c. Ripley patent hand lamp. Height: 3¹/₈".*

The popularity of Ripley's April 5, 1870 patent is evident from the variety of the examples shown here. The first of these, (a), has PATENT PENDING and the number 100 on the base.

Both the size and shape of (b) is almost the same, however the cast iron handle has a tiny thumb rest and a groove that fits over a raised mold seam. This would prevent lateral slippage. On the side it has the company name, RIPLEY & CO. embossed in an arc above PAT'D, and the date APRIL 5 1870.

The lamp (c) is marked PAT<u>D</u> APRIL 5. 1870 on the side. There is a raised area in the glass below the cast iron handle. This and the slight changes in the design of the handle were likely considered minor improvements.

Every variation of a lamp that is discovered adds evidence to the probability of its success.

*d. Ripley metal-band lamp. Height: 3¹/₄".*

The unmarked lamp (d) conforms to the patent illustration and description of Ripley's patent No. 151,435 dated May 26, 1874. Examples with the patent date on the shoulder are known. The patent describes a method of uniting a metal band and font, or similar article, by placing the metal band or handle within the mold. The bowl is then blown, filling out the mold so as to protrude slightly beyond the upper and lower edges of the band. In the completed article the band is seated in a recess encircling the lamp bowl. As with his other metal-handled lamps, this could be adapted for wall use. A wall holder can be seen on page 83.

Since 1874 was the year Ripley sold out to George Duncan, and two of the 1870 lamps were illustrated in a George Duncan & Sons catalogue circa 1884 (see p. 83), it is sometimes impossible to determine whether Ripley or Duncan actually manufactured a particular lamp.

*a. Ripley's two-handled tableware set.*

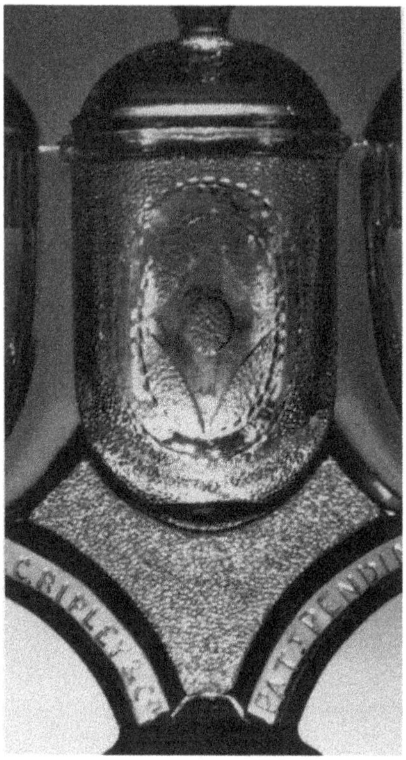

*b. Match-holder section from a clear-glass Wedding lamp.*

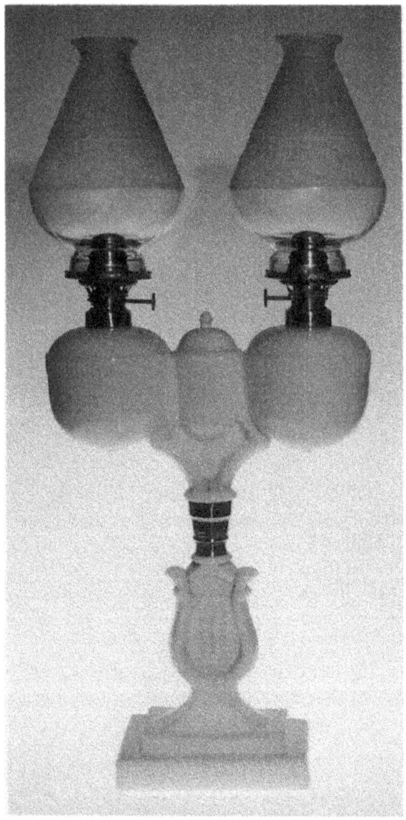

*c. Ripley Wedding Lamp.*

*d. Wedding lamp illustration*
*Courtesy the Sandwich Historical Society Glass Museum.*

Daniel Ripley's penchant for double handles extended to his design for a double-handled tableware set that included a pitcher that can be poured from either side. Both the match-holder section of the Wedding lamp (b) and the September 20, 1870 patent drawing for the lamp show the same stippled pattern. Height of these pieces are: spooner 5⅜", sugar 4¾" and creamer 6".

The opal or opaque white Wedding lamp (c) is enhanced by the addition of a pair of frosted chimneys with a raised animal design. This is a popular way among collectors to exhibit pairs of special chimneys. Patented Ripley bases were made in this lyre design and in two sizes of the design opposite, with or without the crosses. The only known illustrations of Ripley lamps by a manufacturer are shown opposite. These are from an 1884 George Duncan and Sons catalogue that also included Duncan's successful Three-Face pattern lamp.

The white opaque lamp (c) was also called milk or opal glass. In the Lovell 1877-78 catalogue illustration (d) the Ripley patent fonts have a pair of Oregon shades and a base commonly combined with other fonts in the same catalogue.

a.

There are examples of all of these hand lamps in black and white or color in this chapter. Only the small brackets for the cast iron handles always seem to be missing. While the top row of lamps appear to be probable Duncan products, it is difficult to be certain of the other marked examples.

When George Duncan bought out Ripley in 1874, the details of the sale and subsequent arrangements would have to be known to correctly determine the manufacturer. This holds true for the baptismal fonts and for other known variations.

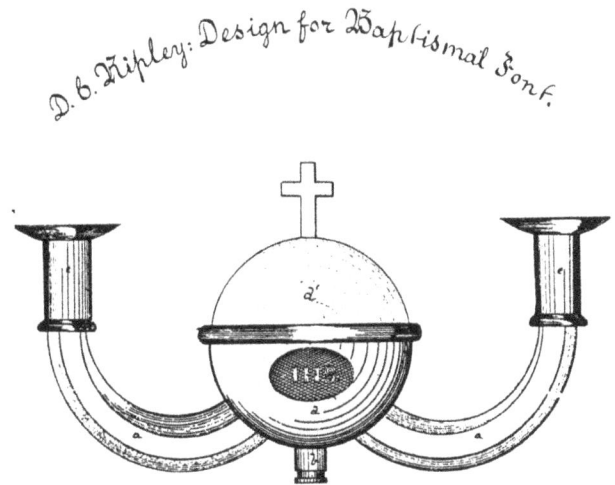

b.

c.

Daniel C. Ripley's patents for the candlestick on the left and the base or pedestal for the baptismal font as well as the Wedding lamp bases conform to his design patent No. 3,834 dated Feb. 1, 1870. This describes glassware or lamp stems with a web center section, upon which any ornamental design can be pressed. The web being comparatively thin, almost instantly solidifies when released from the mold, and possesses sufficient strength to hold the semi-plastic side stems in place while cooling and solidifying.

The design patent No. 3,842 dated February 8, 1870 for a baptismal font, (c), granted to Daniel C. Ripley, was described as "an improved design consisting of a bowl arranged on a stem or base and between radially diverging arms, with outer ends being fitted with candle sockets." Ripley in describing the baptismal font as well noted, "On this a cover may be used if so desired." This option suggests an example without a cover is not necessarily incomplete.

*Illustrations from George Duncan & Sons catalogue circa 1884. Courtesy Corning Museum of Glass.*

b.

c.

*a. Patent No. 73,122 Jan. 7, 1868.*

The above patent issued to Daniel C, Ripley Sr. was described as, "A Lamp which is constructed with a pressed base A, and one or two handles B and a globe blown thereon." Reissues No. 3035, July 14, 1868 and No. 3,078, Aug. 11, 1868 were obtained for minor improvements to the January 7th patent.

Several variations are illustrated in this chapter. Although patent specifications stressed a base intended to receive a blown font, many were entirely pressed. Some of the latter have had the number 1 or 2 in the center of the base, partly obliterated by a pontil mark. Others have indentations made by a snap tool or clamp. These details and the lack of mold seams on the shoulder are evidence of a pressed font. The salient differences in the examples pictured are noted below.

Fonts (b) to (f) inclusive were mold-blown and all on this page are relatively rare.

b. Base marked PATENT APPLIED FOR. Height: 4½".

c. The blown fonts with the ribbed band were blown in three-piece molds, and the plain fonts in two-piece molds. The base is marked PATENTED JAN 7th 1878.

d. and e. Both are marked as above but each has had a different plunger, which is an indication of a large production. Note also the differences in the shape of the handles. Both are 4½" high.

f. Single-handled example with the base marked RIPLEY & CO PATD JAN 7th JULY 14th AUG 11TH 1868. Height 4½".

d.

e.

f.

g.

h.

i.

j.

k.

l.

m.

g. The dates on this are the same as on (f) but there is not a D after PAT. It has a pressed font and it is taller and heavier than the others on this page.

There are numerous factors to be considered when speculating about which company made a specific lamp, candlestick or baptismal font. Collars should be observed. Ones made before 1876 would not likely be used on lamps sold in 1884.

h, i, j, and k. All of these lamps have the name RIPLEY & CO. and the three patent dates of example (l). Examples (i) (j) and (k) have pressed fonts, while (h) appears to have been blown.

h. Examples such as this with a stippled web between the handles range from having a well-defined wafer at the bottom of the font to a mere thickening of the glass. The number 2 in the center of the base is almost hidden by a pontil mark. Height 5⅝".

i. This example without a web has a clearly-defined pressed wafer between the top of the handles. The number 2 on the base within a band having fine concentric rings is also very distinct. Height: 5⅝".

j. Bases of lamps with the square stippled center support were marked with the number 1. Height: 5".

k. The vine pattern pressed on the font is in high relief. This example has a slight greenish tint. Height: 5".

l. Two-handled lamp with blown font. When inverted, the base markings read: PAT^D JAN^Y 7^{TH} JULY 14^{TH} AUGT 11^{TH} 1868. A No. 1 Atwood undated collar was used. Height: 4½".

m. There is a thin strip of glass that joins the circular handles and provides a base upon which to blow the font as described in the Ripley patent. The collar is one that is often found on lamps of the early 1870s. This lamp is unmarked. Height: 5½".

a. Ripley's Warrior or Conquistador Lamp.

b. Front view of Warrior.

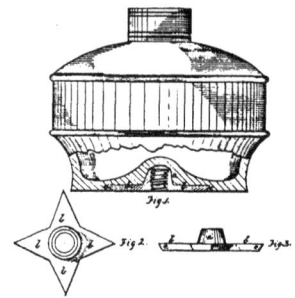

c. Daniel C. Ripley patent.
No. 177,425 May 16, 1876.

Ripley's patent claims refer to a method of embedding a metal socket in glassware as the article is formed, to connect two or more pieces of glassware. As the glass cooled and shrank, the metal insert became firmly embedded due to its peculiar shape.

d. Ripley's patented font.

The patented feature of this lamp has nothing to do with the outstanding acid-etched figural stem. Another view is shown in figure (b). The blown font has raised panels with a roughed finish and a brass wide plate collar. The hexagonal black glass base is marked, PATENTED MAY 16 1876 on the underside. This refers to Daniel C. Ripley's patent (c). The later patented lamps opposite made by **Ripley & Co.** were identified only by paper labels.

Another example (d) marked PATENT PENDING clearly shows the distinctive patented socket that could be used to connect fonts to bracket or hanging lamp fixtures, as well as to stand lamps.

Many companies produced special lamps for the Centennial and this may have been the inspiration for this example. Height is 12¼".

This example has the words PATENT PENDING in raised letters, faintly marked above the horizontal mold seam. Height is 3¼".

Examples of the last lamps patented and made by Ripley & Co. are shown on this page. Composite lamps (a) and (b) are the only ones known to me. The example (a) has no patent date or identification. It does, however, have the same cast iron plate as (b) under the base.

Example (b) has a badly stained paper label covering the iron plate. The only legible printing is the date July 20. This and the patent below serve to identify these lamps.

Ripley's claim was for a hollow stem that could be decorated. Also claimed was a pressed-glass stem with a perforated diaphragm and socket pieces continuous with the stem to obviate metal parts. This refers to the brass parts usually found between the bottom of the stem and the brass ring on the base. See page 79.

The narrow brass ring was retained for improved appearance and a better joint between the parts.

a. Ripley's 1880 Fancy lamp.

b. Decorated Fancy lamp.

D.C. Ripley Pat.
No. 230,340
July 20, 1880

There were frequent references to Ripley's new fancy lamp in the *American Potter and Glassware Reporter* from June to December 1880. In December they reported, "The firm has sold an immense number of their fancy lamps." Until an original name is found, the contemporary description "fancy" may as well be used.

An announcement of a new line of Ripley & Co. lamps was made in the June 26, 1884 *PGR* issue. They were described as having engraved fonts and square stems colored inside.

In the November 15, 1881 patent No. 249,676, a one-piece hollow stem, per se, was not claimed as this had been commonly produced before. The single patent claim succinctly describes the novel aspects.

"A transparent pedestal and base or foot formed in a single piece, the walls of the pedestal being of substantially uniform thickness throughout, and adapted to display internal decoration or ornamentation, in combination with a disk or plate adapted to hermetically close the pedestal and foot in order to protect any ornamentation applied to the inner surface of the pedestal substantially as specified."

D.C. Ripley Patent
No. 249,676
Nov. 15, 1881

c. Ripley patent model.

The patent model (c) was mentioned in the Nov. 15, 1881 patent. There was no paper label and the font was broken off, but the pattern on the base can be used to identify other Ripley lamps and perhaps tableware. I have seen the base with another font.

*a. Adams Bouquet lamp.*

*b. Adams Vase lamp.*

## A DRIVE.

### Bouquet Lamp.

This Lamp is a very large and showy article, having a bouquet of pretty, artificial flowers inserted in the centre of the stand and protected all around by the glass vase of the lamp. It is very large, standing 12 inches high.

Price, with No. 2 Burner, $6.00 per dozen.

Bouquet Lamp.

*Vogeley-Adams patent July 25, 1882 No.261,64.*

*c. Vase lamp with replaced decoration.*

**A Drive!** This is a superlative you may want to adopt to describe lamps of the 1880s. Another interesting term for a hot item was, "It's off the toboggan!" At any rate the lamps shown on these two pages all have, or have had, artificial floral or leaf decorations. These were supported by a cork wafer with a printed (usually green) paper label.

It is known that while they were all made by Adams & Co., the labels all included the Ripley & Co. Nov. 15, 1881 patent date for his one-piece hollow stem lamp. The answer to this puzzle that in the past has caused some confusion regarding attribution may be found in the 1882 patent application files of S.G. Vogeley and A.A. Adams.

*d. Adams Temple lamp.*

*e. Adams Corner windows.*

*f. Adams Hollow-stem No. 90.*
*Courtesy Corning Museum of Glass.*

Adolphus A. Adams applied for his 1882 patent for a hollow-stem lamp or other article, on May 3rd. On May 15 he received a notice from the Patent Office advising him that his application was rejected "on reference to the patent to D.C. Ripley No. 249676 of Nov. 15, 1881 which substantially anticipates the invention." Several amendments were made and a patent was issued for the revised document on July 23. In order to manufacture these lamps they likely had to incorporate the Ripley patent and pay him a fee or royalty.

The Temple lamp is embossed on the shoulder of the base below the columns: PATENTED MARCH 2O 1883 JULY 23 1882. The first date is for a patent granted to Samuel G. Vogeley who joined Adams & Company. This

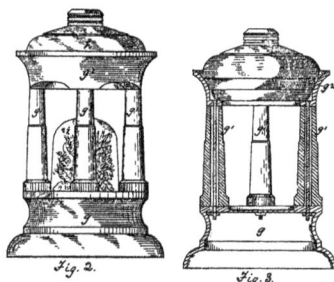

*S.G. Vogeley patent*
*No. 274,233 Mar. 20, 1883.*

patent was for a complex mold "for lamps and other articles of glass or earthenware, consisting of a base or foot and top ring or annulus connected together by two or more columns, all formed in one piece substantially as and for the purposes described." These purposes included holding a lamp font or other similar articles such as flower baskets, pots or epergne.

Instead of round columns Vogeley made some alternative suggestions. "They may be made in the shape of statuettes, limbs of animals, stems of plants, leaves or other forms which are suitable to constitute the shape of supporting devices of the upper ring." He also referred to the dome which he called a shade. He said it could be placed between the columns and could contain flowers, a statuette or other ornament. Only a font such as shown in the example (d) having indentations that correspond with the tops of the pillars can be considered to be the matching one.

The original names for the Vase and Temple lamps (c) and (d) were found in the May 3, 1883 issue of the *AP & GR* by Jane Spillman. In OL-1 I gave the name commonly used locally.

Since then two possibilities have arisen that may have prompted the general use of the Applesauce name. One suggestion is that if the font is removed and the stand inverted, it becomes an elevated bowl. On the bottom of these domes which contain flowers, there is sometimes a cork disk with the remains of a green paper label with the words: FRUIT BOWL/PATENTED/ NOV. 15 1881/ JULY 25 1882. Temple however is the original and more appropriate name. It appears that from the quantity of glass and lamps made by Adams & Company and found in Ontario, Canada, this was a well-established market.

In OL-1, I called the lamp (e) Corner Windows. The square lamp (f), Adams No. 90 was identified in *AP & GR*. Its round counterpart was numbered 150. It was also noted that the projection above the stem was to prevent the hand from slipping up to the greasy font.

All of the lamps with hollow stems that include internal decoration held in with a cork disk have a printed label with the 1881 and 1882 patent dates. These acknowledge both Ripley and Adams patents.

*a. Bradford Variant.*

*b. Bradford.*

Attributing the Bradford Variant lamp to Adams & Company is based upon the resemblance of the base to that of the Bradford lamp above. The Bradford lamp illustrated in OL-1 p. 262 (d) is without the stem decoration. It was also made with a frosted font. The example above has a green printed label which reads: PATENTED/ NOV.15, 1881/JULY 25, 1882. These dates are explained on the preceding pages.

A second characteristic relates this lamp to an Adams lamp with a Diamond and Dot font, shown on page 92. When viewed through their collars, each of these lamps has a hollow font peg and two triangles can be observed on opposite sides of the peg.

The engraved design on the black glass base of the Bradford Variant lamp base helps to reduce its massive appearance. A squat or crown shade would enhance its appearance. Height: 12½".

*The American Pottery and Glassware Reporter* described the small patented lamps like Bradford as being unique and pleasing to a high degree. Other lamp designs with decorated hollow stems will likely be found in the future. Height: 8½".

*a. Adams Minerva goblet.*

*b. Lamp stem, obverse detail.*

It was Eason Eige, former chief curator of the Huntington Museum of Art, who discovered the Minerva lamp (c) which served to identify this pattern as a product of Adams & Company. Two of the three Greek Warrior figures used on the goblet (a) are included on the lamp stem.

Unlike the other examples of Diamond and Dot fonts shown on the following page, this one has a filler.

*c. Minerva lamp with font and base detail found on Adams lamps.*

a. Thousand Eye with Diamond and Dot font.

## No. 206. Stand Lamp

Large and showy lamp, full crystal. The cut does not do the lamp justice.

Per doz.
No. 206, height 12¼ in.,
with No. 2 burner .... $4 75

No. 206. Stand Lamp.

c.

## No. 207.  Stand Lamp.

Fancy bowl, ebony foot, brass trimmings; very showy and a good seller.

Per doz.
No. 207, height 12½ inches,
with No. 2 burner ....... $7 75

No. 207  Stand Lamp.

d.

c. & d. Illustrations from *The American Potter and Illuminator Vol. 5 No. 4, April 1886.*

The advertisements above do not mention color although many of these lamps have been seen in light blue, deep amber, green, canary, and crystal (clear). These lamps were very popular in the 1880s and 1890s.

Examples with black glass bases and with a more massive appearance could have shades or big bulge chimneys, while an attractive crimp-top chimney would perhaps be adequate with lamps like (a). They were all around 12" tall.

The manufacturer of the blue Web Vase lamp (b) has not been identified, although it was probably made in the Midwest during the 1880s or early 1890s. It is a most unusual and distinctive lamp, and it appears to relate to others in this chapter. The thin web of glass between the three handles is similar to Ripley's patent lamps and could serve the same purpose. In other ways the ingenuity of Adams lamps comes to mind. Another example in canary has been seen.

The removable font is almost a necessity for a lamp such as this. Even when it is empty, it is very awkward to carry.

b. Web vase lamp.

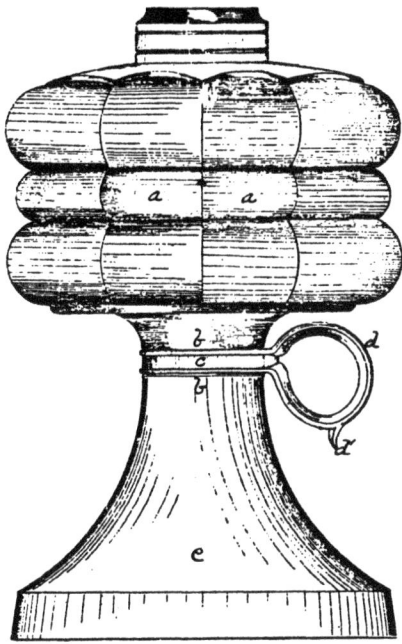

*John Adams patent illustration No. 110,815 January 10, 1871.*

*a, b & c. Adams Ten Panel lamps.*

This drawing serves to identify the three Ten Panel lamps (a, b & c) pictured here. They are very different from the patent examples with the iron handles found in collections today.

The two examples (d) and (e) are marked on the base: PATENTED. JAN. 10TH 71. BY JNO ADAMS. Two of the three known handle designs are shown. The third design that I have seen used with a plain font had a tang fused to the base. This was described as an alternative in the patent.

Grape and Festoon (e) has been the popular name for this pattern for decades. Jane Spillman's article on Adam's & Company in the *Glass Club Bulletin* clearly documents many patterns including this one. It appeared in an Adams catalogue circa 1871-72. Spillman noted the name Grape and Festoon given to the pattern by Ruth Webb Lee was originally Myrtle.

She also credits J. Stanley Brothers with the identification (in 1940) of the original name of the Thousand Eye pattern. It was described as "Sensation" in the *American Pottery and Glassware Reporter,* February 19, 1885 issue. It is unlikely that knowledge of these original names will be adopted in place of the commonly accepted and more descriptive ones.

Blakeslee's distinctive patent Sept. 29, 1868 burner made by Benedict and Burnham, combined with what is commonly called a petal-top chimney, is an appropriate and attractive choice.

Height of the lamps is about 6".

*d. Adams plain iron handle.*

*e. Grape and Festoon with iron handle.*

The clear-glass lamp (a) is an example of the catalogue lamps with opal feet and reeded handles and the only one I have seen. It is marked in the drip-trough or groove top as they called it, PATENTED JULY 1872. This refers to the July 29, 1872 patent for a glass mold issued to John Bridges, and assigned to Adams & Company.

Some Bridges fonts are incorrectly marked July 2, 1872. Reeded handles, so common on English and Continental lamps, are rarely found on American lamps. Height: 4⅝".

The patent drawings below show the construction of the stand lamps. The patent specifies separately-made blown or pressed fonts, to be glued in place.

Spring clips held in annular grooves were suggested as an alternate means of securing the font. The patent also noted that two colors could be combined as in (b) or ornamentation placed between the bowl and a colorless cup-cavity as illustrated. The only clear-glass examples that I have seen have the same ribbed pattern as (c), between the smooth walls of the font. Other examples should yield more information.

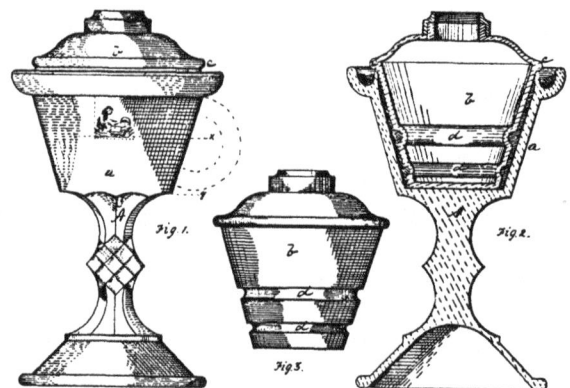

No. 183,274. Patented Oct. 17, by John Adams and Jacob Bonshire. The patent was assigned to Adams & Company.

The above pages which I photographed at the home of the late Lowell Innes appeared in his book *Pittsburgh Glass 1797-1891*. They are from a lamp catalogue published by J. P. Smith, Son & Co., Pittsburgh, Sept. 15, 1876. Since one of the lamps illustrated was patented on October 17, 1876, the supplement would have been issued after that date. These pages are particularly interesting because the lamps were all made by Adams & Company and involved three patents and four patentees.

The most conspicuous characteristic of the lamps is the combination of clear and opaque white (opal) glass. At least two of them were also made entirely of clear glass. An example of each design is pictured here. Although only one is dated. The others can be identified by the patent specifications and illustrations.

Both patents for the lamps with a white body and clear shoulder include a drip-trough and a method of combining clear and white or colored glass. Fusion was difficult because each type of glass has a different coefficient of expansion and lamps often fractured during the annealing process. Earlier patents by the Atterbury brothers and Benjamin Bakewell offered different solutions.

b.

c.

Adams described this mold and method of manufacture: "I press up a foot, or foot and stem, *a*, having a cup or bowl section, *b*, with an annular grooved flange, *c*. This foot is then removed from the press, and placed beneath a mold section, *E*, and forms therewith a matrix within which a bowl, *e*, may be blown or formed, uniting with the foot and cup section so as to constitute a complete lamp shown in Fig. 3."

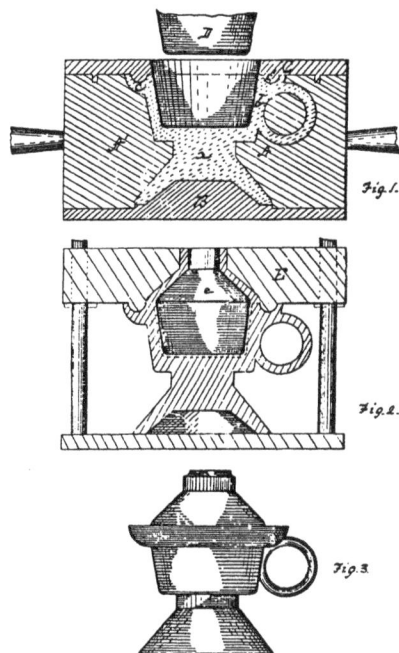

*No. 177,087 Patented May 9, 1876 by A. Adams and assigned to Adams & Company.*

Both the font (a) below and the footed hand lamp (b) have blown fonts and were likely examples of this patent.

*a. Bracket or hanging lamp font.*

*Adams 1876 patent hand lamp, with an opal sun chimney.*

# Illumination.

## At the Illumination on Monday Evening,

it is recommended that Lamps be used instead of candles. One Parafine Lamp s t before each window, or in each front room, having the blinds raised and the curtains drawn aside, will give sufficient light to illuminate the whole street opposite, and will be free from the objection of dirt and danger.

Let there be a general display! let every house and every room bear testimony to the fact that Yarmouth is celebrating her first Centenial birthday.

Yarmouth, June 8, 1861.

*From the collections of the Yarmouth County Museum, Yarmouth, Nova Scotia.*

This notice conveys the early acceptance of kerosene (Parafine) use in a small Nova Scotia port town, as well as the use of light to establish a festive and celebratory mood. For the past decade Black Creek Pioneer Village in Toronto, Canada, an 1860s village recreated and expanded on the site of an early nineteenth century settlement, has staged special pre-Christmas events.

In the evenings the village homes are aglow with kerosene lamps. Costumed interpreters explain the roles citizens played in those days. All this is further enhanced by the blend of fragrant aromas of pioneer cooking and baking and the taste of roasted chestnuts. The sounds of the choir singing hymns and spirited Christmas songs and the jingling of sleigh bells all play a part in a lively learning experience.

*a.*

*b. Photograph courtesy Black Creek Pioneer Village, Toronto, Canada.*

## Triple Flute and Bar

All examples on this page are variations in color and shape of the Triple Flute and Bar pattern. The example (b) shedding light in the living room of the Doctor's House at Black Creek Pioneer Village in Toronto, Canada, is illustrated in OL-1 p. 80 with related forms.

Lamp (d) is illustrated in OL-2 p. 25 with other examples and information. Here an 8" Ives shade holder and burner and Ives style shade have been added. This combination with exceptionally well-preserved gold bands measures 15" to the top of the shade.

These fonts are also found in other shades of blue, green, and canary. The tall green lamp (a) with solar lamp type stem and base would be considered a banquet lamp. It measures 15⅞" to the top of the collar. A flat hand lamp with an applied handle can be seen in OL-2 p. 98 (f), in clear glass.

*c.*

*d.*

a. *Atterbury opal and blue bas-relief tulip lamp.*

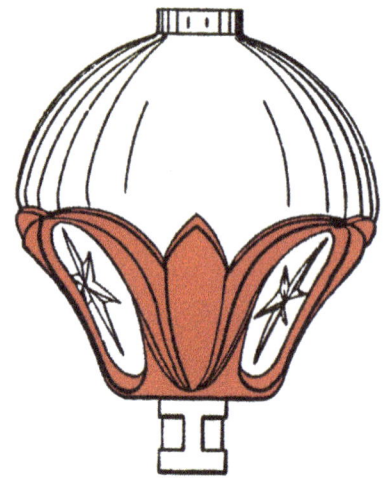

b. *Colored illustration for the June 3, 1862 patent, granted to Thomas and James Atterbury, and to James Reddick, also of Pittsburgh.*

# Atterbury & Co.

This lamp is a combination of pressed and blown techniques and examples are found with variations in shape and in the definition of the tulips. This is one of the better ones, and like the others I have seen, has the number 2 inside at the bottom of the font.

Height to the top of the collar is 11½".

According to an article in the Aug. 24, 1879 issue of *Crockery & Glass Journal*, the Atterbury company was founded in 1835, and the Atterbury brothers, Thomas and James, took over the operation in 1860. As innovative and creative glassmen, they were certainly in the right place at the right time to achieve success in the four decades of tremendous interest and output in glass tableware and kerosene lamps. Their many invention and design lamp patents which often included other patentees, usually related to the appearance of the product. Most were dated, and the patents and illustrations can give clues to identify the glassware or lamps.

The tulip lamp (a) is marked PATENTED MARCH 4 & JUNE 3 1862. This patent described a method for producing a design in two colors in bas-relief for lamps and hollow glassware.

Today these lamps are found in clear, or occasionally opal, with blue tulips. See OL-1 p. 127 for another example. Red was the color suggested in the patent so that it is reasonable to assume that a font like the colored patent illustration (b) might be found.

a.

b.

c.

d, e, f.

g. *Detail of bill.*

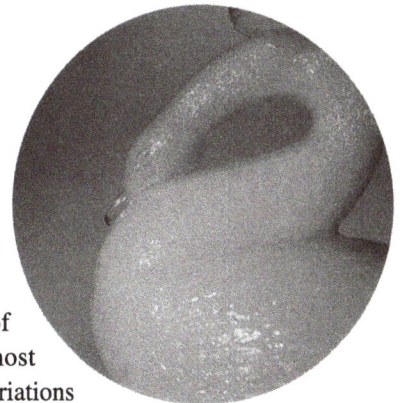

## Atterbury Swans

The many sizes and color combinations of Swan lamps have made them among the most popular of the Atterbury lamps. There are variations in the colors and opacity of the alabaster glass. For those lamps with the swan fonts, the definition of the swans is inconsistent.

The two-piece lamps had swans or plain fonts. They feature the successful screw connector patented by Thomas and James Atterbury on September 29, 1868, No. 82,579. This date and another patent date, Nov. 16, 1869, No. 82,579 appear on the one-piece lamps. Roland H. Smith assigned this patent for a method of connecting lamp fonts to bases, to the Atterbury brothers. The patent described another type of screw connection which doesn't seem to have been used in these examples.

Most one-piece swan lamps have clear glass fonts without a pattern. The rare exception, (c), has a Scroll and Rib font that was popular with Atterbury. Another example is shown on page 124 (b).

One of the most interesting and usually overlooked details is the clear glass bill, and to some extent the clear tail feathers of the two-piece swans. Altering the lighting and viewing through the camera lens will sometimes enhance obscure features. The small checks that often appear at the swans' bills likely occurred during the annealing process.

None of these lamps is illustrated in the 1872, 1874 or 1881 Atterbury catalogues. This suggests they were made either before, after or in between those dates.

*a. Atterbury/Dithridge chimney.
Photograph by Eileen White.*

## Atterbury Lamps

This chimney was patented by Thomas Atterbury Nov. 30, 1875, No. 170,431. It was assigned to Dithridge & Co., also of Pittsburgh. It was an improvement on an earlier patent by the Atterbury brothers, August 14, 1866, No. 57063. The purpose of the patent states that it is for "Tools for flaring and crimping chimneys, & c." The effect created on the chimney above is not specifically described or illustrated in the complex patent, that mainly illustrates smoke bells. Presumably Dithridge & Co. manufactured these chimneys so that joint attribution is appropriate. It is shown here on an

Atterbury Scroll lamp with Saucer base that was illustrated in their 1872 catalogue.

The font of lamp (b) is marked PATD APRIL 10, 1883. This patent No. 275,562 issued to Thomas Atterbury, was for a mold for forming "a guard or drip-flange" on lamps and other articles, or for ornamental purposes. Atterbury claimed it was an improvement on the patent of John Bridges of July 23, 1872, No. 129,781. See OL-1 p. 188. Atterbury also claimed that he was the owner of the Bridges patent. These lamps are found in a typical Atterbury blue shade and in canary featured here.

In profile it clearly resembles a Lomax patent lamp. Apparently George Lomax also noticed this and brought suit against Atterbury who claimed to be ignorant of the infringement!

The base is dated March 12, 1878. This refers to patent No. 201,266, granted to R. S. Merrill for a lamp stand formed with an internal receptacle combined with an "independent clock movement susceptible of being bodily fitted into and removed from said chamber." Small clocks made by Seth Thomas were used in another lamp stem like the one shown in the Merrill patent illustration. Parker & Whipple and The Yale Clock Company also made small clocks. These two companies were involved in litigation regarding patents and reissues for these small clocks, from October 1883 until

*d. Ripley/Atterbury Wedding lamp.*

October 1887. Perhaps it should be stated "If it fits — use it."

Lamps bases (c) and (d) above and opposite, were given the name Eureka by Atterbury & Co. The example (c) is a translucent grayish shade with white flecks distributed throughout. This and the spatter glass base are the only ones other than white, that I am aware of.

Ripley Wedding lamp fonts present a good opportunity to display unusual burners and chimneys. On July 14, 1868, Robert R. Crosby patented a cone-shaped chimney that had "an abrupt or nearly right angle" at the bottom of the cone.

The 6¾" chimneys opposite are marked PATD. JULY 14, 1868, and the roughed finish that enhances the bright lines is exceptionally well executed.

The 7½" chimneys above are marked PATD. FEB. 1877. This was the date and shape of an F. S. Shirley patent that was supposed to have been "provided with a corrugated radiating surface" below the cone, and "roughed to form a reflector." I have never seen an example with a corrugated radiating surface and this is not shown in the Mt. Washington advertisements. These chimneys may be attributed to Mt. Washington. They also are examples that reveal the background of primary source information that can confirm, and sometimes confuse, research. See pp. 22 and 23.

*b. Atterbury/Merrill Clock Lamp.*

*c. Atterbury Eureka base.*

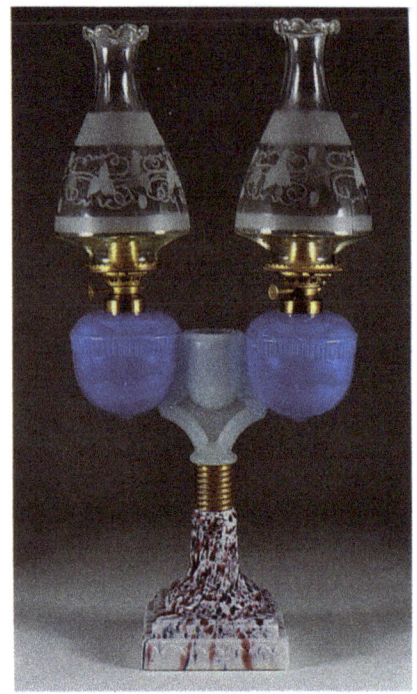

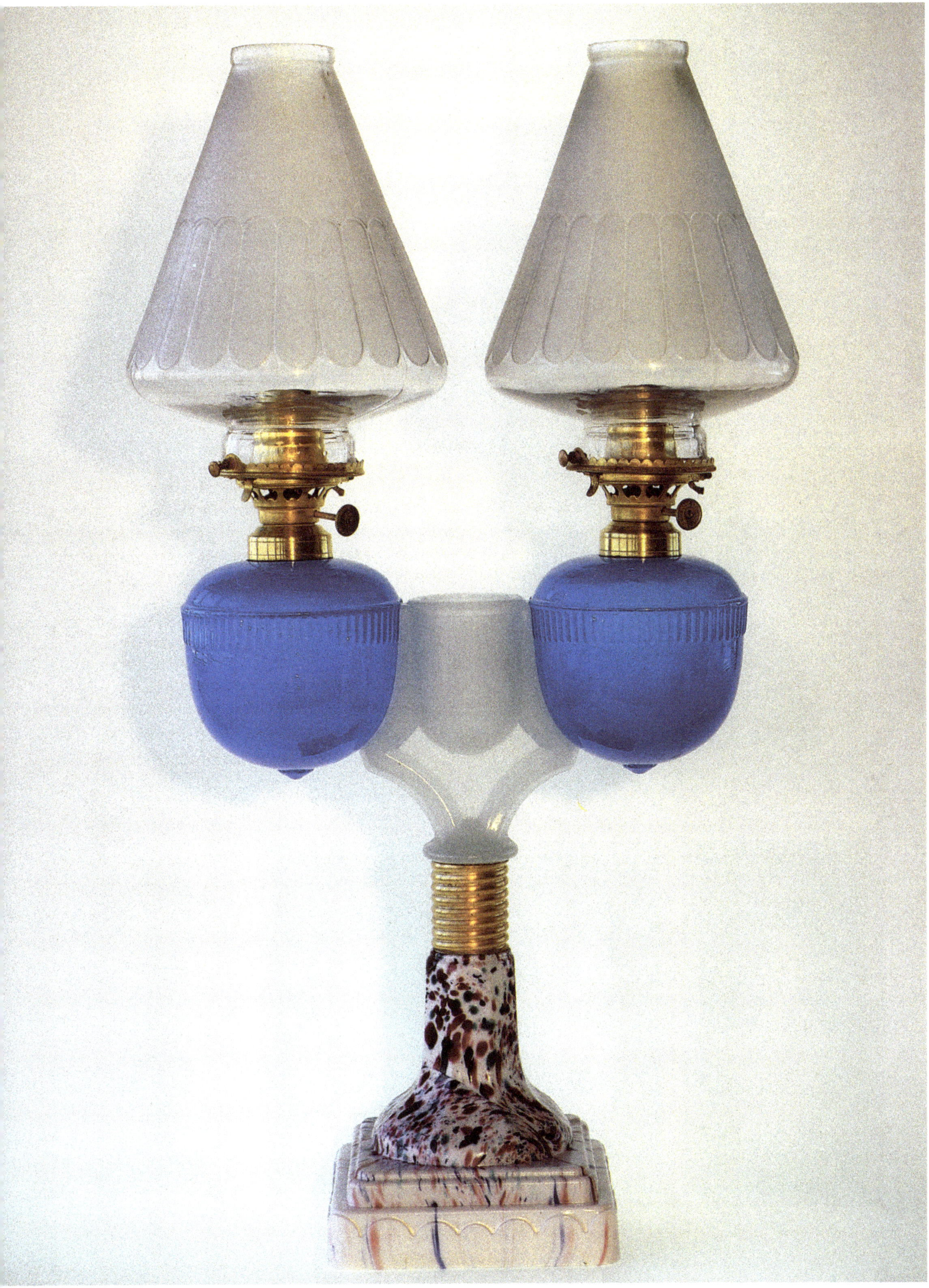

## Atterbury Figural With Vine Font

Goddess of Liberty was the name chosen for another Atterbury lamp illustrated in OL-1 p. 132. It would also be appropriate here. Both lamps have the same Vine$^{ON}$ font with a threaded peg, however the connectors are different. The patent for this lamp is pictured and described on page 79 in this book, where it led to confusion regarding the Atterbury lamp pictured there.

The glass quality and design of the opal stem shown separately here in three different views, (b), (c), and (d), are superior to other Atterbury glass pieces and could compete with any other glass manufactured during the period. On the other hand, they also produced pieces of such poor quality that one might wonder what, if anything, would be judged a "second."

In the Dec. 8, 1875 issue of *CGJ*, p. 17, the following amusing and informative comment was made about this lamp: "Their hexagon foot stand lamp, with bust stem, is an elegant article. This can be taken apart and screwed together at will. This has no point, but works well together with glass screws and sockets. The busts are either in opal, black or turquoise, and the bowls ribbed, imitation cut, or frosted."

The bust of the spelter lamp stem (e) is the same as the glass stems. This is known to have occurred with other glass figures. Height of (a) to the top of the collar is 12¾".

a.

b.

c.

d.

e.

# Atterbury, Ripley & Duncan Hand Lamps in Color

Lamps on the top row are Atterbury patented single-handled, footed hand lamps. They have the Atterbury Filley[ON] ribbed pattern on the fonts. When compared to the three Ripley lamps below, the handles are noticeably thicker and more rounded. They are marked on the underside of the base: FEB 11th & JUNE 3rd, 1862 RE-ISSUED JULY 20th, 1869. All have later collars. Sizes are: (a) & (b) 5", and (c) is 5½".

Three different styles are represented in the Ripley footed hand lamps. The deep amethyst example is quite a departure from the usual pinks and blues, although none of them is common. The single-handled lamp is marked on the underside of the base to be read from above: RIPLEY CO. PATD JAN. 7 JULY 14 AUG. 11 1868.

The second Ripley with the white transparent alabaster font is marked on the underside of the base: RIPLEY & CO. PATD JAN. 7th JULY 14th AUG 11th 1868.

The center-post example is a translucent blue with tiny flecks or bubbles. It is indistinctly dated as above. Height is 5".

a, b, c.

g, h.

d, e, f.

The two Atterbury shoe lamps above have been referred to as night lamps, miniature lamps or novelties. They were probably intended to be the latter.

George Duncan & Sons probably made (i). This is a rare departure from the usual popular colors or combinations. See p. 83 for the catalogue illustration.

i.

# Color and Decoration

Colored glass, color combinations, and surface decoration are considered among the most interesting and appealing aspects of kerosene lamps. The variety pictured here includes two slip burners designed to support chimneys from the inside.

Lamps made in America may have had surface decoration applied by Americans or foreign artists. In December 1879, *The Crockery and Glass Journal* (*CGJ*), printed a full-page notice describing the Atterbury new building. It included:

"This department is assigned for decorating purposes, and that lets a good-sized [cat out of the bag.] For a long time past, the Messrs. Atterbury have been engaged in manufacturing opal ware in fancy designs, which has been decorated beautifully by artists whom they have imported from Belgium and France." They do not mention lamps, but say they have "shipped immense quantities from East and West, to South America, and even to Europe, and sold in jewellery and fancy stores in our own city to-day as imported wares."

Bohemian glass was frequently acknowledged as superior to American glass in *CGJ*. It became the bench-mark that American glassmakers sought to achieve or surpass. Some of the largest and best-known importers, including F. H. Lovell, advertised Bohemian glass and lamps.

In the May 7, 1877 issue of *CGJ* on page 15, an article titled "The Boston and Sandwich Glass Company" described the stock in their agency or showroom in New York City. The article concluded, "The agency in New York is in charge of Mr. C. E. L. Brinkerhoff, who is not only well known to the trade, but has the reputation of not asking for goods more than they are really worth. "A penny saved is a penny earned;" and if goods equally beautiful can be bought for a less price, who cares if they were made in America or Bohemia."

*Who cares indeed!* Today American glass collectors care very much. Their concern is reflected in the difference they are willing to pay for a lamp if it is described as Sandwich or if it is called Bohemian. The phrase "Kiss of Death" comes to mind!

On this page all lamps except (c) are known to have been made by Atterbury & Co. They are unusual colors and combinations. Atterbury gave the name Star to lamps (a & b). This is probably best remembered by the fact that there are no stars in the design! These alabaster glass examples measure 8½". Lamp (c) has an alabaster font and opaque base. This is a similar combination to the Star lamp. The bottom two alabaster heart fonts vary in opacity. Base (d) has lavender glass that appears to have been the result of a heat or light sensitive formula. More of these are illustrated in OL-2 p. 41. Lamp (e) has an opaque, black glass base.

*a, b, c.*

*d.*

*e.*

f.

g.

h.

Fonts (f), (g), and (h) are probably of Bohemenian origin. The surface of (f) is ruby stained and frosted. An enamelled decoration was applied to *both* the inside and the outside surface and then outlined in gold!

The painted design on the font (g) was illustrated in the 1868-69 F. H. Lovell & Co. catalogue along with others that have been identified as Bohemian in the price lists. Green streaks on the base may, or may not, have been intentional. Variations of the font design (h) have been seen on ball and slant shades and on hall globes. The patented base made by the New England Glass Company is also described on page 68. Both glass quality and gold decoration are excellent.

Lamps (i) and (j) have bright colored decoration on opal glass. The colors are the same, although judging from the fonts and general appearance, they are probably a decade apart. Base (i) with a rather chunky appearance is uncommon and would probably date around 1870. This is the first decorated example that I have seen.

The late composite lamp (j) would have been one of the more expensive models produced around 1880. It has

an Argand burner and opal glass chimney. These were described in an article about Atterbury & Co. in *CJG* Dec. 8, 1875 p. 17. "They also have other new features in the shape of opal shades and Student chimneys for Argand burners, in opal or plain glass, which, it is claimed, gives a better light than the Argand Student chimney, now in general use."

Measurements for these lamps to the top of the collars are: (f) 10", (g) 10", (h) 11", (i) 11½", and (j) 12½".

i.

j.

*a. Ives/Iden spelter figural lamp with bronze finish.*

*b. Cast-iron Tucker Mfg. Co. vase lamp with bronze finish.*

*c. Perkins & House Argand table lamp with original finish.*

# Metal Finishes

While almost all metal figural lamps were made of spelter, they would originally have had a surface treatment. Most had an imitation bronze finish that now has a pewter-like appearance with only a trace of the original finish in the crevices. A few were brass-plated, and others had colorful polychrome finishes.

In the 1867 Ives' Patent Lamp catalogue, the example (a) is illustrated with another Iden font and Ives burner, shade and shade holder. See OL-2 p. 38. This is not an Ives shade, however it is an excellent color choice.

Cast-iron and heavy are the most obvious characteristics of this vase table lamp (b). Along with three other similar styles they were advertised as "a very heavy indestructible lamp." This was probably the reason one of them that was advertised in the 1868-69 F. H. Lovell catalogue, appeared 50 years later in a 1918 Handlan Railway Supply Company catalogue.

Examples that I have seen have a dark-brown finish that doesn't interfere with its well-detailed cast design. Most of the inner fonts have been spun metal, but glass ones were also made.

Brass was chemically treated to produce bands of bright or dull gold on both lamps and burners (see p. 168). It is amazing that there are examples to be found that have escaped rigorous cleaning. The font of this Perkins & House Argand lamp is in excellent condition. Other examples are in OL-1 pp. 190 & 191. An informative account of these lamps made by the Cleveland Non-Explosive Lamp Company was published in *The Rushlight*.

Bearers of beer or wine barrels present an odd topic for lamp bases (d) and (e). With either the glass or metal barrels, they are an expression of rare talent and imagination! The bronze metal finish is excellent.

Approximate heights to the top of the collars are: (a) 14", (b) 11", (c) 9½", (d) & (e) 10".

*d. Beer Barrel lamp with blown glass font.*

*e. Beer Barrel lamp with cast metal font.*

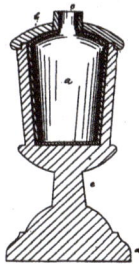

## G. M. STEVENS
### Deering, Maine
### Lamp
### Patented Dec. 28, 1875    No. 171,540

"The object of my invention is to produce a lamp which is not liable to break, one which will not become moist by the exuding of the combustible contents of the same, and one which is and can be made rich and ornamental in form and appearance."

a.

b.

c.

d, e, f, g.

# Wood and Paper Lamps

Although the name Stevens has become associated with all wooden lamps, it really applies only to the Stevens patented lamp above. The main difference is the patented bayonet connection to secure the metal liner and wooden top to the body of the lamp. The only examples that I am aware of are the above shape that is made of walnut.

The many examples of birch and maple lamps with metal liners that have survived indicate that they were very popular. I have seen other shapes and sizes. The group (d to g) includes a mica chimney patented by G. M. Bull, January 9, 1872 , No. 122,560.

Lamp (h) was illustrated in *CGJ*, in a June 6, 1889 F.H. Lovell & Co. advertisement. They were shown in five sizes and were called Paper Lamps. There was also a paper oil can.

The example (h) has a paper label on the bottom with the name L. H. Thomas and Patent applied for. His application was applied for on January 19, 1889, and it was granted on May 14, shortly before the advertisement appeared. The cylindrical form was more convenient to make. The interior coating recommended was nine parts glue to one part glycerine or sugar. Lamp (i) is usually referred to by collectors as a papier-maché lamp. These have been seen in different colors.

After filling the wooden match-safe (j), a simple up and down motion will deposit a single match ready to use as shown (k). This one has the name H. LANGFORD, marked with a steel stamp, inside on the central post. A somewhat similar design patent issued to Nicholas Altmyer, March 2, 1897, is illustrated in the Patent Office Gazettes.

h.

i.

j.

k.

*a.*

*c.*

## Colored Glass

Solid color hand and stand lamps found today, are usually ones made after the 1880s. The one in my son Randy's hand above (a) with the Egyptian motif, probably dates from the early 1870s.

Examples of 1860s or early 1870s plain or patterned solid color lamps, are more rare today than overlay lamps and almost as rare as examples such as (b). Red and blue glass threads were pulled against a white body to create this striking footed hand lamp. I photographed it at the home of the late Lowell Innes.

Most old colored glass chimneys found today have a slip base and are primarily found in the colors illustrated

here. Many have been reproduced in blue, amber, and green. They do make a significant contribution to the over-all appearance of a lamp with matching colors.

The blue chimney in photograph (a) was likely made during what was head-lined as the "BLUE GLASS CRAZE." Detailed accounts were published in the 1870s about experiments with humans, animals and plants using light filtered through blue glass. Amazing results were claimed by doctors and professors whose work included watching identical twin girls grow up. Outstanding success was acclaimed for the one confined to a blue glass envi-ronment. The stories grew from serious to suspect to silly — especially the report from Prof. Givodam! Neverthe-less it *did* sell glass.

Blue glass was just one of the many colors used for fire grenades. These bottles, filled with a liquid, served as fire extinguishers when they were

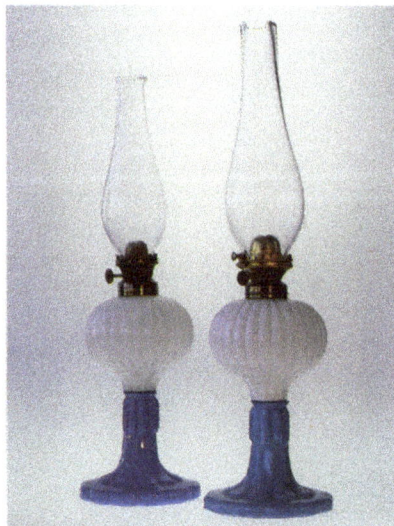

hurled at the source of the fire. Today they are collected chiefly by bottle col-lectors, however they would be an appropriate adjunct to a lamp collec-tion or display.

The example (f) has the word STAR inside of the star within a circle. On the plain band around the middle are the words in raised letters: HARDENS HAND GRENADE FIRE EXTIN-GUISHER. On July 14, 1885, a design patent, No. 16,159 was granted to Thomas Atterbury for this bottle. He assigned it to the Harden Hand Fire Extinguisher Company of Chicago, Illinois. Earlier on May 27, 1884, Thomas Atterbury obtained an inven-tion patent for a glass fire-extinguisher bottle with ribbed upper and lower sec-tions, and a band of thinner, more frag-ile glass, in the middle. This example appears to incorporate both patents although it is not dated. Dr. Arthur Peterson describes the Harden bottles in *Glass Patterns and Patents.*

The Hayward Hand Grenade Fire Extinguisher Co. of New York City, another major manufacturer, made their bottles in many colors. In an advertisement in Trow's NYC 1888 directory, they claim the liquid used was "Absolutely harmless to flesh or fabric."

Lamps (d & e) are about 7½". The bottle (f) is 6½".

*b.*

*d. & e.*

*f.*

*a.*

*b.*

*c.*

# Hobbs Lamps

Additional examples and advertisements contribute more information about Hobbs table lamps. The illustration (a) from an 1893 United States Glass Company catalogue was shown on page 320 in OL-1 and named Foster. It was also made in flat and footed hand lamp forms and identified as No. 9805. Hobbs well-known Snowflake lamps were also shown as No. 341. They were described as follows: "The Bowl and Foot of these lamps are screwed firmly together by a metal socket, which obviates excessive breakage in transit. The socket is covered by a pressed glass sleeve, which completely conceals the metal, producing a brilliant effect and making practically an all glass Lamp. Sold also without the sleeve." The last sentence was included with the Foster lamp but not with the Snowflake. The No. 9805 lamps were also described as "Optic Screw Socket Lamps."

The Snowflake lamps showing a pattern that looks more like a daisy, were available in "Crystal, Ruby or Sapphire Opalescent." Those without a pattern like (b) were available in the same colors.

The example (c), photographed by Eileen White, was illustrated in an 1892 Butler Bros. wholesale catalogue. It was called a "COTTAGE" Sewing Lamp and priced at $6.40 a dozen, complete with chimney and burner. A package included four each of ruby, pearl and turquoise opalescent. Three and a half dozen lamps in mixed colors without chimneys sold for $5.47.

The very successful clinch connector patented by John L. Hobbs in 1870 is seldom seen with colored bases. Here their Loop and Rib Band font (d) has a light gray base. Hobbs also made black glass bases and chocolate glass bases (e) in this square style and their clover leaf base. The full-rib font serves to identify two Hobbs all-glass lamps on the next page.

*d.*

*e.*

## Hobbs Lamps

a, b, c.   *Three Hobbs clinch-connector lamps dated May 24, 1870.*

f.

g.

d, e.   *Hobbs clinch-connector lamps dated May 24, 1870.*

On page 55 we see that fonts (a) and (c) found on the ship *Bertrand* were made as early as 1865. These "patterns under glass" or "plunger pressed designs" as they may be called, are also illustrated in OL-1 on pages 150 and 151. The Bellflower pattern (b) so popular with other manufacturers is the only example I am aware of that has been attributed to the Hobbs, Brockunier & Company.

It was while actually using and later photographing one of these lamps that I discovered a surprising phenomenon. When filled with kerosene (d), the pattern almost disappears. To illustrate this peculiarity, I thought I could photograph a font containing water (e). The pattern changed very little! This was due to the different indices of refraction of the two liquids.

This effect was described as a disadvantage in a later patent. Cleaning the irregular surface is another disadvantage. The approximate height of the three lamps is 11½".

The Hobbs Full-Rib font (f) shown with a clinch connector on the previous page, and the same bases of (f) and (g) serve to identify them as made by Hobbs.

# Nickel-Plate
# Opalescent Lamps

Banbury is the name that I gave to this lamp, pictured with a clear base and similar font in OL-2, p. 104 (i). In their Book 9, on p 25, William Heacock and William Gamble show an advertisement from a U.S. Glass Company catalogue circa 1892. It features several of these opalescent stand lamps as well as flat and footed hand lamps. The factory (N) designation indicates they were made at the Nickel-Plate Glass Company in Fostoria Ohio.

The example (a) below has also been seen with a vertically striped font. These lamps are greatly enhanced with matching chimneys. If one is fortunate enough to find an opalescent chimney, it should only be used for display and not subjected to heat.

Both the lamp and chimney (b) are exceptional. The silver vertical opalescent stripes on the font may be the result of an air-trap technique. This lamp is 9" high, and the opalescent stripe chimney is 7⅞".

*a.*

*b.*

# The Enigma Lamps

Several of these lamps also appeared in OL-2 pp. 36 & 37. It seemed reasonable to assume that Atterbury & Co. made the bases with threaded pegs that screwed into their patent dated brass screw connectors. They were like those with the threaded connectors shown here. At least it seemed reasonable until I discovered the promotional newsletter opposite, published in June 1869 by the Ansonia Brass Company.

Before discussing the HOT CAST PORCELAIN LAMP STAND, a few aspects of all of these bases should be noted. The colored ones show varying degrees of iridescence. Where the surface is chipped, a solid color is revealed about 1/32" below the surface. This could be due to a heat sensitive process. The underside of the maroon or mulberry bases is less marbled and has a distinct blue shading.

Bases *without* the threaded connectors have a narrow waist-like feature near the top. The bottom vertical portion of the base is either plain like (a) or those on p. 37 in OL-2. Others have a small but definite step like (d) or a small horizontal rib like (f). These variations were of sufficient significance to be detailed in the 1877-78 F. H. Lovell Co. catalogue. It is probably worth noting that most of the Mt. Washington fonts on Plate 113 in that catalogue are combined with bases like (a). These are only line drawings and the price list describes all of them as Opal Lamp Stands.

The clear font of lamp (a) with ruby and white looped threads has the same broad turnip-shape and wide wafer characteristics of many Mt. Washington fonts.

Lamp (b) from the Ken Kercheval collection has a threaded connector, but is it an Atterbury or a Hot-Cast Porcelain base? The font is pressed, and the expanded Star and Punty pattern is usually found on earlier lamps. See page 7.

a.

b.

c, d, e, f, g.   *Related lamps of unknown origin.*

We take pleasure in informing our friends that we have the exclusive sale of the

## HOT-CAST PORCELAIN LAMP STAND,

manufactured by the AMERICAN HOT-CAST PORCELAIN COMPANY. These Stands are made of a new material, patented both in this country and in Europe, which combines the *Strength of Marble with the Hardness and Durability of Quartz—* of which it is largely composed. The principal ingredient is a mineral found only in Greenland, and known as "Cryolite." In regard to points of strength and durability, we guarantee these Stands to SURPASS ANY OTHER STYLES IN MARKET, and in finish, they equal the BEST OF FLINT GLASS.

The accompanying Cuts represent our

## NEW STANDS WITH SCREW SOCKETS.

This arrangement renders *Cement* or *Plaster* unnecessary, and we wish particularly to call your attention to it, *as by it* the Peg and Stand can be connected more quickly, and firmer than by any other method. These *Stands* with this *Socket* can also be used with the old style of Peg and when so used save all risk of loosening the *Socket* from the Stand, by the use of wet Plaster in setting the Peg.

We also Manufacture this and other Patterns of Stands for the old style of Sockets. Time, labor and freight are saved by using the Screw Socket.

The old style of Peg can be used with this *Stand* and *Screw-Socket.*

| Sizes, | 3¼ | 3¾ | 4¼ | 5in. |
| Price per doz. | $1 44 | $1 77 | $2 22 | $3 61, with Screw-Socket. |

*per cent. discount.*

Packed in boxes of 6 dozen each. Sample orders solicited.

OPAL, GREEN, BLUE, AND Variegated COLORS.

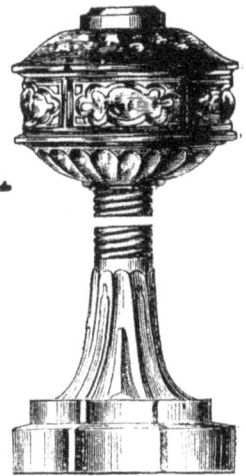

A. W. MACDONALD & CO., PRINTERS, 37 PARK ROW, NEW YORK.

*a. Ansonia Brass and Copper Co's. Price current for the trade.*

Questions immediately spring to mind at the sight of this advertisement that was published in trade papers I found. They were published by the Ansonia Brass Company in Meriden, Conn. This reinforces the potential that ephemera has for research.

Some of the questions are:

*Where* was the American Hot-cast Porcelain Company located?

*Who* were the owners, managers, and personnel?

*What* did their product really look like?

*What* patent do they refer to?

The answers have thus far eluded me. Perhaps at a future date some of the answers will be found, and the information presented on these pages will be part of the conclusions.

There are several coincidences to be considered in the search for answers. Some of these are:

1. The very obvious similarities between this advertisement and the one for the Atterbury screw connector shown on page 129 in OL-1.

2. The description of the colors: "OPAL, GREEN, BLUE, AND VARIEGATED COLORS."

3. The design of the base that matches the ones pictured with the threaded connectors.

4. The design of the font that clearly matches the design patented by Henry Whitney of the New England Glass Company on May 10, 1870. This was *after* this advertisement appeared. See page 68. The photograph of the font that served as the patent illustration makes it obvious that the font had been produced and made *without* the threaded peg shown in this advertisement.

5. The engraved design on the shoulder of the fonts in the advertisement might well be intended to represent the engraving on the font in the detail (b). This font is shown in OL-1 p. 166 (b), where it was found combined with the Whitney design patented base. A better illustration of this base is on page 105 (h) in this book.

Clearly the quality and colors of the bases need to be compared with each other and with glassware made by different companies. The search will be interesting.

*b. Engraved font.*

The significant dates that relate to these lamps are:

September 29, 1868. The Atterbury screw socket patent.

July 1869. The advertisement (a).

May 10, 1870. The font in the 1869 advertisement was patented.

Among the companies associated with the advertisement and these lamps are:

Atterbury & Co.
The New England Glass Co.
F. H. Lovell & Co.
The Mt. Washington Glass Co.

*This advertisement was repeated in September 1869.*

a. Hobb's X-Band and Loop.

b. Hobb's Diamond Cluster Melon.

colors. The blown Diamond Cluster font is clinched on.

The Hobbs Rib and Optic Band font (c) is clinched on to the connector. These connectors described in OL-1 on p. 24 are usually marked with the patent date, May 24, 1870. Of course the fonts found on the ship *Bertrand* in 1865, (see p. 56) were not indented for the clinch connector. This font is often seen with either brass and marble bases or with cast-iron bases.

Neither of the plunger-pressed designs, (d) Chevron Band or (e) Concentric Circles, can be attributed to any manufacturer at present.

c. Hobb's Rib and Optic Panel.

d. Chevron Band.

# Hobbs and Similar

Among the many Hobbs, Brockunier & Company distinctive lamp types were the fine quality, large, almost round, pressed-glass fonts circa 1870. Some were all glass, and others like (a) and examples in OL-1, were either set in plaster or clinched on. These were often combined with one of the Hobbs monumental style bases with ribbed stems.

The most graceful of separate glass bases, Hobbs or otherwise, in my opinion, is their clover-leaf design (b). It was made in chocolate glass and probably other

e. Concentric Circles.

## Pillar-molded Cut Font

Although this pillar-mold font is not clinched on to the connector, it is reasonable to believe that it was made by Hobbs, because they were known to have used this technique extensively. The importance of the font is enhanced by the deeply-cut geometric design on the shoulder.

Height to the top of the connector is 7" and to the top of the collar is approximately 11¾". These lamps are greatly enhanced with appropriate trimmings.

Hobbs bases are often found with fonts that appear to be Bohemian in origin. They probably were, unless like Atterbury, they employed foreign decorators and sold them as the more desirable glassware of the day.

*f. Detail of the cut design on the shoulder of the font.*

*g. Hobbs lamp with pillar-molded font.*

a. Hobbs Wheeling Panelled.

b. Hobbs Wheeling Plain.

c. Hobbs Wheeling with Plain Cable base.

# Hobbs and Related

In OL-1 pp. 210 & 211, there are several lamps credited to the Central Glass Company partly on the basis of a cable design on their bases. Since that time, additional lamps have appeared that indicate this feature was also used on lamps made by other lamp manufacturers.

The Hobbs lamp (a) has the font called Wheeling Panelled on an all-glass lamp in OL-1 p. 157 (e). On the same page, lamp (j) with a clinch connector has a font like (b) only without the filler perched on the edge.

Lamp (c) with a font that matches (b) was likely made by Hobbs, and its cable base is shown in (d). This same base with a plain font is illustrated in OL-1 where it is called Shelby with Cable Base.

Thus, Hobbs is identified as a maker of lamps with the cable base decoration on the bottom of the font. This cable design may have been supplied to several manufacturers by the same mold maker.

The appearance of lamp (e) with a scalloped cable base is rather insignificant and yet it has the date July 1872 in the drip depression. See OL-1 pp. 188 & 189. This was for the John Bridges patent that was assigned to Adams & Company. With the knowledge of that information and the confirmation that Adams & Company made the Grape and Festoon pattern (see p. 93), the cable design can be attributed to at least three manufacturers.

d. Detail of base (c).

e. Adams-Bridges font with Scalloped Cable Base.

Hobbs is the name generally used to describe the company that started in the early 1860s as J. H. Hobbs, Brockunier and Company. For nearly two decades before that time, there were several name changes that involved principals of the company, including members of the Hobbs family.

In the late 1880s the company became the Hobbs Glass Company. This name remained until it joined United States Glass Company in early 1891. At one time it was said to be the largest, and one of the finest, glass manufacturers in the United States.

The clinch connector on lamp (b) and the matching patterns establish the fact that both of these 1870s pressed lamps were made by Hobbs Brockunier & Company. This is a detail that is often overlooked. *Unless there is a horizontal indentation in the top half of the connector and a corresponding indentation in the font peg, the complete lamp cannot be considered to be a Hobbs lamp.* It could be, but that would have to be determined by other factors.

The all-glass lamp below with pressed font and base is 8³/4".

*f. Hobbs Fruit Medallion.*

*g. Hobbs Fruit Medallion, early composite lamp.*

*a. Hobbs Optic with amber-stained, acid-etched font.*

*b. Hobbs stand lamp.*

*c. Hobbs lamp with patented drip depression.*

# Hobbs Lamps

There is an 1893 U.S. Glass Company catalogue illustration in OL-1 p. 323 showing an Optic lamp. They were made at factory "H," indicating they were products of the Hobbs factory. They were also made in a night lamp or miniature size, with a matching shade.. The better known Optic lamps are the ones with the opalescent Seaweed pattern advertised by the Beaumont Glass Co. It was also called Coral[ON] by Hobbs. See p. 180 (a).

Fonts with a similar foliate design were described as engraved. This example has an amber stain like the Hobbs Frances Ware, and the design has been acid etched. Colored fonts were not mentioned, however both the stand and the night lamps were described as being available with clear or ruby stems. The stand lamps were made in four sizes: 8", 9", 10" and 10½". This example is actually 9¾".

Lamp (b) has the font that is pictured with another base on page 110. It is also found with their patented clinch connector base. This relatively plain base matches many other glass items shown in Hobbs catalogues, as well as the lamp (c).

The drip-trough at the shoulder of lamp (c) is dated Pat'd. Sept. 29, 1863, Jan. 9, 1877. The first date, is for a patent issued to Michael B. Dyott for a hand lamp with a drip-trough and a handle that would not project as much as usual. He obtained several other lighting patents, and operated a lighting business under his own name in Philadelphia. This Michael B. Dyott was the nephew of the well-known Philadelphia glassmaker, Thomas B. Dyott.

The second date however, was not for a patent, but for a reissue of the Dyott patent. This actually was assigned to George Lomax who was also a witness to the reissue. Lomax was associated with the Union Glass Co. in Somerville, Mass. He was the patentee of the very successful Sept. 20, 1870 pressed glass fonts with a drip-catcher. If it weren't for the matching Hobbs base, it might be suspected that lamp (c) was made by The Union Glass Co. At some point in time, George Lomax must have made an arrangement with the Hobbs Glass Company to use his patent.

These dates in the drip depression of lamp (c) in OL-1 p. 188 serve to identify that lamp as a Hobbs, *not* an Adams lamp. New evidence often shifts the direction of assumptions and conclusions.

# The Hobbs Hands

It has now been established that the lamps shown here are probably all Hobbs lamps. The font (d) matching the dated font (c) opposite is part of the proof. The fact that it is combined with the distinctive hand bases of lamps (e) and (f) probably indicates a common origin. This still may be questioned because it can be observed that there are slight differences in the proportions of the hands.

There is however, much more significant and interesting proof that Hobbs made hands like these. I was fortunate to witness the restoration of a breathtaking Hobbs eight-arm, twenty-four light glass chandelier, as a "work in progress." Both the chandelier and the undertaking deserve the description breathtaking!

In the summer of 1995, I chose to visit the Oglebay Institute Mansion House Museum in Wheeling, West Virginia. The Curator of Glass Holly McClusky, offered to take me to the important event that was taking place at the School of the Visitation de Mount de Chantal. This is a local private girl's school that moved to its present location in 1865. When we arrived the chandelier located in the music room had been lowered from the high ceiling so that it could be disassembled, cleaned and reinstalled properly. Hundreds of glass parts were arranged on tables. These included rows of "hands." This undertaking, spearheaded by the Pittsburgh Chapter of the National Early American Glass Club, is documented in *The Glass Club Bulletin,* No. 176, Fall 1995 issue.

There are additional chandeliers as well as lamps to be seen at the Mansion House Museum. One of these includes Little Samuel figures that were mentioned in a trade journal as being also made in a table lamp form. Both the hand and Little Samuel figures are part of glass lighting fixtures illustrated in a United States Glass Company, Catalogue H.

The fonts (e) and (f), now confirmed as Hobbs, may be discovered on other bases. Also, other fonts have been seen on "Hobbs Hand" bases.

*d.*

*e.*

*f.*

b. *Atterbury flat hand lamp marked* PATENTED FEB. 11 & JUNE 4, 1862. *See the Bertrand p. 57 (l).*

a. *The first lamp patented and made by Atterbury.*

# Atterbury's Earliest Lamps

At first glance the information in raised letters around the collar appears to read PATENTED FEB 11 1865. That date does not apply to Atterbury or to a date patents were issued. The number 5 was inverted. It was intended to be 1862, and it referred to the Thomas Atterbury patent No. 34,345, for creating a pattern between smooth inner and outer surfaces. The only examples of this patent known to me include the date June 4, 1862 of another Atterbury patent.

The manufacturing technique caused air to be trapped between the walls of the font, which produced a silvery effect. This Scroll and Rib design was further developed and used on other Atterbury lamps at a later date. The lamp is 9¼" and I think, warrants a larger base. The font peg has two wide rectangular indentations like that of a font found on the ship *Bertrand*, see p. 56 (f).

There are certain characteristics that can be attributed to the major American lamp manufacturers. These primarily involve design and quality. The differences may be subtle, but when woven into the fabric, they present an individual picture or personality.

After studying many lamps by many makers, a new discovery will almost announce its manufacturer, or at the very least, give direction to the search.

a. O.K.<sup>ON</sup>.

b. Sun<sup>ON</sup> with Squat Octagon<sup>ON</sup> base.

c. Saucer lamp<sup>ON</sup> with handle.

More lamps and greater access to patents and catalogues have allowed the expansion of knowledge of this interesting company and its lamps. The expression "Perfection is dull" seems to apply to Atterbury lamps because in spite of their imperfections, they are charming and have a primitive "country look." We also know they were capable of producing first-class glass.

There are copies of the Atterbury & Co. 1872, 1874, and 1881 catalogues on microfiche at Corning. In addition I have photocopies that I made in Washington many years ago. These are presently undated and will be referred to as such. As well, I have prints from microfilm loaned to me by Dr. Arthur Peterson. The latter two sources contain some additional information that will have to be correlated at a later date.

O.K.<sup>ON</sup> This name, and all others used on this page are the original names given to their lamps by Atterbury. This is a welcome relief to authors who have chosen to provide names to facilitate communication among dealers and collectors. At some point one runs out of different descriptive names and resorts to Christian names, surnames, street names, and so forth. Inevitably some original names surface later, and the author is chastised for not using the "birth name."

The font and base above were pictured in the 1874 catalogue. Lamp (c) is described in the 1872 and 1874 catalogues as "Saucer White Foot Handle."

Maguire was the name given by Atterbury to the distinctive pattern (d), that I called Ribbed Belt in OL-1. It was illustrated in an undated catalogue on Squat Octagon<sup>ON</sup> bases, in 3¾" and 4¼" sizes with screw connectors. It also appeared as all-glass stand lamps with two different styles of their Prism foot<sup>ON</sup>. Here it is on a Eureka<sup>ON</sup> base.

Also in the same undated catalogue, the Atterbury Octagon<sup>ON</sup> lamp (e) was pictured almost as shown. There were, however, two interesting differences. The first one was that the white stem between the threaded brass connector and the top ridge or step was colored gold. When photocopied, the gold appeared black. See OL-1, p. 149.

The second difference was that the catalogue includes the Octagon name for both the font and base, and the illustration clearly shows that it had eight sides. I was convinced that it had eight sides until it was pointed out to me that in the photograph, the font appears to have 10 sides. When the lamp was inspected, it was found to actually have 12 sides! The panels or sides were very indistinct and difficult to photograph. Height is 10¼".

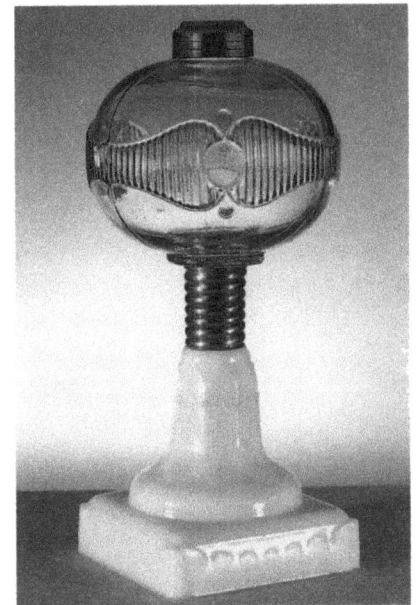

d. Maguire<sup>ON</sup> with Eureka<sup>ON</sup> base.

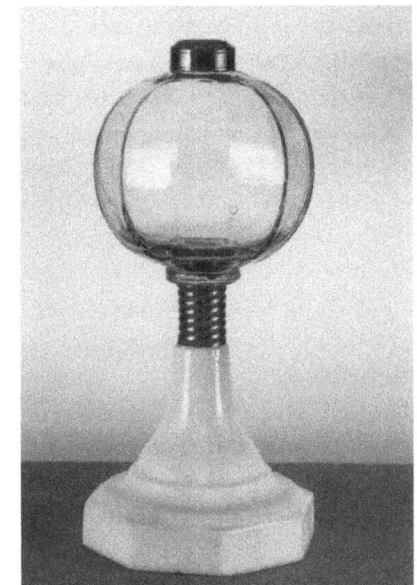

e. Twelve-sided Octagon<sup>ON</sup> lamp.

*a. Wm. Penn<sup>ON</sup> profile.*

*b. Wm. Penn<sup>ON</sup> front view.*

*c. Atterbury Rib and Leaf Band.*

*d. Atterbury hand lamp No. 25.*

# Atterbury Hand Lamps

Years of speculation about the head lamp (a) have been put to rest with the discovery of price lists that corresponded to the Atterbury catalogues. I am not aware of any other lamps that represented living Americans. The closest thing could be Uncle Sam whom I failed to recognize and called John in OL-1 p. 177 (b). Other views of this well-detailed cast-iron figure show the characteristic hat and rolled-up newspaper more clearly.

Lamps (a), (b), and (c) are examples of Atterbury hand lamp patents. Rib and Leaf Band is the name that I gave to the line illustration of this lamp in OL-1 p. 147. In the 1881 Atterbury catalogue it was listed as No. 22c.

The panelled hand lamp (d) was only listed as No. 22. One of the cata-logue price lists gave numbers only to 19 patent handle lamps. Wm. Penn was numbered 21, and Ohio and Shell had names only.

In OL-1 p. 147, catalogue illustrations show the lamp (e) named Sherman and another of similar shape and size named Ohio. This is the way they appear only in this catalogue that at present is not dated. In all other catalogues examined, only the one (e) appears, and it is always named Ohio! The one catalogue that I had consulted earlier had transposed the names.

The base and handle of this lamp is pressed, and like some other supposedly pressed patented handle lamps, it has been illustrated with what appears to be an applied handle. This was probably just due to a little artist's license.

*e. Atterbury Ohio<sup>ON</sup>.*

Maguire<sup>ON</sup>, called Ribbed Belt in OL-1 was shown in two sizes in an undated Atterbury catalogue, on Squat Octagon<sup>ON</sup> bases with screw connectors. It also appeared as all-glass stand lamps with two different styles of their Prism<sup>ON</sup> design bases. There is a considerable difference between these three Maguire lamps.

The smallest lamp (a) is so short that a person with a large hand would have difficulty taking hold of it. It is marked with the same dates as the lamps with the larger handles.

The bases of the lamps (c) and (d) with the extended pressed handles are marked on the underside: ATTERBURY'S PAT FEB. 11TH& JUNE 3D 1862. The letters are rather crudely formed and spaced.

*c. Maguire<sup>ON</sup> with extended handle. The patents refer to the handle and base being pressed in one piece.*

*a. Maguire<sup>ON</sup> double handle.*

*b. Unmarked Maguire<sup>ON</sup> footed hand lamp with applied handle.*

*d. Filley<sup>ON</sup> with extended handle.*

These lamps with extended handles may have been successful in terms of manufacture and strength, but they were awkward to carry. The mold seams on the extended handles are very sharp and cut into your finger, unless the handle is grasped by a fist. Height is 5".

*a. Atterbury patented drip-catcher.*

*b. Blown Scroll and Rib.*

*c. Wave handle with Diamond foot<sup>ON</sup>.*

The bases of the two stand lamps above are the same size and design. Each font may be attributed to Atterbury & Co. for different reasons. Lamp (a) is marked in raised letters on a stepped band around the collar,

PATD APR 10 1883. This refers to the patent No. 275,563 granted to Thomas B. Atterbury for a mold to produce a blown font with a flange. The specifications made reference to the Hiram Dillaway patent, but not to the George

Lomax patent. A later *Patent Office Report* mentioned that Lomax was considering taking legal action against Atterbury, and that Atterbury claimed he was unaware of any infringement. Both the Dillaway and Lomax drip-catcher fonts were pressed. See OL-1 for information about these lamps.

Font (b) is the same as the one shown with a Swan base on page 99c. These two lamps are 8".

Lamp (c) was described as "Wave handle with Diamond foot" in the Atterbury 1872, 1874, and 1881 catalogues. They were illustrated in three sizes.

James S. Atterbury and Thomas B. Atterbury received a Design patent Aug. 29, 1870, No. 4298, for the lamp bases (d & e). The Chieftain and Shelley font designs were used with their screw socket connectors.

*d. & e.   Chieftain<sup>ON</sup> and Shelley<sup>ON</sup> with patented bases.*

# Atterbury All-glass
# White Base Lamps

All three of these Atterbury opal or white base lamps are illustrated in their catalogues or patent illustration. The patent date marked on the underside of the bases is June 22, 1875. This patent, No. 164,669 granted to J. S. and T. B. Atterbury, was for a method of attaching clear glass fonts or bowls to an opal or colored stand or base. In their specifications they stated, "We are not aware that a lamp with an opal or white glass stand and clear glass bowl has ever before been made and united together without a brass socket or cement." They also claimed that lamps made this way could be sold for thirty per cent less than those joined with a socket.

Lamps (f) and (g) have their Panel[ON] bases. See also OL-1 p. 130. Original names are given from their catalogues and price lists. In the 1874 catalogue, colorless Grecian fonts are shown with connectors and white Octagon bases, or in clear all-glass stand lamps.

The Band[ON] font appears in the 1881 catalogue as an all-glass lamp with an amber base like p. 148 (f) in OL-1, and also with a screw socket and white Octagon base.

Crystal[ON] appears as a clear all-glass extra heavy lamp in three sizes, in the 1874 catalogue. In the 1881 catalogue it is shown as in the 1874 catalogue and with an amber foot.

The clear Illuminator 6¼" diameter shade holder and opal shade are both appropriate and attractive. The lamp is 8¾".

*f. Grecian[ON].*

*g. Band[ON].*

*h. Crystal[ON].*

*a. Atterbury Hercules.*

*c. Atterbury Tucker^ON font.*

# Atterbury Hercules

Hercules is the name collectors have given to the footed bowl with this base. It has been attributed to Atterbury & Co. and the lamp form (a) here confirms the attribution. The pressed boss shoulder was also used on Atterbury's patented lamp pictured on page 65 and further described in OL-1 on p. 132.

There is no patent date on this lamp. Perhaps it was not made according to the patent specifications. These stated the portion of the lamp from the join at the edge of the font to the bottom of the base was pressed in one piece. This may not have applied to this lamp.

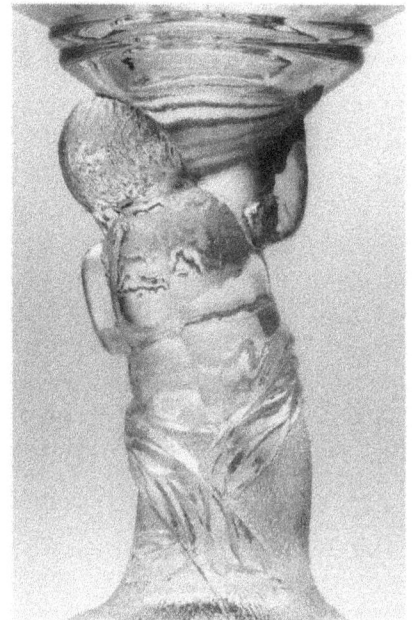

*b. Hercules detail.*

If depicted today, the figure, especially the view (b), would likely have a more svelte appearance. The font is 5" in diameter and the height is 8¼".

The Atterbury Tucker^ON font (c) was named and pictured in their 1872 catalogue. It has the July 1861 patent date around the filler opening. This was for the Jacob Reighard patent assigned to Atterbury. The reason for naming it Tucker is not known at present. One possibility is that its shallow form fits in the Tucker cast iron bracket and hanging lamp font holders. See p. 184 (a).

a.                        b.                        c.

## Eaton/Onion Variations

The pictures and the primary source account presented here may initially create more conjecture than conclusions. In the future, however, it is probable that part of this information will be woven into new theories and opinions.

Lamp (a), a large lavender Eaton or Onion lamp (to use one original and one common name), is pictured for comparison. A catalogue illustration and other examples are shown in OL-1&2. Recently, similar examples in green alabaster have appeared at auction sales. They have different connectors and are said to have originated in France.

I have not had an opportunity to examine lamp (b) with the Atterbury connector, but have been told by the owner that the font and base pegs are threaded. The next lamp (c) was found with a recently cemented collar of foreign origin. It has some features that clearly relate it to Eaton lamps and others that are obviously very different. These include the one-piece form and the ledge at bottom of the scalloped base.

The glass is white, translucent, and slightly granular, with a waxy texture that closely resembles the base of the Triple Dolphin lamp in OL-2 p. 72 (c). This has since been identified as a lamp sold by Dietz & Co. in London. This lamp may be English.

Another related example is the font (d). It has a recessed hollow peg and a filler, combined with the same shape and number of ribs as the Eaton lamp (a). The effect is light and graceful when mounted upon a gas bracket.

d.

# Iron Base Lamps

The Close patent lamp (a) is one of the most unusual, and particularly interesting, early patented lamps. It required a custom molded font and three identical cast sections for the base. When fastened together by means of screws or rivets, the sections formed a base that firmly clasped the font. The lower part of the font is marked in raised letters PATENTED MAY 27 1862 BY C T CLOSE. This patent, No. 35,363, was obtained by Charles T. Close of New York city. The bronze finish appears to be original.

The burner is dated Oct. 14, 1862, June 21, 1863, and Dec. 10, 1867, and the chimney is embossed R V B.

Both the font and base of lamp (b) are typical of the 1860s. The cast iron figure of a hunter is attached to the cast tripod base. It is dated April 8 and Aug. 25, but the year is indistinct and patents for the appropriate years do not seem to apply. The wide plate collar, flattened font, and rather crude engraving are typical of 1860s lamps.

Spelter took over in the 1870s as the metal used for figural bases. Much better detail could be achieved with this softer metal. Figurals in great variety were immensely popular in the 1870s and 1880s.

The slip burner is stamped on the cone THE MAGIC SUN PAT MAR 1 1869. The thumbwheel is marked, PATD Jan 24, 1871.

Height to the top of the collar of (a) is 9", and (b) is 9½".

*a & b.*

## MAIZE LAMPS.

*SEND FOR SAMPLE PACKAGE*

*a. Pottery and Glassware Reporter Vol. 21 July 11, 1889.*

## Advertised Lamps

Our knowledge of lamps of the kerosene era is rounded out by lamps that were advertised in trade journals and magazines. This represents relatively few compared with examples extant and in catalogues. Only one damaged example of the Maize lamps made by the W. L. Libbey & Son Co. is known. Other examples of this lustrous yellow and green glassware are in museums and private collections.

The Princess Lamp (b) with its nautical theme was from the opposite end of the price scale. It was advertised in the May 23, 1895 issue of the *Crockery and Glass Journal* by the famous chimney maker, Thos. Evans Co. Also advertised in *CGJ* in September 1886 was the Dewdrop lamp made by the New York Lamp Co. It has been seen with different color combinations.

*b. Princess lamp.*

*c. Dewdrop lamp.*

# Mechanical Lamps

Mechanical lamps have had a lengthy history among members of the Rushlight Club, and articles have been published in *The Rushlight*. Lamps photographed and studied here include examples from the former collections of Carlton Brown, Larry and Mabel Cooke, Edward Durell, Brent Rowell, and the author. This subject was introduced in OL-1.

Catalogues, including one with photographs, price lists, patent records, and archives provide a substantial record of this category. The basic principle of these lamps was that of creating a controlled draft surrounding the flame, by means of a fan operated by a clockwork motor. The intention was to provide a smokeless flame without the use of a chimney. Such an advantage would have been significant for public places and for transportation lighting. This could outweigh the higher initial cost.

Different and distinctive are words that describe this category of lamps. They were made in the 1860-1900 Victorian period in both the United States and Canada and were exported to distant parts of the globe. This might suggest that they could be found in far away places, but only time will tell. They are not particularly plentiful in North America possibly because it was unlikely that they would be saved for their beauty, or for their convenience if required for an emergency. Novelty was probably the main reason they were saved.

Many patents associated with these lamps are annotated on pages 266 & 267. Not only do the patents describe the improvements, but of perhaps greater interest, they provide the names and involvement of those associated with the subject.

In broad terms this subject could be referred to as early and late kerosene mechanical lamps of the nineteenth century. The F. H. Lovell & Co. illustrated wholesale catalogues and separate descriptive price lists have provided the best records of American mechanical lamps offered for sale. These records are incomplete, however they do afford an overview. They were first described in the 1875 wholesale Price List as:

## MECHANICAL LAMPS

The draft is produced in these lamps by means of a small Fan Wheel, turned by machinery placed in the base, and which will run 8 hours without re-winding. This is the only Lamp known that will burn without a chimney, without smoke or smell, and will not blow out. And owing to this great merit they are coming into general use.

No. 3296.   No. 3297.   No. 3298.   No. 3299.   No. 3300.

No. 3301.   No. 3302.   No. 3303.   No. 3304.

*a. From the the 1877-78 F.H. Lovell & Co. catalogue.*
*Courtesy The Sandwich Historical Society Glass Museum*

The 1877-78 F.H. Lovell & Co. price list claimed the lamps would for run 10 hours. In 1881 their claim returned to 8 hours.

Line illustrations (a) are from plate 192 in the 1877-78 catalogue, however the same cuts were used in the 1875 catalogue. Not shown here is No. 3305, a cigar lighter similar to No. 3304. There was also a Station Lantern and a "Brass Finish" side bracket lamp. These lamps represent most of the currently known catalogue illustrations of early mechanical lamps. There are different early examples extant shown on the following pages.

Wholesale prices quoted were per dozen and they were essentially the same as in 1875.

| | | | |
|---|---|---|---|
| 3396 | Bronze Mechanical Lamp | No. 1 Burner | $78.00 |
| 3397 | Nickel Plated Mechanical Lamp | No. 2 Burner | 90.00 |
| 3398 | Bronze Mechanical Lamp | No. 2 Burner | 78.00 |
| 3399 | Nickel Plated Mechanical Lamp | No. 1 Burner | 84.00 |
| 3300 | Marine Nickel Plated Mechanical Lamp, complete | | |
| | | No. 1 Burner | 120.00 |
| 3301 | Nickel Plated Mechanical Lamp | No. 2 Burner | 90.00 |
| 3302 | Bronze Mechanical Lamp | No. 2 | 120.00 |
| 3303 | Bronze Mechanical Lamp | No. 2 | 72.00 |
| 3304 | Plain Bronze Mechanical Lamp | No. 2 | 90.00 |
| 3304 | Gilt Bronze Mechanical Lamp | No. 2 | 96.00 |

Lamps 3304 were described as having "arms."

a. *Lamp described as a "Brass Pendant. Complete with Spring Balance Fixture" from the 1875 F.H. Lovell Catalogue.* Courtesy: The Sandwich Historical Society Glass Museum.

This example (a) is of particular interest because it is the only illustration of an early mechanical lamp hanging form and of a shade. Hanging forms, absent from the 1877-78 catalogue, returned in the 1881-82 catalogue where they were called a "Saloon Pendant complete."

There is one lamp, No. 3302, among the group of illustrations opposite, that can be identified from advertisements and an article, in 1875 issues of the *Crockery and Glass Journal*. Accompanied by the same illustration, the article states, "The Patent Mechanical Lamp Co., of which Mr. S.C. Brower is president, 138 Chambers Street, New York, are the sole manufacturers."

While at the home of Larry and Mabel Cooke taking photographs for my book *Primitives & Folk Art*, I included the mechanical lamp (b). This and the example (c) are now in the collection of Brent Rowell who has provided the descriptions.

b. *Mechanical lamp with cast lion decoration.*

This ornate mechanical lamp, thought to have been made by Michael B. Dyott of Philadelphia, was most likely made from the late 1860s until perhaps the early 1870s. The following note about this lamp was found in the files of the former owner Mabel Cooke: the lion lamp shell is identical to a non-mechanical lamp [in a New Hampshire collection] which has an original label marked "Dyott's Patent Stellar Lamp, Mfd. By M. B. Dyott 114 So. Second St., Philadelphia."

A small brass tag, soldered on the tin band encircling the glass font, reads "Patented Nov. 10th 1863." This was for the George A. Jones mechanical lamp patent. The font's underlying drip cup is stamped "Dyott's Patent May 29, 1866." The base contains a De Keravenan-Jones patented clockwork motor topped with a 1¾" extension tube.

The example (c) contains the same patented clockwork motor, however it is topped with a 5-inch long extension tube. This example also has the glass font holder and the drip cup patented by Michael B. Dyott.

c. *Mechanical lamp with applied cast decoration.* Photograph by Brent Rowell.

Thought also to have been manufactured in the late 1860s or early 1870s, this imposing lamp is the largest mechanical table lamp known. It is a full 18 inches in height. It is extraordinary not only for its size, but because it retains its original finish, key, and original manufacturer's label. The label reads as follows: "DIRECTIONS for using the ATMOSPHERIC COAL OIL LAMP....Remove the Oil Fount from the Stand to trim and fill; unscrew the burner to fill; trim the Wick same as in other Lamps. Wind up the movement before lighting and to insure a good light, the movement should be wound up every four or five hours. The movement should be taken out once a year and the pivots oiled. M.B. Dyott, Manufacturer, No.114 South Second Street, Philadelphia."

The Gothic cast spelter decorative band was also used on a lamp in the circa 1865 Dietz catalogue.

*a. Early mechanical brass lamp with lacquered finish.*

*c. Early mechanical brass lamp with gilt finish.*

*b. Jones patent metal font.*

*d. Dyott patent glass font.*

There is nothing to suggest from the external appearance of lamps (a) and (c) that their interiors would be different. While they closely resemble the lamps from the Lovell catalogues, there does not seem to be an exact match. Lamp (c) shown in OL-1 is included here for comparison.

Lamp (a) is stamped PATENTED. NOV. 10TH 1863 for the George A. Jones motor patent. The dull gray non-ferrous metal font (b) has a tin tip. It would likely have been manufactured between 1863 and the next patented improvements that were included in lamp (c).

Any oil seepage would have dropped onto the fan blades. Like the font (a) the blades are non-ferrous. They are somewhat bent, but not broken. The motor differs in construction from (c), and there are no visible patent dates. There is not any indication that it has ever been disturbed. In fact, a lack of cleaning has left a curious sooty deposit on the underside around the key and the air intake holes. It appears that the forced draft has sucked in smoke. The fact that the presence of soot inside the lamp shell is commonly found indicates they weren't entirely smokeless!

Lamp (c) has Dyott's patented metal drip cup supported below the glass font. It is stamped Dyott's Patent May 29, 1866. Like lamp (a), it has the Jones 1863 date stamped on a brass strip, soldered to a metal band that supports the glass font. Both lamps are about 15" and have about a ¼" space between the body of the lamp and font.

The date of Dyott's font patent, May 7, 1867 is not visible on this glass font. This is unusual because it was a patent office requirement at the time. If Dyott was involved with the manufacture of these lamps, he perhaps reasoned that it was not necessary, since the inner font was completely hidden.

Lamp (a) has an unmarked thumbwheel, while lamp (c) has an undated one marked G. W. Brown & Co. Although shades for these stand lamps were not indicated in the 1870s catalogues, they were promoted extensively with the later mechanical lamps.

Michael Boyd Dyott was a lamp dealer in Philadelphia who often advertised in the *Crockery and Glass Journal*. He obtained several patents in addition to those for mechanical lamps. One of the most successful was his January 6, 1863 spiral burner, that continued to be advertised into the late 1880s.

Although these burners were practical for hanging and bracket lamps, few are found today.

Another Dyott patent for a glass lamp, that included a drip trough as part of his claim, was granted September 29, 1863. This patent was reissued to George Lomax on January 9, 1877. Lomax patented the most famous drip catcher flange on September 20, 1870. These patents were for a method of manufacture, not for the concept.

Dyott was the nephew of Thomas B. Dyott, the famous early nineteenth century glassmaker etc. He was the subject of a fascinating biography, *Bottles, Flasks, and Dr. Dyott* by Helen McKearin, noted American glass historian.

# Late Mechanical Lamps

The illustration (a) from Robert Hitchcock's earlier patent drawing was used in an 1880 promotion flyer advertising the Hitchcock Lamp. Twenty-three railway companies, including two in Canada, were listed as users of their car lamps. Cross section illustrations were commonly used in mechanical lamp promotion, to convey the operation of these lamps.

Lamps (b), a sidewinder, and (c), a stemwinder, were the two basic Hitchcock models. The painted one was pictured in Hitchcock's own 1887 catalogue that used photographs to illustrate many ornate styles. Photographs were rarely used for this purpose and serve to validate their stock.

The painted example (b) is stamped in a single line around the shade holder rim surrounding the cone, HITCH-COCK LAMP-PATENTED WATERTOWN. NEW-YORK UNITED STATES OF AMERICA. This same information is on the thumbwheel and the inner font has the name and patent date Nov. 30, 1880. It now has a dull brass finish, with evidence of gilding in the decorated area. The painted white flowers have a touch of blue.

The late June Kelm, past president of the Rushlight Club, sent me details and photographs of a Hitchcock lamp with a brake. This would have allowed the motor to be restarted without completely rewinding it. It would have been a significant improvement, particularly in public places where several lamps had to be lit each evening. The shape of the base was smaller and slightly different.

A worn paper-thin layer of nickel-plate coats the embossed brass lamp (c). While it was very worn on the outside, the interior is very clean, without any sign of soot. The lamp itself however is of much lighter, and no doubt cheaper, construction than any other mechanical lamp that I have examined. To accommodate the wider offset sidewinder motor, the earlier Hitchcock shape adopted a Wanzer-like profile. This gave the table lamp a more stable appearance. The inner portion of the rim is embossed: THE IMPROVED HITCHCOCK LAMP NEW YORK, and the outer area PATENTED NOV 30 1880 JULY 20 1886 DEC 17 1895 MADE IN UNITED STATES OF AMERICA. It is a very quiet motor. The design was featured with elaborate art-glass shades, in a late 1890s or early 1900s catalogue.

The 1881-82 F. H. Lovell catalogue is the last known reference to the early mechanical lamps pictured on page 130. It appears that Hitchcock did little advertising in the 1870s. Perhaps it was beyond his capabilities or means. His name appears in connection with S. Elwood May's advertisements in 1882 & 1883. See p. 134.

During the 1883-1884 period, negotiations must have been underway between Robert Hitchcock and F. H. Lovell & Co. who had dropped the line of early mechanical lamps from their catalogue a year earlier. Perhaps this connection was made through Rosewell P. Flower, a wealthy New York businessman, partner, and financial supporter of Hitchcock, who later became governor of New York State.

F. H. Lovell & Co. printed several separate small catalogues in English and in Spanish from June 1, 1884, to one dated 1886 only. On the cover they claimed to be Hitchcock's sole agent. The focus changed from commercial to house lamps in many styles. All the new styles however, incorporated the old basic well-constructed Hitchcock form.

While there have been accounts of Hitchcock lamp sales before 1880 referred to in *The Rushlight*, I have not seen any examples and expect there are very few extant. Transportation and commercial examples are also rare.

Both lamps are 12".

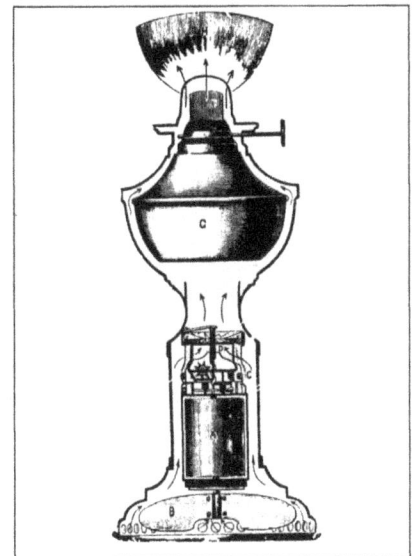

*a. Interior construction.*

*b. Hitchcock Stemwinder lamp.*

*c. Hitchcock Sidewinder lamp.*

# New Ideal Lamp

In June 1882 S. Elwood May, a business associate of Robert Hitchcock, placed an advertisement in the *Crockery and Glass Journal*, that was repeated about four times. He included a small illustration of a Hitchcock lamp and the claim that he was the sole wholesale agent for Hitchcock lamps. May also stated that, "As this is the headquarters, and I control the whole production of the company, I can offer you the bottom prices."

There were a few repetitions of this advertisement, followed by a more urgent appeal in December 1882, for agents stating, "If I can't get lamp men, I will be forced to look to other dealers." This apparent lack of success gave rise to another attempt. In September and December of 1883 there were full-page advertisements promoting a new mechanical lamp that closely resembled the basic Hitchcock design and included an additional hanging lamp, bracket lamp, and a chandelier. He called it the IDEAL LAMP. On June 10, 1884, S. Elwood May became the assignee of a mechanical lamp patent granted to W. H. Rogers of Brooklyn, New York.

This led to the production of the lamp (a). The following information is stamped on the rim. N.Y. — MAY'S NEW IDEAL LAMP PAT'D JUNE 10. 1884. Since May owned a factory, he could (and did) produce a substantial product. It is brass with a heavy nickel plate. It was found with a shade holder, but not necessarily this one. The squat 5" glass shade was the most popular choice for mechanical table lamps. Height to the top of the cone is 12½".

Both this and the lamp from the Edward Durell collection have soot inside the top portion of the shell. This suggests some smoke was recirculated by the fan.

*a. S. Elwood May, New Ideal Lamp. Patented 1884.*

*a. Hitchcock wire harp lamp.*

# Hitchcock Lamps

The Hitchcock harp lamp was the first and probably also the last hanging version to be made with this basic lamp. After the retirement of the early-style mechanical lamps from the large F. H. Lovell 1881-82 catalogue, and the efforts of S. Elwood May to promote Hitchcock and similar lamps in 1882 and 1883, there was a serious attempt by Lovell to introduce a new line.

In 1884 and 1885 Lovell introduced separate small export catalogues in English and Spanish featuring Hitchcock lamps. They included commercial and transportation lighting, as well as the two hanging lamps and the Faience table lamp illustrated here (b). Only a price list exists for the Lovell 1886 large format catalogue. It priced Faience mechanical lamps at $15.00, $18.00 and $20.00 each depending upon the quality. They also listed non-mechanical Faience lamps at $12.00.

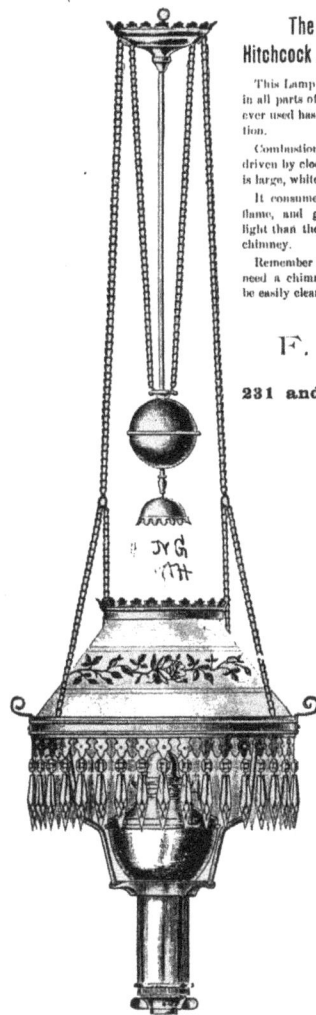
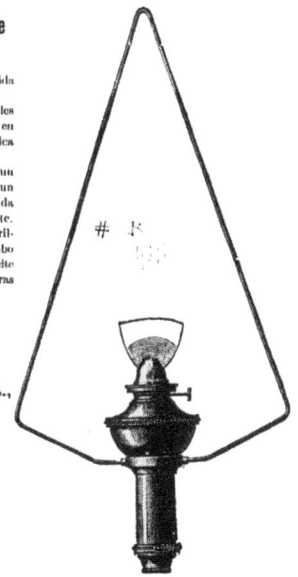

No. 647.
Hitchcock Nickel Pendant, $4.00 each. | Lira y lámpara, $4.00 cada una.

No. 648.
Hitchcock Extension Nickel Library Lamp, complete, each, $10.00.
Lámpara de Hitchcock, con extension, completa, con lagrimas de vidrio y pantalla adornada, cada una, $10.00.

Hitchcock Faience Lamp, complete, each, $18.00.
Lámpara de Hitchcock Faience, toda completa, cada una, $18.00.

No. 649.

Hitchcock Nickel Extension Chandelier, 2 lights each, $20.00.
Hitchcock Nickel Extension Chandelier, 3 lights each, $30.00.
Hitchcock Nickel Extension Chandelier, 4 lights each, $40.00.

No. 650.

Araña extension para la lámpara de Hitchcock, niquelada, con dos luces, cada una, $20.00 ; con tres luces, cada una, $30.00 ; con cuatro luces, cada una, $40.00.

*b. Illustrations from the F. H. Lovell small 1884 and 1885 catalogues.*
*Courtesy The Sandwich Historical Society Glass Museum.*

In 1887 Robert Hitchcock produced a catalogue with about 30 pages of photographs. It has been reprinted in *Lamps and Other Lighting Devices*. There were many hanging lamps and parlour lamps included. Also pictured were both single and double student lamps, as well as their commercial and transportation lamps.

Hitchcock claimed to be sole manufacturer at this time, while Lovell claimed to be sole wholesale agent. Perhaps Hitchcock wanted to tap directly into the export market so successfully established by Lovell.

# Electric and Hitchcock Lamps

# F. H. LOVELL & CO.

## Electric and Hitchcock Lamps, Chandeliers, Brackets, &c.

### DRUMMOND ELECTRIC LAMP.

(EMBOSSED.)

Gives the light of 80 candles.

Is made of Brass, and cannot break.

Finished in Nickel, Rich Gold, and Brass, as desired.

It combines all the advantages of the Rochester Lamp, which it closely resembles.

The top of the Lamp can be removed and the Lamp easily cleaned and re-wicked.

The wick always moves smoothly and evenly, there being no ratchet to get out of order.

One Lamp will light a large room brilliantly.

For the Drummond Electric Fount see Plate No. 5, No. 620.

Lamps completed with 10-inch Plain or Decorated Shade, as ordered.

#### PRICE LIST.

WITH DECORATED SHADES.

| | | |
|---|---|---|
| Brass, | $36.00 per doz. |
| Nickel, | 38.00 " |
| Rich Gold, | 38.00 " |

WITH PLAIN SHADES.

| | | |
|---|---|---|
| Brass, | $30.00 per doz. |
| Nickel, | 32.00 " |
| Rich Gold, | 32.00 " |

Particular attention given to orders for export.

Goods packed by experienced packers.

Gross, net weight and measurement of each package given when required.

MANUFACTURED BY

No. 600.

FABRICADA POR

### F. H. LOVELL & CO.,

Lamps, Chandeliers, Glassware, &c.

### F. H. LOVELL Y CA.,

Lámparas de todas clases, Cristaleria para la mesa, etc.

#### 118 JOHN STREET and 233 PEARL STREET, NEW YORK.

*Illustration from the F.H. Lovell & Co. 1888 Export Catalogue.*
*Courtesy The Sandwich Historical Society Glass Museum.*

The F. H. Lovell 1887 and 1888 export catalogues printed in English and in Spanish promoted "Electric and Hitchcock Lamps" on their covers, however the the latter were relegated to three simple examples on one page. Clearly, taking advantage of the popular kerosene lighting scam of the 1880s was of greater significance. Throughout the world *electric* was the magic word in lighting, and America was where it came from. Before there was a real understanding of what it involved, kerosene could masquerade as electric lighting.

In their large domestic and the smaller export catalogues, Lovell advertised the Drummond as an electric lamp. This was their own brand of Argand or center draft lamp. Of course an electric burner was also available! Others advertised electric chimneys, electric wicks, and electric oil. This deception was a very common practice with many manufacturers, especially those introducing new and improved Argand burners. Today trade card collectors value nineteenth century cards that were used to promote kerosene lighting referred to as "electric." Lovell chose this dubious method to exploit the situation, whereas the Hitchcock catalogue made no reference to electric lighting.

In the early issues of *The Crockery and Glass Journal* beginning in late 1874, whenever electric lighting was mentioned, it usually referred to carbon arc lighting used primarily outdoors or in very large public interior spaces. This could easily lead to some confusion about Edison's development. It should be kept in mind that this was a trade publication with its own biases. The information the general public received would have been presented in a different manner.

# Wanzer Mechanical Lamps

Lamp (a) photographed by the author is reproduced with the permission of the Wellington County Museum. It is unlike any others I have seen or heard about. Information provided by the museum gives its height at 30 cm, diameter at font 12¾ cm, and the diameter at base 14 cm. It is marked Bowman-Heath and with the date Nov. 13/89 Hamilton. The date is not known to me and the connection to Richard Wanzer and his lamps remains to be investigated.

Wanzer was the second-best known name in mechanical lamps. Whereas Robert Hitchcock was born in Ontario, Canada and became successful in the USA, Richard Mott Wanzer was born in New York State and became successful in Hamilton, Ontario, Canada. This, of course, poses a bit of a dilemma for chauvinists. Both men died in 1900 at a time when the demand for household use of mechanical lamps had all but disappeared.

Wanzer moved to Canada from Buffalo, New York, where he formerly resided. He was one of the most successful entrepreneurs able to take advantage of a loophole in the Canadian patent law. This restricted grants of patents to British subjects who were actual residents of Canada. It did not however restrict a foreign resident from copying American inventions and profiting from them in Canada. In February 1861 the *Scientific American* reported that the laws "ought to be modified so as to give foreign inventors a chance to protect themselves against a wholesale appropriation of their inventions."

In retaliation Canadians were required to pay $500.00 to obtain a US patent that would only cost a US citizen $15.00. United States patent commissioners in their reports routinely complained about this situation, however it was not until 1872 that reciprocity was accomplished. Obviously restrictions did not impede Wanzer's ventures. Pirating the patents of successful American sewing machine inventors, he produced his own highly successful brand which he marketed in Canada and overseas.

When supply and demand factors adversely affected the sewing machine business, Wanzer gravitated towards the production of mechanical lamps. This time his use of the inventions of others took a more respectable route. He made arrangements with Abel G. Heath of New York, to assign his Canadian lamp patent to him Sept. 27, 1886. Later on March 22, 1887, Heath obtained a US patent for this lamp. For the second patent Heath assigned to Wanzer on September 18, 1888, his address was given as Hamilton Ont. Canada. One of the witnesses was W. A. Lovell. Could there have possibly been a connection with F. H. Lovell & Co.? All of this occurred at the same time as the Lovell and Hitchcock promotion was in high gear.

From the outset, Wanzer aggressively sought to market his lamps. After a brief announcement in the Niagara Falls (N.Y.) *Gazette* on February 29, 1888, there followed the next week, March 7, an announcement of the incorporation of the Wanzer Lamp Co. in Albany as a New York State Company. It stated: "The incorporaters are Frank L. Wanzer, Hamilton, Ont.; Oliver V. Mercer, Philadelphia, Pa.; Edward B. Wyman, New York; W. Caryl Ely and Lawrence Van Cleef , Niagara Falls." Frank Wanzer was the son of R. M. Wanzer. In the 1890-91 Niagara Falls City Directory, Van Cleef was listed as a freight agent for the NYCRR, and Edward Wyman was listed as superintendent of the Wanzer Lamp Co. Frank Wanzer was also listed in the 1888 Philadelphia City Directory.

Most of the Wanzer lamps that I have seen are marked on the shade-holder rim, THE WANZER LAMP PAT 1886 WANZER & Co HAMILTON ONT CANADA. US models are marked as either Niagara Falls or Philadelphia, and British lamps are stamped as example (b).

*a. Mechanical lamp in the collection of the Wellington County Museum and Archives R.R.1, Fergus, Ontario, Canada.*

*b. Wanzer sidewinder lamp with black enamelled cast-iron base. The burner is stamped: THE WANZER LAMP PAT 2833-87. This refers to his British patent. This may not be an original combination. In the past, parts have been known to have been exchanged.*

Wanzer lamps were advertised as being available in brass or nickel plate. Patented reflector shades and heating attachments were also made.

THESE Library-slides are made especially for the Wanzer Lamp, of the best Polished Bronze Metal, with a rich gold finish and having the celebrated Parker Automatic Spring Extension, which never breaks or wears out. Any style of 14 inch Shade can be used. . . . .

THESE Lamps can be removed from the hangers and used in any other attachment.

THE WANZER LAMP is the simplest, safest, and most economical yet offered to the public. . . . . . . . .

PRICE quoted does not include Glassware and Prisms.

No. 3585, LIBRARY-SLIDE.    Rings Pierced for Prisms.

*a. One of three library lamps illustrated in a catalogue published by The Wanzer Lamp Co. Niagara Falls N.Y. Courtesy the Strong Museum.*

The stepped conical base used for Wanzer lamps made in Hamilton, Ontario, was adapted for use in the Wanzer hanging lamp. All mechanical hanging lamp bases underwent some modification when adapted to hanging forms. This catalogue served to promote a variety of Wanzer products. They included two more hanging lamps and vase lamps with dome shades that they referred to as "Fancy lamps." There were patented "nursery attachments" for heating food or water, and patented reflectors "Good for Old People and Weak Eyes."

Of particular importance was "THE WANZER PATENT PORTABLE COOKER." This "Marvel of usefulness and economy" was comprised of a series of utensils stacked upon a frame over a Wanzer lamp.

The June 7, 1898 *Hamilton Evening Times* reported that "Mr. E. M. Wanzer Will Go Back to Buffalo." There was no mention of his business failure that was featured in later accounts and biographies. According to this article, over thirty thousand Wanzer lamp and cooking lamp and cooking appliances had been sold in Canada and foreign countries.

The article described Wanzer's many achievements during his thirty-eight years in Hamilton. World-wide distribution of his products was emphasized. Gold medals for the superiority of his sewing machines were awarded in the United States, England, and Europe. In Austria he was knighted by the Emperor and received the Iron Cross.

Announcing his future plans, it was stated that, "He now proposes opening out in Buffalo as general manager of the Wanzer Lamp and Cooker Company." He died two years later and was buried in Hamilton. Several biographical articles have acknowledged his role as one of Hamilton's most illustrious citizens.

The straight-sided Wanzer lamp (b) has been found with the Niagara Falls and with the Philadelphia identification on the shade-holder rim. These were very well constructed and heavy; more like the May lamp. Four different keys have been found with Wanzer lamps. The catalogue illustrates the same style as on the May lamp. Two are perforated and one is solid. Soot is usually found in Wanzer lamp interiors.

*b. Wanzer nickel-plated lamp stamped on the shade-holder rim: WANZER LAMP CO. NIAGARA FALLS U.S.A. PAT. MCH. 22-1887.*

# A Pucca
# With a Punkah Top

This, in part, describes the rebirth of mechanical lamps in England. After the men behind the success of mechanical lamps in North America died in 1900, sales for domestic use dropped dramatically. The reprinted Sherwoods Ltd. of Birmingham catalogue in *Early Twentieth Century Lighting* contains nine pages of mechanical lamps and parts. There are three named lamps. One is the Pucca with a modified Wanzer profile. It used the same clockwork and key as the Wanzer and was available with a Punkah or wind proof top.

In this catalogue, almost all of the oil and candle lamps had Punkah tops and some had Punkah burners. These were made for India and perhaps other countries that cooled their houses with large swinging cloth fans mounted on a frame. The Wanzer lamps were like those made in Hamilton, Ontario.

The third lamp was the Kranzow shown here in what they described as "Sherwoods Special Service Outfit." This container with "1 doz. Wicks and Oil Can, with Strong Brass Padlock and Key" was intended for "Jungle, Camp, and Up Country use."

*a. Kranzow mechanical lamp.*

The Kranzow was a stemwinder more like the Hitchcock lamps. Some had a stop or brake, however it was not like the Hitchcock with a brake. That example had the air intake holes close to the top of the stem.

*b. Metal travelling box.*

The majority of these twentieth century mechanical lamps was illustrated with simple 10-inch slant or dome shades or with 5-inch squat shades. Kettle holders and cooking rings were available for all of the lamps.

*c. Signed base of Kranzow clockwork motor.*

*d. Side view of Kranzow clockwork motor.*

*e. Sherwood's patent burner for the Kranzow lamp.*

a.

# Banquet, Parlour, Student, and Piano Lamps

These were the special lamps. They were more impressive, more expensive, more creative, and more useful for special needs. Just a sampling is offered here.

The Bradley & Hubbard lamp (a) was reputed to be from a house in Port Hope, Ontario. I had hoped to be able to photograph it in its restored original house, but this could not be arranged. A second choice was to photograph it in the drawing room of a nursing home in what remains of my family's summer home in that town blessed with so many fine nineteenth century homes and churches. See also p. 146 (d).

The Bradley & Hubbard entry (b) at the 1876 Centennial in Philadelphia, could not fail to impress. The imposing font appears to be cut glass although this is not described. It was illustrated in the 1877-78 F. H. Lovell & Co. catalogue and noted in their price list as #2880 Bronze lamp complete $16.00 each. Possibly some of these lamps still exist.

b. From THE ILLUSTRATED CATALOGUE OF THE CENTENNIAL EXHIBITION, PHILADELPHIA, 1876. By John Filmer 1876.
*Courtesy The Corning Museum of Glass.*

BRONZE PARLOR-LAMP.

No. 9110.
Alto, 10 pulgadas.

*a.*

No. 9108.
Alto, 10 pulgadas.

*b.*

*c.*

## Vase or Parlour Lamps

*Illustrations from the F. H. Lovell & Co. Catalogue circa 1890. Courtesy The Sandwich Historical Society Glass Museum.*

There is an example of lamp (b) in the Old Dartmouth Historic Society-New Bedford Whaling Museum in Massachusetts with information that it was decorated by S. R. Bowie & Co. in New Bedford. The notation on the catalogue indicates that it was Bradley and Hubbard that assembled the lamp. Wholesale prices for No. 9108 were $70.00 per dozen. This was an export catalogue with lamps probably destined for South America.

Vast quantities of these cylindrical vase lamps were assembled in the U.S. with imported or domestic vases. Illustrations of Bradley & Hubbard and Edward Miller vase lamps are very similar. Relatively few had matching shades originally, and even fewer examples exist today.

The mystery of how a two ring slant shade (b) & (c) was held in place with no visible means of support is solved by the catalogue illustrations (d). Composite lamps with shades would have been considered parlour lamps in more modest homes.

UN NUEVO PATENTE.

PORTA-PANTALLA DE VIDRIO DE "ARGAND,"

*d.*

# Student Lamps

The basic requirement of a student or study lamp was to provide an unobstructed light on books or papers. Most had a vertical adjustment and shades to shield the eyes. The common ones used the Cardan principle, with the font and reservoir on opposite sides of a central post.

Cardan lamps provided a continuous flow of fuel from a large reservoir to a small font, thus maintaining fuel at a constant level close to the flame. The following drawing (Fig.1) and description are from *Chemical Technology* edited by C. E. Groves and William Thorpe, published in London by J. A. Churchill 1895.

"What is known as the bird-fountain principle, in which the passage of air into the reservoir permits escape of the liquid, appears to have been applied to lamps as early as the sixteenth century by Cardan.

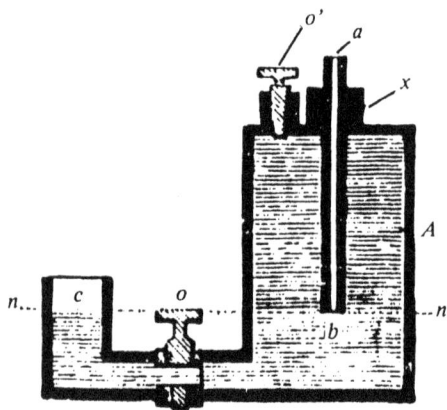

*Fig. 1*

"Fig. 1 represents an arrangement of this character, $A$ is an oil vessel with a stopcock $o$, an air-tight stopper $o'$, and a tube $a\,b$, open at both ends, inserted through an air-tight stuffing box $x$. The stopcock $o$ being closed and the stopper $o'$ being withdrawn, the vessel $A$ is filled with oil. On the stopper being replaced and the stopcock opened, the oil will rise in the branch $c$ to the level $n$, corresponding to the lower end of the tube $a\,b$. If the burner of a lamp be attached to the branch $c$, and the oil gradually consumed, the

level will remain constant, a few bubbles of air passing from time to time from the lower end of the tube $ab$ into the vessel $A$, and a corresponding volume of oil flowing into the branch $c$." The transfer of air and oil can create an audible gurgle.

Most kerosene student lamps use this principle, however for filling they usually have an independent container with a valve. When this is filled and inverted in the reservoir, the fuel is released. This obviates the need for a stopcock and tube $ab$.

Syphon Study Lamp.

*a.*

The Syphon Study Lamp (a) offered a different solution to the separate reservoir. It was illustrated in the Edward Miller & Co. 1881 Catalogue. There were also two designs of bracket lamps with either plain or engraved fonts, and a two-arm counterbalanced chandelier. Examples of the bracket lamps and student lamps are known.

The student lamp and chandelier are pictured with double-tube burners patented by H. C. Alexander, March 26, 1878, No. 201,730. The illustrations of the bracket lamps do not show burners.

In the late 1870s lamps with horizontal cylindrical fonts were patented

and became very popular. Probably the most popular was the Spencer lamp (b). C.F. Spencer of Rochester N.Y. obtained one patent on Aug. 12, 1879 and another on Oct. 21, 1879 for this type of lamp that could also function as a bracket lamp. H.H. Barnard and G. V. Hanna also of Rochester patented a similar lamp on Oct. 21, 1879. All of these patents were assigned to Henry E. Shaffer also of Rochester. A Manhattan Brass Co. (CGJ) advertisement January 1, 1880, offered the August 12, patented, nickel plated lamp.

None of these lamps was described as a student lamp in the patents, but they are often referred to as such today. On the other hand the Lincoln Leader lamp was advertised as a Student Lamp. The fonts would obstruct the flame to about the same degree, however the adjustable aspect of the Leader might have been a slight advantage.

*b. Spencer lamp.*

Student lamps rivalled the best banquet and parlour lamps and were not simply relegated to the office or study. There were single suspended lamps called Library Pendants, as well as multiple arm chandeliers.

# The Lincoln Lamp and Leader Burner

The Bridgeport Brass Company Leader student lamp patented by W.O. Lincoln Oct. 28, 1879, had a horizontal cylindrical font with a sleeve that permitted vertical adjustment. This was illustrated in the U. S. Patent Gazette drawing in Fig. 1.

It was evidently a very successful lamp, no doubt due to its simplicity and compact form. It was advertised for many years along with the Leader burner patented by S. R. Wilmot, Sept. 18, 1877, No. 195,241. It was necessary to use a flat or oval burner-chimney combination because there is not enough space to accommodate a standard round chimney. The font must be elevated to install or remove the flattened chimney, and the burner must be in the correct position relative to the post when it is tightened. In order for this to happen the collar must be mounted so that the thread is in precisely the proper position. The height is adjustable from 13" to 18".

Both the lamp and burner are often referred to by the names of their patentees.

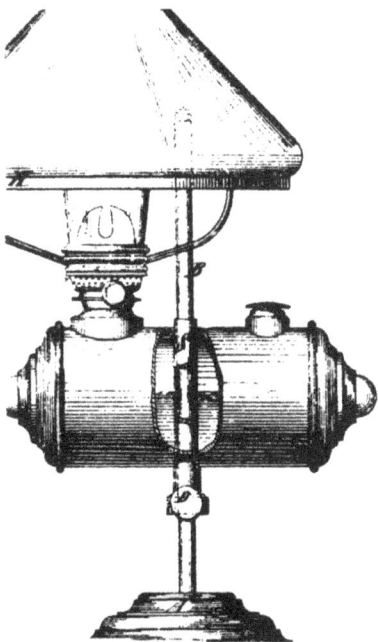

Fig. 1. Interior view
U.S. Patent No.221,078.

The Leader Student Lamp.

# Early Banquet Lamps

The American solar and kerosene banquet lamps of the 1850s and 1860s were spectacular! The public was presented with a visual tour de force when it came to impressive, decorative lamps. The workmanship was extraordinary, and the design could be interpreted as everything from vulgar to exquisite, depending upon one's taste and background. Fortunately there were enough decorators and collectors who fancied them to endow them with sufficient value to preserve examples for us to admire or to ponder over.

It has been considered that Americans promptly gave up their solar lamps for kerosene lamps when the fuel was available. One alternative was to have a factory conversion of their old solar lamps to accommodate the new fuel. There is however, the appearance of solar lamps in catalogues long after 1860.

The Dietz catalogue, circa 1865, has a plate showing two dozen of them. It has been assumed that these were for burning lard oil. The price list for the 1877-78 Lovell & Co. catalogue notes twenty five "SOLAR LAMPS FOR SPERM, COCONUT OR RAPE SEED OILS." They ranged in price from $2.50 to $18.00. Since they had a substantial overseas market, there is no way of knowing what market they were expecting for their different products.

The shades as a group are extremely varied. All are frosted with engraved or cut designs that range from excellent to exceptional. All are variations of familiar shapes, with the exception of (e). However, the Lovell illustration (f) confirms that this rare shape was original. A smaller example is also known.

The solar lamps of necessity had metal fonts, and it seemed to be fashionable to hide them behind a band of sparkling prisms. This left the stems to express the art of the glass maker.

Lamps on the opposite page have some of their special features noted below.

(a) The glass colors used in this stem are probably the most striking and rare of the combinations of cased glass used for lamps of this solar lamp period, or of the 1860s kerosene lamp period. The outer layer is a deep blue — almost amethyst! Next is a thick white layer of glass that sharply outlines the design. The inner layer or core is a deep ruby glass. All other features of this lamp are secondary to this stem!

(b) This lamp has a delicate foliate design engraved on a ruby plated stem.

(c) In contrast to (b), this lamp has a cylindrical stem with a bold geometric shape. The strong profile gives visual support to the exceptional bold shade. It is impossible to know if

*Most of the catalogue illustrations of solar lamps depict examples with metal stems, and at least half of them had marble bases. The use for kerosene was enormous, and they were also used with girandoles. Inevitably there came a time when fashion declared them obsolete. Gardeners in the town of Sandwich took advantage of the situation, recycled the little squares and laid a herringbone front walk!*

the shades shown here were original choices, and even if they were, was the selection a random one? In balance, the choices seem admirable.

(d) A true transitional lamp! This lamp appears to have had a factory conversion from solar lamp to kerosene. In its later life, it was wired for electricity with a minimum of invasive alteration. The light blue stem was cut to a thick layer of white on a clear glass base layer. Most of the original gilt accents remain.

(e) The Sandwich Glass Museum was fortunate to receive the gift of this lamp from Lois and Jack Hirshmann. It is exactly as shown in the 1868-9 Lovell catalogue. It was also listed in their price list circa 1873, in assorted colors for $26.50 each, complete.

(f) Illustration from the 1877-78 F. H. Lovell & Co. catalogue.

Both illustrations (e) and (f) courtesy The Sandwich Historical Society Glass Museum.

a.

b.

c.

d.

e.

f.

a.

b.

c.

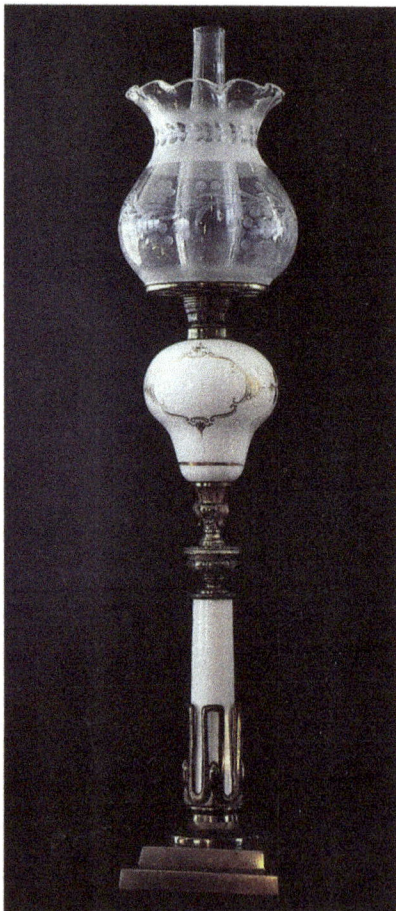

d.

e.

f.

These lamps would be considered parlour lamps by reason of their size or because they have a shade that has added height and importance. Their salient features are noted, and height, if given, is to the top of the shade rather than the collar.

(a) Compared with cased or overlay glass fonts, clear cut glass fonts are rare. This lamp with an Ives burner shade-holder combination, and Ives-type shade, would be considered an important decorative addition to a room. Height, 21".

(b) Blue and green combinations were often seen in the 1860s and 1870s. Although one would expect a double marble base, this lamp is usually found with only one piece of marble. Height, 19".

(c) Cast spelter lamp of the 1860s illustrated on plate 29 in the Dietz catalogue.

(d) The Bradley & Hubbard lamp from Port Hope is also illustrated on p. 140. This lamp of cast spelter and brass has little of its original gilt finish. The font holder has beaded diagonal bands with a foliate design and a central boss. This is the same as on the piano lamp on page 160. The main portion of the stem is a Corinthian column mounted upon a cylinder with a raised design featuring cherubs with musical instruments. An ornate plinth is supported by claw feet. I believe the cased gold decorated shade was the original choice. Height, 36¼".

(e) An even larger example of an astral lamp with a longer stem and this cast brass base has been seen. It is another example of early Art Nouveau design that appeared briefly around the 1860s; disappeared, and then enjoyed a glorious reappearance in the 1890s. There would likely have been a polychrome decoration in the center of the gold cartouche on the font. Height, 31".

(f) Markings on this lamp are described in detail in OL-2 pp. 128-9. It was made in England by Coalport expressly for the Chicago 1893 World's Fair. It is included here because interesting new information related to this lamp has been found. See page 165. Height, 32¾".

(g) The lamp on the right has some similarities to the Coalport lamp (f). They are both about the same size and are embellished with surface decoration. They were obviously among the most expensive kerosene lamps offered at a time when the wealthy would likely have also had gas lighting. It would appear that there was still some appeal for these lamps as a decorative if not functional accent. This matching shade is almost ¼" thick and would effectively subdue the light. Both have P&A Duplex Burners.

This lamp was wrapped and kept in storage for many years by a Chicago area family. The original delicate tassel attached to the extinguisher almost disintegrated when exposed to air. Cotton was sewn onto the ends of the wicks to extend their use.

Perhaps the most significant feature of the lamp (a) with the tomato red cased shade is the fact that *it really is* a bronze lamp. Bronze was used to describe any metal lamp with a brown finish, but this is the only one that I have seen other than the expensive Tiffany or similar lamps. The Argand burner and the 7½" shade ring confirm that it was imported.

It appeared in the same F. H. Lovell & Co. Spanish export catalogue circa 1890, as the lamps on p. 141. It was shown with a ball shade and holder like (c) opposite and priced at $60.00 per dozen. It is 17¾" to the top of the shade.

All of the lamps on this page are vase lamps. The parlour lamps (b) and (c) and the banquet lamp (d) are referred to as Junior size lamps. They are about half the size of their full-size counterparts and were likely intended for the bedroom or boudoir.

The Junior Banquet lamp (d) has a ruby satin etched shade and an onyx stem. The metal parts are exceptionally ornate. It is 16½" to the top of the shade. All of these lamps were probably made between 1880 and 1900.

*a.*

*b.*

*c.*

*d.*

a. Composite lamp with matching Illuminator shade.

b. Annie; A Mary Gregory type vase lamp.

c. Enamelled Dogwood lamp.

A rather commonplace late composite lamp is upgraded to an inexpensive parlour lamp with the addition of an illuminator base and a shade matching the stem. The lamp (a) and lamp (b) are decorated with hand-painted scenes and are considered to have been made by the Sandwich Glass Company.

This type of lamp would have been very affordable and was featured in many mail order catalogues from the 1880s to well into the twentieth century. Such an attractive lamp could add a cheerful ambience to even the lowest wage earners' humble abode. All else would literally fade into darkness.

According to the Ray Barlow and Joan Kaiser, the Mary Gregory diaries revealed that Mary Gregory and her sister Emma who worked for the Boston & Sandwich Glass Company during the early 1880s spent much of their time painting brown-toned winter scenes on opaque white glass. In her diaries, reference is made to two co-workers who also painted designs on glass. One was Annie Leary, and the other was Annie Nye. This lamp shade bears the inscription Annie/ Oct. 14/ 1884. A round portion of the acid-etched pastoral scene has been polished to accommodate the engraving. Perhaps there was some connection there.

The information I received when I first purchased the lamp was that the base and shade were the original combination. It is now in the Sandwich Museum collection. It is 19½" to the top of the shade.

Few of the better quality vase lamps have survived without at one time being converted to electricity; and the lamp (c) is no exception. Fortunately it was only a slightly invasive procedure with a metal inner font that could easily be returned to kerosene use.

The P&A Harvard burner and shade holder were seen in many of the Lovell and other catalogues of the 1880s. This appears to have been the decade when these lamps were most popular.

An unusual background was chosen for the dogwood blossoms and olive-green leaves. There is a geometric design with four-lobed black and blue elements against a reddish brown color.

The design on the shade is etched upon a textured, stippled, and frosted background.

This lamp is 21¼" to the top of the shade.

a.

b.

c.

d.

# Parlour Lamps for the Modest Home

Many consider the lamps on these two pages to be most typical of the kerosene Victorian parlour lamps. It is the matching shade and base that are associated with a cozy parlour. All of these lamps with the exception of (e) have shades that not only have their colors and textures illuminated when lit, but also shine down upon the matching base. The glass is therefore not only back lit but lit directly to show its different qualities.

Collectors owe a debt of gratitude to the late Bill Heacock for identifying so much American glass of the Victorian era. Although the two lamps (a) and (b) closely resemble each other, they are products of two major glass and lamp manufacturers. (a) This pattern, commonly known as Cosmos, has been identified as a product of the Consolidated Lamp and Glass Company. It was originally called Daisy. In addition to tableware pieces, this lamp was also made in a miniature size.

The lamp (b) is shown in the Fostoria catalogue. See page 164. The maker, the Fostoria Glass Company, called this design Mayflower.

The makers of the other lamps on this page are not yet identified. There were enormous quantities of these lamps made and sold through mail order catalogues. Lamps (a) to (d) are not vase lamps. They have very large capacity fonts. All on this page have raised or embossed designs except (d) which would likely have been the most inexpensive.

The vase lamp (e) is a type commonly referred to as a Gone-With-The-Wind lamp or its abbreviation GWTW. This name arose from the appearance of similar lamps in the movie of the same name. Now it is recognised as an obvious anachronism because the movie was set in the Civil War period, and these lamps did not appear until a few decades later. This lamp features raised water lilies painted in blue with deep green leaves. The overall height to the top of the ball shade is 21½".

e.

a. Undecorated vase lamp.

b. Mt. Washington Burmese vase lamp.
Photograph courtesy The Corning Museum of Glass.

# Better Quality Lamps

These three lamps range from average to the most expensive parlour lamps. Lamp (a) has a mat finish shading from pale pink to a deeper shade. It has a rather bland appearance and while it would likely have been more expensive than those on the opposite page, it could not compete with the other two lamps.

The second lamp (b) is perhaps the best-known American parlour lamp. The delicate shading from pale yellow to pink was used not only for the shade and base, but also for the chimney. It is difficult to imagine that it was ever intended for use. This type of glass was named Burmese by the manufacturer, the Mt. Washington Glass Company, in New Bedford, Massachusetts. The enamel decoration consists of a fishnet draped over the 10" dome shade and base. The net covers realistic fish and a final acid treatment imparted a mat finish to all the glass.

Shading from white to a deep pink, this Diamond Quilted vase lamp (c) has an acid etched satin finish. It is mounted on a square pressed glass base. The base resembles some Adams lamp bases, but details of the design are not the same. Height to the top of the shade is 16", and the shade diameter is 10".

c. Diamond Quilted parlour lamp.

# Mt. Washington, Royal Flemish and The Brownies

When scholars next their voices tried,
The Brownies came from every side;
With ears to knot-holes in the wall,
To door-jambs, thresholds, blinds, and all,
They listened to the jarring din
Proceeding from the room within.

a. Royal Flemish banquet lamp.

b. Illustration from The Brownies by Palmer Cox. Courtesy Dover Publications.

This Royal Flemish medium size mold-blown banquet lamp (a) was made by the Mt. Washington Glass Company. It was also made with the Brownies decoration. Height to the top of the shade is 23⅝" circa 1890.

Collection of the Corning Museum of Glass, Gertrude Christian Melvin Endowment.

*Courtesy The Corning Museum of Glass.*

It was a Brownies lamp that first brought my attention to these fascinating figures that were created by Canadian Palmer Cox in the late 1800s. Tales of the nocturnal activities of these long limbed, pot-bellied elves fascinated children then and would likely do so today if they were readily available.

The Brownies would appear late at night to do good deeds that would make people happy and the world a better place. Their delightful antics recorded in verse were very successful in the world of children's literature. Part of their success was due to the the distinctive nature of the illustrations that portrayed large numbers of Brownies in action, in a variety of situations and locations.

The appeal of the stories for children is just one part of the current interest in Brownies. The promotion and marketing of the figures was akin to methods used today. *Brownies were everywhere!* They promoted all kinds of products. There were rubber stamps and buttons with Brownie images, and the figures were used in many advertisements including kerosene burners. The Kodak Brownie camera was pictured with a Brownie in a French advertisement after the camera was introduced.

Cox himself capitalised on the images by obtaining design patents for handkerchiefs and rulers. These were liberally decorated with Brownies. Toys and games also promoted the Brownie images. Dolls were ready made, sold in kits or hand made like (c).

The Mt. Washington Glass Company made lamps and other glassware decorated with enamelled Brownies. The example (d) is in the collection of the Strong Museum in Rochester, New York.

*c. Hand-made Brownie doll.*

*d. Mt. Washington Brownie lamp. Courtesy The Strong Museum.*

*a. Textured gold and polychrome vase lamp.*

*c. Signed Handel parlour lamp.*

*d. Cased green vase lamp.*

# Parlour Lamps

Over the years, when many of these lamps were modified for electricity, some of them lost some of their original parts. The monetary value of retaining a lamp in its original kerosene condition in the mid to late 1900s was insignificant compared with the price it would bring if it were wired! Today the reverse is true. Perhaps when the rarity of some examples is realized the significance of alteration will diminish. After all, the conversion from kerosene to electricity was part of a natural evolution.

*b. Venetian glass parlour lamp.*

The lamp (a) has had individually applied raised dots covered with a gilt finish. This surrounds bands of bright polychrome fruit. The result is spectacular! Because it does not seem to relate to any known glass or lamp maker, it may have been custom made. Height to the top of the shade is 17".

Lamps (a) to (c) have had some of their original parts removed. These may have been replaced with suitable ones by later owners. Lamp (b) was made by the Phoenix Glass Company who advertised this type of glass as Venetian.

The shade of (c) is signed "Handel 6116." Some changes have been made since this picture was taken to restore it to a condition that would be closer to the original metal parts. Those who electrified it years ago were not concerned about retaining the integrity of the lamp.

Clear glass was coated with a thick layer of colored glass. The ball shade was coated with a maroon red layer, and the base of the lamp was shaded from a moss green to the color of the lamp shade. The orchid and leaf design was protected with a resist, and acid was used to create the cameo effect. Gold was then applied to enhance the glass. Height to the top of the shade is 21⅞".

Little light would be transmitted by the dark green cased vase lamp (d). It would however create a pleasant ambience.

Lamp (e) below has a hand painted orchid design on a green ground, accented with gold. It is signed with the Pairpoint trademark. Height to the top of the shade is 18½".

Ken Wilson provided me with illustrations of three circa 1900 Pairpoint Art Nouveau lamps. The bases were quadruple plate and the shades were hand painted. Panel shades like the one below were offered separately.

*e. Pairpoint Orchid parlour lamp.*

a.

b.

# Tiffany Lamps

Design, materials, and workmanship have earned Tiffany Studios their reputation as producers of the greatest lamps made in America. Although many were made for kerosene use, most found today have been electrified. These two are not only exceptions in that regard, but also possessed provenance backed up with ephemera.

These lamps were originally transported to Ontario's cottage country by train and steamboat. Each of two daughters of a wealthy American family who summered at Ahmic Lake near Magnetawan received one of these lamps as a wedding present. They were used at the cottage from the time they were received until the property was sold. I believe that was sometime in the 1960s.

Martha Langford, a local girl, worked as a maid for the family at the cottage in the summer, and at their U. S. residence in the winter. When that property was sold, Martha was asked to choose a few items as tokens of appreciation. Martha chose wisely in selecting the Tiffany lamps. Later she passed along the lamps to her daughters. Both lamps saw daily use until the mid-1950s when electric power reached the area. After that they were used occasionally as reminders of the past.

Lamp (a) with stylised natural form base and geometric shade has its original 12½" chimney with a monogram containing the letters K, G & Co. and the words MADE IN GERMANY. Plume and Atwood Duplex burners with extinguishers were used in both lamps. The glass shade is mottled green with amber used on the decorative band. Inside the edge is the stamped bronze label marked TIFFANY STUDIOS/NEW YORK and the number 26846. The ring of the removable shade holder has the letter U stamped in one area of the underside, and T.G. & D.C., in another area. The ampersand is rather indistinct. Overall height to the top of the shade is 18½".

Lamp (b) has the same bronze Tiffany labels as lamp (a) except for the number which is 1453. Both shade and base are illustrated in different combinations in *The Lamps of Tiffany* by Dr. Egon Neustadt. He notes that the pansy design which covers more than half the shade is repeated four times, with each repeat using different color schemes for the pansies. Both the colors and the textures of the glass used for the pansies are skilfully handled to create a feeling of authenticity. According to Neustadt the base was described in the Tiffany catalogues as "Greek Model".

This lamp is approximately 21" to the top of the shade. Both shades are 16".

a. Dragon Shade detail.

In the late 1880s and 90s, many major lamp manufacturers offered their own particular brand of Rochester type center draft lamp. This Juno lamp which has its original wick escaped electrification. It was made by Edward Miller & Co. The brass font has a relatively sophisticated antique bronze finish. Most were shiny brass. The wrought iron type base was very much in vogue in the 1890s. Height to the top of the shade is 23".

b. Juno Center draft lamp.

Dragons, griffins, and similar imaginary creatures embellished home furnishings in the late Victorian era. The cased shade (a) with etched design is filled with gold. When illuminated from behind, the design appears black.

c. Composite creation.

The designer of this lamp let his or her imagination take flight! Starting with the top there are two cast brass beetles and two cast flies attached to the wide plate brass collar. The blown font has a conventional design with a roughed finish.

A polychrome enamelled china or pottery insert is held in place by spun and cast brass mounts. Even the round slate base is rare. The grotesque creatures that form the cast brass handles complete this tour de force!

The final touch is the frosted shade showing a Japanese influence. It is as unrelated as the other parts and in that sense is consistent. Height to the top of the shade is 17½".

d. Polychrome griffin.

This frenzied creature has the potential to star in a horror film. The action portrayed and the color combinations qualify the shade as a rare departure in color and design. Like lamp (c), it is difficult to imagine who these things would appeal to.

e. Bradley & Hubbard parlour lamp.

This lamp was advertised as a B & H table lamp. Both the cast metal shade frame and the lamp base in dark green "Verde Gris" finish are signed with the triangular-shaped Bradley and Hubbard trademark.

B & H also supplied these slag glass shades for Rayo center draft lamps. Height to the top of the shade is 20½".

# Meriden Britannia Co.

The 1886-87 Meriden Britannia Co. catalogue illustrates over 3,000 sterling, gold, and silver-plated articles. It includes almost every utilitarian and decorative category imaginable. Wholesale prices are quoted and special finishes are described.

Founded in 1852, the company began making pewter and Britannia ware but soon switched to the production of silver-plated wares. In 1862 three Rogers brothers, who perfected silver electroplating, worked at Meriden under contract to supervise their method. In 1881 a branch began operation in Hamilton, Ontario.

On the basis of a signed matching vase in the collection of the Jones Museum of Glass and Ceramics, the shade (a) is attributed to the Fritz Heckert Studio, Petersdorf, Bohemia, circa 1880s. It is blown, shallow cut, and enamelled in a Persian design.

*b. Meriden vase lamp No. 485.*

*a. Meriden vase lamp No. 410.*

Both of these vase lamps have at one time been wired, however they still have their original Duplex burners and could be restored to kerosene easily. The catalogue illustration shows this copper finish lamp with a silk cord and tassels draped around the shoulder of the lamp.

The base of this lamp is stamped ROGERS SMITH/ & CO/ MERIDEN CT / QUADRUPLE within a shield, and the number 485. This corresponded with the catalogue number. Without shades, lamp (a) sold for $36.50 and (b) sold for $35.00. I believe both shades are original. They would also have been expensive.

Instructions with lamp (a) note that the lamp is enamel finished and should only be cleaned with a damp cloth.

The distinctive design of the amber cased shade (c) was patented by Joseph Kittel of Dresden, Saxony, Germany. It could have been made in Germany or in America.

*c. J.J. Kittle Lamp globe U.S. design patent No. 15,556, Nov. 18, 1884.*

The shape and color are well-suited to the lamp. Sizes to the top of the shades are (a) 14"and (b) 16".

*a.*

*b.*

*c.*

*d.*

*e.*

# Student Lamps

The lamps selected here were chosen to illustrate a wide selection of both lamps and shades. Whether they were the original combinations or not, most of the shades and some of the chim- neys chosen add substantially to the appearance and, of course, to the value of the lamps. There is an outstanding selection of student lamps and shades illustrated in *Lamps of the Victorian Era* by Richard C. Miller and John E. Solverson published by Antique Publications, Marietta, Ohio.

Lamp (a) has added cast decoration on its distinctive Manhattan Brass Co. reservoir. The cased yellow, etched, and gilt dome shade is exceptional

b. Another Manhattan Brass Co. lamp with cased raspberry satin shade and colored chimney.

c. Lamp marked on gallery which serves to adjust the wick: PATENTED MAR 10. 1863. REISSUED MAR. 29. 1870 C.A. KLEEMAN/C.F.A. HIN- RICHS N.YORK SOLE AGENT.

d. Silver plated brass student lamp with embossed decoration. Cased blue 6" shade and colored chimney.

e. This rare and unusual student lamp is unmarked. The reservoir is consider- ably lower than the font. In this exam- ple the relative level of the oil in the reservoir is maintained by a separate inner reservoir that floats on mercury. This reservoir rises as the oil is depleted, and the supply to the burner is maintained. Height, 22" to the top of the post.

# Double Student Lamps

These lamps, and those with three or more arms not only produced more light, but in many instances were more elaborate. Some such as the Harvard and Tiffany types were significant decorative objects. Like chandeliers, they present excellent opportunities to display important shades. Brief descriptions follow:

a. The double Spencer lamp is marked on one side of the tank C. F. SPENCER PATD JULY. 4. 1876. The other side is marked C. F. SPENCER PATD DEC 21 1875. This marking is indistinct. The 5½" shades are cased, canary shaded, satin glass. These lamps are usually found with six-inch shade holders.

b. Several examples of this ornate Harvard Double Student lamp are known. It was made of heavy cast brass by The Plume & Atwood Manufacturing Company. The ribbed shades are maroon, cased glass.

c. Tiffany purchased student lamps from the Manhattan Brass Co. and further embellished them with their own applied designs. A chain-like design decorates the reservoir. This double post example has a pair of ribbed cased shades in turquoise shaded to white.

d. This unmarked nickel-plated example appears to be early. It was found without shades. Those chosen are early, circa 1870, lightweight glass used with an illuminator base.

e. Sometimes a snapshot serves to record a lamp until one can return to take a better photograph with a more favourable background than a busy antique shop. Unfortunately a customer accidentally broke the lamp before I had the opportunity to return. On the other hand it does serve to record a rare lamp. I have heard that separate fonts have been found but not a complete lamp.

*a.*

*b.*

*c.*

*d.*

The lamp is marked I. P. FRINK, but not with an expected patent date. The fonts have the fillers marked CHINNOCKS PATENT SEPT 4 1877. This patent granted to Charles Chinnock of Brooklyn N. Y. was for "an improvement in filler-mouths for lamps & c." The cap was funnel-shaped with a covered opening.

The specifications, but not the claims, mentioned the cap could be combined with a wick tube, and that this would be the subject of another patent. The later patent was used with small night lamps made by the Union Glass Company.

Height of center post is 22½", and the width of each font with holder is 14½".

*e.*

*a.*

*b.*

160  Piano or floor lamps

# Piano or Floor Lamps

Both these names were commonly used to describe the lamps shown here. They were most popular in the 1880s and 90s and while there were inexpensive ones advertised in the mail order catalogues, many were made for the wealthy. Some were combined with ornate tables with onyx tops.

The solid and plated brass lamp (a) opposite is heavy enough to warrant large ball-bearing castors under its tripod feet. This allows it to be moved effortlessly across the floor. The three-dimensional dragon forms create a spectacular base to this Bradley & Hubbard piano lamp with adjustable height. The font is the same as that used on the banquet lamp on page 146.

(b) This heavy silver plated, adjustable brass and cast iron lamp was also made by Bradley & Hubbard. It was illustrated in the circa 1900 Hubbard-Spencer, Bartlett Co. Catalogue and priced $35.84. The hand painted Handel shade is signed and numbered 839.

On the right (c) is a piano lamp that appears to be a Rochester table lamp mounted upon a stand. The illustration is from *The Meriden Britannia Silver Plate Treasury*, courtesy Dover Publications. This is a reprint of the complete 1886-87 catalogue of the Meriden Britannia Co. Prices included in the catalogue indicate they were among the most expensive articles offered.

Because so few of the fabric shades of that period have survived, it is easy to ignore the fact that they were very much in vogue. This is a more restrained style. Some top heavy ones with frills and flounces must have been difficult to keep fresh and clean, particularly on hot and humid summer days.

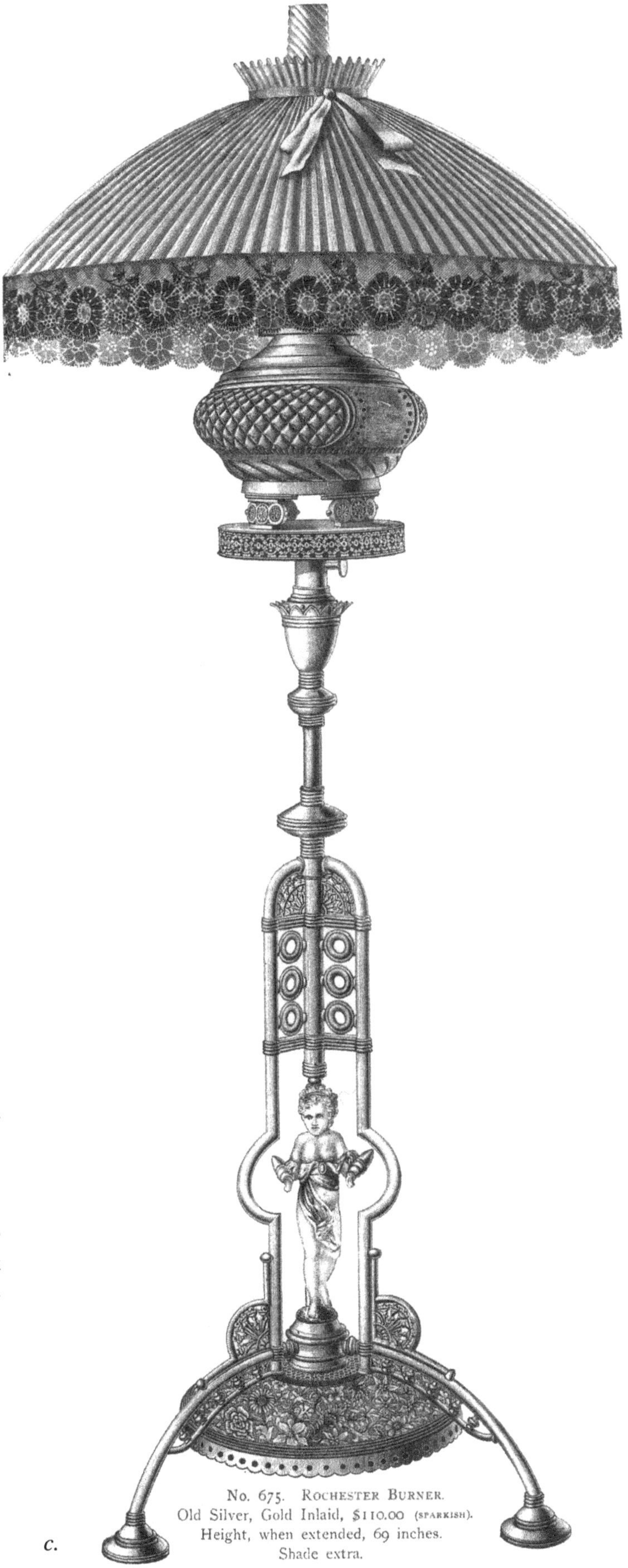

*c.*

No. 675. ROCHESTER BURNER.
Old Silver, Gold Inlaid, $110.00 (SPARKISH).
Height, when extended, 69 inches.
Shade extra.

*Fostoria Glass Company Catalogue. Late 1900s.*
*Courtesy David B. Dalzell Jr.*

# Fostoria Lamps

Shortly before the Fostoria Glass Co. closed in Moundsville, West Virginia, in the 1980s, I had the opportunity to view several of their lamp catalogues and to photograph this one. The number of lamps illustrated in color was amazing. The ones in this catalogue represented the smaller vase and vase-type lamps. Most were considerably larger.

I was told that several years earlier a large number of similar catalogues had been borrowed but not returned. I am not certain where the ones that I saw are now. When it is recognised that old catalogues have a monetary value, they are usually stored — carefully it is to be hoped!

For a thirty to forty year period between 1880-1920, these lamps were very popular and very inexpensive. Some were priced as low as a dollar. They were also made by many manufacturers. There were so many styles produced that unless examples are found in a catalogue or unless they are signed it is difficult to identify a particular lamp. A few still retain their original paper labels.

Many of these lamps that were advertised in mail order catalogues had their metal parts covered with a thin layer of 18k gold. Some had transfer decorations while others were hand painted. The quality varied considerably.

a.

b.

c.

*d.*

*g.*

*e.*

*h.*

*f.*

*i.*

*j.*

*m.*

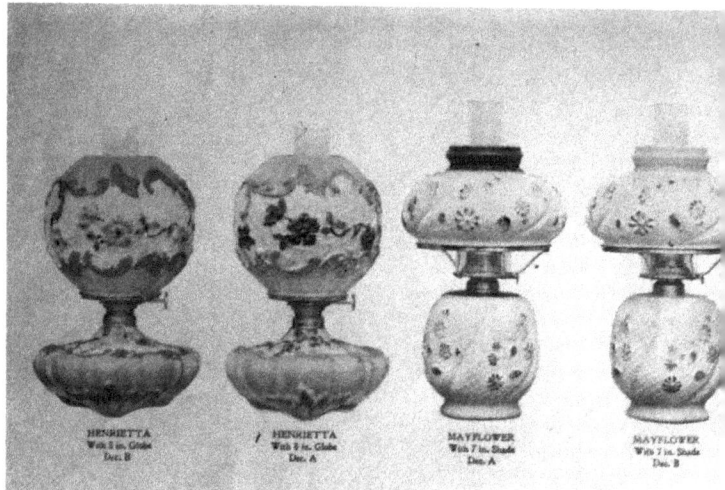

*k.*

*n.*

*l.*

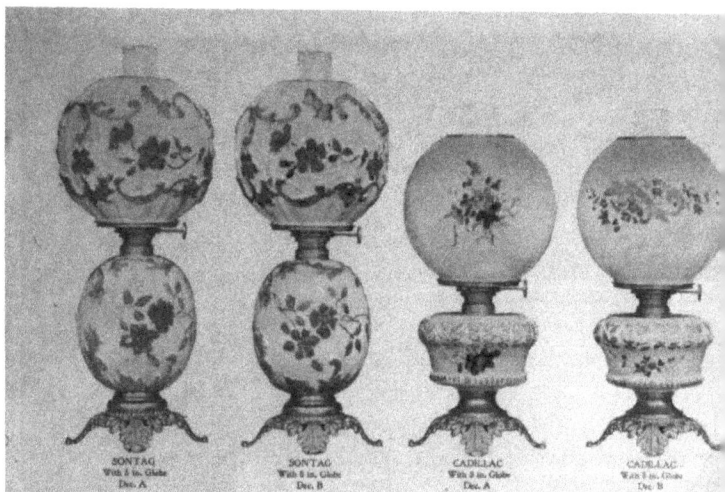

*o.*

# Coalport China at the Columbian Exposition, Chicago, 1893

This picture will be important to anyone interested in Coalport China. It is from an untitled book belonging to a private collector who graciously loaned it to substantiate the lamp on page 146, and in OL-2 on pages 126-7. It contains photographs of displays from various countries.

Of greatest personal interest is the verification that the signed lamp was actually used in the Coalport display. Unfortunately there were no medals associated with this display. The English trade paper, *Pottery Gazette*, quoting from an issue of *Truth*, published an exchange of letters between the Coalport company and the management in charge of the Exposition. Coalport objected strenuously to the way the awards were handled.

In their last communication Coalport stated, "As the awards seem to be all of equal value and about one for every competitor, we fail to see of what use the award for this company's exhibits can be, and we must therefore respectfully decline to receive same, an official communication to this effect having been sent to the Hon. Commissioner representing this country.

In conjunction with other houses who have spent thousands of pounds upon their exhibits, we are placed side by side with the undermentioned in the matter of awards:" Included in this list were Miss M. Butterin, London, Plaque, Flowers: Miss Hainsworth, Harrogate, Nightdress Sachet; and Miss Batt, Witney, Four Pairs Embroidered Baby-shoes.

The letter concludes with "We consider further comment is needless." It was signed by the managing director of a firm representing The Coalport China Company.

This might give cause to reflect upon the importance of awards emphasised in product advertising of the time.

The choice of shades for the banquet lamps would have concealed much of the decoration on the font, however these shades were very much in vogue at the time.

# Wall, Bracket, Hall and Hanging Lamps

These lamps were all classed as fixtures. They were either attached to the ceiling or to the wall. They had, however, a greater degree of portability than their gas or electric counterparts that required connection to a central system. Simple harp lamps could easily be moved to another ceiling hook, and for some of the wall or bracket fixtures, the removal of a lamp or font was optional.

The earliest significant record of these lamps in the 1861 Starr catalogue (see page 44) did not include hall lamps, but rather "Harp, Hanging Lamps, Chandeliers" and a two-arm fixture they called a "Saloon Pendant." They had simple tin side lamps with reflectors that were similar to those made for decades, and often referred to as wall lamps. Most of the fixtures appeared ornate, heavy, and made of spun and cast brass. Examples of these lamps are extremely rare.

Taking a leap of four years to the next available illustrations in the Russell & Erwin Manufacturing Company and the Dietz & Company catalogues circa 1865, we find that ornate brass, both heavy and light, still continued to be popular. Simple, graceful designs in both brass and iron were also featured. Many of these had foliate ornamentation.

A few examples of wall and bracket lamps from the Russell & Erwin catalogue are illustrated on this page. Some of the same illustrations also appear in the Dietz catalogue and in later F. H. Lovell & Co. and Bradley & Hubbard catalogues.

There are brief descriptions, but not prices, given at the back of the catalogue. In the top row are bronzed tin Side Lamps. The next row features cast iron in a simple classic design called " Bronze in Relief, Basket Bracket," and the busy ornate example was listed as "Bronze and Gilt, with Basket." These illustrate the wide range offered at this early date. The simple lamp has a font with a shell pattern on the shoulder that is included with hanging lamps in this chapter, and a bellflower pattern is shown on the other font.

The easily identifiable cast iron leaf bracket, No. 199, appears to be the same cut as found on plate 14 of the Dietz catalogue and on plate 18 of the Lovell 1868-69 catalogue. I have not seen this attractive bracket.

Interesting examples of fonts to fit the No. 5251 "Bronze and Relief Mammoth Bracket" are known, however I have neither seen nor heard of any brackets of this size. The large fonts that have been seen have #3 collars and include the bellflower pattern and sometimes a patented filler.

Surprisingly the word "font" is used rather than "fount" commonly found in catalogues of that period.

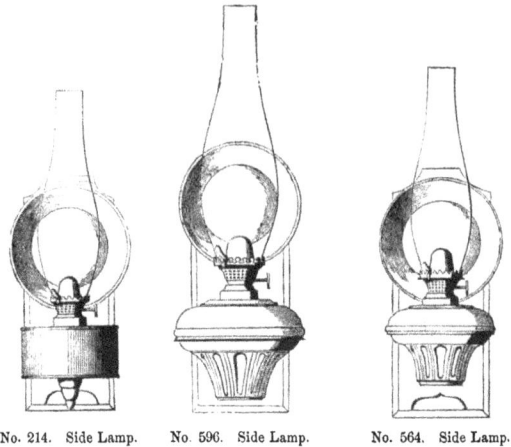

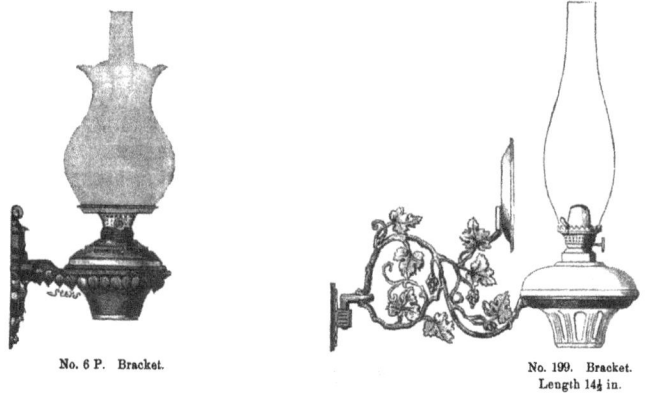

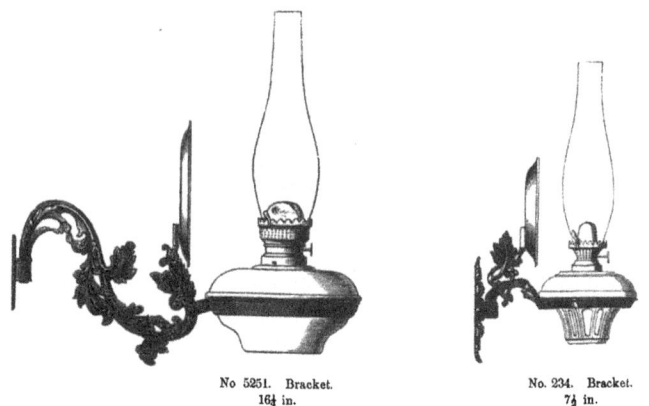

No. 214. Side Lamp.　No. 596. Side Lamp.　No. 564. Side Lamp.

No. 579. Bracket. 12 in.　No 5 P. Bracket.

No. 6 P. Bracket.　No. 199. Bracket. Length 14½ in.

No 5251. Bracket. 16¼ in.　No. 234. Bracket. 7½ in.

*Illustrations from the Russell & Irwin 1865 Catalogue.*
*Courtesy The Association for Preservation Technology.*

*a. Cast iron chandelier.*

*b. Hall lamp.*

Cast iron hanging lamps were the subject of many patent improvements. The way these were implemented and combined as well as the variety offered will interest collectors and historians for years to come. Bradley & Hubbard were masters of their craft, producing extremely heavy fixtures with multiple arms and lights that were made to appear open and lacy like example (a). Other examples like (c) and ones illustrated in this chapter appear more massive. The patented font holders on these two lamps were made by Bradley & Hubbard and help identify other B&H lamps.

The popularity of cast iron fixtures gave way to brass during the 1880s. The brass hall lamp (b) and the brass library lamps with colourful art glass shades were typical of the 1880s and 1890s.

Examples (a) and (b) are from a Hubbard, Spencer, Bartlett & Company catalogue.

*c. F. H. Lovell & Co. Catalogue 1877-78. Plate 142.*
*Courtesy The Sandwich Historical Society Glass Museum.*

# The Angle Lamp
# The Light That Never Fails

*Double Rose Floral Angle Lamp.*

*The Rose Floral pattern is very scarce dating from the earliest known catalogues.This double hanging lamp is circa 1896-1900. The lamp is polished brass and the finish may be original. The wick knobs are embossed "The Angle Lamp Company." The bottom set screw to secure the elbow globe and the early closing tab were signs of pre-1900 lamps.*

*The clear elbow-globes are marked "The Angle Lamp Co. N.Y." and "No Under Shadow." The white chimney-tops are early, indicated by only a slight outward turn of the petal tops. The earliest tops were nearly straight.*

Angle lamps, sold from about 1896 until 1929, were primarily sold in hanging and wall styles. Few were adapted for table use.

The chief inventor was Thomas M. Fell, a mechanical engineer and inventor, from Brooklyn, New York, and Tenafly, New Jersey. Between 1871 and 1890 Fell was granted 18 patents. The Fell Manufacturing Company was formed in 1888 to manufacture and sell oil (kerosene) lamps.

The name Angle Lamp or Angle Lamp Co. is inscribed on burner knobs, on oil tank fonts, and on glass globes (elbows). Most oil fonts have the following words inscribed on top: THE ANGLE LAMP Co. N.Y. PATENTED IN THE U.S. AND FOREIGN COUNTRIES.

Angle lamps were made in an assortment of styles for hanging or side (wall) mount. It was only later that table models or bracket stands for table use were offered. The metal fonts were plain or embossed with attractive floral, leaf, grape, pin wheel, or fleur-de-lis designs. Prices in 1900 for single burner wall lamps were $3.00 to $4.00. A hanging lamp with four burners cost $9.60 in tin and $10.80 in brass. At $45.00 an eight-arm chandelier was the most expensive.

The company used the terms "globe" for elbow and "top" for chimney. As a general rule, lamps were sold with clear globes and white chimneys, however decorative globes and chimneys were offered at higher prices. The figured globes and tops were made of clear glass and etched on the outer surface with attractive designs — birds, bellflower, floral bands, and wreath-and-torch. Colored chimney tops were an extra expense. The most common were white opalescent. Pink opalescent, amber, ruby, and blue tops were colorful and attractive. They are rare today. Reproduction glass has been made for many years.

Travelling salesmen started out selling lamps primarily to businesses for use in public places — stores, churches, halls, hotels, billiard rooms, and factories. In 1899 Angle lamps were advertised for use in the home. Ads in *McClure's*, *Munsey's*, *The Rural New-Yorker*, *Ladies World*, and *Farm Journal* proclaimed the lamp's merits.

Sears Roebuck, Montgomery Ward, Butler Bros., and Charles William Stores sold Angle lamps in their catalogues in the 1920s. Montgomery Ward started selling Angle lamps about 1914. Sears and Montgomery Ward continued to offer replacement parts until the early 1940s.

The company promoted two advantages — Angle lamps were dependable with steady, unvarying light ("Never Fails") and they provided strong downward light for reading and working ("No Under Shadow").

The claim for superior light originated from the patented arrangement of the burner, globe, and chimney top. The "upward draft...draw(s) the flame of the burners outwardly and upwardly in a curved form in such a manner that light will shine downward so that the lamps will have no undershadows." Early catalogues proclaimed, "That great feature No-Under Shadow distinguishes it from every other light." This claim was advertised widely and was the company's first slogan. The words "NO UNDER SHADOW' are found inscribed on wick raising knobs of early lamps as well as along the upper rim of some glass globes.

By 1899 the slogan "The Light That Never Fails" was widely proclaimed. This slogan may be found on letterheads, in advertising, and on the cover of catalogues printed from the early 1900s until the early 1920s. Rudyard Kipling's book *The Light That Failed*, published in 1898, was widely circulated as well as reprinted in serial magazines of the time. It appears that the company adapted the words from Kipling's book title to their advantage.

This brief account of the Angle lamp was contributed by J.W. Courter, author of *Angle Lamps Collectors Manual & Price Guide*.

# Metal Finishes

The finishes described here apply mainly to gas wall and ceiling fixtures, to gas and solar table lamps, and to girandoles and candelabra made of brass. Other non-lighting brass articles were also finished by the method described in an article that appeared in the April 11, 1875 *Crockery Journal.* The basis of this account was a 24-page pamphlet published by Cornelius & Baker, a major manufacturer of lighting fixtures located in Philadelphia, Pennsylvania. This pamphlet was referred to in an 1859 article in *Philadelphia and its Manufacturers: A Hand Book* by Edwin C. Freedley. The Rushlight Club has recently published a reprint of the 24-page pamphlet. It has one identical illustration of the factory building and one that is different. These two publications were provided by Ken Wilson.

Significant excerpts were also published in *Lamps and Other Lighting Devices 1850-1906,* originally published by Pyne Press.

The *CGJ* account provides an understanding of the word "ormolu" and the complex method of achieving that golden effect without using gold in the process. Ormolu was a mixture of chemicals that produced a minutely pitted surface on brass that had been prepared for this purpose. The object was to attain a soft mat gold color that would contrast with highly burnished shiny portions having different shades of gold, although no gold was used in the process. Surviving examples indicate a variety of final results and a range of quality.

Some examples of cast brass fixtures have textured areas that are actually minute depressions, whereas the textured areas of cast iron fixtures frequently have a raised stippled pattern. Surviving examples of ormolu finishes indicate a range of quality.

This 1875 account is clearly a summary of the original 24-page pamphlet, although it is not mentioned.

## Gas Fixtures

The manufacture of gas fixtures is of modern date, and has become one of the most important industries of the day. A few years ago the majority of gas fixtures used throughout the world were manufactured in Europe, principally in England and France, and chiefly by small manufacturers.

The extent and importance of the manufacture of gas fixtures in this country will be apparent on reflecting that in nearly all the houses in the great cities, and in nearly every village having a population of four or five thousand, they are now in use. There are a great number of isolated residences in the country, the owners of which manufacture their own gas by private methods, and whose houses require the gas fixtures. The demand for these wares is increasing every day.

Entering a manufactory, the visitor proceeds, perhaps, first to the modelling rooms. A single firm having in their employ several designers or artists who occupy separate rooms, in different parts of the building, and who do not intercommunicate, each depending upon his own unaided genius in devising sketches for the models. Thus greater originality of design is accomplished. Following a design which is given to him, sketched upon paper, the modeller begins to mould into required shape a mass of prepared wax. After the design is "roughed out" he consummates his task with the aid of tools made of hard wood or steel. When the pattern, frequently the work of weeks, is completed, it goes into the hands of the "caster," who makes a mould of it in brass, which is sent to the "chaser," and is elaborated into, a standard pattern from which the caster may multiply an infinitude of copies. It is a very nice operation to make a mould from an original wax pattern, the fragile material rendering it necessary to use every precaution in obtaining brazen facsimile of the original. Much depends on the "chaser." When the first brazen copy of the pattern is placed in his hands, the embellishments on its surface are faint, and require to be deepened. The partially developed fibres and veins of leaves and flowers, the feathers of birds and fur of animals are by him made distinct. He uses small steel chisels, of various shapes, with which the necessary indentations are made by sharp blows of a light hammer. The completed pattern is returned to the caster. In casting a drooping feather, or a crumpled vine leaf, for instance, it is found more expeditious to flatten the pattern. After the casting is finished, the proper curves are given to the hitherto flat surface by means of wooden mallets and other tools.

In the casting rooms, where many men are employed, the heat from the furnaces is very great, and becomes almost stifling, in conjunction with the sulphurous fumes of the liquid mass of copper and spelter, forming brass, which is glowing and seething in black-lead crucibles placed in the midst of firey anthracite. Each caster works at a wooden trough, into which he carefully sifts prepared sand, slightly moistened. Thus prepared the sand is placed in flasks, and the process of moulding, sufficiently understood by general readers, is proceeded with. After the crucibles have been emptied into the moulds, a few minutes suffice for the lately moulten brass to chill into a hardness which permits the flasks to be opened, by removing the clamps when it is a matter of surprise to note how faithfully the finest chased work has been transferred from the original pattern to the copy. The castings are conveyed from the foundry to the filing department.

Here scores of files create a constant din, not musical to all ears. The castings are first "edged up" with coarse rasps, and then finished with finer tools. In many instances a number of castings must be joined to form one piece. The several parts are conveyed to the soldering room, where they are properly fitted together, care being taken to leave one edge more prominent than the other. The sections are then put into their proper places, and retained in position by iron wire. Particles of brass solder, which look like brazen saw dust, are wetted with water and carefully applied along the projecting edge of the section. The entire piece is then placed in a furnace, where the solder is melted. The work then undergoes another filing. The joints must be made with the utmost care, for the subtle gas would escape through any tiny opening left in the work. Before the castings leave the filing and soldering rooms, there is frequently much to be done in the way of the twisting of branches, crumpling of leaves, drilling of holes, etc., etc.

The castings are taken after the re-filing, etc., to the dipping room. Here everything is done by the means of chemical agents. The room is a perfect laboratory in itself. There are ranges of monstrous stone jars filled with divers coloured acids, of different degrees of strength; pans and kettles filled with various liquids; and hot, luke warm, and cold water is flowing in abundance. When the castings leave the hands of the filers, they are dirty and discoloured and more or less sand and other foreign matter clings to them. The first act of the dipper is the taking up of a casting with a pair of tongs, and dipping it into a jar of acid. Only a moment is required to remove by this process every particle of dirt from the surface of the piece. The chemical would soon devour the piece itself if sufficient time were given it. But the dipper speedily takes out the cleansed metal and places it in water, which arrests the ravages of the acid.

The operation of plunging the metal into the acid is called "pickling." The colour of the metal is rendered by it essentially brass-like, as the "pickle" has devoured the foreign substances on its surface. The article thus cleaned is dipped into a jar, the contents of which are a mystery to us. This has the effect to give the surface a rich sulphur colour. This operation occupies but a moment. The piece of metal is again washed in clean water, and is then plunged into a chemical combination called "ormolu;" in a few minutes the colour of the metal is changed to a dirty yellow. The ormolu is then washed off, and the surface of the metal is found to have been eaten into minute molecules. One more dip into an acid, which gives the brass, a rich pale gold colour, finishes the chemical ordeal. After the piece is again cleansed in water, it presents a rich and uniform, though dull gold colour. This dullness forms a good foil, and contrasts finally with the prominent parts of the design, which are afterwards richly burnished, the ormolu having prepared the surface for that operation.

In an apartment joining the dippers is another one in which the coating of the brass which has passed the ormolu process is carried on. The galvanic battery is here put in use. The piece of brass is put in connection with the battery, and is made to form the negative pole of the instrument. A bar of pure silver acts as a positive pole. The brass is then held in a solution, and the bar of silver is played around it under the surface for a few seconds, which suffices to precipitate upon the negative pole, or piece, a coat of silver thick enough to bear without injury the action of the burnishing instrument.

Burnishing is an important process in the manufacture of gas fixtures. The tools used are of a great variety of shape, and during the process of burnishing are frequently dipped into a dark coloured liquid, which on inquiry we find to be simply small beer. The parts of the surface of the metal which are not burnished are "dead," or "matted" as they come up from the ormolu. Much of the beauty and the character of the work depends upon a judicious selection of the parts to be burnished. It is to the proper development of the design, what lights and shades are to a good picture. The process of lacquering, which is a very important one, is carried on in a room supplied with stoves, which are kept in all seasons constantly heated. Here the various articles are placed upon hot iron after being carefully brushed. When heated to a certain degree, the articles are taken to a table, were the lacquer is applied with fine, flat brushes. Some articles are dipped into the lacquer, and "slung" backwards and forwards, in order to make it certain that the lacquer is properly spread over their surfaces. The lacquer must be scientifically prepared and skilfully applied to ensure a rich and lasting gold colour, unaffected by the action of the atmosphere.

The different parts and ornaments after undergoing the processes described are ready to be placed in the hands of the fitter or finisher, and are selected and taken to the respected places for putting them together. One room is occupied entirely by a number of men who are constantly employed in fitting together such gas work as chandeliers, pendants, brackets, etc.; another room is devoted to the numerous class of solar lamps designed for standing upon the table, or to be suspended from the ceiling or against the wall. Some of the ornamental work is painted in party-colours, to please fanciful taste; some is bronzed in different shades, while other work is covered with a coating of fine gold, or tastefully enamelled.

It should be kept in mind that although this article was published in 1875, it was based upon information printed in 1859 and the lamps including the solar lamps referred to would have been of that period. There were still solar lamps advertised in the F. H. Lovell 1877-78 catalogue although it is not certain if they were manufactured in the manner described, or if they were old stock. As previously mentioned, they were listed as "SOLAR LAMPS FOR SPERM, COCONUT OR RAPE SEED OILS."

*a.*

*b.*

Combination wall and hand lamp, signed in raised letters on the corrugated reflector:

# DIETZ

## No 11 TUBULAR HAND LAMP

Little remains of the original shiny coating on the curved reflector. The entire tin lamp has no sign of its original finish although the burner appears unused. As a hand lamp, it is somewhat awkward to handle, but as a windproof wall lamp, it would function very well.

It is stamped on the back PATENTED/ JUNE 9 74/ JAN 14 79. I have not been able to locate a January 14, 1879 patent that appears to relate closely to this lamp.

The patent for the other date, June 9, 1874, No.151,703 was granted to John H. Irwin of Philadelphia. He obtained over a dozen kerosene lamp and lantern patents. A significant and easily recognisable part of this and other Irwin patents was the use of the flanged unit seen at the back of the reflector. Irwin called it an "air injector."

One or more of these distinctive air injectors are frequently seen on Dietz lanterns and street lamps. They served to diffuse the draft at the air-intake, in a situation where outside air is brought into the burner through a tube or tubes.

Instead of using a common round tube most frequently seen, this lantern has the air injector placed at the top of a double-walled reflector. The burner is similar to those used on Perkins & House lamps. Height to the top of the air injector is $8^7/_8$".

## A Lamp for the Doctor's Office

At Black Creek Pioneer Village in Toronto, Canada, this lamp was chosen because it would be most suitable to direct a beam of light towards a patient during nighttime emergency operations or dental surgery which the doctor performed.

Silvered reflectors used primarily with bracket lamps were common throughout this kerosene period. They could be considered spotlights of the kerosene era, and they functioned surprisingly well in the absence of ambient light. In this instance, the lamp can be rotated to direct the light 360 degrees, to the operating table or the dentist's chair. Not everything then can be thought of as the "good old days"!

The bracket arm is marked PAT PENDING, which is unfortunate from a research standpoint. The font is marked in raised letters on the panels, PAT JULY 29 1862. This was the date of the Charles S. Orpen patent No. 36060, for a reservoir or font with a socket, designed to fit over a gas fixture, in conjunction with an elastic rubber sleeve. This must have been a successful patent judging from the numbers that have been found.

# The 1888 H. Leonard & Sons Catalogues

It is an overworked description, however "amazing coincidence" does apply here. The only two H. Leonard & Sons catalogues that I am aware of happen to be different ones for the same date! One is a regular wholesale one with cuts shown here, and the other is a retail one that was combined with a cook book. The comparative retail prices are in parenthesis beside the lamps.

Three of the more expensive lamps offer interesting comparisons. No. 1020 is $1.60 as shown and $2.10 for a Double Joint model. Each of these would have included the Baccarat shade like (a). Today these shades are found in amber, ruby, and blue.

The cast brackets themselves were only ten and fifteen cents each. Six- to ten-inch reflectors were listed elsewhere in the retail catalogue for fifteen to thirty five cents each. No. 118 with Electric Fount and Reflector was $2.10. One wonders what was so special about the Electric Fount other than the name!

The five-inch squat shades can appear too large when used with some table or late composite lamps, whereas they can often be used to advantage with a bracket lamp. It is a good way to display a special shade.

*a. Amber shade signed BACCARAT.*

Perhaps Edward Miller supplied H. Leonard & Sons with the bracket lamps shown here. The Baccarat shade above is shown on No. 1020 with the pattern reversed. Miller advertised that he was sole agent for Baccarat.

It has been suggested that the unmarked examples may have been made by others. In 1887 the E. P. Gleason Mfg. Co. catalogue these shades were advertised as "SAND BLAST SQUAT GLOBES."

See also pp. 260-261 H. Leonard & Sons.

### BRONZE IRON BRACKETS—ONLY.

*(.10)* No. 120.

*(.15)* No. 121.

*(.15)* No. 0100.

No. 1144. Double Swing.

*($1.00)*

No. 1020. Brass. Rich Gold Finish.

*($1.60)*

*($2.10)* No. 118.

| | | | | | Per doz. |
|---|---|---|---|---|---|
| No. 404, French Bronze, | 7 inch spread, | A Ring Pin............................ | | | 50 |
| No. 120, | " 8 " | B " ............................ | | | 85 |
| No. 121, | " 11 " | B " ............................ | | | 1 25 |
| No. 0100, | " 11 " | B " ............................ | | | 1 25 |
| No. 118. | " 14 " | B Ring T. S....................... | | | 2 50 |
| No. 118, | " 14 inch with Elec. Fount and Reflector, comp. (see cut) | | | | 17 50 |
| No. 461½, | " 12 " | B Cup T. S....................... | | | 2 50 |
| No. 461½, Ebony & Gold, | 12 " | B " ............................ | | | 3 00 |
| No. 1144, French Bronze, | 18 " | B " ............................ | | | 8 00 |
| No. 1020, Rich Gold, | 12 " | with Fount, no Trimming.......... | | | 13 25 |
| No. 1020, Double Joint, | 18 " | " " " .......... | | | 17 25 |

For prices complete, see page 239.

### BRONZE IRON BRACKETS—COMPLETE.

No. 461½ Bracket.

All Prices Complete with Fount, No. 2 Sun Burner and Chimney.

| | | | | | | | | | | Per doz. |
|---|---|---|---|---|---|---|---|---|---|---|
| No. 120. | Pin B. Ring, F. B. with 6 inch glass reflector (see cut page 238)...... | | | | | | | | | 4 50 |
| " 120. | " | " | " | 7 " | " | " | " | " | | 4 65 |
| " 121. | " | " | " | 7 " | " | " | " | " | ........ | 5 00 |
| " 121. | " | " | " | 8 " | " | " | " | " | ........ | 5 50 |
| " 0100. | " | " | " | 7 " | " | " | " | " | ........ | 5 00 |
| " 0100. | " | " | " | 8 " | " | " | " | " | ........ | 5 50 |
| " 118. | Thumb Screw, B. Ring, F. Bronze, with 7 inch glass reflector........ | | | | | | | | | 6 50 |
| " 118. | " | " | " | " | 8 " | " | " | " | ........ | 7 00 |
| " 461½. | " | " | B. Cup, | " | 7 " | " | " | (see cut). | | 6 25 |
| " 461½. | " | " | " | " | 8 " | " | " | " | | 6 50 |
| " 461½. | " | " | " | Eb. and Gold, | 7 " | " | " | " | | 6 50 |
| " 461½. | " | " | " | " | 8 " | " | " | " | | 7 00 |

Each.

No. 1020. Rich Gold, complete with Etched Crystal Globe, Unique Burner and

Pearl Top Chimney (see cut page 238)....................................... 1 70

No. 1020. Double Swing Joint, same trimmings..... ................... 2 00

*a. Side view of lamp stand.*

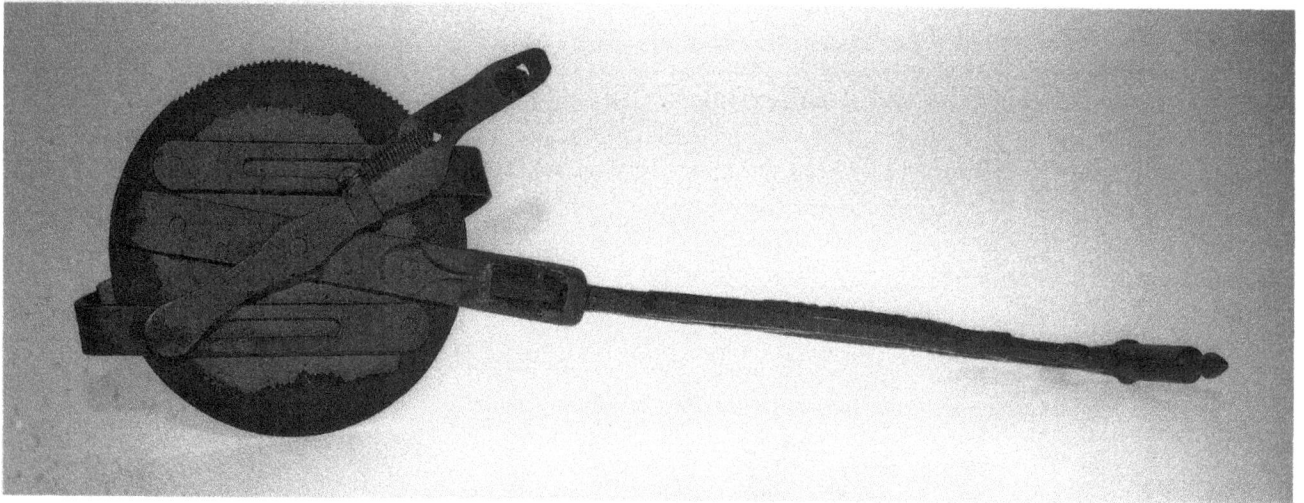

*b. Bottom view of lamp stand.*

# Elisha Bacon 1875 Patented
# Lamp Stand

This is an instance where a rare single example can establish that a particular patented device was actually manufactured. The requirement to mark dates on patented objects is a great boon to researchers and collectors. Elisha Bacon of South Avon, New York, obtained a patent March 23, 1875, No. 161,088 for this lyrical-looking contraption.

Bacon described it as follows: "The object of the invention is to produce a lamp-stand which, while capable of being used to advantage in any of the purposes to which such devices are commonly applied, is more especially designed to be used in connection with musical instruments — pianos, organs and the like — for the purpose of placing the lamp in such a position as to throw the best possible light upon the music."

The patent illustration differs considerably from the example above. It shows a plain tubular arm that doubled back to place the font holder close to the wall or to a piece of furniture.

The clamps and springs were intended to hold a lamp with an indentation above the base that would allow the arms that extend outwardly from the holder to firmly clasp the lamp. The spring allows fonts of varying widths from about 4¾" to 7¾" to be used.

One rubber cushion is missing from a clamp, and a replacement pin was used to attach the base plate to the arm.

Overall length is about 13½".

# Roelofs Patent Lamp
## Supporting Bracket

This lamp bracket was an improvement over another Roelofs bracket patented about four months earlier. In his first patent Sept. 28, 1880, No. 232,761, the font support consisted of four arms, and the wall mount was different. This exceptionally large one was not pictured in the illustration of the January 25, 1881 patent No. 237,048. That date was cast on the arm of this bracket.

The improvement was the use of only two arms to support the font. This meant the bracket could be cast in one flat piece. The custom-made blown font with a filler is 3¾" high and the arm length is 10⅜".

Anthony Roelofs of Philadelphia patented another lamp holder, July 18, 1882, No. 261,385. This was for a ring holder that also required a custom molded font.

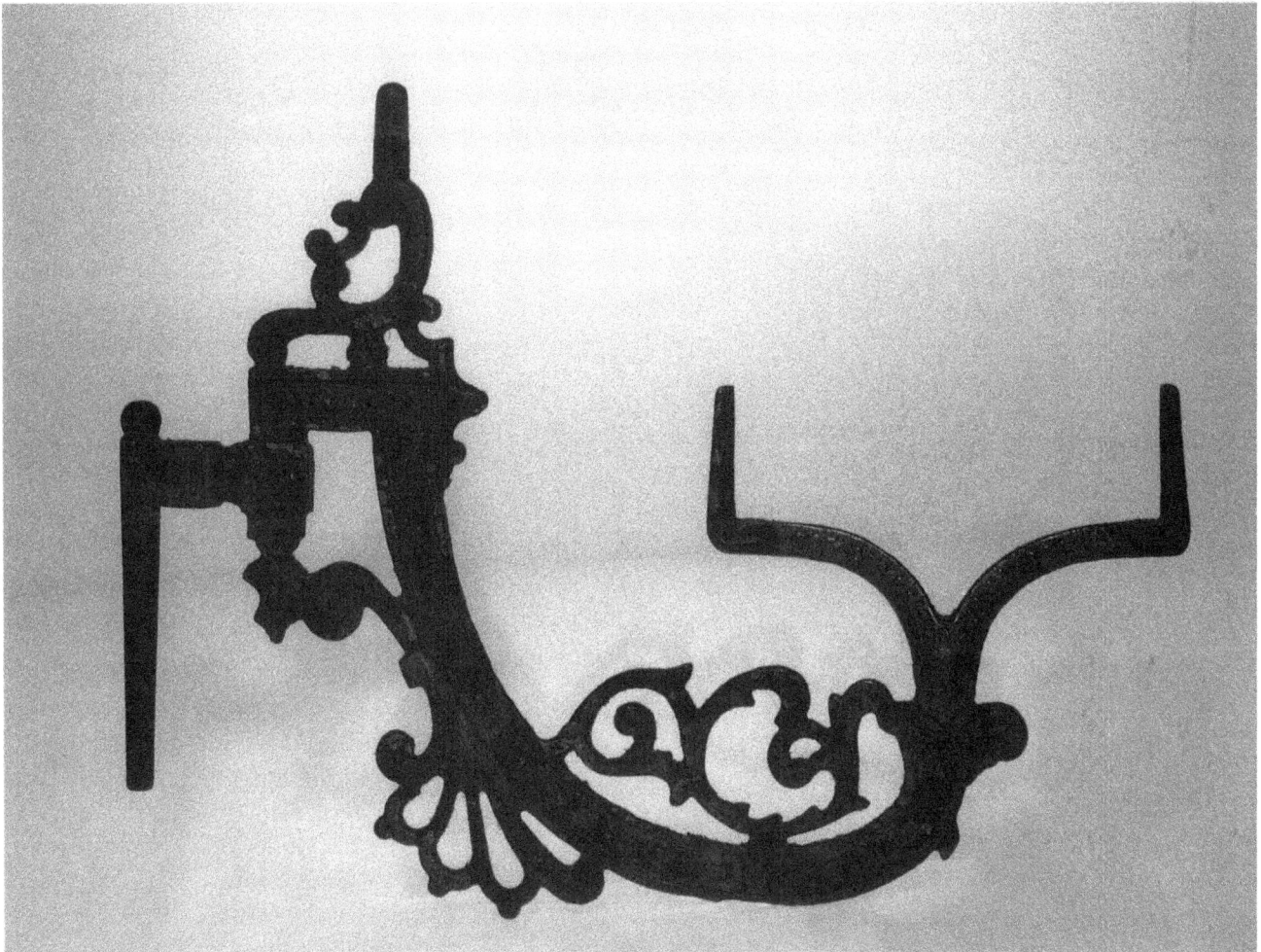

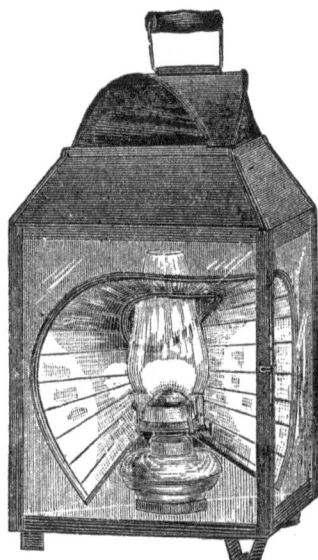

# Wheeler Reflectors

Wheeler, like Ives (for a time), had a distinctive, readily identifiable style that even extended to their descriptive letterhead above.

In 1981, The Rushlight Club reprinted a 48-page booklet titled *The Wheeler System of Reflectors*. This catalogue of examples, promotional literature, and instructions contains testimonials dated from 1884 to 1887, the likely date of publication. On the cover of the booklet they display a medal of the Massachusetts Charitable Mechanic Organization awarded in 1887. There are about forty lamps illustrated including the one shown here. The illustrations (b) and (c) are from *The Iron Age*, a monthly trade magazine.

*b.*

*c.*

Wheeler designed lamps and lanterns with segmented mirrors for all manner of industrial, commercial, farm, transportation, and domestic situations. Lamp (b), style No. 414 wall-bracket lamp, was described as "THE VERY BEST REFLECTOR MADE for general use."

It claimed to throw just as strong a light diagonally to each side as it does to the front. They recommended it for domestic uses as well as for public halls, billiard-rooms, reading rooms, offices, shops, etc.

It was priced at $2.25. All the lamps were individually priced, presumably for retail trade.

The lamp (d) opposite compares most closely, but not exactly with style No. 365 in the booklet. It was described as, "A headlight reflector for use with oil, for hand, table or wall use." Also mentioned is the handle in the back, and the fact that it throws a strong light in one direction.

The effect of the flame reflected in each mirror segment is very impressive. This is not conveyed in the line illustrations, but it must make a dramatic presentation with each of the many different configurations offered in the many styles.

There were student lamp shades and a cast iron hanging lamp with a 14" shade mounted just under the weight ring. The reflector shade was $1.50 and the complete lamp was offered for $4.25.

They manufactured large chandeliers for churches, opera houses, and halls with twelve or more fonts. I. P. Frink was another manufacturer who advertised large chandeliers with mirrored reflectors.

The lamp (d) was purchased with the Argand burner shown. It does appear to be like the one in the Wheeler booklet.

*d. Opposite is a Wheeler stand, wall or hand lamp. Height to the top of the reflector is 11³⁄₈".*

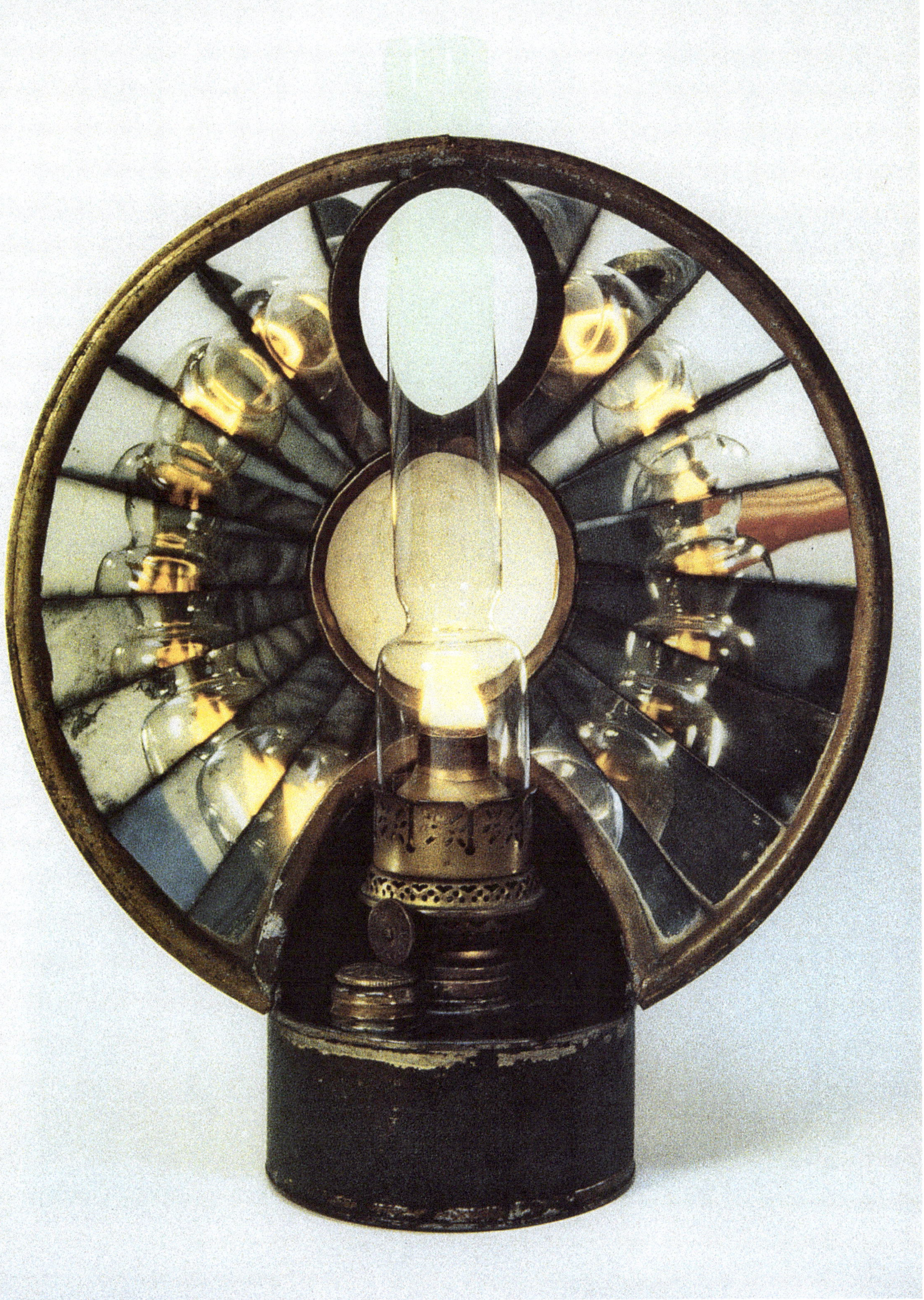

a.

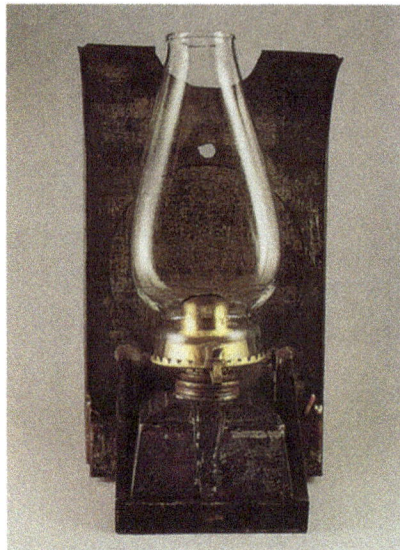

b.

c.

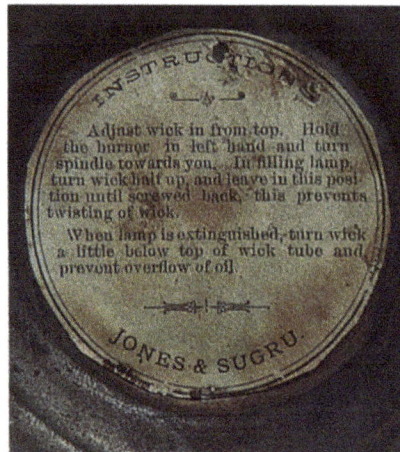

d.

e.

f.

# Portable and Fixed Wall Lamps

Wall lamps were useful for general room illumination as well as to light halls, stairways, and passageways. Most were inexpensive, and many were patented.

(a) The first lamp pictured has a saucer-like tin tray attached to a wire support that hooks over a nail. The tin hand lamp fits snugly upon the tray.

(b) This is a plated tin fixed wall lamp with a corrugated glass reflector.

(c) The brass font can be removed from the heavy brass wire holder to be filled elsewhere.

(d) This fixed tin wall lamp with traces of red paint on the removable font also has two receptacles for matches. Perhaps one was for burnt, and one for new. It also has a Drummond burner and chimney, made for and sold by F. H. Lovell & Company.

(e) and (f) The lengthy printed instructions identify this lamp. They also emphasise what a nuisance it must have been to fill fixed wall lamps. The rectangular Leader burner with its flat chimney would have been a good choice for wall lamps.

# Early Brass Bracket Lamps

These are probably the earliest brackets pictured in this book, and they retain most of their original finish. This ormolu finish is described on pages 169 and 170.

The fonts, burners, and chimneys used are typical of the 1860s. The burner (a) made by The City Mfg. Co. is dated March 3, 1863, for a patent granted to W. H. Smith. See p. 236. The burner on (b) is the more familiar 1859 E. F. Jones patent. Both have the patented Oct. 8, 1861, E. & E. D. Dithridge No. 1 chimneys. They were described in the patent as "a lamp-chimney with a round base and top and an oval-shaped bulge for the purpose of adapting it to the ordinary round mounting of lamps in which flat round wicks are used, and also for bringing the air equally in contact with the blaze."

The brackets relate to gas fixtures in terms of the cast brass metal, the finish, and design. The burnished highlights on the wall mount (c) contrast beautifully with the mat ormolu background. It is an elegant and unusual fixture.

There are wall attachments with holes in the centers for gas fixtures, closely resembling (d). They are pictured in catalogues. The S. E. Southland's 1859 catalogue shown in OL-1 on page 18, illustrated a similar lamp.

The font and chimney (a) measure 14⅜" and (b) is 11⅝". The length of (c) is 9¼" and (d) is 11".

*a & b.*

*c.*

*d.*

a.

b.

# Brackets
# to Hold Lamps

These brackets were designed to hold stand lamps. All examples were covered by the A. Thurber patent of April 22, 1884, No. 297,317. It is remarkable that the three versions have different finishes.

The bottom bracket holds a Hobbs Optic<sup>ON</sup> lamp with a blue Coral<sup>ON</sup> pattern. The sand-blasted chimney with a sawtooth frosted design is similar to, but not the same as, ones shown in the 1877-78 F. H. Lovell & Co. catalogue. This one has a U. S. mail train running around the middle! The engine is complete with cow-catcher, engine headlight (kerosene of course), a bell, and other details. On the side of the coal car are the bold initials U. S. M. This is followed by a very long car with UNITED STATES above the windows, and the number 1 below. It may be a good representation of the trains of the time.

All three brackets were found in Ontario, Canada. Their condition is really exceptional, suggesting that they may have been stock from an old general store. The top two have colored enamel finishes. The bottom one (c) has a copper-bronze finish.

c.

## Early Iron Bracket Lamps

These bracket lamps closely relate to the Russell & Erwin 1865 catalogue illustrations shown on page 166. Lamp (a) has an iron bracket that resembles No. 5251 in the catalogue, although its overall length of 12¼" is 4" shorter.

The most unusual feature of this bracket is the ring that was drilled to hold prisms. The only hanging lamp that I have seen drilled in this manner is an Ives lamp that is earlier than those pictured in this chapter on page 189.

Ideally the center of the reflector should be directly behind the flame, however such a combination is often difficult to find.

b.

a.

The bracket (b) above closely resembles No. 579 in the Russell & Erwin 1865 catalogue. They both have simple arms that have four concave sides. This 11" one with a small knob is one inch shorter than the one in the catalogue.

The identical illustration also appears thirty years later in an 1895 F. H. Lovell & Co. catalogue that was "devoted to goods especially adapted for Railroad use." There it is mistakenly described as a Ring Bracket for B flat font, instead of the basket font holder illustrated.

Another lamp in this 1895 Lovell catalogue is the one with the Baccarat shade from the 1888 Leonard catalogue illustrated here on page 173. Unfortunately the page with the prices is missing.

*a. Early cast iron bracket with blue glass font.*

The Ripley patented glass font (b) has since been replaced with the original one as shown in an advertisement. An article in the January 16, 1879 issue of the *Crockery & Glass Journal* suggested that it was the beginning of the end for the Ives company; however The Ives Patent Lamp Company advertisement in the August 21 issue of the same year included two bracket lamps and a chandelier.

This bracket with PAT APL FOR worked into the design on the flat arm has an original bronze finish. It is thinner and more finely detailed than most. The original font design was patented Feb. 2, 1875, No. 8041, by Frederick R. Seidensticker of West Meriden, Conn., assignor to Bradley & Hubbard. Seidensticker assigned many patents to B&H.

The other lamps shown in the advertisement have the Ives' ribbed shoulder fonts that were designed for use with their first hanging lamps in the 1860s. They were used in many lamp advertisements in the 1870s.

The blue font, the concave bracket arm, the 10" silvered reflector, and the imitation gas cock are all important features of this circa 1870 lamp. Since gaslight was associated with houses of the wealthy it was fashionable to mimic the valve. This later changed to a decorative form like (b).

It appears that the original finish had rusted and was overpainted with flat black paint. This could be restored. The large reflector has been used to spotlight a painting across a sixteen-foot room. Height and width of the bracket itself is 14".

*b. Ives/Bradley & Hubbard lamp.*

*a.*

*b.*

(a) All parts of this rare and exceptional combination are white opalescent blown glass with a varying degree of opacity. The striped chimney, the hobnail or Dew Drop[ON] shade, and the Waffle Cube pattern font serve to illustrate the range of effects that can be achieved with one type of glass. Not pictured is the matching smoke saucer with opalescent stripes.

Today some collectors like to combine parts of the same period to create a stunning effect. Height is 12¼".

The original finish on the Bradley and Hubbard bracket (b) is pristine. It can serve as a model for refinishing poorly restored iron lamps or ones in need of restoration. The 1877 design patented font holder used on many B&H lamps is described on page 68. The N. L. Bradley patented, threaded font holder that prevented oil seepage was used on this, and the Ives bracket (c) opposite. It is dated January 31, 1871, No. 111,430. Outside measurement of bracket from font holder to wall is 15".

# Bracket Lamp Assortment

This varied sample of styles begins with (a), a design that was pictured in the 1868-69 F. H. Lovell & Co. catalogue, in bracket and chandelier forms. See p. 186. There is a connection with Hiram Tucker who obtained several patents for finishes applied to iron in the 1860s. It has its original dark bronze finish. Lamps (b) and (c) have the same design. One is brass and one is iron. The arm of the brass lamp (d) has a fixed position.

The Atterbury lamp (e) must have been very successful. The bracket arms have been found in different styles. There are variations in the shape of the fonts, the position of the pegs, the dates, and the ribbed bands. Because they are rare, it is difficult to record the variations.

This bracket was also in the same catalogue as (a). It has bold and simple lines. The bracket (g) has a fixed arm, and the font may not be the original one. At the present time it is difficult to assign dates to brackets (d) and (g). The others are likely 1860s and 1870s.

*a.*

*b.*

*c.*

*d.*

*e.*

*f.*

*g.*

# Early Hall and Hanging Lamps

These lamps are the same as, or closely resemble, lamps advertised in the 1860s or before. The first two, (a) and (b), with cast arms and flat rectangular stamped chain links, are similar to the hanging lamps in the Southlands catalogue in OL-1 p. 18. Both have an excellent original finish. The example (a) appears unused. The font and trimmings are also from the 1860s.

The brass font (b) could be from a later date, however the shade with the ruby edge was pictured with Mt. Washington shades referred to on page 18. A patent that described applying such an edge referred to it as tipping. The choice of trimmings can make a significant difference to the appearance of these lamps. The overall length is about 25".

Lamp (c) would have been an economy model for a modest home. The simple wire frame has plated, stamped tin applied accents, and the font holder ring is cast iron. The font itself is a translucent white alabaster glass that goes well with the roughed Oregon shade and smoke bell. Length is about 23½".

The lamp (d) is almost the same as one pictured on page 424 of the Russell & Erwin 1865 catalogue. There are two lamps on that page having frames made with this lightweight, hollow ribbed tubing. The lamp is difficult to clean and fill. The complete font is not removable, therefore it is necessary to remove each component of the trimmings separately. The top and bottom of the spun brass font are joined just above the cast brass ring holder. This is not an easy lamp to take apart and reassemble, especially if one has to use a stool or chair.

*a.*

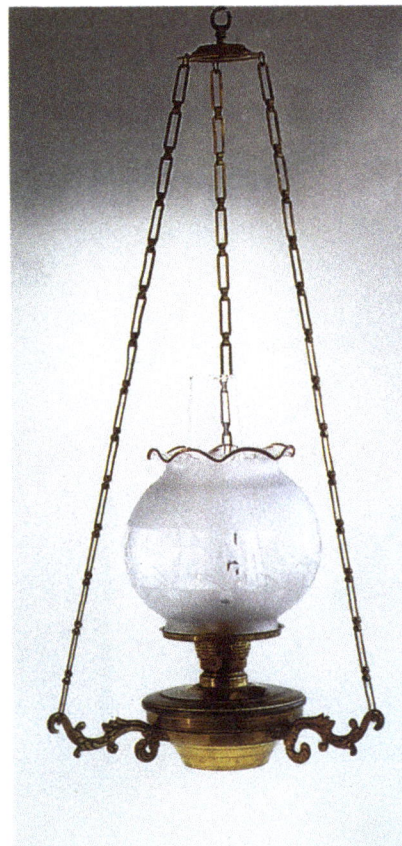

*b.*

*c.*

All parts of (d) are brass with the exception of the top loop, and a reinforcing ring inside the top of the font. The dull patina appears to be the original finish. The trimmings are appropriate and the length is about 38".

*d.*

## F. H. Lovell Lamps

This lamp was pictured in both the 1868-1869 and the 1877-78 Lovell catalogues. The prices are not available for the 1868-69 catalogue, however a price list for a circa 1873 catalogue provides information on this and other Lovell lamps. The lamp here, number 7662, illustrated on plate 27, was described as Brass Harp, and the wholesale price was $27.00 per dozen.

Brass and iron were often effectively combined in early bracket and hanging lamps. The rope twist harp and cast font holder provide an attractive setting for the dramatic engraved 5" Oregon shade and smoke bell. The chimney with a roughed band improves the appearance. For actual use, only reproduction Pyrex chimneys should be considered to replace rare old ones. The early Jones burner and shade holder combination is an appropriate choice.

The same circa 1873 price list notes the bracket lamp with a reflector (without the blue font), on page 182 (a) was $22.50 per dozen.

Also noted was the cast iron vase stand lamp on page 106 (b) and the Tucker double bracket lamp on page 184. These were priced at $5.75 each. The iron fonts were described as "Velvet Heads" and elsewhere they have been described as "Velvet Cups." An inner glass font is attached to the metal shoulder. Perhaps the metal fonts were originally lined with velvet. Shallow Atterbury Tucker fonts will fit the Tucker iron font holders.

a.

b.

# Hall Lamps 1880–1900

Brass gradually replaced iron as the favoured metal for hall and hanging lamp frames, and ruby glass was a popular choice for hall shades. Colorful stained glass was used in entrances and around windows in late Victorian homes. A ruby glass shade would have matched the intense red color commonly used for stained glass.

Lithophane was a type of porcelain made primarily in Europe during the Victorian era. It varied in thickness and when backlit, pictures were created by the amount of light transmitted. The depth of shade depended upon the thickness. Both flat panels and molded shades were made.

Two 4½" × 5½" panels were used in this extension hall lamp, pictured with a punched brass frame. The first panel (a) depicts two children, or perhaps a mother and child, taking a walk on a windy winter's day. This medium is well suited to the subject. The second panel (b), a domestic scene, includes what appears to be a lard lamp. Flat ruby glass accents frame the panels. A strong photographic light was used to give definition to the panels.

The hobnail or Dewdrop shade (c) is solid ruby glass. These shades often have an outer layer of clear glass that gives them a lighter appearance and sparkle.

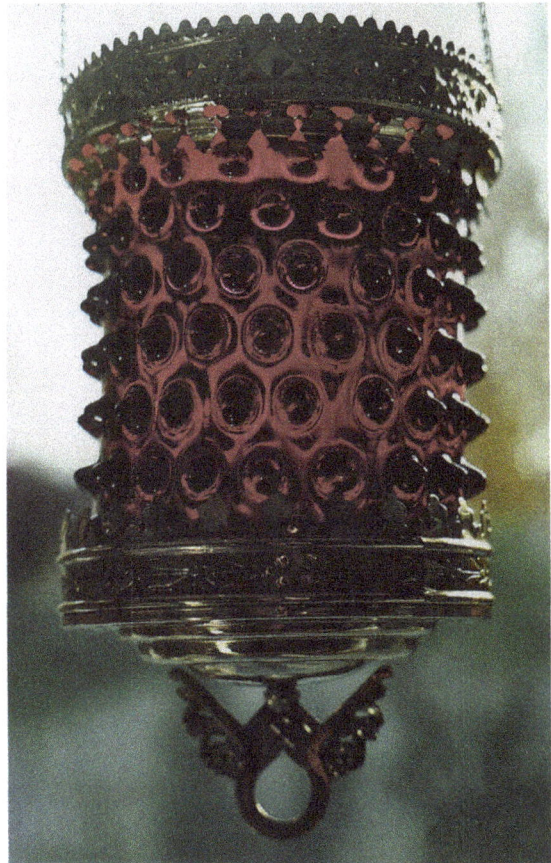

c.

*a.*

*e.*

# Fancy Iron, Wrought Iron and Colored Glass

According to turn of the century advertising, these lamps were "just the right thing for the Moorish Room, Alcove, Cozy Corners, Vestibule or Small Halls." The term *wrought* was generic. It described any metal that was black, twisted, curved, curled or spiralled.

Smoking was all the rage, especially cigars. There were public smoking rooms as well as designated areas in private homes. The dominant theme was Turkish or Moorish, and these lamps helped to set the stage.

They are generally inexpensive today, partly because their age has been suspect or their condition is sometimes poor. Some are complex and elaborate with interesting glass panels. The colors and shadows they create can add an interesting decorative touch.

It is possible to create a bracket by using an enlargement of the advertisement as a pattern.

*b.*

SPRING AND SUMMER CATALOGUE (NO. 45), 1901.

This cut illustrates a fancy iron lantern with colored glass sides, handsome designs, very strong, well made goods, being the very latest idea for halls, smoking rooms, Moorish rooms or Turkish divans. The bracket is separate from the lantern, but it adds very much to the appearance of each to have both.

No. 135. Fancy iron lanterns with colored glass, in entirely new designs, can be used for halls, Moorish rooms or Turkish divans, each ................ $8.50

Other styles and sizes in iron and brass, $2.00 to 7.50 each.

Bracket, $1.50 each.

T. EATON C?., 190 YONGE ST., TORONTO.
Courtesy Eaton's of Canada Limited

*c.*

*d.*

a. Ives' reflector hanging lamp with high shade by day.

b. Ives' lamp at night.

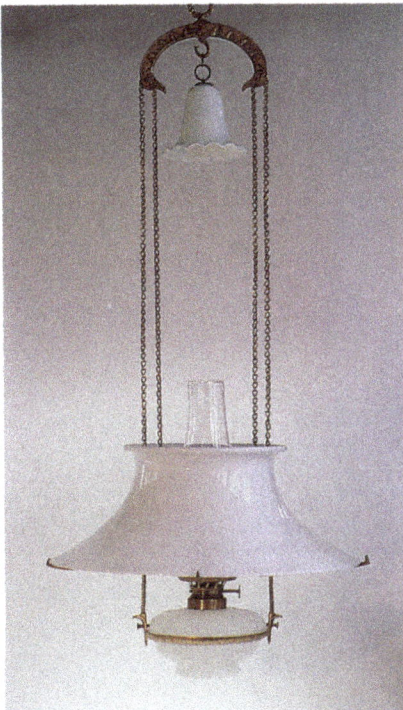

c. Ives' short shade.

A simple description of these two pages might be "from the ridiculous to the sublime!" Although form follows function was not a recognised concept until almost a century later, it was a factor in this daring departure from all that had gone before. When the font is pulled down, the shade, shade holder, and chimney balance the font and oil. This allows the font to be filled through an aperture in the burner while the cone is elevated with the shade holder. The font could be removed if desired. When the shade and holder are lowered, the attached cone slides over the wick tube. The relationship of the burner parts is maintained by set screws attached to the ring font holder. These are secured by the ribbed design on the shoulder of the font.

The bottom of the font is shaped to enable it to be pulled down easily and to stand on a table if removed. The easily recognised font with the ribbed shoulder is illustrated in catalogues and advertisements with other Ives' lamps and Bradley & Hubbard lamps. They were made with either alabaster or opaque white glass. The shades were listed as Enamelled Reflector Shades. The "less is more" principle promoted by Meis Van der Rohe in the 1930s is apparent here.

Although these lamps are relatively rare, the one with the short shade (c) is most often seen. Sadly, the later Ives' production lapsed into indistinguishable popular styles.

The length is about 29" and the shades are just under 14".

a.

b.

From the 1860s to the 1880s, cast iron dominated the production of hanging and bracket lamps. After about 1865, most ceiling fixtures either had an integral or a separate means of extension.

After the simple Ives' lamps, it became a challenge to patentees and manufacturers to produce a novel means of counterbalancing and extending the fixtures.

Counterbalancing usually involved either the weight of the frame itself or weights (usually lead) were added to the crown ring or a separate container. This must have added considerably to the cost and problems of shipping although it was rarely mentioned. In fact, in *The Heritage of Light* by Loris Russell, an advertisement for a Bradley & Hubbard cast iron lamp is reproduced. It appeared in a supplement of the "London Reflector" described as "A HIGH-CLASS MAGAZINE FOR THE COLONIES."

The advertisement was placed by Prince & Symmons, Kerosene & Petroleum Lamp Manufacturers and Exporters. Canada was clearly their targeted market and the heavy cast iron Bradley & Hubbard lamp was described as "Finest American Iron Casting." The shade was listed as "FRENCH OPAL." It must therefore, have been economically feasible to sell heavy B&H cast iron lamps to Canadians that had been shipped via England. This appears to have been what they were attempting unless they were acting as agents.

Lamps (a) & (b) made by Bradley & Hubbard were advertised in the F. H. Lovell & Co. 1877-78 catalogue. They utilise the considerable weight of the frame to counterbalance the extension. Lamp (a) could only retract about 15" when not in use and if the smoke bell is removed. With a smoke saucer, it could have about a 10" range of adjustment while lighted.

Lovell noted lamp (b) could be lowered 4" for lighting and trimming. That would be about the equivalent of standing on one's tiptoes. Only the shade on (b) may be original. Other glass parts are old replacements. The overall lengths as pictured are (a) 41" and (b) 32".

The 1877-78 Lovell Wholesale Price List showed (a) No. 2996 at $122.00 per dozen, and (b) No. 2992 at $92.00 per dozen, complete with shade. Both lamps have been lightly painted over the original finish.

_a._

## George Bohner Lamps

George Bohner, of the firm George Bohner & Co., Chicago, obtained several lamp patents. The first was for the lamp pictured above. The cast iron font holder has the following information indented on the outside at the bottom, BOHNER LIBRARY LAMP PAT APRIL 30 1872. Simply stated, the patent was for a lamp whereby the weight of the ring and shade would counterbalance that of the font and holder.

The September issue of the _Crockery and Glass Journal_ advertised Bohner's Patent Extension Library and Hall Lamps showing drawings of each. The one titled "Fig. A Extended for Lighting" shows one hand holding a lighted match to the wick while the other hand is pulling down on the bottom of the font to elevate the shade. There is no explanation as to how the chimney has become mysteriously elevated or how this "no hands" approach was achieved. Overall length is 32". This example with the original green and bronze finish has the original shade and a rare smoke bell with a green edge.

_b._

Only one out of three patent dates can be deciphered on this lamp, however it is enough to identify it as a Bohner lamp. It is a reissue of his April 30, 1872 patent. The large crown hides a separate heavy iron ring. Overall length is 42".

This lamp has contrasting massive and delicate features. The hand painted shade is likely original, and the font with a large drip catcher flange is marked patent applied for.

*a. Bradley and Hubbard Centennial lamp.*

This lamp was patented Oct. 31, 1876 by John A. Evarts of West Meriden, Conn., and assigned to B&H. It was for "An improvement in extension lamp fixtures" and was a variation of a shade-ring, ring-weight, and shade combination to serve as a counterbalance.

*b. Bradley & Hubbard lamp from:*

**THE ILLUSTRATED CATALOGUE**
*of*
**THE CENTENNIAL EXHIBITION
PHILADELPHIA, 1876**
*Courtesy The Corning Museum of Glass.*

# Wallace & Sons

This company, based in New York City, made the nickel-plated lamp pictured here. It was illustrated in a George F. Bassett & Co. New York, 1883 catalogue. Part of the description included, "It is made of SOLID WROUGHT BRASS, beautifully finished in GILT or NICKEL PLATE. It will not break like lamps made from castings. The weight does not touch the Crown and break the Shade. IT HAS TWO AND A HALF FEET EXTENSION. It has a DRIP CUP and CUT FOUNT WITH A BRASS CAP OIL GUARD (the latter an entirely new feature), a double protection against damage by overflow." The price per dozen, all complete, was $36.00, packed 1 dozen in a case. The shade is 14".

The frame is stamped with a June 6, 1882 patent date. This patent No. 259,087 was issued to Edson L. Bryant of Ansonia, Conn., who assigned half his rights to Wallace & Sons, of the same city. Their factory was probably located there.

The stated object of this invention was "to produce the fixture from sheet metal in such a manner that the extra cost of sheet metal over common cast-iron is more than counterbalanced by the saving of labor in the construction of the device." He went on to claim many other advantages including the application of stamped decoration and cleaning. He also claimed that it was much stronger than the common cast-iron construction and more attractive than wire. Wallace & Sons had previously made two popular wire lamps, the "Rival" and the "Royal." These were similar to the B&H lamp on the next page.

Edson L. Bryant also patented the nickel-plated sheet metal covering plate for the font. This was patented August 29, 1882, No. 263,474. The patent suggested the collars for the burner and filler openings could be soldered onto the plate. This would require a corresponding glass font and metal plate openings. The end result was a very neat appearance that could be plated to match the frame.

Wallace & Sons used their patented "Surprise" burner made without rivets or solder on these lamps. They also sold them separately. The wire loop extending from the right side of the burner activates an extinguisher. I think the "surprise" must be that one has to push it *up* rather than follow a natural instinct to push it down to extinguish the light. Possibly this is a reaction conditioned by using electric light switches.

This lamp has passed unscathed through the period of time when it was popular to strip nickel-plated brass objects. Nickel-plating required an additional manufacturing process, and therefore it was considered more desirable and expensive. In time, having the original finish will again become more desirable and expensive.

*a. Wire frame extension lamp.*

*b. The Hero<sup>ON</sup> lamp.*

*b. The Hero^ON lamp.*

*c. Ball shade hanging lamp.*

# Hanging Lamps

Hanging lamps made with wire frames appeared in advertisements around 1880 in the *Crockery and Glass Journal* and the *Pottery and Glassware Reporter*. They were made for 10, 14 and perhaps 12 inch shades, as well as for 7 inch X. L. Illuminator or Radiator shades. One of these was advertised as having an "Extreme Length" of 62 inches. The extension feature was important as they stated, "This lamp is designed for the Library, Parlour, Office or any place light is needed at any desired height.

In 1881 Wallace & Son who made the nickel-plated lamp shown on the previous page used the same weight and pulley with a wire lamp. It was called their 14 inch Standard Library Lamp, and they also advertised a wire 10 inch Rival Library Lamp. They used at least two other pulley arrangements. Both cast-iron parts and stamped brass parts were used. These lamps appear to mark the transition from the use of cast iron to the popular brass hanging lamps of the 1880s and 1890s.

The New England Glass Company and Bradley & Hubbard both advertised the same wire frame "Hero" lamp (b) noting which part of it they made. As with all of these lamps, the shades were white or opal glass, either plain or with painted designs. The NEG shades had colored bands and a floral design like the one on the previous page. The Hero lamps also had the star peg fonts like the one on the centennial lamp on page 192.

Other major lamp manufacturers that advertised their own brand of wire extension lamps were Edward Miller & Co., The Manhattan Brass Co., the Ansonia Brass Co., Charles Parker, and The New York Lamp Co.

Of the hundreds of hanging lamps illustrated in trade papers and catalogues, this style (c) with a ball shade represents only about one per cent. They offer a splendid way to display an exceptional shade such as the cased blue dragon shade here.

Red and white dragon shades are also illustrated in this book. A much smaller dragon shade about 5" was made to match a small font with the same dragon in bright yellow. The gilt design is usually found to be in excellent condition.

*a.*

*b.*

## "Jewels of the Night"

It is easy to become mesmerized by the sight of daylight shining through colored art glass shades and fonts, smoke bells, ornaments, prisms, jewels, and sometimes chimneys. How these lamps must have transformed even a modest home at night with colors splayed around rooms furnished in dull and sombre tones. All else would have been subdued while all attention would have been focused upon these spectacular "jewels of the night."

Over the years, broken and missing parts have sometimes been replaced so that it requires the expertise of an experienced dealer or collector to confirm original lamp parts. Ornaments and parts were often sold separately so that the later addition of such parts is considered acceptable today.

Library lamps that are considered to be original or to have the proper parts are far more expensive than examples with inappropriate substitutions. With that in mind, it is possible to select an attractive but not authentic lamp that may be satisfactory from a decorator's point of view.

Lamp (a) is known to be complete. Although the other two lamps (b&c) do not have all parts in view, they do present an impressive visual impact.

*c.*

a.

b.

c.

d.

# Library Lamps

Very few correct and complete kerosene library and hanging lamps of the 1880s and 1890s are to be found in museums. Those pictured here are from private collections and offer a rare opportunity to view a very spectacular group of lamps in color. Few catalogues of the period illustrated glass in color so that these lamps come to life in the color photographs. The most colourful description that I have come across was in a June 11, 1885 *CGJ* cover advertisement for the Bridgeport Brass "LA FAVORITA" extension lamp. Among other things, they mentioned cut jewels in "Amethyst, Emeralds, Sapphires, Opals, Agates, Rubies, and Topaz." Clearly these lamps were intended to dazzle the beholder!

Unfortunately, examples in private homes can be awkward to handle and very difficult to photograph in close quarters. Ambient light that includes daylight, and various types of artificial light as well as reflected light and colors, dramatically affect the color of the glass and background. Nevertheless, after viewing the examples pictured on these six pages, it will be easier to imagine the actual appearance of the dozens, if not hundreds of such lamps, that appeared in catalogues and advertisements of the period.

Few original names of parts or types of glass are used by collectors and dealers today. Most of the descriptions adopted here have been provided by the owners and are understood by those familiar with the field.

Trade papers frequently refer to the 1880s and 1890s as difficult economic times, and perhaps these lamps added a cheerful note. Advertisements also emphasised imported drawing-room lamps with Kioto, Bohemian & Longwy decorations. These would have been beyond the means of the average household, however they might afford a modest form of one of these colourful highlights.

The Bradley & Hubbard lamp frame (a) opposite also appears on the front and back covers of this book and on the title page as illustrated in an 1885 *CGJ* advertisement. The owner who described it as B&H's finest has provided in current terms, some important features of that lamp and others on these two pages.

The patented spreader that holds the chains apart below the motor has a self-adjusting roller system that assures a level lamp. Leading authorities have agreed that (b) is a rare original ten-inch hanging lamp frame. The faceted cut-glass "jewels" as they were known were a part of kerosene and of electric lamps. Here they enhance the amberina glass shade and amber prisms.

Parker hanging lamps, possibly the most sought after today, are generally considered to have the finest extension devices or motors ever made, and in general were the best made lamps. The example (c) with a light and elegant frame has a matching high-dome shade, font, and match holder.

Both the exceptionally delicate cast-brass frame with floral motif and the rare and unusual art glass shade vie for attention in the example (d). Deep amethyst and purple glass have been used to create this rare and possibly unique shade. The motor has a patented outside tension adjustment.

Lamp (e) on the right introduces a rare combination of colors, textures, and forms. It might be said to be the essence of a grand, sophisticated Victorian Era library lamp. According to the owner, the textured shade is Pelaton glass. It relates well to the hammered and embossed brass parts. Ubiquitous Victorian Griffons are incorporated into the design in a restrained way. Even the round weight appears to be in greater harmony than the optional spreader and motor would have been.

*e.*

*a.*

*b.*

Any one of the library lamps on these pages would be considered very special if not sensational by collectors. Most of the information about the lamps has been provided by the owners who have had years of experience handling and observing a large percentage of the known extant examples.

Lamp (a) above has a Rochester lamp frame made by Edward Miller & Co. It has a New England Peach Blow hobnail shade. Beside this (b) is an outstanding amberina hobnail shade with matching prisms and a cranberry (ruby) chimney. The all-original frame has a jewelled brass font.

On the opposite page are library lamps that exhibit a compelling array of frames and glass parts. The first of these, 199(a) with a high-dome hobnail shade, has an original frame with brass ornaments. Several of these decorative ornaments were patented. Lamp (b) is a Parker lamp with matching shade and font in pink cut velvet satin glass. Lamp (c) has an acid-etched design on cranberry glass. It is attractively displayed in a handsome Rochester cast-brass frame.

Lamps (d, e, and f) all have an irregular wavy or scalloped bottom edge. The example (d) is a rare original Parker lamp with a diamond quilted cranberry or raspberry shade. The

brass and silver font with floral decoration is suspended inside the shade.

The lamp (e) probably has the most spectacular frame that Parker, and possibly any manufacturer, made for what is now called a petticoat shade. The combination of the brass font and multicolored jewelled frame that corresponds with the shape of the hobnail shade is remarkable.

In the 1889 Henry & Nathan Russell & Day catalogue, this lamp (f) with some differences in the frame was offered for $162.00 per dozen wholesale. It was one of their most expensive library lamps. The description included 'With Ruby Vase and Ruby Diamond Shade."

Since museums apparently have not collected, displayed or studied these lighting fixtures, the bulk of our current knowledge and expertise must come from collectors and dealers. In the future, the vast stock of primary source material housed mainly in museums may be combined with the expertise of those who have had many years of hands-on experience to bring about an accurate reconstruction of this subject.

*a.*

*b.*

*c.*

*d.*

*e.*

*f.*

*a.*

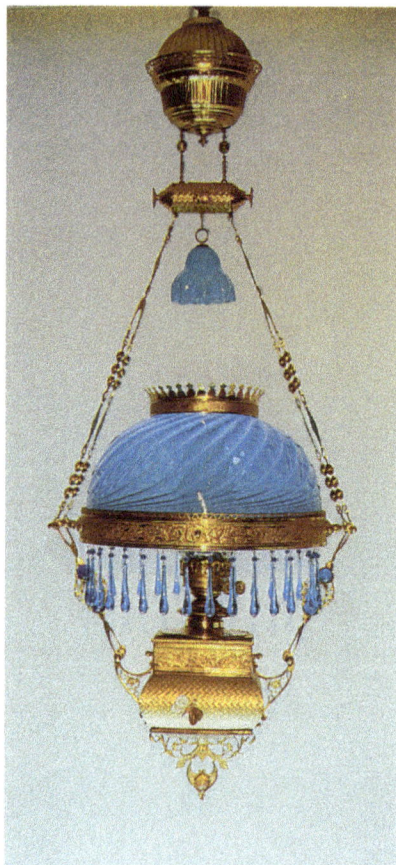

*b.*

*c.*

*d.*

There is little doubt that the surge of interest in these lamps peaked in the 1880s. This group demonstrates efforts to incorporate a dazzling array of innovations and embellishments designed to capture the attention of the buyer. Many of them are yesterday's or even more recent add-ons. As we try to visualize them in a parlour, they should be imagined in beams of sunlight, as well as illuminated by an open flame. It is obvious that every decorative component was made to transmit or reflect light.

Major functional improvements were also introduced or incorporated. Part of the reason for this, was the uncertainty of future production with the prospect of electric lighting on the horizon. At that time there was significant worldwide distribution for kerosese lamps.

Some important and unusual features of these lamps are noted here:

(a) The matching shade and font in light blue mother-of-pearl, ribbed air-trap glass. This is also referred to as cut velvet. The ornaments suspended from the shade holder ring and the deep blue jewels make an impressive statement.

(b) This opalescent blue swirl shade has unusual blue teardrop accents. The square Parker font is embellished with a cast brass dragonfly.

(c) The upper part of the hobnail dome shade is clear glass with a frosted finish. Below this are extraordinary ornaments consisting of hollow perforated brass balls suspended from round jewelled medallions.

The spreader allows the lamp to be rotated a full 360 degrees and to remain in a fixed position. Match holders were useful accessories and have developed into a popular area of collecting. The one used here is colored glass with a rabbit and rooster in relief.

(d) The frame, chains, and ornaments combine to create a very feminine effect. They balance the striking high dome blue opalescent shade.

## "Beautiful Beyond Description"

A line illustration of this lamp was included in an 1895 catalogue titled:

LONDON TEA COMPANY-U.S.A. It was sent to me from Australia many years ago by Ron Page. Lamps in the catalogue were offered for sale or as premiums with orders for the purchase of merchandise. There were minor differences in the frame design and common prisms were used, however the shade and font were unmistakably the same. The catalogue description began:

"ROCHESTER SPRING FIXTURE LIBRARY LAMP No. 201.

This new Lamp is beautiful beyond any description we can give."

Then follows the caveat, "Exactly like the above cut, *except* with decorated shade somewhat similar to shade on Lamp No. 271."

Turning to No. 271, a low dome white glass shade was offered for only fifty cents less than one with an ordinary hand painted decoration. It was titled a BARGAIN LAMP.

This leaves room for a good deal of speculation about the reasons for the substitution of inexpensive glass. The glass in this example has been described by the owner as "Cranberry Zipper Pattern Glass" Perhaps it was no longer being made at that date.

Other lamps included a Rochester parlour lamp with the Mt. Washington design patented, matching vase and shade. This was described as "Ribbed Bisque Decoration." It was priced at $7.50 or offered as a premium with a $28.00 order. This was about twice the price of other parlour lamps and would compare with the cost of a good library lamp.

*a.*

# Chandeliers

Two-arm chandeliers were an appropriate choice for the dining room. More utilitarian ones with longer arms were made for use over store counters. The earliest examples evolved from brass and iron gas fixtures, often adapting or mimicking tubing or valves. Compared with library lamps, there are few two or three arm chandeliers to be found today. One reason for this is the difficulty of finding matching fonts and shades. Smoke bells have been reproduced in opaque-white glass with a colored edge.

Lamps (a) and (b) were made in the 1860s. Like chandeliers in the 1865 Russell & Erwin Catalogue, they were not adjustable and may have required a separate extension device, a ladder, or a tall person to reach the burner. It is obvious that burners designed to allow lamps to be lit without removing the chimney and shade were a great advantage.

The brass lamp (a) also shown in OL-1 has more appropriate Mt. Washington shades and choice early blue fonts added here. It has tubular, stamped, and cast components. The iron lamp (b) has solid, plain, and rope-twist rods and solid imitation valves. Later, less realistic and more symbolic imitations eventually became the decorative drops found on almost all chandeliers. The soft metal rod holding the smoke bells is original. This arrangement was later patented. The basket font holders have two similar fonts with fillers patented in the 1860s. One is dated September 18, 1860, and the other is marked July 2, 1861.

The original bronze finish has deteriorated, however it has not been painted and should be carefully restored.

Both the outstanding original finish and the slightly bizarre design set this circa 1870 chandelier (c) apart from others of that date. Patents for the extension device featuring a spring and clutch first relate it to the Tucker Mfg. Co. and later to Bradley and Hubbard. In the 1860s, Hiram Tucker of New York, obtained four patents for special finishes on iron. Tucker cast-iron lamps are occasionally found with excellent original bronze type finishes. Other patents link these manufacturers as well as Ives & Co. This lamp is one of a pair purchased in San Francisco, California.

*b.*

*c.*

a.

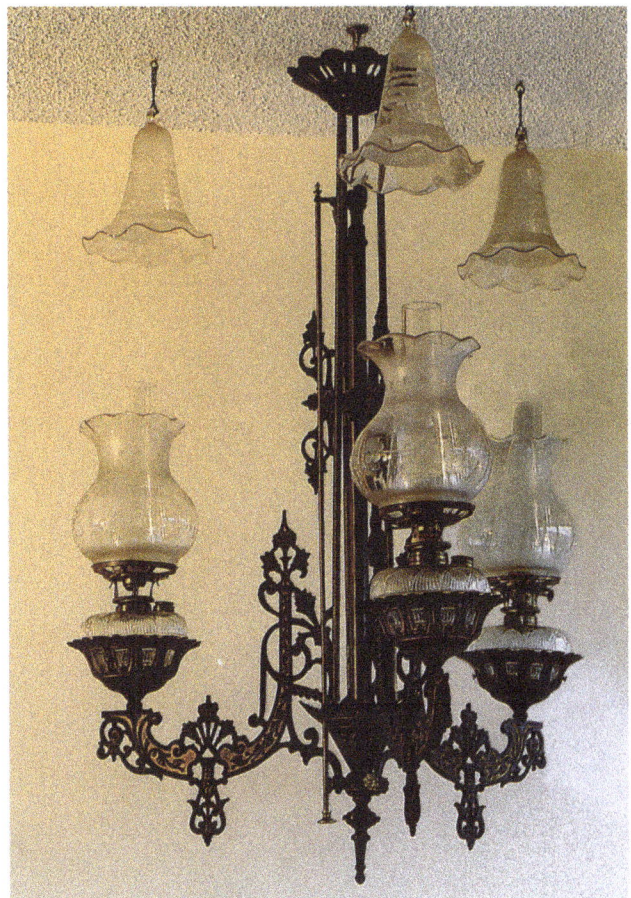

b.

# Bradley & Hubbard
# Cast-iron Chandeliers

There is no question that Bradley & Hubbard dominated the world production for cast-iron lamps. The first of these (a) is brass plated. This was an option advertised by B&H but seldom seen today. There is no extension component and the Illuminator bases and shades, while not original or common, were used with chandeliers as well as double hanging or bracket lamps.

The examples (b) and (c), probably made in the late 1870s or 1880s, retain their original finishes in outstanding condition. The frames are enhanced by the choice of trimmings. Both lamps are very heavy and although they are equipped with extension devices, using them might involve some risk.

Lamp (c) with Lomax fonts has a ceramic insert surrounding the central post. These embellishments seen also on parlour and banquet lamps were reserved for the finest examples. It is surprising that chandeliers do not appear to have been subject to the jewels and ornaments that were so much a part of the hanging library lamps.

c.

*a.*

*b.*

*c.*

# Lovell & Hinks Lamps

The three-arm cast-iron chandelier above is extraordinary for several reasons. The first is that the cast portion of the arms are three dimensional. This allows the curved rod to be slipped through to support the font. This is more apparent in the circa 1880s James Hinks & Son Limited catalogue illustration (b). Hinks were listed in Birmingham and London, England. All other cast-iron arms on hanging lamps and chandeliers that I have seen have been flat castings.

A two-arm example appeared earlier in the American F. H. Lovell 1868-9 catalogue on Plate 31. At the present time the reasons this lamp with different font-holders and trimmings appeared in catalogues widely separated in time and geographically is not known. Cast parts of the other Hinks lamps on this page are also found in American catalogues. The fonts and trimmings are clearly of English origin.

Hinks was a noted manufacturer of the finest quality lamps and patented burners. Several of these are illustrated in OL-2 pp. 131-132. There appears also to have been a relationship with Hiram Tucker.

At the bottom of each Hinks catalogue page is a reminder that glass was extra. The more ovate globes and high-shoulder fonts are characteristics of English manufacture. The slotted hangers swivel for positioning.

*d. & e.*

James Hinks and Son catalogue.
*Courtesy The Corning Glass Museum.*

*a.*

*b.*

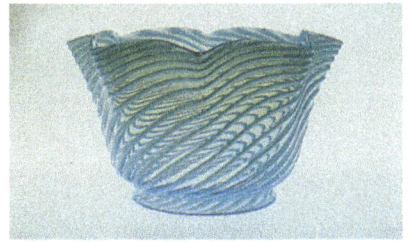

*c.*

*d.*

*e.*

*f.*

*g.*

*h.*

*i.*

*j.*

*k.*

*l.*

# Colorful Art Glass Shades

The colors and techniques used in the creation of lamp shades during the 1880-90 Victorian period produced an astonishing variety for homeowners to choose from. Today individual shades are particularly suited to bracket or hall lamps, or are used on banquet and vase lamps. If two or more matching shades are found, they would be appropriate and impressive on a chandelier. The selection illustrated has mainly four- and five-inch bases. Some may have been imported. They are briefly described here.

a. Figured art glass with two ruby glass applied flowers and blue edge.

b. Transparent blue hobnail with white opalescent fluted edge.

c. Opalescent blue swirled ribs with fluted top.

d. Opalescent and translucent, textured yellow-green art glass.

e. Translucent opalescent art glass shaded from custard to salmon pink. Color changes when back lit.

f. Cameo amber glass shade with a clear acid etched surface.

g. Hobbs Glass Co. hobnail shade with intense contrasting color.

h. White threaded shade with ruby threaded fluted edge.

i. Mt. Washington deeply etched Cameo glass shade. This type of glass was also used for a library lamp with a matching shade and font.

j. Yellow or vaseline hobnail with ruby crimped edge.

k. Opalescent white shaded to pink with applied blue medallion.

l. Signed Baccarat roughed ruby globe.

*a.*

*b.*

*c.*

*d.*

*e.*

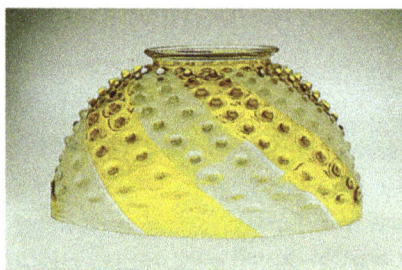

*f.*

*g.*

*h.*

# Library Lamp Shades

Most library lamps were advertised with fourteen-inch shades, however some were made to accommodate ten-inch to eighteen-inch shades in two inch increments. Ten-inch shades were primarily used on center draft, vase or student lamps. All of those illustrated on these pages are referred to as dome shades, and collectors generally prefer a high rather than a low dome shade.

The shades were supplied to the lamp frame manufacturer or they may have been supplied to a wholesaler or retailer. The glass shade manufacturer may also have purchased frames to assemble and sell their own complete lamps.

(a) and detail (b) This is one of a few shades that appears to be a unique example of an experimental technique. The color change and the spidery effect surrounding the hobnails are rare and unusual. The shade would appear to be difficult to duplicate.

(c) to (g) are many variations of hobnail dome shades with and without opalescence.

(h) The amber and white can be recognised as a Hobbs Glass Company product known as Francesware.

The shades on this page include many different colors and glassmaking techniques, most of which were also used on other examples of Victorian Glass of this 1880 to 1900 period. One multicolored dome shade that I saw recently had a surface with thin layers like flakes or shreds of glass that lifted off the shade. If one attempted to run one's hand over the surface, it would likely be inflicted with many small cuts.

The art glass featured here includes enamelling and pink satin quilted mother-of-pearl with a yellow lining.

Many exceptional shades such as (j) were pictured in Hobbs Glass Company catalogues. It is also known that many other glass manufacturers including Sandwich and Mt. Washington also made library lamp shades. Unfortunately there are no known catalogues or other means of identifying most of the shades.

Library lamps with matching shades and fonts are popular with collectors. Smoke bells and match holders are often selected to match or compliment the shades. In addition there were jewels and ornaments such as the crown (p) used as further enhancement. Some of these were patented.

*i.*

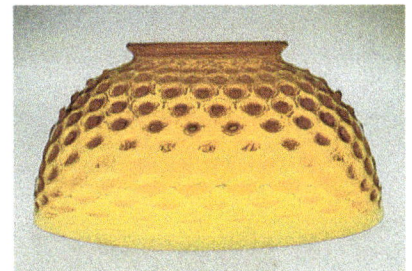

*j.*

*k.*

*l.*

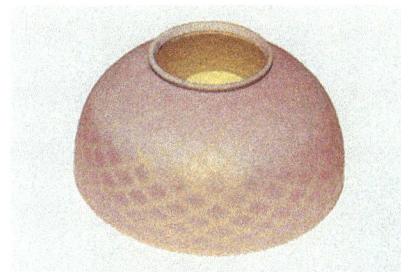

*m.*

*n.*

# Miniatures and Night Lamps

*a. Henry C. Hutchinson chimneyless burners patented Jan. 3, 1865, No. 45,719.*

*b. Bloxam miniature, flat hand, and small stand lamp.*

*c. Glow lamps sold widely in the 1890s and early 1900s.*

Night lamps, using whale oil, burning-fluid, and later kerosene were practical and economical nineteenth century alternatives to candles. They could provide a sufficient amount of light to guide one in passageways and on stairways as well as to enable one to check the time or rekindle the fire. A low flame could burn for many hours or even all night.

Special chimneyless burners such as the distinctive Hutchinson examples (a) and others opposite were very successful commercially. Each thumb-wheel is stamped HUTCHINSONS/ PATENT. The absence of a patent date suggests these examples may have been made in the 1880s after the patent had expired. Height 4¼".

Night lamp was the common name for all, however those made in diminutive forms of full-size lamps as in (b) have come to be known as miniatures. They have always been popular with collectors. The Bloxam pattern was made in an unusually wide range of sizes and colors. The sizes of these lamps from left to right are 4¾", 4¾" and 7½".

The Glow Night Lamps (c) were patented August 27, 1895, No. 545,313 by R.J. Robertson, a British subject residing in Chelsea, Mass. The original glass burners have been reproduced (d) allowing the safe use of these lamps. Approximately 4½" high.

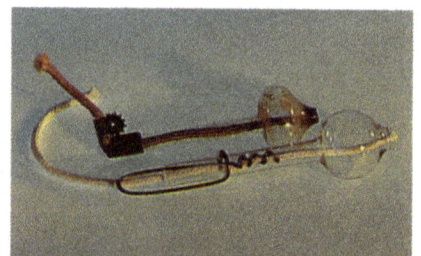

*d. Original (top) and reproduction Glow-Lamp burners.*

*a, b, c, d, e. Metal chimneyless or no-chimney burners.*

# Early Night Lamps

Attempts to patent a successful night lamp began early in the kerosene era and produced many distinctive and interesting forms that were intended to appeal to a specific segment of the market. While some of the examples that are found today may have been made close to their patent dates, many of them continued to be sold long after.

If thumbwheel markings are in two rings, they are noted as (or) outer ring or (ir) inner ring. Additional patent details are found in the appendix. The first example (a) has home-made characteristics. It is marked PUTNAM & CO / PATENT APPLIED FOR. There is not a patent date nor record of a kerosene patent granted to that name.

Burners (b) and (d) are two variations of the D. Symonds patent that used wood as an insulator around the wick tube. They are both marked with his name and the patent date; Mar. 7, 1865.

The more familiar burner (c) has raised letters on the thumbwheel that read (or) J. SANGSTER / PATENT (ir) MARCH 25th 1862. The fluted cone was one of his claims to improve the draft.

Also patented in 1862, the burner (e), called the "No-Chimney Eagle Burner," was advertised by the Bridgeport Brass Co. in *CGJ* as late as Sept. 6, 1880 and possibly later. In 1880 brass hand lamps with "gilt" finish were $1.50 per dozen wholesale. This was about the price of a regular or a chimneyless burner. Similar ones including patented examples, were in use before the 1860s.

The burner (f) is stamped on the winged portion below the burner: TISDEL & NASH'S PAT MAR 24, 1863. It was described as "An attachment for converting burning fluid into coal oil lamps." This appears to be a later version intended only for kerosene, that fits over a small flat wick tube. The wick case is stamped MADE BY D. SELLECK NORWALK CONN, and the thumbwheel is marked NATIONAL BURNER.

One of the most successful night light burners (f) was the Ne Plus Ultra, patented January 24, 1860 and made by Holmes, Booth & Haydens in the 1860s and 70s.

*f.  Tisdel & Nash burner.*          *g.  Ne Plus Ultra burner.*

*a.*

**Grand-Val's Perfect Time Indicating Lamp.**

Light and Time combined in this simple, beautiful and economical adjunct to every household in the world.

A pleasure to the well—a treasure to the sick.

Silently recording each fleeting hour, yet avoiding the monotonous ticking of a clock—so annoying to the invalid.

**The Model Night Lamp of 1881.**

LIBERAL DISCOUNT TO THE TRADE.

Please address orders to the

**Grand-Val Time Indicating Lamp Co.,**

**38 MURRAY ST., N. Y.**

L. E GRAND-VAL,
General Manager.

A. MEYERSBERG,
Sole Agent.

## Time-indicating Night Lamps

Both of these very similar lamps were advertised in the *Crockery & Glass Journal in* 1881. The advertisement above appeared in the January 6th issue, and the lamp (a) was on the cover of the April 21 issue. It was described as the "IMPROVED/ TIME-INDICATING NIGHT LAMP/ THE PRIDE OF AMERICA," and advertised by the Bristol Brass and Clock Co. New York.

There were no patents claimed in the advertisements for these novelties. Both lamps had a graduated time scale so that the level of the fuel (illuminated by the lamp) indicated the time. The lettering and the beehive and plain shades are minor differences. In her book *Evolution of the Night Lamp*, noted authority Dr. Ann Gilbert McDonald pictures both lamps.

# Candelabrum
# With Candle Lamps

Opaque white glass fonts made to resemble candles were equipped with string wick burners and shade holders. Most are found on single candlesticks, or occasionally on pairs. The five with identical shades illustrated here on gold plated candelabrum are a rarity. Similar candelabrum were advertised in late 1900s mail order catalogues.

The shades consist of four layers with a beaded glass fringe. The layers include mica, rigid fibreboard about ⅛" thick, pink silk, and an embossed punched metal outer layer.

a.                    b.                    c.

# Night Lamps

The diminutive night lamps in this column are well documented in books and articles on night lamps. To gauge their size, the small brass Fire-Fly[ON] lamp (b) and (d) illustrated in the 1877-78 F. H. Lovell catalogue is only 3¼" to the top of the shade, and the small hand is mine. Brief descriptions follow.

a.  Raised letters on the font clearly identify this lamp with a similar burner and chimney as (b). Marked on the font are the words: LITTLE HARRY'S / NIGHT LAMP, and on the reverse, L.H. OLMSTEAD / NEW YORK. Around the base it is marked PAT MARCH 20 77. This is the date of Olmsteads patent No. 188,533.

b. & d.  One of F. H. Lovell's smallest with an Olmstead burner and chimney.

c.  Raised letters on the font read UNION/NIGHT LAMP, and on the reverse, PATD APL 24-77. The amethyst chimney has the letter U. When rotated, the collar cap reveals a filler opening. It is incorrectly marked CHINNOCK / PAT. MARCH / 1876. The correct date was September 5, 1876.

e.  One of C.W. Cahoon's patented burners often found on night lamps is illustrated below on the same lamp used to advertise the Savage burner (g). The lamp was probably the illustrator's own because it appears on the Union Attachment on the opposite page and in the Fish Heater advertisement on page 73.

d.                              e.

*Illustrations from the F. H. Lovell & Co 1877-78 catalogue.*
*Courtesy The Sandwich Historical Society Glass Museum.*

*f.  Savage & Hawley burner patented May 5, 1863[1].*

Removed from 202 FULTON TO 286 GREENWICH ST.

**THE LONG-LOOKED FOR FOUND AT LAST!**
A BRILLIANT LIGHT FOR EVERY FAMILY.

*g.  Advertisement that serves to date this lamp in the 1860s when compared with New York City Directories.*

# Lanterns and Heaters

Lanterns and heaters were among the most creative items that used kerosene. The demand to provide something with a special feature or refinement inspired the examples included in this chapter.

One might question the stability of the Union attachment (a) below that would appear to hold much more liquid than the ubiquitous lamp, once again used in the illustration. Perhaps the name of an illustrator should be reserved for the lamp.

Although claims for "The Perfect Lamp Chimney Stove" (b) are exaggerated like much of today's advertising, it really was a clever, simple, and useful device. It consists of a heavy, ferrous metal ring and two flat slotted pieces of the same metal. When fitted together, they would support a kettle as shown. The only problem with this is the size of the kettle. If it is in scale with the heater, it would be about 4" in diameter. Perhaps just right for the proverbial "Spot of Tea."

*a.*

## A ✱ BLESSING ✱ TO ✱ EVERY ✱ HOUSEKEEPER !
### SAVES BUILDING HOT FIRES IN SUMMER !

# THE PERFECT
# LAMP CHIMNEY STOVE

### BOILS, FRIES, STEWS,

Coffee, Tea, Meat, Eggs, Oysters, Potatoes, Fruit, &c., &c.

Is perfectly safe and always ready for use in the DINING ROOM, NURSERY, SICK ROOM, OFFICES and SHOPS.

For the purposes above mentioned, and numerous others, it takes the place of expensive spirits and oil stoves. When your lamp is lighted this handy little device can be attached to the top of a chimney, no matter what size or style, and without altering or affecting the light. It will concentrate all the heat and prevent the smoking of the chimney. Twenty-five pounds weight can be placed on top of any Lamp chimney with perfect safety. The ordinary kitchen utensils can be used. Each stove is packed in a neat box, and READILY RETAILS FOR 25 cents; but a single trial is needed in any community to make them popular; all want them as soon as they see how useful they are. Agents coin money selling them; a sure sale at almost every home; money and profits picked up fast every day. Agents sell the stove for TWENTY-FIVE CENTS. To introduce them, and to secure agents, we will send a sample stove, by mail, postage paid, to any address for only fifteen cents; this is ten cents under the retail price, and the offer is made only for the purpose of introducing them, and to secure agents, through showing their extraordinary and wonderful usefulness. This is one of the practical inventions of great usefulness of this progressive age, and will prove a blessing to hundreds of thousands. Now is the time; soon all the agents that are wanted will be secured, and then the offer made above will be withdrawn. You can take your sample and go right out and take orders for fifty a day; you can just coin money. Postage stamps taken for amounts less than $1.00.

WILLIAMS-CIN

### TERMS TO AGENTS.

| | |
|---|---|
| Sample Stove, by mail | $ .15 |
| One dozen Stoves, by mail | 1 60 |
| 3 dozen Stoves, by express | 3.50 |
| 6 dozen Stoves, by express | 6.50 |
| 12 dozen Stoves, by express | 12.00 |

This little stove so useful to all can be sold in every family. Send for a sample and be convinced.

**Special Offer:** We will send 1 dozen Stoves and 1 dozen Gem Wick Starters by mail post paid for $2.00. Send all orders to

# HOWARD M'F'G CO., 26 Washington St., Providence, R. I.

*b. Instructions packed with "Stove."*

a. *Manhattan Brass Co. hurricane lantern.*

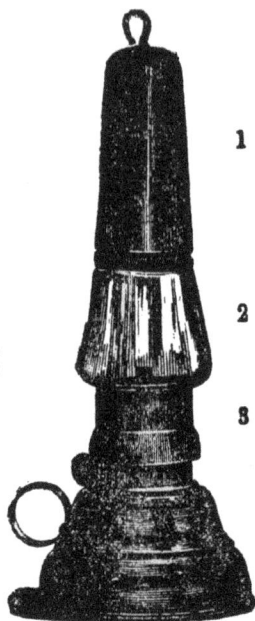

# Hurricane Patent Lantern

**THE BEST,**

**SAFEST,**

AND

**Cheapest**

IN THE

**WORLD,**

Is designed to burn

1

**KEROSENE OIL,**

*heretofore so much*

2

*dreaded,*

3

WITH

**PERFECT SAFETY**

The Lamp is packed, and must have only as much oil in as will be absorbed by the cotton, (all the rest being turned out,) thus rendering it entirely non-explosive, impossible to take fire, and free from dirt or grease spot, in case of an accidental fall or upset. Making it therefore a *perfectly safe, sure and cleanly light* under all circumstances.

Then it combines, with the above advantages, *compactness, beauty and perfect steadiness,* even in the *heaviest gale of wind.* It is therefore peculiarly adapted to in and out door use; the smallest size for the family, whether in the hands of children or servants, around the house, yard or cellar, is invaluable, whilst the other sizes for stables, builders, or watchmen, for railroads, steamboats, &c., are equally serviceable.

It is also the most economical, giving the greatest light at least cost of oil.

## DIRECTIONS.

The brass cone, (No. 1) on top of the Lantern, unscrews from the glass globe, (No. 2) but needs to be removed only to clean, or replace the glass if accidentally broken. The glass globe (No. 2) also unscrews from the bottom brass (No. 3) which contains the burner, and must be removed, together with the cone, (No. 1) in order to light the Lantern. After lighting you must turn the wick well down before replacing the cone and globe, and regulate the height of the flame after they are on again. When the lamp requires filling, first turn the wick well up into the globe, (to prevent twisting whilst screwing the bottom brass off from and on to the lamp, and thus preventing the free passage of the oil through it,) then unscrew the bottom brass (No. 3) from the lamp, and after saturating the cotton well with oil, (pouring back into your can all that will come out on turning the lamp upside down,) replace it before turning the wick down again. When the wick requires trimming, lift the little square cap or cone off the tube holding the wick, and cut square across the tube.

*Heavy Kerosene* of good quality must be used. Care must be taken in putting on the glass, as *too* tight a screw will break it. If you wish to use the Lantern as a lamp in the house, you have only to take off the top cone (No. 1.)

## ASK FOR A HURRICANE LANTERN,

### THEY ARE FOR SALE BY ALL THE DEALERS.

Thitchener & Glastaeter, Printers, 14 & 16 Vesey St., N. Y.

*McGurk collection.*

Protection against draughts was a major factor in the design of any lantern, and many have patented features that relate to this concern. Some, such as the advertised one shown above, also had packing in the font that would absorb excess oil. The name "hurricane" has become a generic term for similar lamps and could apply to any of the lamps shown here except (h) opposite.

All of these lamps except (j), a nearly identical substitute, were pictured in *The Illuminator Vol. 1 No. 1 January 1987.* They are from the collection of Frank Brown, noted dealer and collector, and I am pleased to include them here.

There are markings of some sort on all of them and patent dates on several. Many are marked with the same patent dates. These are included with the end notes. Note that all of these examples have chains and ring handles. These would have been convenient for hanging on a nail, but not as convenient for carrying.

The first of these (a) above is also illustrated in the advertisement from the McGurk collection. It was part of a larger Manhattan Brass Co. New York advertisement. The patent dates, also found on other lamps, can therefore be presumed to have been owned or leased to that company.

b. Cone dated, PATD DEC. 24TH 1867. Glass dated PAT. 5 APRIL 1864. Bottom of font dated PAT, MAY 8.1855 REISSUED MARCH 19 1867. Burner has a round wick. Height, 7½".

c. Cone dated, PATD DEC. 24TH, 1867. Bottom of font dated like example (a). Height, 8½".

d. Glass dated, PAT 5 APRIL 64. Height, 10½".

e. Cone dated, PATD DEC. 24 1867. Height, 9⅜".

f. Cone marked PAT'D DEC. 24, 1867. Thumbwheel marked M. B. CO. NEW YORK. The patent date is not clear. The cone has provision for a bail handle. Height 9⅜".

g. Cone dated, PATD DEC. 24, 1867. Thumbwheel marked HURRICANE LANTERN CO. NEW YORK. Height, 10".

h. Glass marked BABY. The burner has a round wick.

i. Glass dated 5, APRIL 64. Thumbwheel marked E. M. MILLER & CO. MERIDEN, CT. MADE IN USA. The wire guard is removable.

j. This lantern was also made with a bail handle. The letters H B & H are embossed on the glass within an oval. The thumbwheel is marked HOLMES BOOTH & HAYDENS* on the outer ring and Waterbury*CT* on the inner ring. The date FEB. 6th 1877 is stamped on the globe ring. The patent, issued to George A. Beidler, was issued for the chimneyless lantern burner.

It should be kept in mind that old glass is subject to stress that may cause it to crack when subjected to heat. Since replacement globes are almost impossible to find, lighting these lanterns is scarcely worth the risk.

b.

c.

d.

e.

f.

g.

h.

i.

j.

# Tumbler and Darkroom Lanterns

a.

b.

e.

Three views of the novelty Star Tumbler lantern are shown in (a), (b) and (c). The following information is taken verbatim from the enclosed instructions.

Several of these little lanterns seem to have survived. This is probably due partly to their novelty appeal and partly to their initial success.

The instructions do not suggest that an ordinary tumbler could serve as a replacement, and the very nature of the lantern's construction would make such a repair almost impossible.

The lamp is patent dated January 13, 1874. The only lantern patent on that date was issued to L. J. Carpenter and H. W. Dopp, No. 146,379.

d. Darkroom Lantern.

Darkroom lanterns were able to solve the problem of providing a red safelight, however the heat generated by the flame must have contributed to the problem of maintaining a required even temperature. In the days before air-conditioning, the basement was usually the preferred location for a darkroom because the temperature was relatively constant and because light leaks could be more easily controlled.

This lantern has a protected wick wheel shaft to prevent a light leak from the flame. One of the red glass panels is removable for lighting.

For a considerably more sophisticated and versatile example, see OL-1 p. 59 (e).

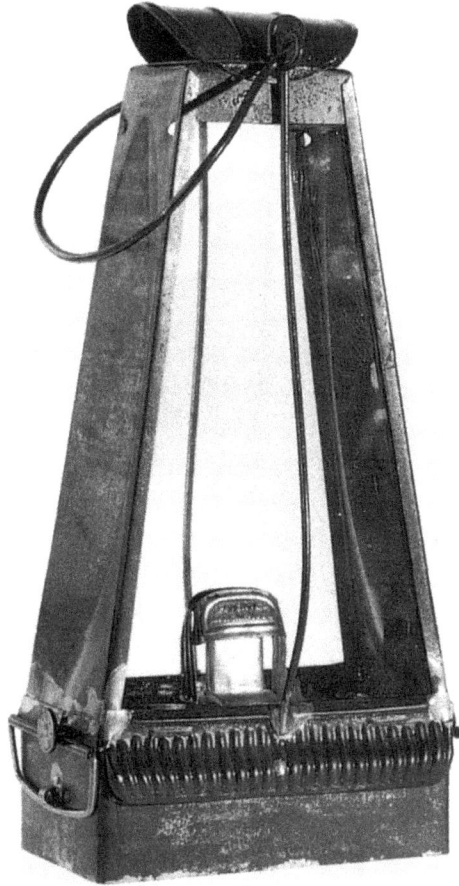

*a. Archer & Pancoast lantern.*

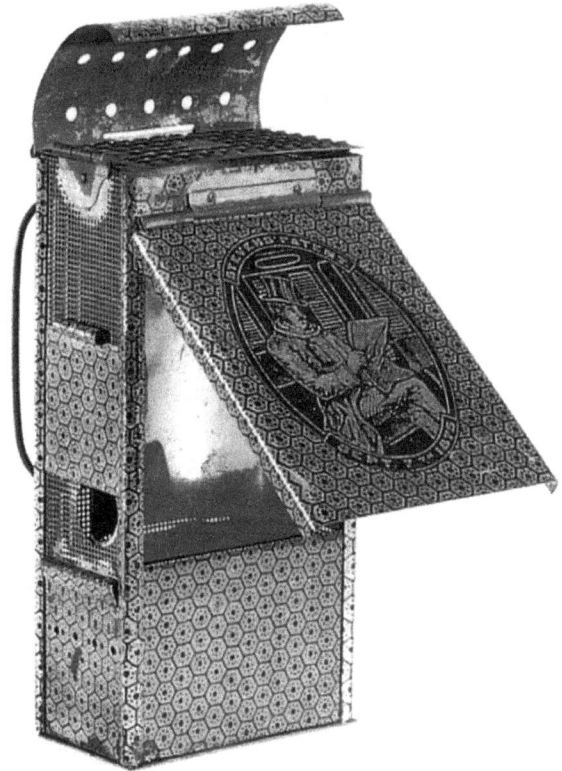

*b. 1875 Stevens/Dietz lantern.*

Variations of this lantern exist in collections. They originally appeared in advertisements and were called Convex or Excelsior by Dietz. The convex name may refer to the creased metal side parts. This feature would have strengthened the side sections while at the same time reflecting the light externally. When the clip below the thumbwheel is released, the top portion may be tipped sideways on its hinge on the opposite side for lighting the chimneyless burner.

On August 8, 1865, James Ives showed this lantern in his patent illustration. In that patent, the burner cone and an attached chimney tipped sideways as part of the upper section.

This particular tin example is faintly stamped with incomplete information: ARCHER & PANCOAST/ PATENT AP—/ NEW YORK. The chimneyless burner is marked on the obverse: ARCHER/ & PANCOAST, and on the reverse PATENTED/ MARCH 1ST 1864. Height without the handle is 8⅞".

John Stevens of Orange, New Jersey patented this lantern on Sept. 7, 1875. He called it a "Pocket Lantern" and said it was especially intended for "travellers, skaters, and others that require light at night." Stevens must have leased or

transferred his patent rights to Dietz & Co. shortly thereafter because on February 10, 1876, J. M. Dietz was granted a British patent for this lantern through his agent, W. F. Lotz.

Both the U. S. and British patent illustrations clearly show the model above with wire handles and clip at the back rather than a bail handle found on the better-known examples. Dietz advertised this later model (c) in the November 10, 1880 issue of the *Crockery and Glass Journal*.

All examples appear to have been decorated in a gold lithographed finish. Height is 5½".

*c.*

*Lantern footwarmer.*

# Footwarmers

Today emergency car kits usually include candles. This idea goes back a *very* long way. In an article giving instructions for travellers, the editor said he was "lately informed by a gentleman that he burnt two wax candles in his carriage, when travelling in Russia, and found that he was thereby kept very comfortable." The editor's footnote stated, "This hint will apply with much force to the numerous Americans who annually scamper over Europe." The article was dated 1813!

If candles can keep you warm in coach or car, it was only logical that kerosene would be even better for this purpose. It was also logical that such heaters should be combined with a lantern. The lantern could provide light to and from a vehicle, or in a home if that was where the heater was to be used. It could also serve as a light for a vehicle. See OL-1 p. 50.

The example above has a cylindrical font mounted on gimbals and a burner with all parts above the wick case, except the wick tube, removed. When the heater is horizontal, the flame is directly below the (replaced) carpeted surface. When held or carried vertically, the light shines through the round windows.

It appears to have been a successful and well used patent. On the side it is marked PAT. MAR 7 in large stencilled letters. I have not been able to locate the patent. The burner thumbwheel dated Jan. 16, 1883 and Feb. 11, 1873, is probably original. It is 9¼" wide, and 12¼" long.

a. *Jacques 1865 footwarmer.*

b.

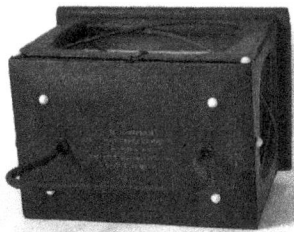

c.

d.

This footwarmer in remarkable original condition does not appear to have been used. The cloth or carpet lining that would have been under the top probably disintegrated. It retains its original bright red stencilled design on a maroon painted base color and white china studs. The lamp and burner are also in original and unused condition.

A mouse has neatly chamfered the two vertical front corners — a true dentil trim! Other views are shown in (b), (c), and (d). When in use, heat would rise from the burner to heat the main portion above the lamp. From there it was directed through the holes seen in (b) into openings in the open top.

The almost perfect yellow stencilled lettering (c) is extremely small. Five lines within 1¼" depth contain the following information.

K. E. OSTROM
MANUFACTURER
ANGOLA, N. Y.
Patented, March, 14th. 1865
By. D. L. JAQUES.

The Ostram initials are slightly indistinct and may not be accurate. The name and date of this patent are not listed in the *Subject Index of Patents for Inventions 1790-1873.*

a.

The construction of this Square Tubular Lantern is complex. This no doubt accounted for its relatively high cost. The main source of air for the burner is drawn into the tubes at the top of the lantern. At the base of the lantern the tubes become hollow rectangles directed towards the bottom of the removable font. There they turn into vertical tubes just over 1" high.

When the font is inserted, two tubes within the font slide over the upright air tubes, and the fresh air supply enters the burner below the cone. The cone is hinged to the top of the font and the blaze hole and therefore the wick is at a 45 degree angle to the reflector. Additional air is drawn in through the row of small holes at the base. This is the No. 6 size.

This 6¼" lantern below with red and green faceted side lights was advertised as a bicycle lamp although it is not marked as such. It is marked on the top in raised letters:

*The*
*Neverout*
TRADE MARK
INSULATED KEROSENE
PATENTED
ROSE MFG. CO.
PHILADELPHIA U.S.A.

The leather-covered spring belt clip, would make it a useful lantern for many situations.

## C. T. Ham Lantern

Large lanterns like (a) could be used around the home, the farm or for commercial use. This example in very good condition has most of its original gold stencilled inscription. The side panels have the wording: Registered 1886.

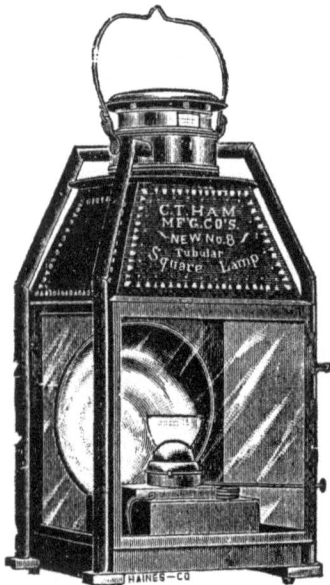

b.

**No. 8 New Improved Square Tubular Lantern.**
No. 6, height 16¾ in., width 8¼ in., depth 7½ in., No. 2 Burner 1 inch Wick, 6 in. Glass Reflector, each................$7.00
No. 7, height 22½ in., width 11¼ in., depth 10½ in. 8 in. Glass Reflector, No. 3 Burner, 1⅛ in. Wick, each...........$8.50
No. 8, height 24½ in., width 13½ in., depth 11½ in. No. 3 Burner, 1½ in. Wick, 10 in. Glass Reflector, each.....$11.00

c. *Neverout Safety lantern.*

*a. Arnold's whale oil stove lantern.*

# Heaters

This interesting lantern is included to show that before kerosene, there were whale oil lanterns used for heat. The cast lid has the wording: ARNOLD'S COMBINED STOVE & LANTERN PATENTED APRIL 11 1854 MANUFACTURED AT MIDDLE HADDAM CT.

When the handle is folded down, it forms a rack about ½" above the top surface. The lantern appears to have had little, if any, use with the tin parts retaining their original Japanned finish.

An 1892 advertisement for the heater (b) on a square base is shown on page 340 in OL-1, and I have seen a third design. The stamped label reads:

FALLS HEATER
PAT. FEB, 23. 1882
BOSTON. MASS.

Whether or not they were successful in operation, they were apparently successfully marketed.

The only markings on the heavy copper and brass center draft lamp are the words U. S. ELECTRIC LAMP on the filler cap. This was just another attempt to capitalise upon the word "electric" at that time. Truth in advertising was ignored.

*b. The Patent Falls heater.*

# Cooking
# With Kerosene

a. Florence Lamp Stove trade card.

b. Back of Florence card (a).

(a) Father Charlie portrayed on a Florence trade card.

"Charlie, what should we do without this dear little Florence stove." Yes indeed, Charlie, what would people have done without lamp stoves and chimney top heaters. They would have had to rely upon the hearth or cook-stove which were not always lit, especially during the summer. Those who could afford it had summer kitchens built at the back of the house.

Cast-iron table-top kerosene stoves had many advantages. They were much safer than the common chimney-top heaters that had only a glass chimney for support and were considered a lamp accessory. They were also much more substantial than those which were fastened to a lamp burner. In addition the larger models were a good substitute for a full-size wood or coal cook stove with an oven.

Most examples had mica windows to monitor the flame and to provide additional light. Charlie would have appreciated that advantage.

d. Stove marked UNION/C. O. & G. S. CO / GARDNER MASS. USA.

There were two basic types. The smallest ones (a) and (b) which included those with a handle for carrying about, consisted of a cast-iron font or reservoir with one to four burners and metal chimneys. Cooking utensils were placed upon an open grid supported by a cast-iron framework.

The larger table-top models usually had a flat surface with stove lids similar to those used on full-size cook stoves. Those were considerably less portable, but could be moved from kitchen to porch without too much difficulty. Cast-iron stands were available for some of these stoves.

The Florence Machine Company, Florence, Mass., was a major manufacturer of kerosene stoves and sewing machines. Pages from their 1885 catalogue reproduced here not only illustrate several models but provide information about their many uses, finishes, and prices. It appears they were most popular between 1875 and 1890.

Although it was generally the smaller models that were advertised as lamp stoves, this was the classification for all of the patents I researched, probably because they evolved from a kerosene lamp.

c. Florence trade card. McGurk collection.

# Florence Kerosene Stoves in Canada

This catalogue indicates Florence stoves were imported into Canada by the E. & C. Gurney Co., Toronto, a well-known Canadian manufacturer. I also have a twentieth century catalogue advertising "Gurney-Oxford" kerosene stoves and heaters. They were made of black Japan sheet metal, white enamelled steel with nickel-plated trim. These they state were "Made in Canada by Canadian Workmen in a Canadian Plant." They were widely used in homes and summer cottages until electricity arrived.

From the complexity of the models it is obvious that they tried to anticipate every possible requirement the housewife could desire.

**No. 3 Florence Cook, with Extension Top "E," Cast Iron Dinner Pot, Patent Jacketed Sauce Pan and Coffee Pot.**

**No. 4 Florence Favorite Cook, with Extension Top "J," and two Flat Heaters.**
The most desirable Laundry Stove for a large amount of work.

**No. 3 Florence Hurricane Cook, with Extension Top "J," Cast Iron Dinner Pot, Large Oven, and Jacketed Tea Kettle.**

This Stove will burn steadily in a strong draft of air, and work in such exposed places with *better success* than any other Oil Stove.

With this Extension Top you can boil a dinner in a 7-inch Cast Iron Dinner Pot; bake at the same time, and cook with jacketed furniture on the Oven.

Our Large Oven is 20 inches long, and will bake four large pies or round tins of biscuit at one baking.

# "Dietz" Stoves,
# Heaters, and Fireplaces

In the 1880s Dietz & Co. offered kerosene stoves that looked like full-size cookstoves, kerosene heaters that looked like parlor stoves and kerosene fireplaces that were intended for use as heaters or stoves. They had mica panels to provide light and create the ambience of another fuel source. Their basic No. 4 Tubular Oil Stove with its 22 parts plus a steam cooker must have thrilled many a housewife who had been accustomed to tending a coal or wood fire.

A slightly smaller No. 3 model was claimed to have been awarded the highest premium over all competitors at Cincinnati Exposition, the New Jersey State Fair, the American Institute Fair, and several other county fairs throughout the United States.

The word "tubular" appears on every catalogue illustration and up to three patent dates are visible on many. The patents related primarily to the drafts created by the design. They were all granted to John H. Irwin of Morton, Pa. This was the same J.H. Irwin that designed the flanged air intake used on the Dietz lantern on page 171. For that invention his residence was listed at Philadelphia.

"Dietz" New No. 4 Steam Cooker, for "Dietz" No 4 Tubular Oil Stove, . . . . $2 50

## "Dietz" No. 4 Tubular Oil Stove.

No 4 Stove, (Improved) with four 4-inch Burners.

*b.*

## "Dietz" No. 4 Tubular Oil Stove.

No. 4 Stove, (Improved) with four 4-inch Burners.

### PRICE.

| | | |
|---|---|---:|
| No. 4 Tubular Oil Stove, each, | | $13 00 |
| " Oven with two Pans, " | | 3 00 |
| " Broiler, " | | 1 00 |
| " Iron Heater, " | | 50 |
| Crated complete, | | $17 50 |
| Iron Stand on Rollers for No. 4 Stove (16 in. high), each | | 2 25 |
| Kettles and Sauce Pan, each, | | 90 |
| Stove Wicks, 4-inch, per doz., | | 50 |

7

*a.*

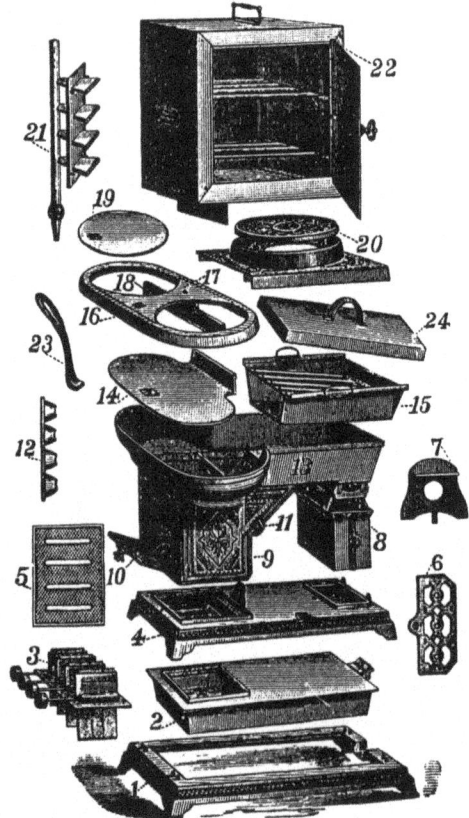

DIAGRAM showing parts of No. 4 Stove.

*c.*

a.

b. *Dietz No. 2 Fire Place Heater dated.*

c. *Dietz No. 2 Fire Place Heater undated.*

No. 2 Fire Place Heater.   Two 4-inch Burners.

d.

The ornate Tubular Parlor Heater above would be very impressive with a yellow flame illuminating the mica windows. One would certainly command attention today. The Fireplace Heaters are the only Dietz models extant that I know of. Two different models are shown in (b) and (c).

The example (b) appears to be the same as the No. 2 model shown in (d). I am aware of about six of these models and expect more have been saved. The example (c) is undated and there are several differences that suggest it was an earlier model.

The air screen and draft deflector arrangements of the upper hearths are very different. In (c) the draft deflector is an integral part of the upper hearth which is bolted to the main stove body. This would make the removal of soot considerably more difficult. The end mica panels are screwed in place; therefore to light the wicks, the screws would have to be removed or the entire upper hearth and stove body would have to be lifted off.

In the catalogue it was noted that the #2 model (d) was suitable for alcoves, conservatories, offices, bath, bed, and sitting rooms. It was claimed to heat an ordinary sized room, produce a bright light, heat a kettle, and warm the feet!

*a. Trade card promoting Mrs. Potts sad iron.*

*b. Summer Girl single burner kerosene heater.*

# Kerosene Heaters

Mary Florence Potts was not only one of the few female inventors of the nineteenth century, but also a highly successful one. The name "sad iron" evolved from a word that meant heavy and became a generic term for irons . It was the detachable cool wooden handle that could be easily transferred to another heated iron that was the significant feature of her invention. As the iron in use cooled, others were reheated. Slight pressure on the knob released the iron and connected it to another.

This is a popular iron with today's collectors, especially when paired with the working toy model for mother's helper. The large iron is marked as follows with raised letters:

H. R. IVES. & CO. MONTREAL
NO. 55 / SIZE
MRS POTTS. IRON PATENT GROUND

This is an example of a kerosene heater introduced on page 222. Although the portability aspect must have been an important feature, not all of them were provided with handles. This example with the name Summer Girl applied with a transfer has a single wick and a mica window that would be useful to view the flame and perhaps offer a little light. It has the following information cast on the top of the base:

PAT'D DEC 26 1898
THE TAYLOR & BOGGS FDY CO
CLEVELAND
NO. 1
SUMMER GIRL

Large heaters specifically designed to accommodate several irons were also made.

# ⊗ Accessories and Novelties

These are the items that round out a kerosene lighting collection. They add another dimension and help us to understand other aspects of day to day living during this period.

In situations without ambient light such as a dark cloudy night in areas where artificial illumination is absent, the amount of light provided by a cigarette lighter would be of some use. Such a meagre light was enough to qualify similar inventions as lamps. One of these was illustrated in OL-1 p. 58 (c). Another is the example (a) that is marked under the cover WATCH POCKET LAMP-FOLMER & SCHWING M'F'G' CO PAT. JUNE. 23. JULY. 21. 91-N.Y.

A round wick fed by a small font is ignited by a spark generated by a flint. The flints are mounted on a cardboard disk that is advanced when the imitation winder is pushed. In addition this motion opens the watch, advances the disk with the flints, creates a spark and the lamp is lit. The invention specifications do refer to it as a lamp or lighter. The two patents for this novelty item were granted to William F. Folmer of New York who assigned it to the manufacturing company.

*a. Watch pocket lamp.*

*b. Lamp interior.*

*c. Make-do lamp.*

When there was a problem with a lamp and a solution was found, the resultant creation is known today as a make-do. In the case of (c) the problem was not with the burner or with the lamp, but rather with the combination of the two. The lamp was made at a time when much narrower lip burners were used, and the longer shaft of the prong burner meant the thumbwheel could not clear the handle of the lamp.

The owner was able to make it work by clipping off a large portion of the thumbwheel and grinding down a portion of the handle. The thumbwheel still does not clear the handle, however it will rotate and slide over the handle.

*a. Shield and Star make-do lamp.*

# Make-do's

Make-do creations were not restricted to lighting, although it was a favourite subject for frugal and imaginative minds. Recycle and reuse may be new terms but they are not new concepts. Example (a) was perhaps the most direct method of transforming a stand lamp with a broken base into a functional hand lamp. An almost amusing attempt was made to enhance it by giving it a coat of red paint.

Bases of broken lamps like (b) were often transformed into pincushions. This was where the housewives could demonstrate their creativity. This is apparent in the many examples found in collections today.

A ceramic drawer knob, washers, and a nut and bolt were used to solve the problem of a broken peg in example (c). Perhaps glue was also used to seal this arrangement or possibly plaster of Paris was relied upon to prevent leaking. On the other hand, since this is the way it was found, it may simply represent a well-meaning but unsuccessful attempt to repair a broken peg.

Practicality appears to have been the only concern when it came to extending the life of the late nineteenth century lamp (d). It is neither pretty nor pleasing but would be quite adequate for the workshop or basement.

Much of the charm of the make-do is the skill and imagination (or lack thereof) used in solving the problem. The examples shown here exhibit everything from fine craftsmanship to apparently reaching for the closest objects at hand to extend the life of a broken lamp.

*b. Pincushion with lamp base.*

*c. Lamp peg repair.*

*d. A practical solution.*

# Thrift and Conservation

In the nineteenth century, thrift and conservation were practised in middle and upper middle class households, as well as in the homes of the poor. They were considered virtues to be encouraged by good wives and husbands and were not looked upon as a status symbols.

Lamps (e) and (f) have had their use extended by replacing broken bases with apparently discarded parts. The Hobbs Wheeling Panelled font (e) still retains its patented connector (see p .116 (a)). This proved to be useful to connect it to the inverted B&H font holder from a bracket or hanging lamp. An inverted bowl (h) in the Feather or McKee's Doric pattern with a broken foot proved to be a good replacement part. The lamp font appears to be a rather crude example of the one pictured in OL-1 on page 104 (f).

The examples (g) and (h) below are outstanding examples of craftsmanship and imagination. They were obviously made by someone who either owned or had access to a workshop equipped with the tools required to produce a professional appearance. The font (g) may have been from a late composite lamp with a damaged base. It has been skilfully encased in a combined metal frame and base. The base itself may have had a former use. It is likely the turned font holder (h) was created to hold a broken font and possibly to appease a chagrined housewife or servant. With its interesting contours and turret top, it may have been as successful as the original lamp.

The creator of (i) has made a serious but rather crude attempt to extend the life of a Ring Punty lamp. It is not possible to determine what form of stem is concealed by the pieces of oak that are held together by fine copper wires, without taking everything apart. The base is cast iron and the repair was all originally painted blue. The final result is a charming primitive lamp that shows the maker adhered to the premise " It's not what you've got that counts — it's what you do with what you've got!"

*e. Font holder base.*

*f. Broken bowl base.*

*g. Metal frame holder.*

*h. Wooden holder.*

*i. Wood and metal base.*

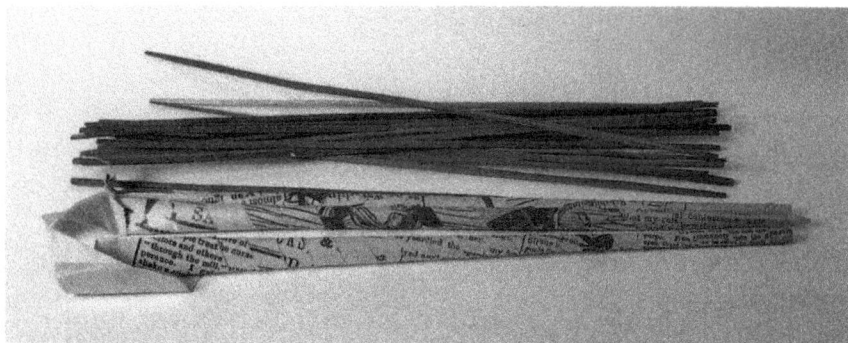

*a. Splints and spills.*

*b. Early wooden matches.*

## Matches and Match Holders

It was a simple matter to transfer a flame from the fireplace or stove using splints or spills, illustrated above, to a nearby candle or lamp. They could be made at home, thereby saving the cost of matches. Today, newspaper spills are routinely fashioned in historic homes open to the public.

The loose matches and their flimsy paper package that have survived well over a century are reminders that matches themselves are a subject to explore. The scored flat wood blocks of matches are the forerunner of the book matches used today.

Match holders (c) and (d) below are patent dated June 13, 1876. This refers to a patent obtained by mold maker Washington Beck of Pittsburgh for a mold to produce match holders and objects of a similar shape.

## Glass Match Holders

In his patent Beck illustrates the example (d) pictured here. He does not describe or name it, but states that the design will form the subject matter of a separate application. I don't know if this was ever done. Such a design patent is not listed as having been granted to Beck in 1875-76 or in 1877 in the United States Patent Office Indexes. In his book *Glass Patents and Patterns*, Dr. Peterson gives the holder the appropriate name Jester. The invention patent essentially describes a mold for a match holder having a flat side with a hole in it.

An article by Mary and Bill Wollett in the July 1984 issue of *Hobbies Magazine* named the match holder (c) as Columbia, whom they describe as the female personification of the United States. Apparently the face of the match holder has also been described as Jenny Lind, the famous songstress. Perhaps some primary source information will surface to confirm an original name.

The match holder (e) below with a Daisy and Button pattern was made for many years. The one shown here is amber, and it has also been seen in blue usually called sapphire, in yellow called canary, and in clear colorless glass called crystal. These were also the most common colors of all-glass lamps.

*c. Columbia or Jenny Lind.*

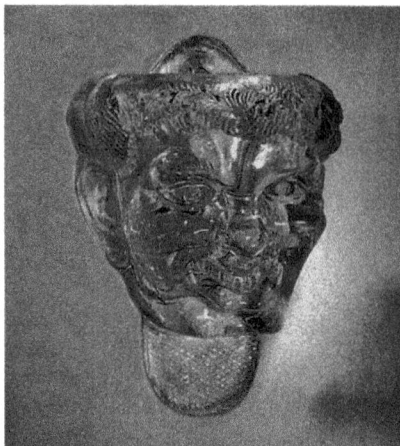

*d. Jester match holder.*

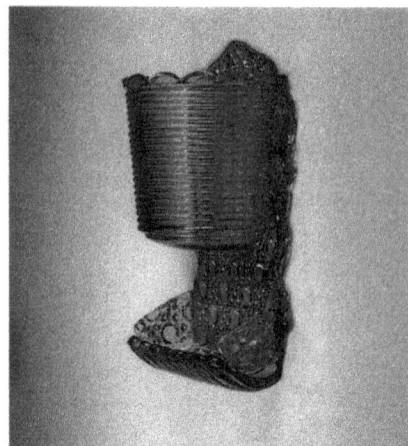

*e. Daisy and Button match holder.*

# Metal Match Holders

Cast iron and tin were the most common metals used, and today cast iron is the most popular. The two examples (f) and (g) are almost identical and were likely made by the same company. The second one was customised for a client who apparently felt it was unnecessary to include the name of the town or city. Perhaps it can be identified if the address still exists. It is marked:

J. H. HARTKE
HARDWARE DEALER
N. E. CORNER 8th & MAIN STS
LOCKSMITHING AND BELL-
HANGING.

The popular example (h) is called the Devil or Mephistopheles by the more sophisticated collectors. All match holders have a rough, textured surface to strike matches. On this holder it surrounds the face.

It is surprising that such a small percentage of match holders provide a receptacle for spent matches. This conjures up an image of guests casually casting their eyes about to spot an acceptable place to dispose of matches. If ash trays or fireplaces were in the room, they could relax. Double match holders like (i) held both new and used matches.

The cast iron acorn match holder (j) has a copper finish and a transfer medallion on the front. The top of the acorn remains in a fixed position while the body, pivoted at the sides, can be tipped to reveal a supply of matches. The striker is at the front of the base. A patent was obtained in the 1860s for this match holder. Many patents were issued for these popular accessories between 1860 and 1900.

This boot match holder (k) has long been one of the most popular among collectors. Some match holders have been reproduced, including this one, and there could be variations in the castings when the molds were reproduced.

f. *Unmarked cast-iron holder.*

g. *Signed match holder.*

h. *Devil match holder.*

i. *Double match holder.*

j. *Acorn match holder.*

k. *Boot match holder.*

*a. Victorian bugs and insects, all match holders, in conference.*

*b. Ruby float lamp.*

Ivy or Flower Stands.

*c. Ivy or plant stand.*

# Victorian Accessories

In keeping with the Victorian fascination with real and imaginary creatures, these accessories were made to add an amusing touch to a room. I thought that to be the case until I encountered a live one like the beetles on the left. It was in the unlikely location beside my parking meter on Queen Street in downtown Toronto. A small crowd gathered and after much discussion, concluded that it must be of foreign origin. Now I wonder why they had an appeal as a decorative element when the real ones were so repulsive.

In their July 1873 catalogue, Bradley & Hubbard advertised a "Beetle Bug Match Safe" like those on the left and a "Large Fly Match Safe" similar to those illustrated. Matches were concealed in the stomach cavity below the wings, and the striker was on the underside.

The long winged creature is also a container. The beetles on the left are about 3½" long, and the cast iron has a bronze finish, adding a touch of realism.

A copper snake (b) is used to suspend a ruby glass float lamp. The slotted copper shield protected the flame. This is clearly a float lamp and the resemblance to the ivy and flower stands (c) and (d) is obvious. Float lamps consist of a wick supported by cork or some flotation material, usually on a layer of oil floating on water. These can be purchased today, and they are still used in temples. Often several are floated in a single container.

Any container could be used, however the ruby one (b) is the only single one that I have seen specifically designed as a float lamp. The B&H and similar stands usually include some sort of flower motif. These were once described in lighting books as float lamps, and the reputation persists in some areas.

Victorian vases and flower stands are always in demand by flower arrangers. They only require a few sprigs to brighten up a side or breakfast table. The reference to ivy is interesting. It was a favourite Victorian plant because it could tolerate near freezing temperatures, and this was important when not all rooms were kept at what we now call "room temperature."

*d. Flower holder.*

*a. Fifield's lamp chimney.*

Several of these combination chimney and cast-iron stove plates have survived until today, indicating a measure of success. The components are heavier than most other chimney-top heaters. Nevertheless it would require a substantial burner and lamp to support a kettle or pot filled with food or water on the 4½" top. This was mentioned in the description.

The patent for this device was granted to Henry S. Fifield of New Hampton, New Hampshire, on January 29, 1878. Fifield claimed his lamp-chimney was provided with a flat ring with grooves extending radially entirely across the surface. He further stated, "It will be readily understood that, when this chimney is in use, and a vessel placed upon it, the heated air and products of combustion within the chimney will impinge against the bottom of the vessel and pass along the same, following the grooves, and ascend around the sides of the vessel. It will also be understood that this chimney may be adapted for use with a great variety of lamps, or with gas-tubes, without departing from the spirit of my invention." Height is 6¾".

The undated Collins-type burner has a convex thumb-wheel marked Chamberlain & Smith in raised letters. Height of the chimney heater 6¾".

*b. Curling tong or iron heater and detail.*

Although the chimney above was found blackened with use (or misuse), the label was preserved. It has the following information: MACBETH CO. / PEARL TOP / PITTS-BURGH U.S.A. / PAT. OCT. 30th. 1883. I was unable to locate a Macbeth patent for October 30, however they did register a trade mark on that date. The label surrounds the opening around the iron tube that passes through the chimney. It provides additional information, but unfortunately not a date. The top of the burner is marked NEW CALCIUM LIGHT BURNER 1870.

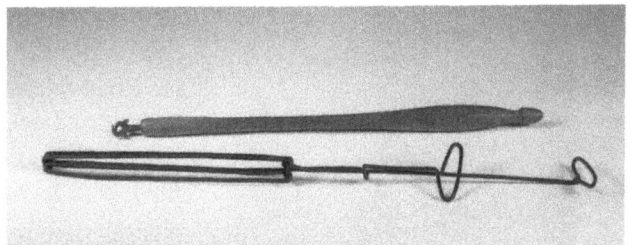

*c. Chimney cleaning devices.*

These are two examples of devices intended to make the daily task of cleaning sooty chimneys easier by holding cloths or papers. Several variations were patented.

*a. Jointed curling tongs.*

*b. Magnifying lens.*

*c. Chimney tidy.*

*d. Home-made safety cage for lamps.*

(a)  Articulated curling tongs had two advantages. They could easily be heated in a readily available lamp chimney and could be folded to be carried in a purse.

(b)  Lenses were used in many ways to magnify a kerosene lamp flame. Some were hung around a chimney, some were incorporated within a chimney, some were fastened to the collar and others could be attached to the burner. One named "The Little Light Increaser" was widely advertised.

(c)  The crocheted chimney tidy allowed the conscientious housewife to give a presentable appearance to a sooty chimney until she or her servants had time to clean it.

(d)  The ever-present danger of knocking over a lighted lamp must have been of great concern to every household with very young or elderly family members. A framework such as the above could be very useful for avoiding accidents. Height of the frame is approximately 13".

LUX·DUX BURNERS

# Burners and Trimmings

These words commonly described the parts above the collar that were either included or priced separately. The Lux-Dux advertisement is a vivid reminder that the domed top of a burner was called a cone. Here they were advertising a burner with three cones in an eye-catching manner.

Although books and articles have described many important burners, there are many more to discover and research. The inventors, their patents, the manufacturers, and the burners can all be factored into the history of this subject. There exists an abundance of primary source information for those who have the time and inclination to explore this challenging area.

An illustrated article published in the *Scientific American* Vol. VIII, No. 24, June 13, 1863 describes the operations involved in manufacturing burners at the City Manufacturing Company. An example of a burner made by this company is pictured on the font on p. 179 (a). It is dated March 3, 1863 and includes the company name. This refers to the patent for the arrangement of perforations in a burner base and cone. The patent No. 37845 was granted to W. H. Smith of New York City. One might wonder if there was any connection with the Mr. L. C. Smith who was head of the department at the City Manufacturing Company.

Another early lip burner marked City Mfg. Co. is in the Mackenzie House Museum, the restored home of the first Mayor of Toronto. It has other dates marked on the thumbwheel. They are Dec. 3, 1861, Sept. 16, 1862, and Aug. 9, 1864. These dates all relate to two patents and a reissue that were issued to Charles W. Cahoon of Portland, Maine, and yet this burner does not resemble the popular Cahoon burners illustrated in the Dietz and Lovell catalogues. See the example on p. 212 (e).

The City Mfg. Co. was located in the Benedict & Burnham Company factory in Waterbury, Conn. The explanation for this situation was perhaps given in this item reported in the *Crockery & Glass Journal*, August 12, 1875. "The Benedict & Burnham Manufacturing Company has from time to time become the parent of several other joint stock companies. Whenever a branch of its business could be better carried on by itself, the property necessary for its prosecution was detached and distributed as a dividend to its stockholders, in the form of stock in a new company, and many of the enterprises of Waterbury originated in this manner."

## KEROSENE LAMP BURNERS

This department is under the direction of Mr. L. C. Smith, who has made some very valuable improvements in the machinery contained in his rooms. It is a remarkable feature in favor of the adoption of machinery generally, that a kerosene lamp-burner which is sold for a quarter of a dollar, goes through one hundred and eleven distinct operations before it is completed. All of these details are not, as many persons would suppose, done by boys or unskilled labor; but a majority of the artizans are, we were informed, paid high wages, and the only reason that the burners and lamp fixtures generally can be made at such low rates is that new and improved tools were employed, which rapidly strike up the articles in question. We have thought it not inappropriate to reproduce here facsimiles of the principle operations performed on a lamp-burner; we must omit some, however, as our space is limited. That so ornate and useful an article should require so much labor seems almost incredible, in view of the low price at which it is sold. NO. 1, is a round thin disk of brass, about two-thirds the actual size; is a blank for the burner body. This blank, after being cut out, is taken to a drop press and formed up by a die into the shape shown in Fig. 2; in another die it is formed as at Fig. 3; and into still another as at Fig. 4. The blank is now slightly thinner than it was and is much harder. The squared shoulder is that part which is screwed into the lamp; and the flanch will afterwards receive the crenulated edge, as in Fig. 5; this is done in a machine provided with dies working very rapidly. The burner body is now approaching its shape, but it must be still further elaborated. There are no air-holes in it, and the scalloped edge we have just seen cut out stands horizontally with the burner, instead of vertically. The body in its present condition is taken to another press and formed up into the shape shown at Fig. 6, and the reader will see that the scalloped edge has also been erected during this operation. The burner is now passed along to a youth, who sits at a punching machine which works at a great speed, he places the burner body on a projecting position of the press, and the punches crush through the hard metal with a crisp sound, and showers the bright little pieces all about. The burner now passes into the hands of another person who puts it into the press again in still another die, and turns it out in the state shown by Fig. 7. The thread has now to be cut on it; for this purpose it goes to a man stationed at a lathe; the burner body is stuck on a swiftly revolving chuck, and chased almost as rapidly as they can be taken up and laid down. It is noticeable that the threads are not formed up, as are some, but are cleanly cut with a sharp tool, thus making much better work. The burner body is now given to another individual at a press, who cuts out at one blow the slot made for the wick tube. The body is now in comparatively a finished state; there are many other minor operations to be done, such as cleansing it with acid, pushing holes in it for the apparatus that holds the chimney in place, &c., it has also to be lacquered or given that shiny yellow appearance which cause it to look as if polished.

The lacquer is simply shellac varnish, applied with a brush by a young woman who sits at a table heated by steam. Before this person there is a revolving wooden chuck in which she sticks the burner; the brush is just held on the brass as it revolves, and it is then thrown upon an endless apron that passes over the steam-pipes. The table is made just long enough to allow the lacquer to dry in its passage over it, and as the burner tumbles off at the further end it is ready for packing. To the body belongs the cone, the wick-tube, the apparatus for managing the wick, and the chimney attachments. The cone is also made out of a blank which is cut and "drawn up" in a die at one operation; this is the blank. (Fig. 1.) After this process is completed it is again formed in another die to the shape shown at Fig. 2. The air-holes at the base are punched by a separate operation. Fig. 3 brings the cone nearer to its final form, and the operation is performed like the others which preceded it, in a die operated by a stamp or a drop press; it is then taken to a machine and is cut out on top for the reception of the wick and to allow the flame to pass; after seeing it burnished on one end and lacquered, we may leave it and proceed to examine the wick-tube.

Here is the blank from which it is made (Fig. 4), also drawn and cut out by one operation. It has no resemblance whatever to a tube, but it will at no distant period confine the wick that draws the oil from the reservoir below; by whose light the reader possible peruses these lines. No. 5 is the first stage, No. 6 the next, and so on consecutively up to the 8th and last; in all these operations the tube has been drawn up, little by little, until it attained the proper shape. It has still to be cut out for the reception of the little spurs which stick into the meshes of the wick and raise or lower it. The spurs themselves are punched out of a brass strip, and the hole in them is not square or round, but is a circle with a segment of it struck off on one side; this leaves a flat place; the shaft which goes through the spurs has also a flat place left on it, and the shaft being forced into the spurs secures them rigidly in place. It is of great importance that these details should be well done, mechanically, since they are not easily repaired when once out of order without a great deal of trouble. We have thus given an idea of the

manner in which a kerosene lamp fixtures (sic) are made. Our account is necessarily discursive in character, as to name and describe separately each of the one hundred and eleven different operations which would involve repetitions not interesting to the general reader. The division of labor and the substitution of mechanical for manual processes alone render the company able to afford the burners at remunerative prices. Some of the most ingenious machinery we ever saw was employed in producing these burners...

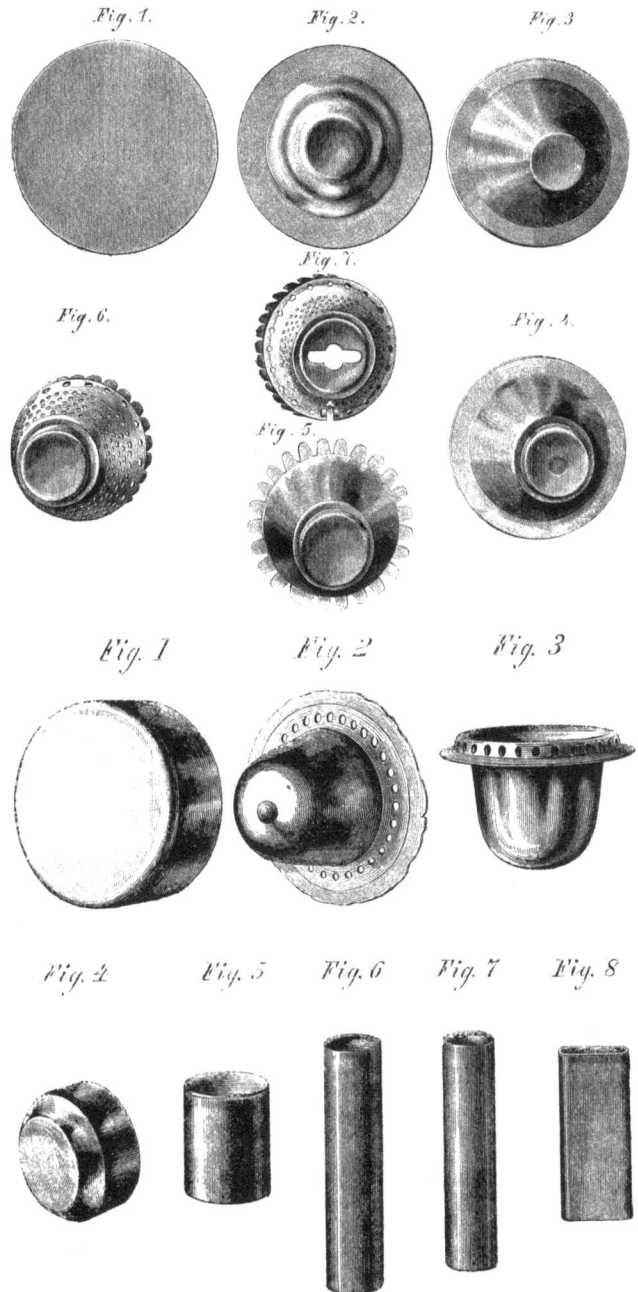

*The top group of figures is reduced about 20% and the bottom group is approximately the same size as the the original printed copy.*

## COLLIN'S PATENT IMPROVED
# NON-EXPLOSIVE SUN BURNER.

This Burner has been greatly improved in its construction, and is now offered as the very best in the market. The Tube being made of thick, heavy metal, and solid drawn, keeps the wick more secure and steady, and the whole Burner firmer and not liable to get out of order. The Tube, being shorter than formerly, causes the flame to draw the oil much lower in the Lamp, at the same time producing a brilliant light.

The Cone and Disc are easily detached from the Tube, as seen in the cut, so that the wick can be easily and properly trimmed, also making it more convenient for lighting, cleaning, &c.

It is simply constructed, and the draft so arranged as to prevent the parts contiguous to the oil from becoming heated to cause the generation of gas, therefore it is *non-explosive*.

The Cone or Diaphragm being more oval than formerly, the Chimneys are less liable to break. It saves one-third in oil, for the reason that no light is hidden below the metallic cone, therefore the whole light is obtained, clear white and cheerful. Light oils can be burned in this Lamp with perfect safety.

**Price 30cts. per doz. additional, Net.** PARK'S PATENT AIR TUBES applied to the No. 1 Sun Burner, renders the combustion more perfect, and completely obviates the smoking and breaking of Chimneys.

DIRECTIONS FOR TRIMMING.—Take off the Umbrella Cone, and trim the Wick level with the top of the Tube, without clipping the corners, and you will have a splendid flame. When placing on, or removing the Chimney, tip the Chimney to one side, so that the pressure will come on one side of the spring. To extinguish the light turn the wick down—never blow it out.

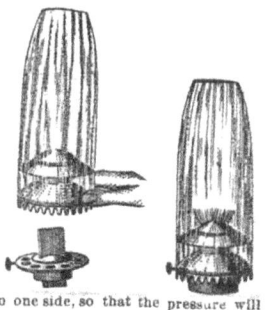

*a. 1869 advertisement in the Ansonia Brass & Copper Co's trade publication.*

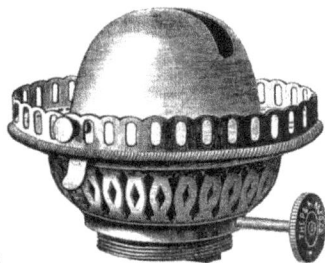

*b.*

**UNIQUE LIP BURNER**

*c.*

**BANNER BURNER**

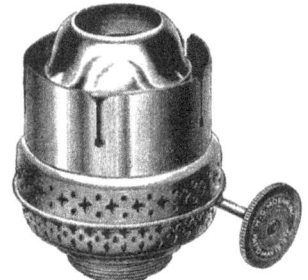

*d.*

**MOEHRING ARGAND BURNER**

# Chimneys and Burners

Chimneys and burners were most commonly described as slip or lip. These apt descriptions determined by the shape of the chimney are simple and easy to use today. The lower end of a slip chimney is straight and cylindrical. It is supported on the inside, the outside, or a combination of both. Prongs, most often referred to as springs in patents, were the most common arrangement. The second method of securing straight-sided chimneys was that used in the Collins and other burners that provided pressure to the inside of the chimneys. Much less popular were burners that supported the chimney both internally and externally.

Chimneys with a flange or flared base were called lip chimneys. The burners that held them in place with a clip or set screw were called lip burners. Lip chimneys and burners were used at the beginning of this period and the larger slip combinations date from the mid 1860s. Burners (b), (c), and (d) were manufactured by The Plume & Atwood Manufacturing Company and were sold throughout the world. Today the round wick Argand burners, especially those combined with shade holders, are more difficult to find.

The F. H. Lovell Co. catalogue illustrates cylindrical slip chimneys were used with both early all-glass and composite lamps into the late 1870s. They were advertised as sun or comet chimneys and came in three sizes that could be nested for shipping. The name sun became popular to describe other chimneys, burners, and just about anything associated with lighting. The cylindrical ones are not as graceful as lip chimneys, however they are more readily available and are definitely appropriate. Slip chimneys in other shapes were also used with Argand and with flat wick, prong, and gallery-type burners. The prong type burner was certainly the most commonly used, and today it is the most common type found.

Also in this catalogue both the Atterbury OK[ON] and Buckle patterns can be recognised. The all-glass example with a cable design in the stem provides a means to identify other Atterbury lamps with this base.

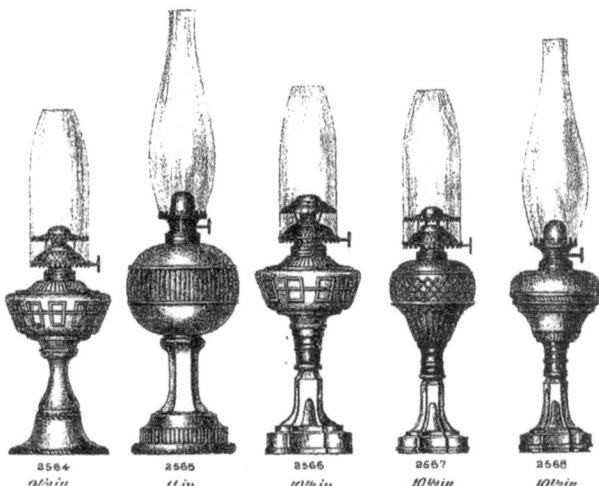

2564
2565
2566
2567
2568

F. H. Lovell & Co. 1877-78 Catalogue.
*Courtesy The Sandwich Historical Society Glass Museum.*

# Prong Burners

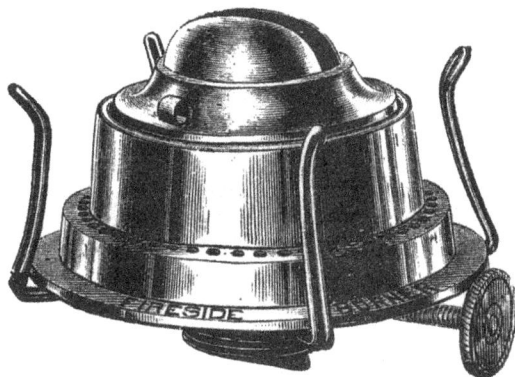

## FIRESIDE BURNER

The most readily available kerosene burners today are the prong burners. They are also the appropriate choice for most of the available lamps and chimneys. In the quest for examples of lip burners during the past decade, little attention has been given to prong burners. A number of years ago I decided to examine boxes containing hundreds of burners that came with lamps acquired in Canada for *Oil Lamps 1&2*. It is likely that they were almost all made in the United States although some are stamped with Canadian names.

After sorting the burners according to manufacturers, they could be put in order. This was done according to patent dates and the quality of materials and manufacture. The Plume and Atwood (P&A) prong burners starting with their best quality Fireside burners introduced in 1873 was chosen for this report. As with most of the prong burner manufacturers, the quality declined as the century came to a close. There were, however, innovations introduced along the way. Scoville burners were found with 52 variations. Some of these were probably twentieth century models.

A flyer, circa 1880, that advertised Plume & Atwood burners claimed that over twelve million of "The Old and Original Fireside" burners had been sold. They claimed, "These Burners are constructed with a close cone, perforated in such a manner that the air supply to the flame is always the same, producing the most perfect combustion, at the same time a large white light, with any of the shapes of Sun Chimneys."

Also advertised in the same flyer were two other successful P&A burners shown opposite. One was the Unique burner for Sun Hinge chimneys. This had springs that were "so constructed that they can be lighted and trimmed without removing the globe or chimney." These were particularly useful for bracket and hanging lamps. The other example was their Astral Argand Burner.

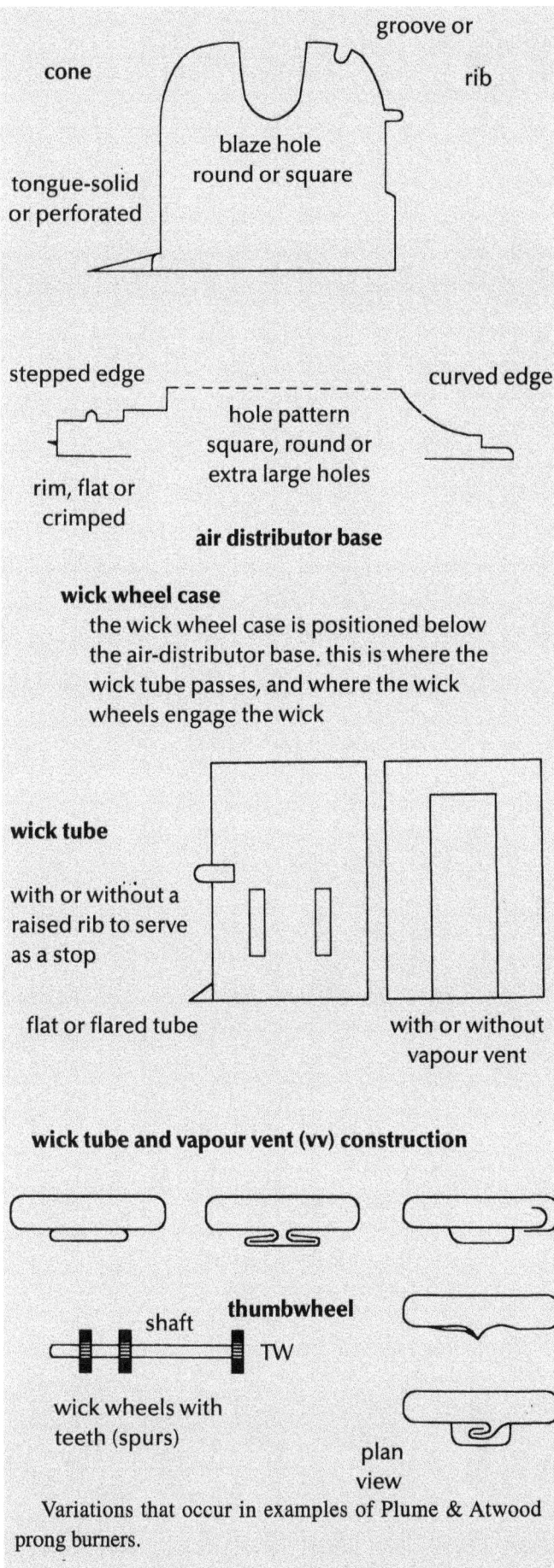

cone

groove or rib

blaze hole round or square

tongue-solid or perforated

stepped edge

curved edge

hole pattern square, round or extra large holes

rim, flat or crimped

**air distributor base**

**wick wheel case**
the wick wheel case is positioned below the air-distributor base. this is where the wick tube passes, and where the wick wheels engage the wick

**wick tube**

with or without a raised rib to serve as a stop

flat or flared tube

with or without vapour vent

**wick tube and vapour vent (vv) construction**

**thumbwheel**

shaft

TW

wick wheels with teeth (spurs)

plan view

Variations that occur in examples of Plume & Atwood prong burners.

# Plume & Atwood Prong Burners Basic Construction

Not illustrated is the wick-wheel or ratchet case that was made in many shapes. It is the section through which the wick tube passes and the wick wheel spurs engage the wick. It is connected to the air-distributor base and prongs by various methods; some of which were detailed in patents.

There were essentially two types of basic construction:

Type 1. These have wick-wheel case extensions that serve as braces. They are soldered to the outer edge of the air-distributor plate where double wire prongs are threaded through slits.

The rim of the wick-case cap is slit or divided and folded over the wick case horizontal lip. Many have a small separate division folded parallel to the wick tube (vertically), above one or both ends of the wick wheel shaft for stability. A few have the end of a wide section bent down for the same purpose.

Type 2. With two exceptions, all other P&A prong burners examined have a variety of prongs that are bent around the edge of the air-distributor plate or chimney rim and continue into the wick-wheel case, clamped between the case and the case cap. The wick-wheel cap extensions form braces that are clamped around the prongs and are fastened next to the chimney rim with two tabs. These are inserted through slits and are folded upwards toward the draft-deflector cone. One exception has a single tab, and some Model burners have two outwardly facing tabs.

The over three hundred P&A burners collected were found to have the following thumbwheel markings. Where there are markings in two rings they are distinguished by (or) for outer ring or (ir) for the inner ring. Starting with a heavier weight brass, the quality gradually diminished as thinner brass plated burners were introduced. A magnet is useful for detecting non-brass burner parts.

1. PAT NOV 26.72  PAT FEB 11.73
2. PAT JAN 16.83 & FEB 11.73
3. P&A. CO. / PAT 1. 16.83 & 8.17.97
4. P&A. M. F. G. CO. / PAT JAN 16.83
5. OL. & L. CO — HAMILTON
6. BANNER. / ONT. L. CO.
7. — BANNER — / O. L. & L. CO.
8. ONT. L. C.O. / HAMILTON
9. (or) * BANNER * / P&A MFG. CO (ir) made in / U.S.A.
10. (recessed center) * BANNER * P & A MFG CO
11. ONT . L. CO / SUNLIGHT
12. * P & A MFG CO*/ MODEL (reverse) MADE IN USA*
13. (or) MODEL */ P&A. MFG. CO. (ir) MADE IN / U.S.A.
14. (or) * GLOBE* P&A. MFG. CO. (ir) MADE IN / U.S.A.
15. P & A. M' F'G. CO. / PAT JUNE 26. 94.
16. (OR) P&A. MFG CO. / WATERBURY CONN. (IR) MADE IN / U.S.A.
17. (OR) P&A. / DORSET DIV. THOMASTON. CONN. MADE IN / U.S.A.
18. EAGLE / PAT 1, 16, 88 & 8. 17. 97.
19. (or) * EAGLE * / P & A MFG CO (ir) MADE IN U.S.A.
20. (or) P&A. MFG. CO. / THOMASTON. CONN. (ir) MADE IN U.S.A.
21. (octagonal) Inscribed as No. 20 above.
22. (octagonal) DORSET DIV THOMASTON, CONN (ir) MADE IN U.S.A.
23. (octagonal) RISDON MFG. CO. DANBURY, CT. (ir) MADE IN U.S.A.

The following eight-prong designs were used on Plume and Atwood burners.

| | |
|---|---|
| 1. Two wire | 5. Flat strip |
| 2. Three wire | 6. Flat shaped |
| 3. Scored flat strip | 7. Perforated & shaped |
| 4. Wire with flat back | 8. Embossed design |

# Trimmings

One of the joys collectors experience today that homemakers would have known in the 1800s is trimming their lamps. The acquisition of a new part has the collector surveying all their lamps to determine which lamp would be most improved by the new part. The next step is to decide where the removed part should go. This can continue until a substantial part of the collection has been altered. In most instances the initial motivation for these exercises is to replicate the imagined original arrangement. It is known that unless a lamp was made with an original matching shade, appropriate choices can only be selected from trimmings made at the same period.

This situation gives collectors free rein to select and rearrange parts in order to give their collection a new and distinctive appearance. The fact that some 1860s parts such as burners and shade holders continued to be manufactured in the late 1870s and 1880s expands the time period that such parts can be considered appropriate. These include Holmes, Booth & Haydens' offerings of the Ne Plus Ultra burner, and early spring and set screw hinge burners. They also offered shade holders that were used in the 1860s. Bristol Brass and Clock offered "The New Dyott Burner" in the late 1870s although the illustration appeared to be the same as the Dyott burner patented in the early 1860s. Fireside and Collins type burners were still popular.

One significant part of the trimmings picture that is almost completely absent is the paper or silk shade. Paper was most popular in the 1860s and 1870s. Both shade holders extant and catalogue illustrations attest to their popularity. Most had printed designs and could be shipped flat.

It was the shades of the 1890s that presented a tour de force that characterised that extravagant lighting decade. Very few exist today, however many reproductions are offered in current magazines. Generally collectors prefer to use glass shades with their lamps but decorators might desire confections patterned after the example illustrated here or others shown in early advertisements or photographs.

From stand lamps to bracket lamps to hanging lamps, the available glass shades and smoke bells or saucers offer the collector an opportunity to personalise a lamp or fixture using most of the same choices that were available in the nineteenth century. This is one of the most satisfying aspects of collecting kerosene lighting. Another is to discover a proper chimney and burner combination and use it to complete a lamp.

Trade papers and magazines featured advertisements for lamp shades that reflected the fashions of the day. Fortunately, if we so desire, we have these examples to replicate long after the have original silks, satins, and laces have turned to dust.

*Advertisement in China Glass & Lamps, Pittsburgh, August 10, 1892.*
*Courtesy the Corning Museum of Glass.*

## ILLUMINATOR BASES.

| | Per doz. |
|---|---|
| 6 inch Illuminator to fit No. 1 Sun Burner | 1 00 |
| 7 inch Illuminator to fit No. 2 Sun Burner | 1 35 |
| 7 inch Illuminator to fit Royal Burner | 1 35 |
| 7 inch Illuminator to fit Grand Burner | 1 35 |

"D" or No. 2 Sun Illuminator Base.

## LANTERN AND STREET LAMP GLOBES.

| | |
|---|---|
| No. 0 Tubular Globe (the regular size) | 48 |
| No. 0 Tubular Globes by the barrel (5 doz.), 45c. doz. Barrel 35c. each. | |
| No. 1 Tubular Globe | 90 |
| No. 2 Tubular Globe | 5 00 |
| No. 3 Tubular Globe for No. 3 Street or Mill Lamp | 6 00 |
| No. 10 Tubular Globe | 55 |
| No. U. S. Tubular Globe | 55 |
| No. 0 Tubular Globe, Ruby Glass | 5 00 |
| No. 0 Tubular Globe, Blue Glass | 5 00 |
| No. 39 Railroad Lantern Globe | 90 |
| Brilliant Lantern Globe | 85 |
| Buckeye (Senior) Inside Globe | 55 |
| Buckeye (Senior) Outside Globe | 85 |
| Buckeye Nested (Senior) | 1 40 |

No. 0 Tubular Globe.

Reflector.

## SILVERED GLASS REFLECTORS.

| | |
|---|---|
| 6 inch Silver Glass Reflectors | 1 25 |
| 7 inch Silver Glass Reflectors | 1 50 |
| 8 inch Silver Glass Reflectors | 1 75 |
| 9 inch Silver Glass Reflectors | 2 00 |
| 10 inch Silver Glass Reflectors | 2 25 |
| 12 inch Silver Glass Reflectors | 3 25 |

For Tin Reflectors see page 251.

## THREE INCH PRISMS OR U DROPS.

| | Per 100. |
|---|---|
| 3 inch Crystal Rich Cut Glass Prisms | 2 50 |
| 3 inch Assorted Colors Cut Glass Prisms | 4 00 |

Jewels, Assorted Colors Cut Glass. These have a Crystal top part, same as shown in cut, with a Diamond shape cut piece attached, in assorted colors, and are intended to be used alternately with Prisms, thereby making a very pleasing effect. ............ 3 00

Prism.

Smoke Bell.
3 in. Smoke Bells, Opal, per doz.... 65 | 7 in. Smoke Saucers, Opal, per doz.. 1 75

Smoke Saucer.

a

## WHITE SHADES FOR TABLE AND LIBRARY LAMPS.

| | Per doz. |
|---|---|
| 6 inch Vienna | 90 |
| 7 inch Vienna or Dome Shade—Case lots 12 doz., 75c. No charge for case. | 1 00 |
| 7 inch Vienna or Dome Shade—Wide top for Sun Chimney | 1 00 |
| 10 inch Cone Shade | 2 50 |
| 10 inch Dome Shade | 3 50 |
| 14 inch Cone Shade (bbl. lots 1 doz., $2.75) | 3 25 |
| 14 inch Dome Shade (bbl. lots ⅝ doz., $4.50) | 5 00 |
| 10 inch Dome, French style tops | 3 50 |
| 10 inch Dome, Corrugated | 6 50 |

DOME

VIENNA

## TIN CORRUGATED SHADES OR REFLECTORS.

| | |
|---|---|
| 14 inch Tin Shade (see cut) Green Top | 2 75 |
| 20 inch Tin Shade (see cut) Green Top | 4 50 |

14 inch Tin Shade.

## DECORATED SHADES FOR TABLE AND LIBRARY LAMPS.

Less 10 per cent discount in original bbls.

| | |
|---|---|
| 7 inch Vienna or Dome—Flowers | 2 25 |
| 7 inch Vienna Green Shades | 4 50 |
| 7 inch Dome Pink Shades | 9 00 |
| 10 inch Cone Shades, Flowers, white ground | 75 |
| 10 inch Dome Shades, Flowers, tinted ground | 6 00 |
| 14 inch Cone Shades, Flowers | 4 75 |
| 14 inch Dome Plain, Flower dec | 7 00 |
| 14 inch Dome Plain, "A" assortment, Flowers | 00 |
| 14 inch Dome Shades, "B" assortment, tinted body, rich Flower decoration | 9 50 |
| 14 inch Dome Shades "D" assortment. Very richly tinted—summer scenes, pond lily scenes etc | 10 50 |
| 14 inch Amber or Blue Dew Drop. See cut | 9 00 |
| 14 inch Ruby Opalescent Dew Drop. See cut | 14 00 |

14 inch Dome Shade, Flower Decoration.

14 inch "Dew Drop" Dome.

| | Per doz. |
|---|---|
| No 1, 10 inch Paper Shades, assorted colors | 45 |
| No. 18, 10 inch Paper Shades, assorted colors | 65 |
| Comic, 10 inch Paper Shades, assorted colors | 75 |
| No. 633, 11 inch Paper Shades, assorted colors | 80 |
| Corrugated Dome, Paper Shades, assorted colors | 1 50 |

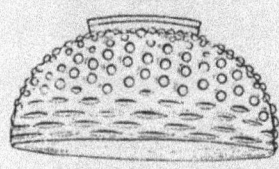

b

# Trimmings From the H. Leonard & Sons 1888 Catalogue

There is a wealth of information to be found in the few wholesale catalogue pages included here. They provide an insight into the comparative costs and options involved in completing a lamp. Inasmuch as there are almost 150 trimmings listed here, I will note only one important item per page.

a. Colored prisms and jewels and U drops

b. 7-inch Vienna or Dome shades with wide tops for Sun Chimneys.

c. The variety and "rich gold finish" of burners offered.

d. Hobnail Globes in amber, crystal or blue.

e. Note the original names of shades and the fact that they were sold with chimneys or filler fonts.

f. Chimneys were shipped six dozen per box.

g. La Bastie chimneys first introduced in France with extravagant claims in the 1870s were still being made in the U.S. in the late 1880.

## LAMP BURNERS.

The Eureka Burner.

Hinge Burner.

| | Per doz. |
|---|---|
| No. 0 Sun Eureka (see cut) | 50 |
| No. 1 Sun Eureka " | 55 |
| No. 2 Sun Eureka " | 75 |

Fireside or Banner same price.

| | |
|---|---|
| No. 0 Sun Hinge (see cut) | 90 |
| No. 1 Sun Hinge " | 1 50 |
| No. 2 Sun Hinge " | 1 75 |
| No. 2, Favorite, rich gold | 1 75 |
| No. 2 Unique, rich gold | 1 75 |
| Grand, rich gold, take No. 3 wick | 2 50 |
| Arctic, brass, take No. 3 wick | 1 50 |
| Sun Duplex, rich gold, take 2 No. 3 wicks | 3 00 |
| Little Giant, rich gold, take No. 3 wick | 2 50 |
| No. 1 Leader, takes No. 2 wick | 1 25 |
| No. 2 Leader, takes No. 3 wick | 2 25 |
| Argand Burners | 1 75 |
| Moehring | 6 00 |
| Harvard | 7 00 |
| Leader Argand | 9 00 |
| Nutmeg | 90 |

| | Per doz. |
|---|---|
| No. 0 or 1 Tubular | 75 |
| No. 10 Tubular | 75 |
| Buckeye, large or small | 1 50 |
| No. 1 Flat Lard Oil | 25 |
| No. 1 Flat Lard Oil with heater | 75 |
| No. 0 Alladin | 1 25 |

The Perfection Burners all use common flat wicks, either No. 1 or 2, are simple in construction, and as easy to trim and take care of as any common flat wick burner. The No. 1, 3 Cone Burner, takes No. 1 wick and the regular No. 2 Sun Chimney. The No. 2 Burners (either 2 or 3 cone) take the No. 2 flat wick and the Shaffer's Perfection Chimney.

| | |
|---|---|
| No. 1, 3 Cone Perfection Burner fits No. 2 Collar | 5 04 |
| No. 2, 2 Cone Perfection Burner fits No. 2 Collar | 5 04 |
| No. 2, 3 Cone Perfection Burner, fits No. 3 Collar | 6 30 |

Leader Burner.

No. 2—2 Cone Perfection Burner.

c

## GAS OR LAMP GLOBES.

<table>
<tr><td></td><td>Per doz.</td></tr>
<tr><td>Opal Squat, 5 inch, imported.........................</td><td>2 00</td></tr>
<tr><td>Opal Squat, 6 inch, corrugated—heavy domestic........</td><td>3 00</td></tr>
<tr><td>Hobnail, 5 inch, assorted colors—see cut below.......</td><td>2 00</td></tr>
<tr><td>Engraved, 5 inch, assorted designs—see cut below.....</td><td>2 50</td></tr>
<tr><td>Etched Squat, 5 inch, rich assorted patterns—see cut, page 253.........</td><td>4 00</td></tr>
<tr><td>Etched Crown, 5 inch, rich assorted patterns—see cut, page 253. The richest crystal shade for chandelier.........</td><td>7 50</td></tr>
<tr><td>Polka Dot, 5 inch, assorted colors, amber, blue, 2 50 doz., crystal opalescent and blue opalescent.........</td><td>3 50</td></tr>
<tr><td>Polka Dot, 5 inch, ruby color—see cut, page 253.........</td><td>4 25</td></tr>
<tr><td>Tulip, 5 inch, assorted colors, amber, blue, crystal opalescent and blue opalescent</td><td>3 75</td></tr>
<tr><td>Tulip, 5 inch, ruby color—see cut, page 253.........</td><td>5 00</td></tr>
<tr><td>Tulip, 5 inch, ruby opalescent—see cut, page 253.........</td><td>6 00</td></tr>
</table>

## PRICES OF TRIMMINGS ONLY.

*For use on any Table Lamps on the following pages.*

No. 1. No. 2 Sun Burner, 7 inch illuminator base, 7 inch Vienna or Dome Shade.........  3 00

No. 2. Same, with decorated (flowers) shade, either shape.........  4 00

No. 3 Trimmings.
Hobnail 5 inch Globe.

No. 3. Unique Burner, Ring and 5 Inch Hobnail Globe, amber, crystal or blue, and pearl top chimney—as shown in this illustration....  5 50

No. 4. Same as No. 3, only with Grand Burner and Ring....  7 00

Engraved 5 inch Globe.
No. 5 or 6 Trimmings.

No. 5. Unique Burner, Ring and 5 Inch Eng'd or Sand Blast Globe—as shown in this illustration....  6 00

No. 6. Same, with Grand Burner and Ring.........  7 20

All with Pearl Top Chimneys.

d

## LAMP CHIMNEYS.

Our main specialty. Our invariable car-load purchases, and superior facilities for handling, make a comparison of prices a favorite occupation. Chimneys are always in demand. You can order a box or two to fill up your order, even if your stock is not entirely exhausted; they will come in very handy in a short time. *Always order chimneys direct*, and we will prove to you conclusively our advantages on Lamp Chimneys, as well as in all other departments.

### ANNEALED CRIMP TOP CHIMNEYS.

Sold by the Box Only. Six Dozen in Box. No Charge for Box.

<table>
<tr><td></td><td>Per box.</td></tr>
<tr><td>No. 0 Sun Crimp Top.........</td><td>1 90</td></tr>
<tr><td>No. 1 Sun Crimp Top.........</td><td>2 00</td></tr>
<tr><td>No. 2 Sun Crimp Top.........</td><td>3 00</td></tr>
<tr><td>No. 1 Hinge Crimp Top.........</td><td>2 25</td></tr>
<tr><td>No. 2 Hinge Crimp Top.........</td><td>3 25</td></tr>
</table>

### H. L. & S. EMPIRE OR QUAKER FLINT.

H. LEONARD AND SONS.

<table>
<tr><td>No. 0 Sun Crimped Top.........</td><td>2 15</td></tr>
<tr><td>No. 1 Sun Crimped Top.........</td><td>2 25</td></tr>
<tr><td>No. 2 Sun Crimped Top.........</td><td>3 25</td></tr>
<tr><td>No. 1 Sun Crimped Top, Hinge.........</td><td>2 60</td></tr>
<tr><td>No. 2 Sun Crimped Top, Hinge.........</td><td>3 60</td></tr>
<tr><td>No. 2 Sun Electric Plain Top.........</td><td>4 70</td></tr>
</table>

### XXX FLINT GLASS CHIMNEYS.

XXX FLINT GLASS.

Each chimney wrapped and labeled—Pure Lead Glass. Five cents extra from open stock.

<table>
<tr><td></td><td>Per box.</td></tr>
<tr><td>No. 0 Sun Crimped Top.........</td><td>2 58</td></tr>
<tr><td>No. 1 Sun Crimped Top.........</td><td>2 80</td></tr>
<tr><td>No. 2 Sun Crimped Top.........</td><td>3 80</td></tr>
<tr><td>No. 1 Sun Crimped Top, Hinge.........</td><td>2 95</td></tr>
<tr><td>No. 2 Sun Crimped Top, Hinge.........</td><td>3 95</td></tr>
</table>

### PEARL TOP CHIMNEYS.

This well advertised chimney fills a want for a strictly first quality article and is the crowning achievement in Pure Lead Chimneys. Its name is a guarantee, and each chimney is wrapped and labeled in a manner that makes imitation impossible. There is only one PEARL TOP. WE HAVE IT.

<table>
<tr><td></td><td>Per box.</td></tr>
<tr><td>No. 1 Sun Pearl Top.........</td><td>3 70</td></tr>
<tr><td>No. 2 Sun Pearl Top.........</td><td>4 70</td></tr>
<tr><td>No. 2 Sun Pearl Top, Hinge.........</td><td>4 70</td></tr>
</table>

No charge for Boxes for Chimneys quoted on this page. Chimneys in less quantities than 1 case, charged at 5c. per dozen extra. Package charged at actual cost.

f

---

## TRIMMINGS—CONTINUED.

Squat Etched 5 inch Globe. No. 7 or 8 Trimmings.

<table>
<tr><td></td><td>Per doz.</td></tr>
<tr><td>No. 7. Unique Burner, Ring and 5 inch Etched Squat, assorted patterns, Globes—as shown in cut—with pearl top chimneys.........</td><td>7 20</td></tr>
<tr><td>No. 8. Same, with Grand Burner and Ring.........</td><td>8 40</td></tr>
</table>

Crown Etched 5 inch Globe. No. 9 or 10 Trimming.

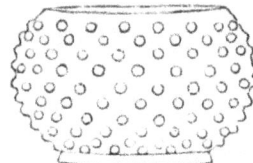

<table>
<tr><td>No. 9. Unique Burner, Ring and 5 inch Etched Crown, assorted patterns, Globes—as shown in cut—with pearl top chimneys.........</td><td>10 80</td></tr>
<tr><td>No. 10. Same, with Grand Burner and Ring.........</td><td>12 00</td></tr>
</table>

Polka Dot 5 inch Globe. No. 11, 11¼, 11½ or 11¾ Trimmings.

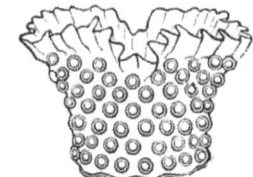

<table>
<tr><td>No. 11. Unique Burner and Ring, assorted blue, amber, opalescent or blue opalescent, P. D. Globes—as shown in cut—with pearl top chimneys.........</td><td>6 75</td></tr>
<tr><td>No. 11¼. Same, only Ruby Globes.........</td><td>9 00</td></tr>
<tr><td>No. 11½. Same with Grand Burner and Ring, and assorted colored Globes.........</td><td>8 00</td></tr>
<tr><td>No. 11¾. Same, only with Ruby Globes.........</td><td>10 25</td></tr>
</table>

Tulip 5 inch Globe. No. 12, 12¼, 12½ or 12¾ Trimmings.

<table>
<tr><td>No. 12. Unique Burner and Ring, old gold, sapphire opalescent, 5 inch Tulip Globes—as shown in cut—with pearl top chimneys....</td><td>7 50</td></tr>
<tr><td>No. 12¼. Same, with Ruby or Ruby Opalescent Globe.........</td><td>10 50</td></tr>
<tr><td>No. 12½. Same, with Grand Burner and Ring, and assorted colored Globes.........</td><td>9 00</td></tr>
<tr><td>No. 12¾. Same, with Grand Burner and Ring, and Ruby or Ruby Opalescent Globes.........</td><td>12 00</td></tr>
</table>

For Chandeliers, add $1.00 per doz., for Filler Founts, to the above.

e

## LAMP CHIMNEYS—CONTINUED.

### LA BASTIE GLASS CHIMNEYS.

Positively Unbreakable by Heat.

Packed about 8 dozen No. 1, or 5 dozen No. 2, to barrel, or in quantities to suit.

<table>
<tr><td></td><td>Per doz.</td></tr>
<tr><td>No. 1 Sun Bulb Plain Chimneys.........</td><td>1 25</td></tr>
<tr><td>No. 2 Sun Bulb Plain Chimneys.........</td><td>1 35</td></tr>
<tr><td>No. 2 Sun Crimped Top Chimneys.........</td><td>1 60</td></tr>
<tr><td>No. 2 Sun Hinge Plain Chimneys.........</td><td>1 60</td></tr>
<tr><td>No. 2 Sun Hinge Crimped Chimneys.........</td><td>1 75</td></tr>
</table>

### ENGRAVED PARLOR CHIMNEYS.

Globe and Chimney combined. Packed 6 dozen No. 1 or 6 dozen No. 2 in box. Five cents per dozen extra from open stock.

Engraved Chimney.

<table>
<tr><td></td><td>Per doz.</td></tr>
<tr><td>No. 1 Sun, Crimped Top, Engraved (see cut).........</td><td>65</td></tr>
<tr><td>No. 2 Sun, Crimped Top, Engraved (see cut).........</td><td>85</td></tr>
</table>

### BAND AND WREATH HAND PAINTED CHIMNEYS.

Extra Large Bulb. A complete Globe and Chimney combined. Packed 3 dozen No. 1 and 3 dozen No. 2 in cases, or 6 dozen of either size; or repacked to suit.

<table>
<tr><td></td><td>Per doz.</td></tr>
<tr><td>No. 1 Sun, Crimped Top (see cut).........</td><td>85</td></tr>
<tr><td>No. 2 Sun, Crimped Top (see cut).........</td><td>1 20</td></tr>
</table>

### LANDSCAPE—HAND PAINTED.

Band-Wreath Chimney.

Combination Globe and Chimney, burnt-in colors, same as the "Lily." The large size Globe on the Chimney makes it a handsome and practical trimming for any lamp. The decoration being put in on white background acts as a shade to the eyes and gives a beautiful, soft light. A trial will convince you that it will please your customers.

<table>
<tr><td></td><td>Per doz.</td></tr>
<tr><td>No. 1 Landscape, Crimped Top (see cut).........</td><td>1 15</td></tr>
<tr><td>No. 2 Landscape, Crimped Top (see cut).........</td><td>1 40</td></tr>
</table>

### LILY HAND PAINTED CHIMNEY.

COLOR BURNT IN.

For use on any lamp. Packed 6 dozen in boxes, either size. Five cents per dozen extra to repack.

<table>
<tr><td></td><td>Per doz.</td></tr>
<tr><td>No. 1 Sun Lily, Crimped Top.........</td><td>60</td></tr>
<tr><td>No. 2 Sun Lily, Crimped Top.........</td><td>75</td></tr>
</table>

g

# Illuminator Bases

White Vienna and dome shades and separate illuminator bases are priced on the previous catalogue pages. They were used on table lamps, bracket lamps, and hanging lamps from the middle 1870s on. Examples of the bases are found today in more than a dozen shapes and are marked with the names of different patentees and manufacturers.

This lamp with a Lomax Utah[ON] font is trimmed with a No.1 Arnold Blackman burner marked on the thumbwheel, PATENTED FEB 11 1868. These burners were given the name XL and illustrated on Blackman's letterhead with the frequently advertised short XL chimney. Here it is also correctly combined with an illuminator base marked A XL and ILLUMINATOR on the upper edge. The slip portion is marked PATD OCT 3, 76. / REISD FEB 13 77. on the obverse, and 1 X on the reverse. The patent refers to one issued to Carl Votti and assigned to B.B. Schneider, a manufacturer whose name is frequently found on illuminators.

This was the start of complex litigation involving the aforementioned as well as others including Hiram Ives, George Pashley, Lovell, and Richard Douglas who registered the ILLUMINATOR trade-mark above on July 3, 1877. He claimed to have been using the mark for six months.

The *Official Patent Office Gazettes* and the *Crockery and Glass Journal* reported on the conflicts that lasted several years. The companies issued dire warnings to each other and to customers who might be risking legal action for using shades made by the opposing manufacturer. This lasted into the early 1880s.

Height of this lamp to the top of the six-inch lightweight shade is $16^3/4''$.

# Combination Shades

In the late 1870s and 1880s, several combination one- and two-piece chimneys and globes were introduced. Few are known to have survived and those that have, should only be used for display. Brief descriptions of those illustrated are given here.

a. In the Dec. 23, 1880 issue of the *Crockery & Glass Journal*, this plain globe and another with engraving on the clear portion were advertised by Edward Rorke & Co., NYC, as "Daylight Combination Globes PATENT APPLIED FOR." They were also made with slip or lip bases.

b. The upper portion of these shades was intended to reflect the light downwards. Given the name Hero [ON] shade, they were patented by Joseph Bourne April 3, 1877, No. 189,180 and assigned to the Meriden Flint Glass Co. They have been described in an article by Ed and Abbie Meyer in the March 1976 issue of the *Spinning Wheel*.

c. The Lovell Drummond radiator base was molded like their chimneys, to be held in place by the clip on the Drummond burner. This was the F. H. Lovell version of the popular illuminator base and shade.

d. Regular or indirect lighting could be achieved with this one-piece reversible Drummond radiator and burner. The patent date shown, Feb. 27. 1877, actually refers to the reissue of a T. B. Atterbury patent for a combination chimney and burner dated April 18, 1876. Atterbury & Co. probably manufactured them for F. H. Lovell & Co. I have seen only one example of the Drummond Radiator base.

e. This combined lamp chimney and shade, was included in the Atterbury & Co. 1881 Catalogue. I have not heard of any examples that have survived. It was patented by T. B. Atterbury, Nov. 5, 1878 No. 209,542.

*a. Rorke combination globe.*

*b. Bourne Hero[ON] shade.*

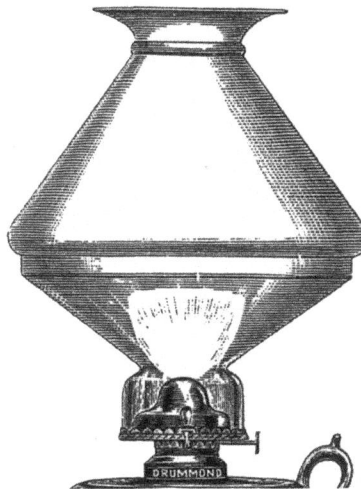

*c. Lovell Drummond radiator.*

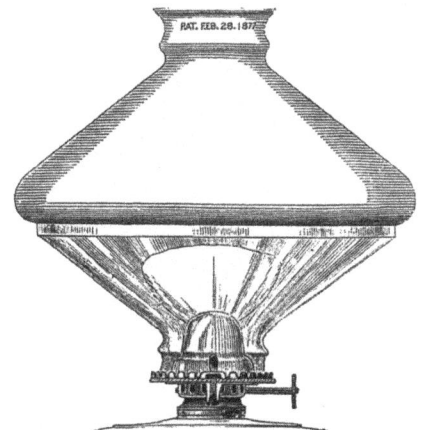

*d. Reversible Drummond radiator.*

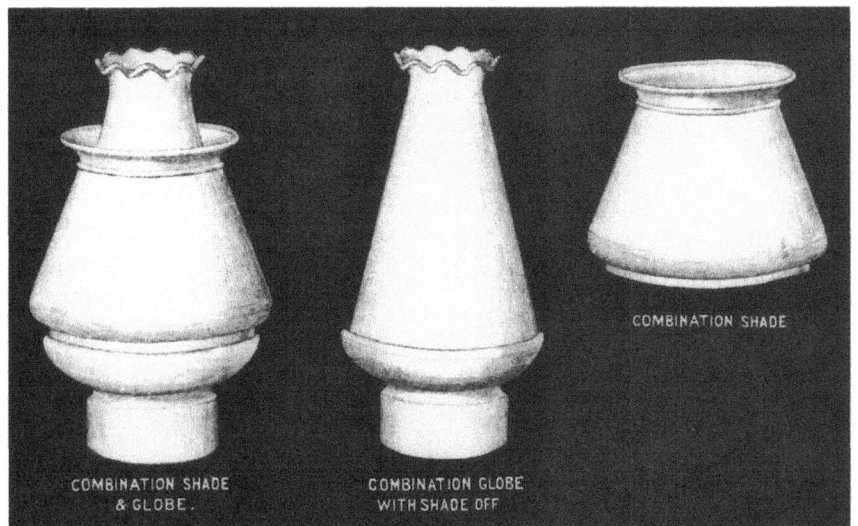

*e. Atterbury combined chimney and shade.*

a. Roughed and cut Oregon shade.

b. Roughed, cut, and engraved Oregon shade.

c. Roughed and cut globe or ball shade matching (a).

# Decorated Oregon and Globe Shades

The magnitude of the output of clear glass shades with frosted designs is generally overlooked. There were several major manufacturers of such shades and chimneys. Some of them illustrated their designs in their own catalogues, and other designs were illustrated in the catalogues of wholesale distributors such as F. H. Lovell & Co.

In the 1877-78 F. H. Lovell Price List, shades were listed in 3-, 3½-, 4-, and 5-inch sizes according to their base measurement. Oregon sizes started at 3" and globe shades, commonly called ball shades today, started at 3½". Oregon shades were less expensive. For example, 5" Oregon shades were $4.00 per dozen, and 5" globe shades were $7.00 per dozen.

The 1877-78 Lovell catalogue plate No.194 was titled CUT AND ENGRAVED GLOBES, however the examples were described as either "Decorated" or "Fine Etched." Precise descriptions of decorating techniques did not appear to be important. There was however a wide price range. A 4" globe was $5.00 per dozen and 4" fine etched globes were $24.00 per dozen. Like today, the terms "etched" and "engraved" appear to have been interchangeable, although the techniques were not. The 4" Oregon and ball or globe shades illustrated here would be suitable for lamps of the 1860s and 1870s. Oregon shades usually had roughed bands on the neck portion. Those with bands of cut ovals or circles often had better quality engraved or cut designs.

a.

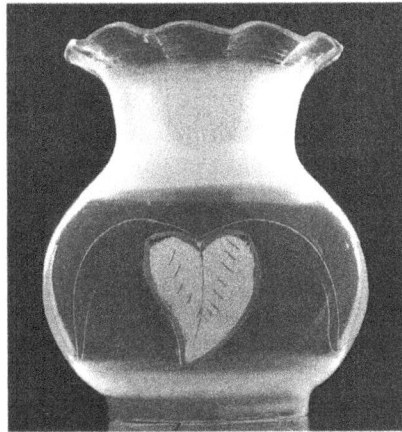
b.

c.

d.

e.

f.

g.

h.

Several techniques were used in the decoration of the globe and Oregon shades shown here. They inspire close examination of shades to try to determine how they were made, and the degree of skill and perfection exhibited in the execution of the decoration. Sometimes the lack of skill can also prove interesting. Brief descriptions follow.

a. With the exception of the squiggles representing tendrils, the center band is very well executed.

b. These crisply defined stylised leaves can also be found in different arrangements on fonts and on other glassware. It is certain they were made by Mt. Washington, and they have also been attributed to Portland and Sandwich glass companies.

c. The varied horizontal bands, particularly the one with cut ovals, create interest.

d. & e. There were many well-detailed scenes created with acid-etched techniques. The sight of the bare flame was diffused by the mat finish, and the yellow flame sparkled in the clear portions. Farmyard, cottage, and hunting scenes were popular.

f. The clearly defined pattern with a serrated edge easily identifies this as a sand-blasted design that became popular in the 1870s.

g. Roughed, cut, and engraved techniques were used to produce this complex design. The center band decoration has also been seen on Mt. Washington chimneys.

h. Another distinctive design was achieved with the creation of a decorated clear window against a frosted background, This technique is popular among collectors.

Many of these designs were also used on chimneys. It may be possible to identify some makers of a particular design, but its use was not necessarily exclusive. All of these shades have 4" bases.

# Squat Shades

Neither the name nor the shape of these five-inch squat shades is as popular with collectors today as those on the previous pages. They were also made in a 4" size. The name Squat is the one that was used in catalogues and advertisements. The wide flared top as in (c) and (d) was called a Crown. They were most popular in the 1880s and 1890s for both kerosene and gas lighting.

These broad shades are usually better suited to substantial late composite table lamps or to bracket or hanging lamps. It is difficult to find matching shades for lamps with two or more arms. The shade (a) is one of a pair used on a two-arm bracket lamp with an original copper finish. It is roughed with a cut design.

Few overlay, ball or squat shades are found today. They are included in the Mt. Washington photographs of shades. Example (b) is white with a clear base and an etched design.

The squat shade (c) with a cut top edge is one of the most commonly advertised shapes. It has a transfer design that was not too carefully applied, but this was also a common fault. In their 1892 catalogue the E. P. Gleason Manufacturing Co., New York, advertised similar shades on Plate 2 as ETCHED SQUATS, CROWNS, AND FANCY CROWNS. The wholesale price for etched squats was $5.00 per dozen and for the etched crowns $8.13 per dozen. Fancy crowns ranged between $8.75 and $13.75 per dozen.

A very significant aspect of these shades that is not apparent here is the manner in which they are transformed when illuminated by a kerosene flame. An acid-etched surface creates a soft glow with the clear areas picking up the yellow flame. A coarse roughed surface can sparkle when back-lit with a flame, and sharply cut edges will pick up a bright edge. An opaque cased or overlay surface does not transmit light, but by contrast, it accentuates the clear portions. The lack of attention that has been paid to these trimmings leaves many to explore.

*a. Roughed and cut squat shade.*

*c. Etched squat crown shade.*

*b. Cased or overlay etched shade.*

*d. Etched squat shade with plain crown.*

# Kerosene Lighting Catalogues, 1860–1900

The discovery over the last twenty years of the existence of a number of lighting catalogues has added information, confirmation, and sometimes confusion to the subject. They only confirm that particular companies offered the lamps, burners, trimmings, and accessories illustrated. If the catalogue is dated, it confirms the products were offered at that date, but not how much earlier or later they may have been advertised or sold. The words "Manufactured by" have to be disregarded. The degree or extent of manufacture by the companies who offered the catalogue should be determined from other information.

The appearance of a particular lamp in a catalogue does not mean it was offered exclusively. Some lamps were illustrated in several different company catalogues. Descriptive price lists accompanied some of the catalogues. This has given us added information and at times provided speculation. Different interpretations may be made, and controversy may be sparked, but that should move us closer to an accurate picture of the past. Some companies advertised imported lamps. Some included such information in their price lists, while others pictured imported lamps and didn't mention it. As the century progressed, the word *imported* was associated with superior quality and upper class prosperity. Lighting examples found today demonstrate that production in America *and* abroad included both good and poor quality. In my opinion, the overall ingenuity, imagination, and enthusiasm that promoted the kerosene era in America far outstripped the rest of the world! Opinions about the design are subjective, but I think those who have collected and studied examples for years sense that these distinctly American products reflect not only lighting, but history itself.

Interpreting the catalogues and price lists may take different avenues. Even if one takes the wrong route, the exercise may heighten an awareness of the factors to be considered. Bronze seldom meant bronze! It usually described a bronze finish on spelter or iron. Also mentioned was fine bronze and French bronze. One can speculate if items prefixed by French, Italian or German were actually imported, or was it just an attempt to provide a degree of sophistication? Were companies such as Dietz, Sandwich, and Lovell importers as well as exporters?

One of the few known pages from the Boston and Sandwich Glass Co. circa 1875 catalogue raises some questions. The Plate No. 76 was reprinted in *New Light on Old Lamps* by Dr. Larry Freeman and in *The Glass Industry in Sandwich* Vol. 2 by Raymond E. Barlow and Joan E. Kaiser. Could the top row of lamps that were advertised as French possibly have been from France? The three-arm shade holder

attached to the collar has most often been illustrated on lamps that have been identified in catalogues as Bohemian. Perhaps it was a European style. The connectors are like those used on the Eaton (or Onion) lamps, pictured on page 17 in OL-2. Could they be a French connection? If the Eatons were imported, it might explain why the glass differs from American lamp bases of the same period. The wide Eaton bases are very vulnerable to chips and bruises, and yet this is a very rare occurrence. Damage to American bases is common. This could be the result of care or coincidence. Shards found at factory sites may have been discarded lamps that were broken in shipping.

There were reports of considerable damage to goods while they were being transported. When one considers rough ocean voyages and the time and the distance required to move people and goods, it is amazing how easily they took it in stride.

The catalogues tell us that in the 1860s Dietz & Co. had offices in New York and London. Russell & Erwin had warehouses in New York, Philadelphia, Boston, and San Francisco, and the F. H. Lovell & Co. 1868-69 catalogue printed in Spanish meant they started their South American trade at an early date. To ship to either Rio or London, about the same distance, would have taken weeks. For Russell & Erwin, shipping or travelling to San Francisco added thousands of miles, and many weeks more, as well as a treacherous route around the Horn to navigate. Even when transcontinental trains began in 1869 making safe passage across the western states possible, shipping around the Horn continued.

Any land transportation from dock to destination had to be a jarring experience. Contact between rough roads and wooden wheels with iron tires must have contributed to a considerable amount of breakage when the cargo arrived at the factory, store or distribution location. These are additional factors that should be taken into account when assessing the validity of shards found on site. The greater part of nineteenth century Canadian pattern glass was based upon shards dug at the site of the Burlington Glass Works in Ontario. While scholars acknowledge the shards represented about 150 patterns, they now also feel it was highly improbable that few, if any, represent glass made in Canada. This mistake is perpetuated in books found in libraries in Canada, and little has been done to correct it.

Descriptions of many of the most significant catalogues that I have been able to study in the past twenty years are given here. As a fellow of the Corning Museum, I have made frequent visits to their library, where most of these catalogues are on microfilm or microfiche, for study purposes.

*For publication purposes, written permission should be obtained from the copyright holder or owner of the original copy.*

# The 1860s

After the *Charles A. Starr Catalogue* (see pp. 44-45) was published in 1861, the next catalogues that featured a variety of lamps and fixtures were published around the end of the Civil War. The *Dietz & Company Illustrated Catalogue* circa 1865 was the first to feature color plates. Its size and scope make it one of the most important lamp catalogues ever published. The recent reprint of this is dated 1860, however a few patented items that were included place the date closer to 1865. Much of the information in the introduction by Ulysses G. Dietz needs to be updated, because so much of the research is related to the 1860 date. There was also the assumption that the lamp prices listed in the S.E. Southlands 1859 catalogue, OL-1 pp. 18,19, were for individual lamps. They were actually prices per dozen. These problems affect the socioeconomic theories presented in the introduction and text.

Included in the introduction are four photographs illustrating one hundred and twenty-two lamps offered by "the London branch." Most of them resemble English or Continental production. There is one curiosity, however, and that is a glass stand with long prisms surrounding a bowl-shaped top. These are known as *lusters* that were used as mantelpiece ornaments. The one in the picture, however, appears to have a font and burner placed in it. This seems to be a logical use, but I have not seen it before.

Fonts pictured on plate 6 that have been generally attributed to Sandwich are now known to likely be English since they have been found with alabaster bases marked with the Dietz name and London address.

Much of Dietz sought after information can be found in the F. H. Lovell & Co. CATALOGUE "C" price list, discovered after the Dietz catalogue was reprinted. According to the Lovell introduction, catalogue "C" could be dated circa 1875. It contains the following significant information:

*Gentlemen:*

*We take great pleasure in informing you that we have purchased the entire stock and business of the old established firm of Dietz & Co., of this city, and enclose with this their Illustrated Catalogue.*

*The styles of Lamps being similar to our own (we having furnished Messrs. Dietz & Co. with nearly all the Cuts); we are prepared to fill all the orders with promptness.*

Catalogue "C" will affect the interpretation of catalogues and lamps of the 1860s and 1870s. This price list contains brief descriptions and prices of about 375 lamps on 51 plates, and the majority of them correspond with the Dietz numbers. Generally, the numbers on plates 1 to 30 run consecutively from 852 to 1096, however the 800 numbers do not correspond.

There are 25 "Solar or Sperm Oil Stand Lamp" prices listed on plates 31 and 32, ranging from $3.50 to $18.00 each. The No. 54 Dietz Patent lamp among the solar lamps in the Dietz catalogue appears to be a kerosene lamp. It was priced at $2.50 each. Also on plate 32 were lamps numbered 5, 36, 507 and 600 to 610.

Plate 33 to the end lists prices for numbers 1091 to 1182. These included Bracket Lamps, Harp Lamps, Chain Hanging Lamps, Hall Hanging Lamps, two Solar Hanging Lamps, and Chandeliers. There were two- and four-light Billiard Chandeliers, Companionway, and Verandah lamps. Unfortunately not all of these lamps nor the lanterns can be identified in the Dietz catalogue. There were lanterns described as Japanned Tin Street, Square, Station, Sugar House, and Boat listed, as well as the Tin Convex, Patent, Vesta, Side, and Champion lanterns.

The 1865 *Illustrated Catalogue of American Hardware of the Russell and Erwin Manufacturing Company*, which included fifteen pages of lighting, contains much more than hardware. It should be consulted by anyone interested in the period. In the Dietz catalogue, the many lamps that were shown in both the Dietz and R&E catalogues are listed. This is the beginning of the discovery of an amazing number of coincidences regarding the frequency with which certain lamps show up in different company catalogues. Also there is a single known page of an undated Boston & Sandwich Glass Company catalogue. It was titled *Catalogue of Petroleum or Kerosene Oil Lamps and Chandeliers*. This is shown in OL-1. Each of the eight lamps pictured is also illustrated in the Dietz catalogue. See Iden & Co. in OL-2 pp. 38 & 39.

The lull in catalogue production during the Civil War may have been just coincidental, or it may have been because the major manufacturers of metal lamp parts were also involved in war related production. During this period kerosene lighting continued at a healthy rate, giving us some indication of production in the absence of catalogues, and the scarcity of advertisements, trade cards, and ephemera. The trade publications did not appear until the 1870s.

Early 1860s Edward Miller & Co. records in the Connecticut Historical Society collection show purchases made from a number of suppliers. These indicate how extensive was the practice of assembling lamps, using parts from many sources.

# The Julius Ives & Co. Catalogues

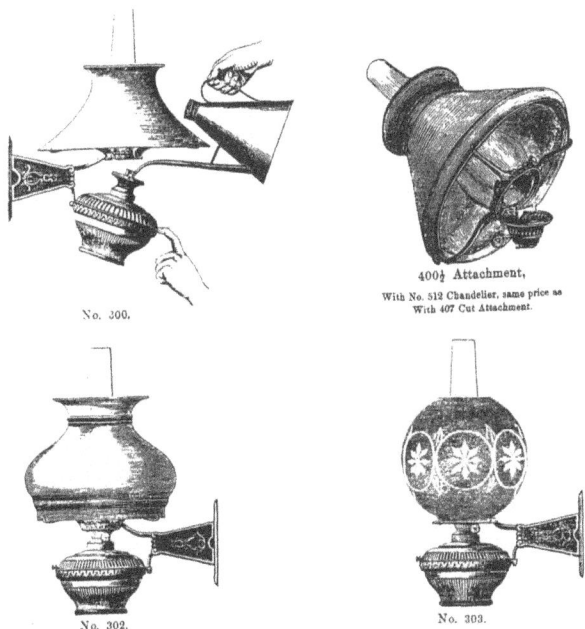

*a. Ives shade holders and shades.*

This company, based in New York, published a small catalogue dated August 1, 1867. It served to introduce Julius Ives patented lamps, burners, and shades. He used 19 of the 29 known pages to offer testimonials praising his products. One was from "Edward Miller Esq.of Meriden Conn." Edward Miller & Co. made the burners used in Ives' most important patented shadeholder and burner combination. Another from Rev. Henry Ward Beecher stated, "Your Hanging and Bracket Lamps we use with great satisfaction. I hope you may sell enough to redeem millions from their bondage to Gas Companies, who seem to spend their skill in making poor gas and large bills." This was the brother of the Harriet Elizabeth Beecher Stowe, author of *Uncle Tom's Cabin*. It appears that Ives was a well-connected gentleman who had a lot of help from his friends. This important catalogue is in the Strong Museum in Rochester, New York.

A great deal of emphasis was placed upon the advantages of Ives lamps over gas lighting. The quality and cost of this rival lighting continued in advertising and articles for more than a decade. An article reprinted from the *Brooklyn Daily Union* described the Ives operation, "The manufacturers of these lamps have a factory in this city composed of three lofts, each sixty feet deep, with all the machinery necessary for making the metal portions of the lamps, and employ quite a large number of men." The article goes on to say that the New York salesrooms have "three lofts about 130 feet deep, consisting of show-room and office, and rooms above for decorative artists, as well as for storage, packing, etc., to such an extent has their business grown in less than two years."

Judging from the familiar lamp bases in his catalogue, manufacture of the metal portions likely referred to his patented items. According to the catalogue these were U.S. patents, October 25th, 1864; February 21st, 1865; July 18th, 1865; and August 8th, 1865. These were also patented in Great Britain, France, Austria, and Belgium. Ives claimed also to be sole agents for Minor's improved, folding pocket candle lanterns, patented January 24th, 1865.

The late Vincent Ortello kindly sent me an 1871 Ives catalogue for my use. It appears to have additional pages from a later catalogue that may at some time be dated from other catalogues or advertisements. Both Lovell and Bradley & Hubbard advertised Ives lamps in their catalogues, and it appears that B&H made the cast iron bracket and hanging lamp parts for his lamp. Edward Miller made the burners, and the manufacturer of the glass parts is not known at this time. In spite of that, any lamp that Ives placed his patented shade-holder upon became an Ives lamp! It was later in the decade that Ives became involved in litigation regarding his patent for the illuminator shades. This continued into the 1880s and took advantage of the trade journals' eagerness to publicise the running conflict. At this same period of time, Ives was defending the validity of his lamp extension device against the accusations by Bradley & Hubbard and the Meriden Malleable Iron Company.

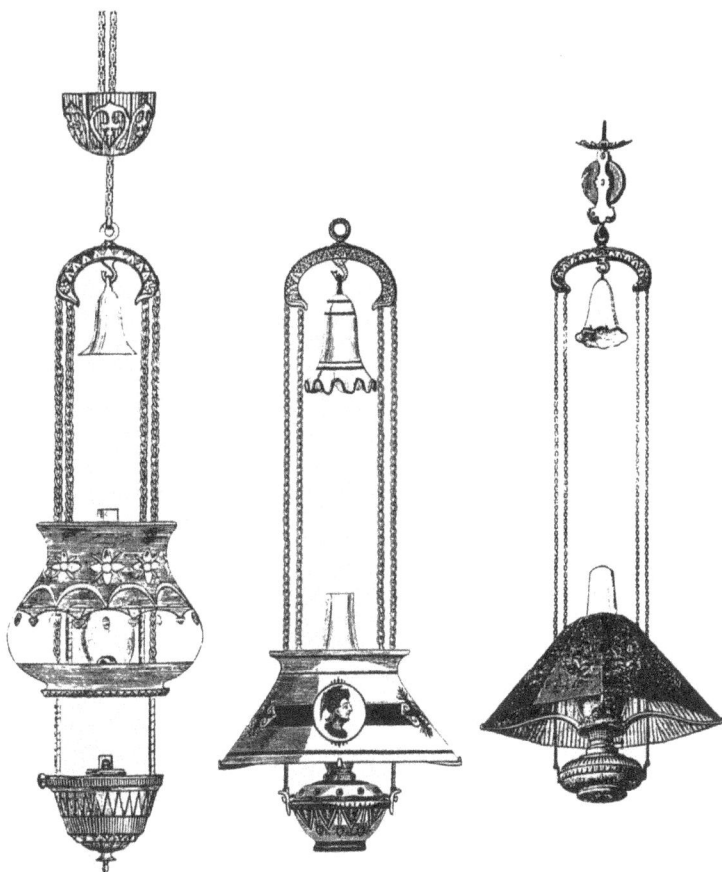

*b. Ives hanging and hall lamps.*

# F. H. Lovell & Co. 1868–69 Catalogue

This catalogue is in English with a cover in Spanish. The price list is missing, however there are descriptive price lists of a circa 1872-3, and an 1874 catalogue, with some matching numbers and descriptions. All of the specified and unspecified descriptions used here are from these sources.

Plates 1, 2 & 3. These plates include almost 100 flat and footed hand lamps, and stand lamps, under 12 inches. All have lip chimneys. Many, if not most, appear to have Jones or similar burners. One has an Adlam's patent burner, and one has a Tom Thumb (Cahoon's patent) burner. There are four pyramidal-shaped metal hand lamps. In the 1872-73 price list, metal lamps are described as brass or as bronzed tin.

Plates 4 to 9. Of the nearly 100 composite stand lamps ranging between 12" and 16", about a third of the smaller ones have lip chimneys and burners as above. The remainder have ball or Oregon frosted shades with designs and many would be considered banquet lamps. Almost every type, pattern, and style of glass font illustrated is in OL-1 or OL-2. There are all-glass bases and marble bases, with brass stems or columns as they are described, as well as two figural stems and a simple cast iron base that appears in the B&H and the Union Glass Catalogues.

Plates 10 and 11 have tall and elegant table lamps, some of which are the same as, or similar to, those that appear in the Russell & Erwin, Dietz, and Boston & Sandwich catalogues. The spectacular lamp pictured on page 145 (e) is included with different cutting.

Plate 12 has lamps pictured and numbered the same an in the Dietz catalogue. Number 1056 is described as "Fine Bohemian Vase Lamp, decorated." With a #2 burner they were $9.00 each! Other examples similar to those on pages 52 and 53 in OL-2 and in the Dietz catalogue were $10.50 to $11.50 each. The smaller composite lamps were about $5.00 to $6.00 per dozen.

Every lamp on plate 13 is described in the 1874 price list as "Bohemian Decorated," and the opaque glass is listed as Opal (white), Dove, Turquoise, Black or Chrysophase (yellow). Some were sold separately at $5.00 to $8.00 each, while others ranged from $41.00 to $46.00 per dozen. Sizes were not given, however the several that I have seen were about ten to sixteen inches high to the top of the collar. All appear to have American burners, shade holders, and either Oregon or ball engraved shades.

According to the 1874 price list, Plate 14 must have been reproduced exactly the same, at that time. It featured 14 Julius Ives & Co. lamps but referred to them only as "Patent Hall and Table Lamps, arranged so as to Light and Fill without removing the Globe or Chimney."

Plates 15, 16 and 17 have lamps that were also pictured in the Dietz catalogue on Plates 29 and 30 and in the Russell & Irwin catalogues on pages 421 and 422. They were described in the 1874 price list as fine bronze or bronze. The many examples extant are all spelter. See pages 38, 39, and 55 in OL-2.

Plates 18, 19, and 20 include over twenty spelter figural lamps with primarily ball shades and a few Oregon ones. These are the same as, or similar to, those in the Sandwich and Dietz catalogues. Impressive figurals and metal stands continued to be advertised into the 1890s. The designs changed considerably, and this catalogue was the last to promote these 1860s styles. Both common and some very special bracket lamps are also on these pages.

On plate 21, there is a rather abrupt change to four Tucker *Italian Bronze Vase* lamps. These cast iron stand lamps all had ball shades. Three were priced at $3.75, and one at $4.25. There was also one urn-shaped vase lamp listed as a "*Fine Bronze Lamp,—complete—Each—$7.00.*" Plates 22 to 26 inclusive are devoted mainly to bracket lamps. There are many cast iron Tucker patent bracket lamps described as "*Italian Bronze.*" Accessories such as shades, globe rings, and shade clasps (shade holders), prism rings, and oil cans were also on these plates.

On plates 27 to 39 there are about eighty hanging lamps illustrated. These form an excellent picture of lamps offered during the 1860s. With the exception of Ives' patent hanging lamps, they include examples that are the same as, or similar to, those illustrated in all known catalogues of the decade. Several of the examples are embellished with fine decorative chains, and many Tucker lamps are shown. These pages offer an exceptional opportunity to study this period stylistically, to compare it with other forms of lighting, and with other periods. Being able to relate it to the later Lovell price lists and catalogues also places it in a unique position because neither the Dietz nor the Russell and Irwin catalogues include prices.

There are also a few more bracket lamps and an insulator that could be inserted between the font and base. Accessories, lanterns, shades, burners, and chimneys are continued on the remaining plates. All of the burners and chimneys are the lip kind. This is surprising because we know from other sources that the cylindrical slip chimneys, also known as Sun or Comet, were widely used at this time. The chimneys are two for ½" burners, six for ⅝", two for 1", and one for 1½". They were from 5 to 11 inches tall. The ⅝" ones included one with a wide ground band in the area surrounding the flame, and five decorative narrow ones above this. There was a metal top one and three without measurements called Tom Thumb, Carleton, and Ne Plus Ultra for the patented burners.

Both the Dietz and this catalogue have pages that do not appear to be part of the original catalogue. Almost all of the stand lamps are familiar to collectors and many are in OL-2.

# Catalogues of the 1870s

The most significant plates of the 1870s catalogues that are known are from the Bradley & Hubbard Company, Meriden Conn., The Boston & Sandwich Glass Co., and the F. H. Lovell & Co. These were large, comprehensive catalogues that included almost every type of lamp and accessory. Only a few pages of the Sandwich catalogue are known, one of which is shown below. The following excerpt is from the February 6th, 1875 issue of *The Crockery Journal*.

## LAMP GOODS

*Upon our table lies an immense catalogue, whose pages, a hundred of them are not less than thirty inches long by fifteen inches wide, are wholly occupied by the most accurately prepared designs of the various lamps and lamp-ware manufactured by the Boston & Sandwich Glass Company. These illustrations, elegantly executed in lithograph, not only give the form and decoration, but the color as well. Lamps for parlor use are shown with wreaths of flowers encircling their globes; lamps for more humble uses are in green, and blue, and red glass,*

*and these colors are faithfully portrayed. There are hanging lamps, and standing lamps, and if we may use the expression, sitting lamps, for some of them are so low in stature that they hardly seem to stand.*

*In some the pedestal is bronze, some of marble, and in some of glass, and all these variations the illustrations faithfully present. Then, when it comes to lamp-ware, such as burners, shade-holders, and the like, there is infinite variety, but everything is shown, a counterpart of the original, in bronze color. Some of the efforts are decidedly gorgeous, especially those intended for use in houses of the best class in localities where gas is unattainable. These include chandeliers with cut glass pendants, and bracket lamps of great elegance of finish.*
—Boston Bulletin

The article continues with a description of more products including lanterns, as well as comments about the expense of preparing the designs and the catalogue itself. If one of these catalogues is found, it will probably have many of the 1860s and 1870s lamps that are illustrated in other catalogues featured here.

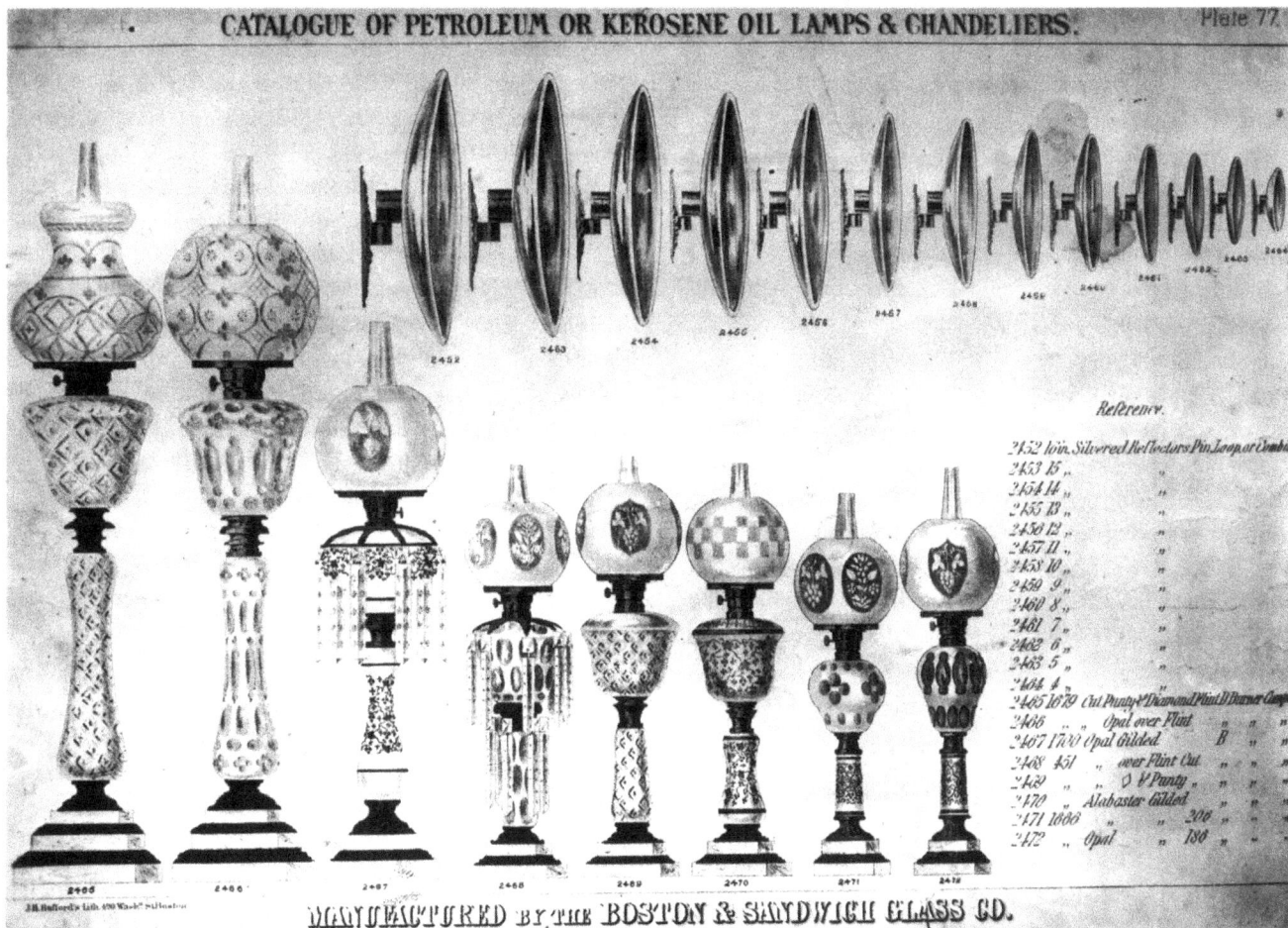

*Catalogue page circa 1875*

# The Union Glass Company Catalogue

This catalogue of "*Kerosene Lamps, Fixtures, &c,. &c.*" can be described as circa 1874. Among lamp collectors this company is best known as the maker of the Lomax patent lamps with the "Oil Guard" trade-mark drip catcher. See OL-1 p. 178, and the Lomax lamps in this book. Like the Julius Ives Co. catalogue, this catalogue appears to be made up of two parts. One contains the lamps, smoke bells, and silvered reflectors, probably made by the Union Glass Company; plus two student lamps. There is an indexed price list after these pages. The second part comprising fifteen pages has no price list and has negative images. It is obvious that most of the fixtures, burners, and trimmings were made elsewhere, and there is no way to determine if the Union Glass Company made any of the glass trimmings in this section.

Bradley & Hubbard cast iron fixtures can be recognised, as well as the F. T. Fracker Sept. 25, 1866, design patented pulley for hall lights No. 2432. This also appears in the Bradley & Hubbard catalogue.

The well-known kitchen lamps and the Utah and Vienna patterns are illustrated in all-glass and composite forms. The Sept. 20, 1870 Lomax patent date was always marked on the font. The majority were named. Some of the font names are listed below with some additional information if available.

Arizona OL-2 p. 83 (j).
Boston Beauty. Also other companies, OL-2 p. 30.
Canada. Like Rand Rib, only with horizontal ribs.
Gem. A favourite name, OL-2 p. 98 (e).
Lawrence. Bullseye with small loop pattern at base.
Leaf. See Inverted Leaf Panel, OL-2 p. 63 (j).
Pillar. Like Rand Rib with small clear ovals.
Reeded, OL-2 p. 98 (d).
Saucer. Plain saucer base hand lamp.
Trenton. A bullseye pattern.
Troy. This is a small lamp, with a square ribbed iron base.
  The font has about six large loops.

One numbered pattern should be mentioned because today it is probably the best known. Buckle (OL-1 p. 171 with the same engraved design) was catalogued as No. 300, Cut Sprig. It was also illustrated without the engraving. Lomax plain and engraved fonts were illustrated with spelter figural bases called bronze, and a variety of shades and shadeholders.

Three designs used for the separate pressed glass bases they called Opal Stands were

Gem: See OL-2 p. 83 (f); Hex: See p. 83 (j); and
Plain See OL-1 p. 165 (i) & (j).

Other glass items include shades, silvered reflectors, smoke bells, and shades with plain or colored edge.

# The Bradley & Hubbard 1873 Catalogue

This July, 1873 catalogue, owned by the American Antiquarian Society in Worcester, Mass., originally had 92 pages, however there are 34 missing pages occurring throughout. From the price lists we have knowledge that they represented the following items:

Pages 9-12 inc. Large and medium chandeliers
Pages 17-20 inc. Chandeliers with patent center drop
Pages 29-32 inc. Chandeliers with two lights
Pages 35-37 inc. As above for stores
Pages 39-40 inc. Medium chandeliers
Pages 53-60 inc. Brackets with baskets and cups
Pages 69-71 inc. Brackets with baskets, cups and rings
Pages 72-73 inc. Bronze lamps
Pages 85-86 inc. Lamp pedestals and stands

Although the missing pages are regrettable, they were mainly composed of hanging and bracket lamps that incorporated many of the components and designs, used in the examples illustrated in the other catalogue pages. Patent-dated examples extant also identify many B&H examples. The non-metal parts would be from other sources.

The catalogue is prefaced with a note to the trade that states that it contains the largest and most complete assortment of chandeliers, brackets, and bronze stand lamps in the trade. They mentioned their improved method of assembling chandeliers, and their patented drip cup font holders. These were not drilled in the bottom.

When ordering, the customer was asked to specify "*the style of finish or bronze, as we are finishing our goods in the following colors, viz: FRENCH, or LIGHT BRONZE, VERDE ANTIQUE, and VERDE and FRENCH BRONZE RELIEF.*" They mentioned that with gilt trimmings they made an attractive and durable finish. I have seen some outstanding B&H fixtures with contrasting finishes on the base and on the relief surfaces. Careful restoration to rescue fixtures from a flat black state can be very satisfying.

More than the first half of the catalogue is devoted to hanging lamps they refer to as chandeliers, pendants, wire or brass rope harp hangers, or chain hangers. Single, more elaborate hanging lamps were labelled Bronze Pendants, Hall Pendants or Hall Lights. There were ball shades, Oregon shades, and slant shades. Some of the latter were supported at the bottom by heavy cast iron rings, some by Ives combination burner and shade holders, while others appeared to be resting on the chimney. The design patented Ives hall lamp was there, but the Tucker patented extension did not appear at this stage. There were lamps that incorporated patented extensions, and the ubiquitous separate spring balance.

No. 2. Alderman. With Match Safe.

*a.*

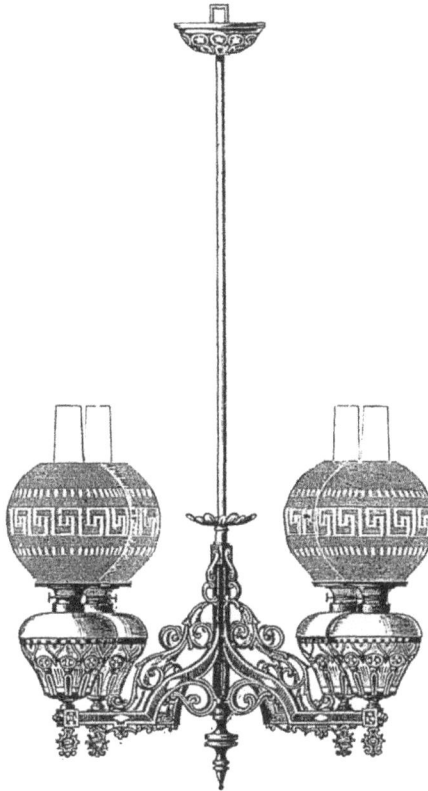

No. 523. 2, 3 and 4 Light. Spread, 24 inches. Length, 36 inches.

*b.*

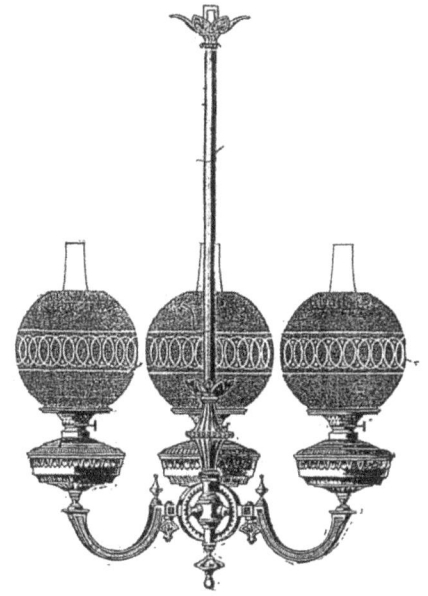

No. 502. 2, 3 and 4 Light. Spread, 27 inches. Length, 42 inches.

*c.*

No. 409. Bracket.
Without Reflector Pos.

*d.*

The Bradley & Hubbard Mfg. Co. was undoubtedly the largest and most important manufacturer of lighting fixtures during the kerosene era. The exceptional amount of documentation that exists includes catalogues, advertisements, patents, and ephemera as well as an abundant supply of examples. Although there are many obvious gaps in the records, it is likely that the potential to fill some of them in the future will provide a more complete picture.

Through their own marketing and through distribution by F. H. Lovell, they became the best known name in American lighting fixtures. They continued to manufacture gas, kerosene, and electric fixtures well into the twentieth century.

| No. 262. Pillar. 12 inch High. | No. 270. Sailor Boy. 11 inch High. | No. 212. Vase. 15 inch High. | No. 301. Fox and Trap. 12 inch High. | No. 292. Vase. 12 inch High. |
| --- | --- | --- | --- | --- |

Numbers designated by a * are shown in Engraving.

[78]

*e.*

## The F. H. Lovell & Co. 1877–78 Catalogue

This catalogue offers a wonderful opportunity to view earlier lighting that was still being offered. This could represent sustained interest, or an effort to unload surplus stock of unpopular styles.

Kirk Nelson, contributed important information about the Lovell catalogues and company, in *The Illuminator* Vol. 3, No. 2, Summer, 1989. Excerpts are included here.

"A recent interview with Lane Lovell provided some very interesting information about the family business. Franklyn (1836-1914) and Orville (1839-1923) were sons of Osterville merchant George Lovell (17?7-1861). Osterville is located about 10 miles south of Sandwich. Following the War of 1812, George and several other merchants established the Dispatch Line, which was the first line of packets to offer regular service between Boston and New York City. George was a prominent figure in the business community on Cape Cod, and was one of the original directors of the Barnstable Bank. The family also maintains he was a shareholder in the Boston and Sandwich Glass Company, but no substantiating evidence has thus far turned up."

"Franklyn Lovell moved to New York about 1859, when city directories list him as engaged in the hardware business at 272 Pearl Street. In 1863 he is listed as a clerk at 240 Pearl, the address of Alfred Bliss and Company. Franklyn is first listed in the lamp business in 1864. This is the same year that F.H. Lovell and Company was founded according to later company literature, although the company was not listed in the directories until 1866. Orville's name first appears in the 1866 directory, and he is listed for the last time in 1890."

The Lovell Company appears to have been a wholesaling rather than a manufacturing establishment up until about 1900, despite the fact that plates from the 1875 catalogue (#'s 92-96) are captioned "Manufactured By F. H. Lovell & Co." Handwritten notations in the 1877-78 catalogue list a number of different firms which supplied Lovell with products, including "Iden," "RD& Sons," "MV&Co," "WHS," Gleason & Cornelius & Son," "R&H," "B&SGCo," and "NEGCo." This is not at all surprising, given the Lovell family's family background in shipping. Orville and Franklyn are actually listed as merchants in the 1889 N.Y. City directory, although the listing reverts to "lamps" the following year. Lane remembers the company's shipping clerk, a Mr. Kobbie, describing the company's early years, when merchandise would arrive and overflow the warehouse right into the streets. Lane also tells the story of several hogsheads of lamp fonts or "pegs" that were stored for decades in the company's attic. These fonts, which he believes were imported from abroad about 1900, were finally sold to a New Jersey antiques dealer in the 1950s.

Toward the end of the nineteenth century the company began to specialize in marine and railroad lighting devices. According to company literature, they acquired factory and warehouse facilities in Arlington, New Jersey, in 1901 but continued to maintain their New York City offices. The company was sold in 1970 to Adams & Westlake Company of Chicago and had since been absorbed by Allied Products Corporation.

The amount of material that survives to document the wares handled by F. H. Lovell and Company is truly staggering."

Nelson goes on to describe many more of the Lovell catalogues and price lists for the domestic and export market. These are on loan to the Sandwich Historical Society. They include the 1884, 1885, 1886, and 1893 Hitchcock mechanical lamp catalogues in in English and in Spanish for export. Several of the Hitchcock illustrations are shown in this book, He concludes with:

"Analysis of the Lovell material has only just begun. This analysis has already helped us to refine the dating and attribution of lighting devices from the period. It should also illuminate our understanding of the relationships existing between wholesale lighting establishments and manufacturers, both domestic and foreign, as well as relationships existing between Lovell and other wholesale firms, most notably the renowned Dietz and Company."

No. 2800.  Fox and Trap.    No. 2804.  Centennial Bell.

*Catalogue illustrations.*

#566

#107

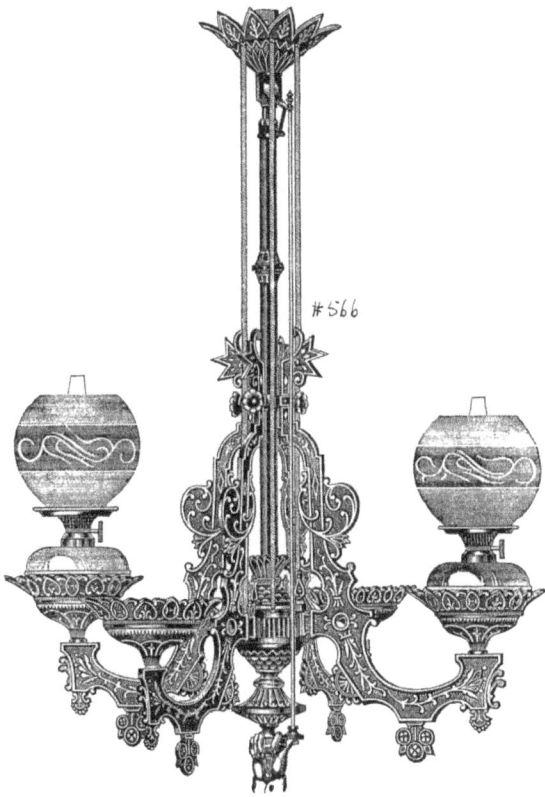

No. 2944.  Bracket.  1, 2 and 3 Light.  Projects 15 in.

70

#489

With the information that F. G. Lovell & Co. supplied the cuts for the Dietz & Co. catalogue and with the knowledge that many of these same illustrations also appeared in the Boston & Sandwich Co., the Ives & Co., the Russell & Irwin Company, and Iden & Co. catalogues, it is safe to say that catalogue illustrations can only tell us who *sold* the lamps. If the catalogue has its original date, it should be kept in mind that this useful information *does not* tell us how much earlier or later they sold the pictured items. Additional information must come from different sources such as the notations on the Lovell catalogues, company records, patents, trade journals, and the lamps themselves.

In addition to the suppliers noted on page 256, we can add the names of Edward Miller & Co., Bradley & Hubbard, Hitchcock Lamp Co., Tucker Manufacturing Co., The Union Glass Co., and many others.

It appears that F. H. Lovell & Co. was the most important lamp merchant in America!

No. 2875.  Crusader Lamp.
Height, 21 in.

No. 2904.

No. 561 Lamp.　　　　No. 1086 Lamp.　　　　No. 371 Lamp.

# EDWARD MILLER & COMPANY

## ILLUSTRATED CATALOGUE

### 1881.

# B. & H. Central
## Draft Table Lamps.
### *Detachable Metal Founts.*

No. 9514.

| NO. | DESCRIPTION. | EACH. |
|---|---|---|
| 9514 | Lamp, as shown above, without Chimney, Shade or Holder. Antique Brass Finish. | $11 67 |
| 09514 | Same as above, but Oxidized Silver Finish. | 13 34 |
| 9515 | Same as above, but complete with Chimney, 10 inch Decorated Bisque Dome Shade and Holder, | 14 17 |
| 09515 | Same as No. 9515, but Oxidized Silver Finish. | 15 84 |

Height to Burner, 12 inches.

No. 9517.

| NO. | DESCRIPTION. | EACH. |
|---|---|---|
| 9517 | Lamp, as shown above, no Chimney, Shade or Holder. Antique Brass Finish. | $7 50 |
| 09517 | Same as above, but Oxidized Silver Finish. | 9 17 |
| 9518 | Same as above, but complete with 10 inch Decorated Bisque Dome Shade and Holder. Antique Brass Finish. | 10 00 |
| 09518 | Same as No. 9518, but Oxidized Silver Finish. | 11 67 |

Height to Burner, 12 inches.

No. 9519.

| NO. | DESCRIPTION. | EACH. |
|---|---|---|
| 9519 | Lamp, as shown above, without Chimney, Shade or Holder, | $19 17 |
| 9520 | Same as above, but complete with 10 inch Decorated Bisque Dome Shade and Holder, | 21 67 |

Body of Royal Copper. Handles, Feet and Ornaments of Oxidized Silver. Height to Burner, 11½ inches.

No. 9521.

| NO. | DESCRIPTION. | EACH. |
|---|---|---|
| 9521 | Lamp, as shown above, without Chimney, Shade or Holder, | $16 67 |
| 9522 | Same as above, but complete with 10 inch Decorated Bisque Dome Shade and Holder, | 19 17 |

Body finished in Antique Green. Handles, Feet and Ornaments Gold Plated. Height to Burner, 12½ inches.

Illustrations from The Hubbard, Spencer, Bartlett & Co. catalogue circa 1900.

## H. LEONARD'S SONS & CO.'S
### Price List and Cook Book.

#### PUBLISHED FOR THE PEOPLE.

#### A GUIDE TO GOOD GOODS AT LOW PRICES.

**NOS.**
**29 and 31**
**MONROE ST.,**
**GRAND RAPIDS,**
**MICH.**

**FOUR FLOORS.**
—
Passenger Elevator.
—
STEAM HEATED.
—
No Rent to Pay.

#### OUR NEW BUILDING,

Erected in 1887 on the ground where HEMAN LEONARD built his one story wooden store in 1845. In 1860 the wooden store gave place to a three story brick block, and this gave place to the beautiful four story block, shown above, in 1887.

We occupy the entire four floors as salesrooms. A ladies' toilet room will be found on the second floor.

The fact that this institution will soon be 50 years old is a sufficient guarantee of its responsibility.

Goods packed for shipment and city deliveries made free of charge.

#### SEE INDEX IN BACK PART OF THIS BOOK.

## 1888 Wholesale and Retail Catalogues

As mentioned on pages 173 and 242-43, the two currently known catalogues extant with price lists from the Leonard Company are from the same date. The retail one was included in a cook book, and the other offered their merchandise to the wholesale market. Fortunately these extensive catalogues had a varied lamp selection which will provide useful information for years to come. These few pages show lamps that may be compared with other examples. A few comparisons are noted here.

A different Harvey (Canadian patent) lamp (here fashionably described as electric) is illustrated with another Harvey burner identified by the large holes above the collar. I have seen one of these. It would have required a special collar and font. Harvey chimneys were widely advertised, indicating a degree of popularity. Not shown here was a Duffield Canadian lamp.

The all-glass lamps and their wholesale prices are interesting to observe. The upper left example appears to be one with opalescent spots. They were only 15 cents a dozen more than the plain lamps, and with all examples, clear and colored lamps were the same price.

Rochester and the other lamps shown were considerably more expensive than the all-glass lamps. The ribbed glass parts of the lower left one were patented by the Mt. Washington Glass Co.

#### FORTY-FIFTH YEAR.

## Illustrated Price List

# H. LEONARD & SONS

### WHOLESALE

### Crockery, Glassware, Lamps, Silverware and House Furnishing Goods.

### Manufacturers and Importers

#### 134 TO 140 FULTON ST.,

## GRAND RAPIDS, MICHIGAN.

EATON, LYON & ALLEN PRINTING CO., GRAND RAPIDS, MICH.

H. LEONARD & SONS, GRAND RAPIDS, MICH.

### THE HARVEY ELECTRIC LAMP.

Let there be more light. The greatest problem of the age: How to obtain the most light at least cost. Solved by using the Harvey Lamp. Excels all other improvements for safety, because it has a cool air chamber surrounding the wick tube and separating it from the oil. The flame cannot come in contact with the oil. Chimneys can be removed with bare fingers while the lamp is burning. The only burner having a central draft around the wick burner. The adjoining illustration represents the Harvey Burner as applied to a glass fount. The fount can also be attached to chandeliers.

*Harvey Burner attached to Glass Fount.*

| | |
|---|---|
| No. 5 Glass Stand Lamp, with Harvey Burner....each | 1 00 |
| Advance " " " " " " .... | 1 00 |
| No. 1 Harvey Glass Founts, with Harvey Burner, " | 75 |
| Harvey Brass Cups.................:......per dozen | 1 25 |

### NIGHT LAMPS.

*The Nutmeg.*    *No. 467.*

| | |
|---|---|
| Nutmeg, assorted colors—per dozen................... | 1 50 |
| No. 467. Hammered brass stands, 9 inches high to top of chimney. The handsomest Lamp in the market—per dozen................... | 2 25 |
| The Peerless; same size and shape as the Nutmeg, hand painted, assorted decoration—per dozen................... | 2 40 |

## OPEN STOCK.

### GLASS HAND LAMPS.—See page 258 for Burners.

No. 713 Hand Lamps—     Per doz.
Crystal .......................... 1 50
Amber.......................... 1 50
Blue.......................... 1 50

No. 704 Hand Lamp—     Per doz.
Crystal ......................... 1 25

No. 700 Hand Lamp, Crystal...... 75

 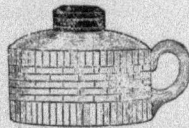

No 707 Hand Lamps—
Crystal .......................... 1 35
Amber.......................... 1 35
Blue.......................... 1 35

No. 702 Hand Lamp, Crystal..... 75

No. 70, Assorted, 3 colors, per doz 1 00     No. 223, Crystal, per doz...... 1 00

No. 709 Hand Lamp—
Crystal ......................... 85
Amber.......................... 85
Blue.......................... 85

No. 221, Crystal, per doz.... 1 00     No. 218, Crystal, per doz.... 1 00

---

## CELEBRATED "ROCHESTER" LAMPS.

Each
No. 2714. Antique Brass. (See cut.) Lamp and Tripod only .. 7 00

Same complete with White Dome Shade and Chimney...... 7 35

Same complete with Decorated Shade.. 7 85

No. 2756. Dead White Satin finish, handsomely decorated Base. Lamp and Tripod only....... 7 50

Same complete with Satin Finish Shade to match.......... 10 50

No. 2714 Antique Brass.     No. 2756 Satin Finish.

No. 2755. Dead White Satin Finish, corrugated Lamp Vase handsomely decorated antique brass trimming. Lamp and Tripod only... 8 50

Same complete with Corrugated Shade to match. Dead Satin Finish....... 11 50

No. 2754. Dead White Satin Finish, handsomely decorated Base, antique brass trimming. Lamp and Tripod only... 8 50

Same complete with Satin Finish Shade decorated to match 11 50

 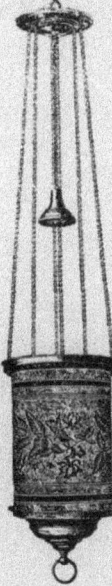  

No. 2755 Satin Finish     No. 2754 Satin Finish.

---

## STUDENT LAMPS.

 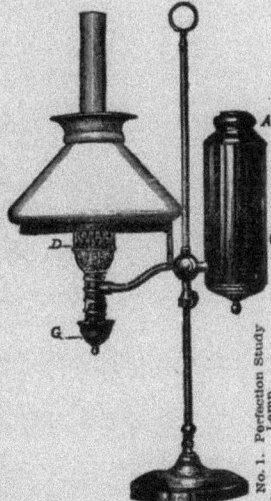

No. 1. American Study Lamp.     No. 1. Perfection Study Lamp.

Each.
No. 1. Nickle, 7 inch Study Lamp complete; either style.................................. 2 75
No. 1. Nickle, 7 inch Study Lamp complete, with green shade.................................. 3 50
No. 1. Nickle, 7 inch Study Lamp complete, with pink shade.................................. 4 50
No. 5. Nickle, 10 inch Study Lamp complete, with white shade.................................. 5 00

### THE DIAMOND REFLECTOR LAMP.

The Burner is of Argand principle, taking a regular wick and chimney, to be found everywhere.

The light is concentrated by a Parabolic Metal Reflector, which surrounds the flame, except that to which the light is to be reflected. The Reflector is adjustable and can be instantly turned in any direction desired, throwing a strong, brilliant light upon all objects in view.

The top of burner, chimney and reflector are removed together to light, and replaced in an instant.

The heat of the flame is all thrown off, the lamp remaining cool and safe to handle or relight after burning any length of time.

No matter how many lamps you have in your home or place of business, an absolute want exists for the Parabolic Reflector Lamp.

---

## EXTENSION HALL AND LIBRARY LAMPS.

Our assortment is entirely too great for these pages. Send for our complete Library Lamp Illustrated Price List. Lamps are wanted and sold in all seasons of the year, and are always considered the most profitable goods a merchant can handle. Keep your assortment full. Every variety of trimmings to be had from us.

No. 567.     No. 1333, 40 in.     No. 1337, 40 in.     No. 463, 40 in. No. 464, 36 in.

| | Each. | Per doz. |
|---|---|---|
| No. 567. F. B. Library Lamp, complete......................... | 1 50 | 17 00 |
| No. 567. E. & G. Library Lamp, complete......................... | 1 65 | 18 75 |
| Trimmed with White Cone Shade, Eureka Burner, Chimney and Bell. | | |
| No. 1333 Rich Gold Hall Light, Ruby Polka-dot Globe, complete | 3 75 | |
| No. 1333 " " " " Amber or Blue Polka-dot Globe, " | 3 50 | |
| No. 1337 " " " " Ruby Polka-dot Globe, " | 3 50 | |
| No. 1337 " " " " Amber or Blue Polka-dot Globe, " | 3 25 | |
| No. 463. F. B. Hall Light, Large Engraved Crystal Globe........... | 2 50 | |

UNITED STATES GLASS CO., PITTSBURGH, PA.
Nº 9810 LAMPS.
— WITH —
NEW CLINCH COLLAR.

This Clinch Collar is spun on under heavy pressure, making a thorough seal without the use of plaster, and cannot be removed without breaking the Glass.

A. Footed Hand. No. 1 Collar.

½ A Footed Hand. No. 1 Collar.

½ A. No. 1 Collar.

SCALE ½.

A. No. 1 Collar.

B. No. 1 or 2 Collar.

UNITED STATES GLASS CO., PITTSBURGH, PA.
Nº 9828 LAMPS.
— WITH —
NEW CLINCH COLLAR.

This Clinch Collar is spun on under heavy pressure, making a thorough seal without the use of plaster, and cannot be removed without breaking the Glass.

A. Footed Hand. No. 1 Collar.

½ A Footed Hand. No. 1 Collar.

½ A. No. 1 Collar.

SCALE ½.

A. No. 1 Collar.

B. No. 1 or 2 Collar.

# United States Glass Company Catalogue

Five designs and a strange type of glass were employed by this company to introduce their "New Clinch Collar." The collar was described on each page as follows, "This Clinch Collar is spun on under heavy pressure, making a thorough seal without the use of plaster, and can not be removed without breaking the Glass."

Two of these designs are illustrated in OL-2. The fishscale design No. 9839 page 115 (k) has a conventional collar. Perhaps this and other lamps in the catalogue were designs made before they began using the clinch collar. Lamp No. 9840, that I called Jewel Clusters in OL-2 page 111 (r), has the clinch collar with a pronounced rib close to the vertical portion of the collar. This rib can barely be discerned on the catalogue pages, but it appears to be at the bottom of the collar.

Each of the lamps except the grape design No. 9828 was illustrated in several sizes of stand lamps, footed-hand lamps, and flat hand lamps. The footed-hand lamp form of the two stand lamps shown in OL-2 appears to have the same handles. No. 9810 has one of the most unusual and most memorable handles that one could find, and it's good to have it identified. I have seen another hand lamp with tiny glass balls in a straight line, forming part of the handle. They do not appear to be either functional or comfortable.

United States Glass Co., Pittsburgh, Pa.
No 9830 Lamps.
— WITH —
New Clinch Collar.
This Clinch Collar is spun on under heavy pressure, making a thorough seal without the use of plaster, and cannot be removed without breaking the Glass.

A. Footed Hand.

½ A. Footed Hand.

½ A.

SCALE ½

A.

B. No. 1 or 2 Collar.

United States Glass Co., Pittsburgh, Pa.
No 9839 Lamps.
— WITH —
New Clinch Collar.
This Clinch Collar is spun on under heavy pressure, making a thorough seal without the use of plaster, and cannot be removed without breaking the Glass.

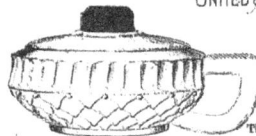

A. Flat Hand. No. 1 Collar.

½ A. Flat Hand. No. 1 Collar.

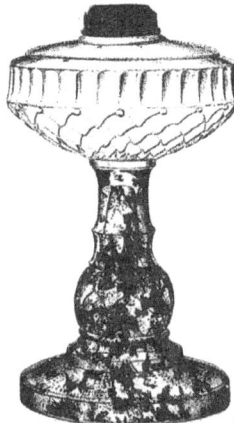

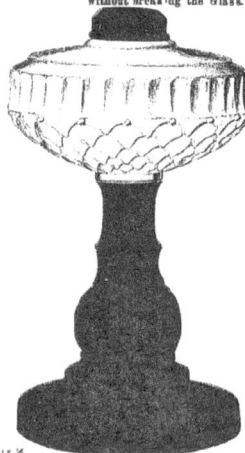

SCALE ½

C. Dec. No. 5. No. 1 or 2 Collar.

D. Dec. No. 5. No. 2 Collar.

E. Dec. No. 6. No. 2 Collar.

United States Glass Co., Pittsburgh, Pa.
No 9840 Lamps.
— WITH —
New Clinch Collar.
This Clinch Collar is spun on under heavy pressure, making a thorough seal without the use of plaster, and cannot be removed without breaking the Glass.

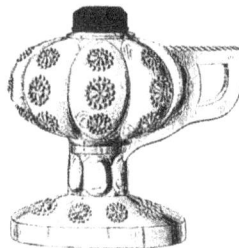

A. Footed Hand.

½ A Footed Hand.

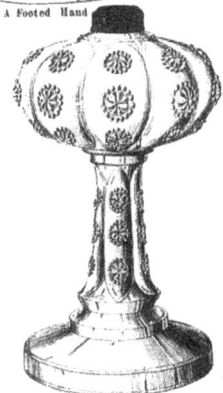

½ A.

SCALE ½

A.

B. No. 1 or 2 Collar.

In clear glass, perhaps the most interesting designs are the No. 9828 grape pattern that could be identified as Grape-1893 USG and the No. 9830 pattern that could be identified as Inverted Daisy-1893 USG. It does seem rather odd to invert the stems and flowers on the font and lamp panels, however they do conform to the shape.

Color is not mentioned in this catalogue. This is surprising since about half of the lamp bases are obviously not clear glass. The lamp base, page 111 (f) in OL-2, was No. 9840 illustrated in the 1893 catalogue. The actual color was a drab gray. Other examples are needed to identify the darker shades shown here.

Catalogue cover designers became very creative during this period. Perhaps it was realized that the currently popular flamboyant motifs would attract more attention than a plain unadorned type face. This exceptional example required greater talents to produce than those of a typesetter.

This USG Co. catalogue is approximately 10"x12". It appears to be complete although the pages are not numbered.

*Courtesy the Corning Glass Museum.*

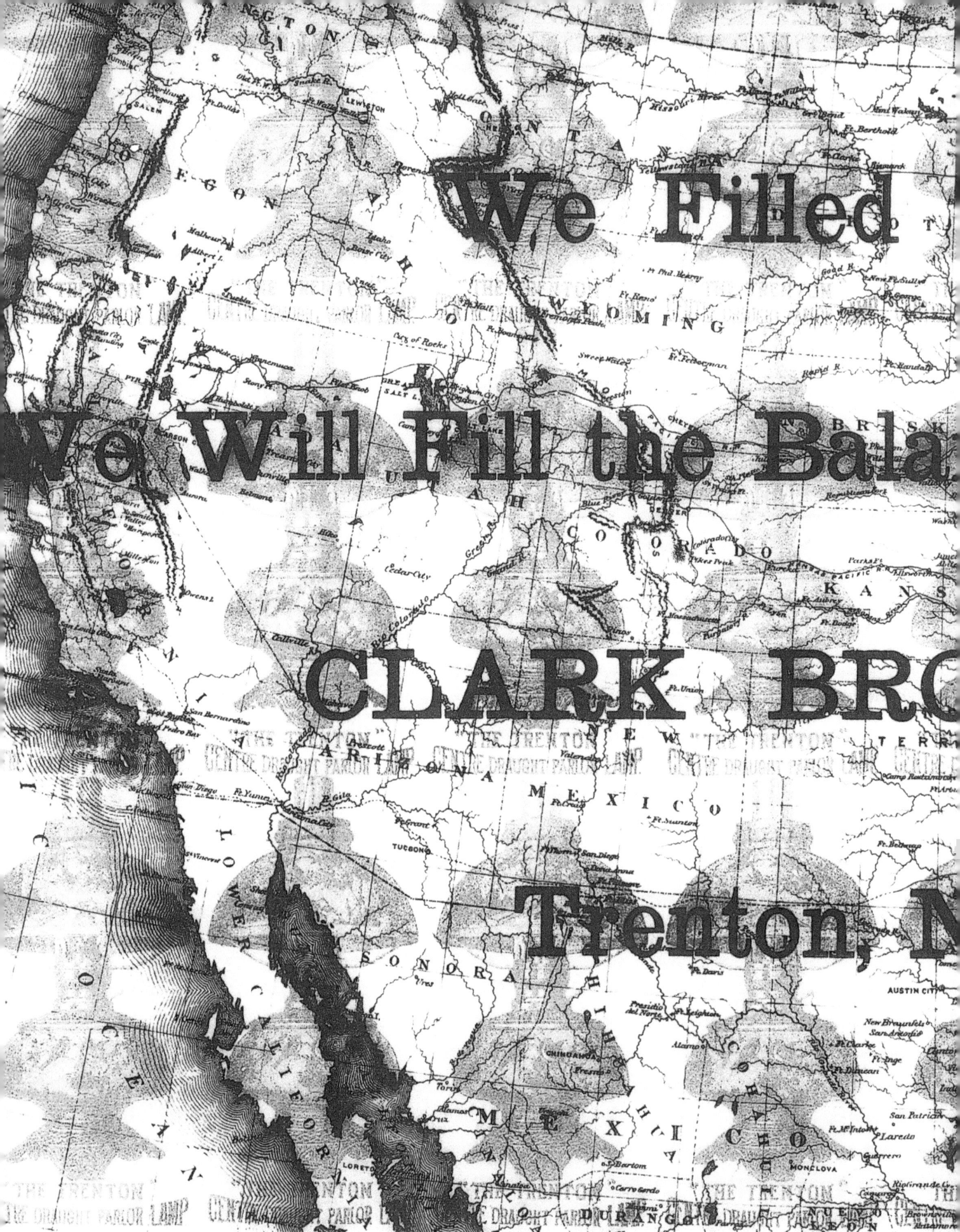

*From a December 1890 Crockery & Glass Journal. This advertisement invites study and comparison.*

is in 1890

of the Earth in 1891

COMPANY,

U. S. A.

"THE TRENTON"
CENTRE DRAUGHT PARLOR LAMP

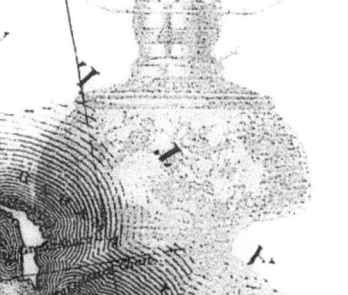

MAP OF THE
UNITED STATES

# Appendix
## Mechanical Lamp Patents

The following analysis of mechanical lamp patents was compiled by Brent Rowell:

30466 10/23/1860 "Lamp" by Francis B. De Keravenan. U.S. patent for a forced draft mechanical lamp; air tubes shown passing through oil font to burner.

37659 2/101863. "Improved Mechanical Movement for Lamps" by F. B. De Keravenan assigned to Joseph H. Bailey and George A. Jones. Patent for the clockwork mechanism which collectors have referred to as the "De Keravenan-Jones" type.

38859 6/9/1863. "Improved Mechanical Movement for Lamps" by F. B. De Keravenan assigned to Joseph H. Bailey and George A. Jones. Equivalent patent in UK (#1154) on 8 May, 1863 to Joseph H. Bailey based on "a communication from Francis B. de Keravenan." Variation of patent 37659 with a different type of blower.

40566 11/10/1863. "Improvement in Lamps" by George A. Jones. Patent for mechanical lamp oil fonts separated from an outer lamp shell by an air space.

UK 97 1/13/1864. "Oil lamps and burners, air supply to—" M.A. Dietz. Patent for mechanical lamp oil fonts suspended from the outer shell by screws.

55075 5/29/1866. "Improvement in Lamps" by Michael B. Dyott. For an air deflecting drip cup beneath font with screen for protecting clockwork.

64508 5/7/1867. "Improvement in Lamps" by M. B. Dyott. Patent for glass fonts for mechanical lamps and method of their attachment.

74695 2/18/1868. "Improvement in Trains for Lamps" by G. A. Jones. Changes in the mechanical movement to allow cheaper manufacture and more reliable service.

74914 2/25/1868. "Gearing for Lamp Trains" by Robert Hitchcock and G. A. Jones. Patent for a hard rubber fan drive gear.

125954 4/23/1872. "Improvement in Lamps for Burning Heavy Oils" by Robert Hitchcock. An adaptation of the forced draft mechanical lamp for burning heavy oils, central draft burner.

134547 1/07/1873. "Improvement in Lamps" by R. Hitchcock. Further improvements in a forced draft heavy oil burning lamp with a new type of wick raiser and rods for heating oil. This patent and 125954 were incorporated into UK 356 (1/29/1873) by J. H. Johnson on behalf of R. Hitchcock et al.

142103 8/26/1873. "Improvement in Lamps" by R. Hitchcock. Complex heavy oils lamp with clockwork combining forced draft combustion and pumping of fuel to wick. Equivalent UK 3212 (10/3/1873) by J. H. Johnson on behalf of R. Hitchcock et al.

145176 12/02/1873. "Improvement in Lamps" by R. Hitchcock. Further improvements in the heavy oils lamp combining forced draft and fuel pump.

UK 4283, 12/12/1874, by J. H. Johnson on behalf of R. Hitchcock et al shows still more improvements in Hitchcock's final patent for heavy oil lamps combining forced draft and fuel pump.

158085 12/22/1874. "Clock Movements" by R. Hitchcock. Patent for the vertical axis cylindrical clockwork movement and gear arrangement which was used in all subsequent Hitchcock "stem-winder" lamps.

UK 1102 3/15/1880. "Air supply to lamps" by J. F. Hoyne on behalf of R. Hitchcock et al. This patent incorporates the vertical axis motor design of patent 158085 into the typical Hitchcock "stem-winder" shell design. Patent also describes a stop mechanism to operate against the winding "key" in the base of the lamp.

234916 11/30/1880. "Mechanical Lamp Shell" by R. Hitchcock. Patent for mechanical lamp shell with a concave bottom on the oil font and a tube below the font to prevent oil and debris from getting into the fan.

287334 10/23/1883. "Clock-work for Mechanical Lamps" by Thomas Silver assigned to S. Elwood May. Horizontal axis clockwork motor employing a variable resistance air governor and a friction wheel fan drive.

300015 6/10/1884. "Clock-work Mechanism" by William H. Rodgers, assigned to S. Elwood May. Clockwork for mechanical lamps employing two mainsprings and a bottom winding mechanism using bevel gears (prototype for the motor used in May's mechanical lamps).

UK 8813 8/8/1884. "Lake's Improvements in Mechanism for supplying Air to Lamps" by William Robert Lake (Patent agent in UK) on behalf of unnamed applicant. This patent is very similar to US 300015.

329600 11/3/1885. "Mechanical Lamp" by Thomas Silver assigned to Orville D. Lovell. Horizontal axis clockwork motor employing a friction wheel fan drive with speed governed by horizontal movement of the driving shaft/wheel.

UK 6346 5/11/1886. "Chimneyless oil lamps" by H. Fricker on behalf of R. M. Wanzer. Patent for Wanzer's (actually Able Heath's) side-winding motor with gear train exterior to the fan/air tube; also describes drip guard and a motor stop mechanism.

345900 7/20/1886. "Forced Draft Lamp" by Robert Hitchcock. Details for a type of mechanical "vase lamp;" incorporates a side-winding mechanism for the vertical axis cylindrical motor.

UK 9755 7/24/1886. "Oil lamp, gas, and vapour burners, air supply to lighthouse lamps." J. H. Ross and Ross' patent Lighting Co. Mechanical lamp with fan driven by a small electric motor in the neck of the lamp; powered by a battery in the lamp base.

359968 3/22/1887. "Kerosene Lamp" by Able G. Heath. Patent for a mechanical lamp with the clockwork mechanism exterior to the central air tube and fan; also for a stop mechanism. The mechanism in this patent is similar to that used in Wanzer mechanical lamps; this patent date was stamped into the deflector rim of some Wanzer lamps: "The Wanzer Lamp Co. LIMTD Philadelphia, PA. U.S.A Pat. Mch 22 1887."

UK 2833 11/23/1887. "Improvements in Lamps for Lighting and Heating Purposes and in Detail Appliances to be Used in Conjuction therewith" by Henry Fricker on behalf of Richard Mott Wanzer. Similar to US Patent 359968 but with gear train on the opposite side of the central tube from the mainspring; additional details include a hood/reflector and ring frame for heating kettles, etc.

376692 1/17/1888. "Adjustable Reflector and Hood-Shade for Lamps" by Richard M. Wanzer assigned to The Wanzer Lamp Company (Limited), Philadelphia, Pa. A reflector and hood/shade designed for Wanzer mechanical lamps; differs from hood described in UK 2833.

389569 9/18/1888. "Kerosene Lamp" by Able G. Heath assigned to R. M. Wanzer. Patent for drip cup attached to bottom of font. Witnessed by W. A. Lovell.

UK 1769 2/3/1890. "Chimneyless oil lamps." T. M. Thompson. For a mechanical lamp with two or more air tubes passing through the font and reminiscent of De Keravenan's first mechanical lamp patent of 1860.

551728 12/17/1895. "Forced Draft Lamp" by R. Hitchcock. Patent for a new design of clockwork motor and blower — the horizontal axis "side-winder" motor used in the new "Improved Hitchcock Lamp."

618123 1/24/1899. "Forced Draft Lamp" by Haward J. Norfolk. Vertical axis clockwork for mechanical lamps with separate fan, gear train, and mainspring compartments for ease of disassembly and repair.

620130 2/28/1899. "Forced Draft Lamp" by Robert Hitchcock. Further improvements on the "Improved Hitchcock Lamp" (patent 551728) aimed at quieter running and cheaper manufacture. Of the five principal patent claims, only two appear to have been implemented; at least one of these claims (the partition in the lower lamp shell) had been described in 551728.

# Notes

General information, quotations, and additional notes are given here as well as information related to specific pages or examples. Notes from *The Crockery Journal (TCJ)*, 1874 & 1875 and *Crockery & Glass Journal (CGJ)*, in and after 1875 are numerous and will usually be indicated by their initials.

## Care and Use:

A statement regarding the use of kerosene lamps is prudent here. There are risks involved in the handling of any artifacts. The greater the value and rarity, the greater care that should be taken. Original finishes are rare and should be preserved, *not destroyed by cleaning!*

The use of reproduction chimneys made of Pyrex is advisable. Chimneys and shades made for use with electric lights can shatter with the heat of a kerosene flame. Chimneys and shades can also shatter with an abrupt change of temperature. Wicks should be turned up gradually and not too high. It is an impressive recreation of history to experience kerosene lighting in the absence of ambient light.

## Research and Patents:

Major discoveries of catalogues and other primary source material have occurred over the past thirty years. The accessibility of this information, as well as information such as patent records and city directories, has improved dramatically. Among my first patent records was a list of mechanical lamp patents given to me by George Sherwood. In those days the only way for me to locate patents was to comb the Patent Indexes and Official Gazettes in Washington. This was before microfilm and at a time when the classification was a nightmare. Researching specific patentees or assignees alphabetically was much easier.

While photographing articles for my book *Primitives and Folk Art* at the home of Mabel and Larry Cooke in the early 1980s, they showed me their collection of *Patent Gazettes*. Between the tools, folk art, a mechanical lamp with lion heads (see p. 131), and the patents, it was a never-to-be-forgotten visit. Not long after, Larry put me in touch with a dealer who had a lot of *Patent Gazettes* to sell. They were only available as a lot — *a three-ton lot!* It was Peter Blundell who travelled to Connecticut to retrieve them for me. He also found a wonderful charcoal portrait of a young Ontario girl dated 1879. This remains with me today, long after the books found another home.

Patent lists compiled by Howard G. Hubbard, John Knowles, Herbert Leflet, and Dan Mattausch, as well as the patent information provided by Kerry Bachler, Abbe and Ed

Meyer, Brent Rowell, and others have been important in building my collection of over five thousand patents. Whether browsing or researching, these records are a perpetual source of pleasure.

In the near future there should be surprising number of nineteenth century catalogues either reprinted or readily available for research. I would like to remind those entering the field of research today of the way it was when there were major problems involved in finding the correct patent listing and numbers and when the slippery sepia-toned copies issued by the Patent Office took weeks to arrive.

Authors of books on glass and lighting that were published decades ago and which are still very useful worked in a different world. Authors in the twenty-first century can build upon the foundation of their achievements while enjoying the benefits of technology that will enhance creativity and presentation.

## Atterbury Notes:

The following news item is from *CGJ*, Dec. 8, 1875, p. 17.

Atterbury & Co., "The White House Factory." This house was originally established in 1835, the Messrs. Atterbury, the present proprietors taking charge in 1860. They report their Western trade as having been good more than at any other house in that line, and their fertility of invention in bringing out novelties cannot be surpassed They have always something new in hand. Among the latest patterns is their new opal bowl lamp with crystal foot. These are joined without their usual metallic or cement fastening, which are so apt to become loosened in time, and the junction is so skilfully made that the parts seem to form one perfect whole. How it is done the Messrs. A. do not tell, but that it is well done no one can deny. These lamps have had a very large sale. Their hexagon foot stand lamp, with bust stem, is an elegant article. This can be taken apart and screwed together at will. This has no point, but works with glass screws and sockets. The busts are either in opal, black, or turquoise, and the bowls ribbed, imitation cut, or frosted. They manufacture also a large variety of screw socket lamps and all kinds of entirely glass and hand lamps. A recent invention is their combination opal globe which does away entirely with the necessity of chimney or shade rings and produces a steady and mellow light.

The sale for this is very large. They have also other new features in the shape of opal glass shades and

German Student chimneys for Argand burners, in opal or plain glass, which, it is claimed, gives a better light than the Argand Student chimney, now in general use. A greater novelty still is their "Air Tube Lamp." This has an air tube passing from the outside of the bowl to the inside of the burner, which furnishes a constant current of air, and this besides preventing smoking, produces perfect combustion. These are only a few of their new articles in their lamp line, and for an idea of the many others, their fine catalogue must be referred to.

This article contains information about many products in this and my earlier lamp books. It is quoted on pages 102 and 105. Some of the comments are difficult to relate to their known lamps, especially the "Air Tube Lamps." The description suggests the Hoyt Lamps made by the Union Glass Co. They were not mentioned in the known Atterbury lamp catalogues.

## Bradley & Hubbard Notes:

The following news item is from *CGJ* Nov. 29, 1877.

### Bronze Clocks and Lamps

It is only of recent years, and very lately at the best, that our people of taste have been willing to acknowledge the possibility of anything really artistic emanating from or being created by American workmen. The very name of our nationality being affixed to an article of virtu, a painting, etc., was enough to condemn it to their self-opinionated fastidious tastes. The art decorations and adornment which graced the mansions of the rich must have a nominal European paternity; there was no room for home-made articles of the sort at any price. There was some foundation for this, so far as certain classes of goods were concerned, for our manufacturers generally aimed at making either plain, durable wares, or when they aspired to anything of a higher grade of finish were apt to be a little too florid in their styles, or else use ornamentation to conceal their defects or inferior material. A great change has taken place, a perfect revolution in respect to such matters, and today we vie as a manufacturing people with our rivals "over the ocean" in both beauty and intrinsic merit in the very choicest products. No house in the country has done more in its way to carrying out this good work, and none has more effectively triumphed in its peculiar branch of manufactures than the Bradley & Hubbard Manufacturing Company, engravings of a few of whose admirable works grace the front page of this issue.

The article continues with descriptions of Bradley and Hubbard products.

p. 7

An article by Jane Spillman in the *The Glass Club Bulletin* Number 183, Fall 1998 that describes the collection of the Technischen Museum in Vienna, illustrates an example of this Diamond and Thumbprint pattern New England compote that they acquired at the Industrial Exposition in New York, 1857.

The pillar-molded kerosene lamp like one in the Huntington Museum of Art has been attributed to J. B. Lyon circa 1859, by the former chief curator Eason Eige.

The burning-fluid lamps are illustrated and identified on p. 30.

p. 18

The round version of the Howe font, also shown in the Mt. Washington Loomis photograph, appears to be the No. 2293 font pictured in *The Glass Industry In Sandwich* by Barlow & Kaiser.

p. 30

In addition to the Samuel Rust example shown and the Samuel Rust patent model at the National Museum of American History, several other examples of lamps that appear to be of the 1830s, have distinctive ribbed knops. The most recently described are in an article by Arthur Green in *The Glass Club Bulletin* Number 186, Spring 2000.

p. 23

July 14, 1868 Crosby patent No. 79,958.
June 15, 1875 Kneeland patent No. 164,380.

p. 26

Although 1880 is considered the beginning of the electric light, it would be a few decades before improvements would provide serious competition to either kerosene or gas lighting. There were many promotional articles and events for this invention, however this simple account that appeared on page 8 of the January 1, 1880 *CGJ* serves as a rather homey personal introduction to one of the most significant developments in history.

### Edison's Light

The laboratory of Mr. Edison at Menlo Park was brilliantly illuminated last Saturday night with a new electric light, the occasion being a visit of a number of the inventor's personal friends. Forty lamps in all were burning from six o'clock until after ten. The various parts of the system were explained by the inventor at length. As a practical illustration of his method of subdividing the electric current, he had two copper wires of about an eighth of an inch in thickness leading to the generating machines placed side by side on cleats along tables nearly the entire length of the laboratory. To these he connected lamp after lamp by merely fastening little wires to each of the parallel supply wires and then attaching them to the lamps. The illumination or extinguishment made not the slightest perceptible difference in the strength of the current.

Twenty electric lamps burned with exactly the same brilliancy as did one when the other nineteen were disconnected. The light given was of the brilliancy of the best gas jet, perhaps a trifle more brilliant. The effect of the light on the eyes was much superior to gas in softness and excited the admiration of all who saw it.

A new feature shown by the inventor for the first time was the method of regulating the strength of the current to be used at the central stations. By moving a little wheel the assistant in charge of this branch of the system was enabled to readily vary the strength of the electric lights from the merest glimmer to a dazzling incandescence. When the latter point was reached, the little horseshoe paper presented the appearance of a beautiful globe of fire. The method of obtaining the vacuum in the little glass bulbs of the lamps was also explained and proved highly interesting.

Some of the questions put to the inventor furnish a sample of the character of those constantly being showered on him by persons whose scientific knowledge is considerably below par. Said one spectator as he curiously examined the little bulb in the process of being exhausted, "But Mr. Edison, how do you extract the vacuum?".

The general laugh that followed put a quietus on further interrogatories from the inquisitive sight-seers. Another spectator solemnly observed that the inventor ought to devise some way to close up pores of the glass, and he seemed at sea when it was explained to him that glass was homogeneous. All sorts of suggestions and of the most ridiculous character from would-be scientists are among the inflictions which the completion of the electric light has brought upon Mr. Edison. Letters are pouring in upon him from all over the country suggesting every modification of the horseshoe filament, from a knitting needle to a small crowbar. Asbestos paper is however, the favorite. About sixty persons have already urged its substitution for the carbon, forgetting that asbestos is a non-conductor of electricity. The little motor for running sewing-

machines and other light work was also shown and created much interest. The electricity consumed for the operation of a sewing-machine is equal to that required to give out an illumination of the brilliance of an ordinary gas jet.

The effect of the exhibition was to convince those present who before were skeptical that Mr. Edison had in reality produced the electric light for household illumination.

No day is yet set for the general public exhibition, but it is quite probable that within a week everything will be in readiness to be seen by all who desire in Menlo Park.

p. 65

See "A Collection of Old Lighting Patent Models" by Bret Farnum, *The Rushlight*, Volume XLVII, No. 3 September 1981. 2384-2389.

In the November 8, 1877 issue of *CGJ*, an article describes an auction of patent rights. A few of the lighting related prices realised are noted here:

A lamp extinguisher $1,200;

An improved lamp chimney, $250; another, $1,000;

An improved lantern for miners' hats and conductors, $1,450;

A safety oil-can, $500.

These prices were among the highest ones listed.

p. 93

*The Glass Club Bulletin* No. 163 Winter 1990-91. Adams & Company, A Closer Look by Jane Shadel Spillman," Blakeslee patent No. 82,480.

p. 94

*CGJ* Dec. 30, 1875. An article described these lamps as Adams & Company most popular new patterns this season. The stand lamp was No. 60 and the hand lamp was their No. 70.

p. 103 i.

This may have been an article made from Duncan molds at a later date.

p. 106

See *The Rushlight*. Volume 65 No. 4 pp. 2-17 "The Cleveland Non-Explosive Lamp Company: Perkins & House's Metallic Safety Lamps," by Marianne Nolan.

p. 130

Mechanical Lamps. Future Hitchcock research could include the relationship of Robert to Wilbur Hitchcock who was also a patentee. One of his patents was for an intricate and interesting electric light shade. According to F. Hollister McQuin who was a neighbour of the Hitchcock family in the early twentieth century, Wilbur was employed by Edison to promote electric light. McQuin said Wilbur would return from trips abroad with interesting gifts. This information is from a taped interview made in the early 1980s.

p. 187

Lithophane reference from *TCJ* Feb. 27, 1875.

A one-piece seven-inch dome Lithophane shade described as a "Pressed Porcelain Shade" was advertised by C. F. A. Hinrichs Lamp Goods. The page illustrated student stand, wall- and hanging lamps.

p. 208

(a) Henry C. Hutchinson Patent No. 45,719.

(c) Another patent, No. 566,882 Sept. 1, 1896 for a metal wick-adjusting device was granted to J. F. Usher of West Medford, Massachusetts. Both patents had the same witness, Frederick L. Emery.

p. 209

(b) & (d) Patent No. 46,730 granted to Dexter Symonds of Lowell Mass. Mar. 7, 1865.

(c) March 25, 1862, Patent No. 34,782 granted to J. Sangster.

(f) March 24, 1863, Patent No. 37,987 granted to A. G. Tisdel & W. Nash of Watertown, N.Y.

(g) January 24, 1860, Patent No. 26,952 granted to George Neilson of Boston was assigned to H.B.& H. See also improvement No. 30,082. This burner and chimney and the Sangster burner were advertised in a Dietz, London, England catalogue c. 1865.

p. 211

The Glow Light Company also made enamelled white, brass seamless "Glow Candles" with nickel-plated shade holders.

p. 212

(a) March 20, 1877 Patent No. 188,533.

(c) September 5, 1876 Patent No. 181,909.

(f) May 5, 1863 Patent No. 38,422 granted to O. J. Savage & George P. Hawley of Ithaca, N.Y.

p. 214

Household lanterns represent a small segment of an important branch of kerosene lighting. The following Aug. 26th 1875 excerpt from an article that appeared in *CGJ* examines the perspective of the subject at that time.

### The Manufacture of Lanterns

No improvement in the method of obtaining artificial light can ever supersede the necessity for portable apparatus for illumination and therefore the manufacture of lanterns is likely to remain an important branch of the industry. Indeed with the extension of the railroad, manufacturing, and commercial enterprises generally, the demand for lanterns steadily increases, and improvements in their construction appear to keep pace with the progressive spirit of the age. The magnitude of the business may be inferred from the fact that over 500,000 dozen lanterns are sold annually in the United States.

For the introduction of the most elegant and serviceable of lanterns now in use, the community is largely indebted to Mr. R. E. Dietz of Nos. 54 and 56 Fulton Street, New York. This is the oldest established lantern business in the United States, the business having originated in 1840. Mr. Dietz having the facilities for the production of lanterns of all descriptions, arranged for the use of oil, kerosene or candles: street lights fitted with gas or kerosene, and is constantly bringing in new and improved styles.

On the cover of the *CGJ* September 5, 1878, The Manhattan Brass Company advertised that they were the "Sole Manufacturers of the ONLY GENUINE HURRICANE PATENT LANTERNS (ALL BRASS.). They also mentioned a special sale of 3,000 dozen to be "Sold Cheap."

p. 215

(b) May 8, 1855, Patent No. 128,14 granted to D. E. Chamberlain. Patent refers to absorbent packing inside the font, used as a safety measure.

(b, c, e, f, g,) Dec. 24, 1867, Patent No. 114,906. Lantern patent granted to Henry Beebe.

(b, c, d ,i,) April 5, 1864, Patent No. 42,249, lantern patent granted to A. H. Woodward.

(j) Feb. 6, 1877. Patent No. 195,744, lantern burner patent granted to George A. Beidler.

p. 218

Footwarmers reference from Archives of Useful Knowledge by James Mease, M.D. Philadelphia. 1813. pp. 322-323

A second hint from these same pages states, "Another salutary precaution recommended to travellers is always to burn a light in the chamber of the inn where you put up at, and as lamps are not always attainable, the following method is recommended for substituting a piece of candle, so as to cause it to burn three times as slow as usual; whilst your candle is alight, form around the wick with the point of your knife, a line of fine salt resting upon the tallow, and the point finishing at the flame, this will cause it to burn very slow, and the salt will descend gradually as the tallow is consumed."

## p. 236

Shades reference from *TCJ* December 12, 1874. "Few persons not in the business have any idea of the enormous trade in the different varieties of kerosene lamps and lamp shades. Of the latest articles which are sold at wholesale by the barrel, each barrel containing nine or ten shades according to size, one house in the trade in Boston, Jones, McDuffee & Stratton, sold in nine months twelve thousand barrels, or one million four hundred thousand glass shades."

## p. 241

Not everyone was enthralled by the voluminous fabric and paper shades of the 1890s, as this excerpt (as much a tour de force as the shades themselves) from an article that appeared on p. 25 in the Dec. 1893 issue of *China Glass and Lamps* reprinted from the *Pottery Gazette* relates:

**Concerning Lamp Shades**

The philosophy of the lamp shade is as complex and as full of contradictions as the Muse of the Mode herself. You may lay down seemingly incontrovertible principles condemning this, approving that, disparaging the other, and yet be snared of a sudden by some charmingly meretricious combination, some unreasonable arrangement that " 'twere lunacy to love," and straightway fall to forswearing and recantation—for the time being at least. The thing of its very nature should be whimsical and short-lived, too. Of course, and in despite of this law of inconsistency, there are certain abominations that no witchery of juxtaposition, no gayety of treatment, could render alluring or even tolerable; and of these the most entirely offensive are such as fail through a bold festivity of intention that simulates chic, that grasps at quaintness, and produces dullness reeking with vulgarity.

Fantasy, in a lamp shade, is one of the cardinal (though not indispensable) virtues; but the impotent attempt is worse than futile, and makes for its deepest damnation. The heads of owls, or of cats, fashioned in crimson paper, with eyes of another color for the light to shine through silk shades meaninglessly be ruched

and beflounced like the worst gowns revived by this veritable rag-bag of a season; blowsy, over-blown simulacra of flowers made in paper, monstrous of size, unpleasant of hue, these and such as these are obviously out of court from the first.

The article continues in much the same vein.

## p. 245

(b) April 3, 1877, Patent No. 189,180.

(b) Article by Ed and Abbie Meyer published by the Historic Lighting Society of Canada.

(c) & (d) *CGJ* Sept. 23, 1875, the Bridgeport Brass Company advertised a Drummond burner and chimney.

(d) Feb. 27, 1877 was not a Tuesday, and therefore not a day that patents were issued. Patent reissues are indexed in the Annual Patent Office Report by subject, by patentee, and by the date and number of the reissue. The date of the original patent is not listed. To obtain this, it was necessary to order a copy of the reissue. This revealed the original patent, number, and illustration. The patent No. 176,160 dated April 18, 1876 and the reissue No. 7,529 dated Feb, 27, 1877 were granted to Thomas Atterbury and assigned by him to his brother James. While the patent illustration bears no resemblance to the Lovell Radiator, the Patent description stating

"— the whole constructed of glass and in one piece, and taking the place on a lamp of the ordinary chimney, and serving the purposes of the ordinary globe and chimney which are made in separate parts," would likely cover the Lovell product. It is also probable that Atterbury & Co. made that reversible shade.

On Jan. 8, 1878, F. H. Lovell was assigned a patent for an "Improvement in combined shade and chimney for lamps." It was made in one piece and closely resembled (d). The patentee was Samuel W. Fowler who also patented the fly-fan sold by Lovell.

(e) Nov. 5, 1881, Patent No. 209,542.

# Selected Reading

This list includes books and catalogues listed in Oil Lamps 1 and 2 that were consulted frequently, as well as new additions. See *Pressed Glass in America* by John and Elizabeth Welker listed here for further information about these and other sources. An asterisk following the listing of the books or catalogues indicates they may be ordered from the source listed.

Alsford, Denis B. Match Holders: *100 Years of Ingenuity.* Atglen, Pennsylvania: Schiffer Publishing, Ltd. 1994.*

American Historical Catalog Collection. *Lamps and Other Lighting Devices 1850–1906.* Princeton: The Pyne Press. 1972.

Antique & Colonial Lighting. *Pilabrasgo Success Oil Lamps and Decorated Vases.* Catalogue No. 13. Reprint. Clarence, New York: 1982.

Auction Catalogue. *The Barlow Sandwich Glass Collection.* James D. Julia Inc. 1996.

_____. *The Oil Lamp Collection of Catherine M.V. and Carl Thuro.* Session I & II. 1989.

_____. *The Oil Lamp Collection of Catherine M.V. and Carl Thuro.* Session III. 1990.

_____. *The Elsholz Collection of Early American Glass.* Richard A. Bourne Co., Inc. Vol. I. 1986.

_____. *The Elsholz Collection of Early American Glass.* Richard A. Bourne Co., Inc. Vol. II. & III 1987.

Baker, Gary E., et al. *Wheeling Glass 1829–1939.* Wheeling, WV: Oglebay Institute. 1994.

Barlow, Raymond E. and Joan E. Kaiser. *The Glass Industry in Sandwich.* West Chester, PA: Schiffer Publishing Ltd., in conjunction with Barlow-Kaiser Publishing, Inc., Vol. 2. 1989.

*Boston & Sandwich Glass Co. Catalogue.* Wellesley Hills, Massachusetts: Lee Publications. 1968.

Bredehoft, Neila and Tom Bredehoft. *Hobbs, Brockunier & Co., Glass.* Paducah, KY: Collector Books. 1997.

Corning Museum of Glass, The. *The Glass Collections in Museums in the United States and Canada.* Corning, New York: 1982.

Courter, J. W. *Aladdin—The Magic Name in Lamps.* Revised Edition. Paducah, Kentucky: 1997. J. W. Courter, 3935 Kelley Road, Kevil, KY 42053. Phone/Fax: (502) 488-2116.*

_____. *Angle Lamp Collectors Manual & Price Guide.* J. W. Courter, 3935 Kelley Road, Kevil, KY 42053. Phone/Fax: (502) 488-2116.*

Cuffley, Peter. *Oil & Kerosene Lamps in Australia.* Victoria, Australia: Pioneer Design Studio Pty Ltd. 1982.

Deitz, Fred. *A Leaf From the Past.* New York: R. E. Deitz Company. 1914.

Dietz, Ulysses G. *Victorian Lighting: The Dietz Catalogue of 1860.* Watkins Glen, New York: American Life Foundation. 1982.

Fairweather Antiques. *Edward Miller & Co. Illustrated Catalogue of Bronzed, Decorated, and Real Bronze Lamps and Cigar Lighters, Meriden, Conn., U.S.A.* 1881 Catalogue reprint. Fairweather Antiques, Meriden, Connecticut, 06450. 1976.*

Haussmann, Carl. *Thousand Eye Ancestral & Related Pattern Glass. Section I & Section II.* Compiled and published privately by Carl Haussmann.

Heacock, William. All of Heacocks's publications are both interesting and useful. Most of them are currently available from Antique Publications, P. O. Box 553. Marietta, OH 45750-0553.

Innes, Lowell. *Pittsburgh Glass 1797–1891: A History and Guide for Collectors.* Boston, Massachusetts: Houghton Mifflin Company. 1976.

Jenks, Bill and Jerry Luna. *Early American Pattern Glass 1850–1910.* Radnor, Pennsylvania: Wallace-Homestead Book Company. 1990.

Krause, Gail. *The Encyclopedia of Duncan Glass.* Smithtown, New York: Exposition Press, Inc. 1976.

Kreuzer, Anton. *Schönheit Der Petroleumlampen.* Universitätsverlag Carinthia. 1990.

Lindsey, Bessie M. *American Historical Glass.* Rutland, Vermont: Charles E. Tuttle Company. 1972.

McCain, Mollie Helen. *Pattern Glass Primer.* Leon, Iowa: Lamplighter Books. 1979.

Maril, Nadja. *American Lighting: 1840–1940.* West Chester, Pennsylvania: Schiffer Publishing, Ltd. 1989.

Measell, James and W.C. "Red" Roettis. *The L.G. Wright Glass Company.* Marietta, Ohio: The Glass Press, Inc., 1997.

Miller, Richard C. and John F. Solverson. *Student Lamps of the Victoria Era.* Marietta, Ohio: Antique Publications. 1992.

Padgett, Leonard E. *Pairpoint Glass.* Des Moines, Iowa: Wallace-Homestead Book Co. 1979.

Peterson, Arthur G. *Glass Patents and Patterns.* Sanford, Florida: Celery City Printing Co. 1973.

*Scientific American.*

First published in 1845 and continuing to this day, this publication provided the best scientific, technical and up-to-date patent information, particularly in the 1860s. At that time the publishers were Munn & Company, a successful patent attorney firm. For this reason the general tone is optimistic and promotional, emphasizing the rewards of a successful patent, and offering suggestions for aspiring inventors. A weekly list of patents issued with occasional comments by the editors is followed by "Notes and Queries," a question and answer column. Their name appears frequently on lighting patents. This and other trade publications, served as newsmagazines with excerpts from national and international publications. Everything from politics to household hints is included. It was my good fortune to be able to purchase bound copies of most of the 1860s issues. This has allowed me to spend countless hours just browsing through the pages.

Sherwoods Ltd. of Birmingham. *Early Twentieth Century Lighting.* West Chester, Pennsylvania: Schiffer Publishing, Ltd. 1989.

Spillman, Jane Shadel. *American and European Pressed Glass in The Corning Museum of Glass.* Corning, New York: The Corning Museum of Glass. 1981.

_____. "The Knopf Collectors' Guides to American Antiques." *Glass Tableware, Bowls and Vases.* New York: Alfred A. Knopf. 1982.

_____. "The Knopf Collectors' Guides to American Antiques." *Glass 2: Bottles, Lamps & Other Objects.* New York: Alfred A. Knopf. 1983.

Swan, Frank H. *Portland Glass.* Des Moines, Iowa: Wallace-Homestead Co. 1949.

The Association for Preservation Technology. *Illustrated Catalogue of American Hardware of the Russell and Erwin Manufacturing Company.* 1865 Catalogue reprint with an introduction by Lee H. Nelson. Baltimore, Maryland: 1980.

The Corning Museum of Glass. *Journal of Glass Studies.* Corning, New York: The Corning Museum of Glass. Vol. 39. 1997.

*The New York Farmer and Mechanic; Devoted to Agriculture, Mechanics, Maufactures, and the Arts.* S. Fleet. Editor. Farmers' and Mechanics' Agency and Record Office, 135 Nassau Street, New York. Vol. 1. 1844.

*The Plume and Atwood Manufacturing Company.* Circa 1906 Catalogue reprint. Simpson, Illinois: J. W. Courter Enterprises. 1975.

*The Rushlight.* This official publication of The Rushlight Club has for over fifty years published illustrated articles and data pertaining to the study of lighting and lighting fuels. The club has also reprinted books, pamphlets and ephemera and can advise members about other sources of information and organizations. Contact their Web Page: http//members.aol.com/amsherwin/web.htm or write to:
The Rushlight Club, Inc.
121 W. First St.
Elmhurst, IL 60126-2802

Thuro, Catherine M. V. *Oil Lamps—The Kerosene Era in North America.* Des Moines, Iowa: Wallace-Homestead Book Co. 1976.

_____. *Oil Lamps II: Glass Kerosene Lamps.* Paducah, KY: Collector Books. 1983.

_____. *Primitives & Folk Art: Our Handmade Heritage.* Paducah, KY: Collector Books. 1979.

_____. "Lighting," *The Canadian Encyclopedia.* Second Edition, Vol. 2. Edu-Min. Edmonton, Alberta: Hurtig Publishers, Ltd. 1988.

*The Rushlight.* "Lomax Lamps" The Rushlight Club. Vol. XLVI, No. 4. December 1980.

_____. "Patented Kerosene Lighting the Inside Story," *The Rushlight Club.* Vol. 52. No. 2. June 1986.

_____. "Classification of Lighting and Related Patents," *The Rushlight Club.* Vol. 53, No. 1. March 1987.

_____. "Joseph Gallinger's Lamps and Patent," *The Rushlight Club.* Vol. 54, No. 4. December 1988.

_____. "Charles A. Starr Joins Mid-Century Lamp Catalogs," *The Rushlight Club.* Vol. 56. No. 3. 1990.

_____. "Pieces of a Puzzle: Globe Naphtha Gas Lights," *The Rushlight Club.* Vol. 58, No. 2. June 1992.

*The Illuminator.* The Historical Lighting Society of Canada. Vol. 1. No. 1-4. 1987.

_____. *The Illuminator.* The Historical Lighting Society of Canada. Vol. 2. No. 1-4. 1988.

_____. *The Illuminator.* The Historical Lighting Society of Canada. Vol. 3. No. 1-4. 1989.

Van Es, James. Lamps. *Chandeliers and Lamp Goods.* Hubbard-Spencer Bartlett & Co. Circa 1900. Catalogue. James Van Es. P.O. Box 1126, Herndon, VA. 20172.*

Welker, John W. and Elizabeth F. *Pressed Glass in America, Encyclopedia of The First Hundred Years.* 1825–1925. Ivyland, PA: Antique Acres Press, 1985.

Whitehouse, David. Glass: *A Pocket Dictionary of Terms Commonly used to Describe Glass and Glass Making.* Corning, New York: The Corning Museum of Glass, 1993.

Wilson, Kenneth M. *New England Glass & Glassmaking.* New York, New York: Thomas Y. Crowell Company, 1972.

_____. *American Glass 1760–1930.* New York, New York: Hudson Hills Press, Inc. Vol. 1. 1994.

_____. *American Glass 1760–1930.* New York, New York: Hudson Hills Press, Inc. Vol. 2. 1994.

Wolfe, John J. *Brandy, Balloons & Lamps: Ami Argand, 1750–1803.* Carbondale and Edwardsville: Southern Illinois University Press. 1999.

In the future microfilm, microfiche, and the Internet will make much more primary source information available at home or libraries.

# Index

1865 Illustrated Catalogue of American
  Hardware of the Russell and Erwin
  Manufacturing Co. . . . . . . . . . . .202, 250
1867 Ives' Patent Lamp Catalogue . . . .106
1875 F. H. Lovell Catalogue . . . . . . . . .131
1877-78 F. H. Lovell Catalogue . . . . . .212
1881-82 F. H. Lovell Catalogue . . . . . .133
1884 and 1885 F. H. Lovell
  Catalogues . . . . . . . . . . . . . . . . . . . .135
1889 F. H. Lovell & Co. . . . . . . . . . . . .107
1892 Butler Bros. Catalogue . . . . . . . . .109
1893 United States Glass Company
  Catalogue . . . . . . . . . . . . . . . . . . . .109
1898 Henry & Nathan Russell &
  Day Catalogue . . . . . . . . . . . . . . . .198
1918 Handlan Railway Supply Co.
  Catalogue . . . . . . . . . . . . . . . . . . . .106
Accessories & Novelties . . . . . . . .227-234
Acetylene . . . . . . . . . . . . . . . . . . . . . . .32
Adams, Adolphus A. . . . . . . . . .88, 89, 95
Adams, John . . . . . . . . . . . . . . . . .93, 94
Adams Bouquet Lamp . . . . . . . . . . . . . .88
Adams-Bridges Font . . . . . . . . . . . . . .116
Adams Lamp . . . . . . . . . . . . . . .92, 118
Adams Vase Lamp . . . . . . . . . . . . . . . .88
Adams & Co. . . . . . .80, 88-91, 93-95, 116
Adams Plain Iron Handle . . . . . . . . . . . .93
Adams 1876 Patent Lamp . . . . . . . . . . .95
Adams Temple Lamp . . . . . . . . . . . . . .89
Adams Ten Panel Lamps . . . . . . . . . . . .93
Adams Corner Windows . . . . . . . . . . . .89
Adams Hollow-Stem No. 90 . . . . . . . . .89
Aladdin . . . . . . . . . . . . . . . . . . . . . . . .32
Alexander, H. C. . . . . . . . . . . . . . . . . .142
Altmyer, Nicholas . . . . . . . . . . . . . . . .107
Amberina Hobnail Shade . . . . . . . . . . .198
American Gaslight Journal . . . . . . . . . . .66
Angle Lamps . . . . . . . . . . . . . . .168, 186
Annie Lamp . . . . . . . . . . . . . . . . . . . .149
Ansonia Brass and Copper Co. . . . . . . .113
Archer & Pancoast Lantern . . . . . . . . . .217
Arnold's Combined Stove and Lantern  221
Art Glass Shades . . . . . . . . . . . . . . . .205
Association for Preservation
  Technology . . . . . . . . . . . . . . .66, 166
Atterbury & Co. . . .56, 57, 60, 65, 98, 100,
     103, 104, 105, 113, 124, 184, 245
Atterbury & Co. 1881 Catalogue . . . . .245
Atterbury 1881 Catalogue . . . . . . . . . . .79
Atterbury All-Glass . . . . . . . . . . . . . . .125
Atterbury Band . . . . . . . . . . . . . . . . . .125
Atterbury Blown Scroll and Rib . . . . . .124
Atterbury Brothers . . . . . . . . . . . . .94, 100
Atterbury Buckle . . . . . . . . . . . . . . . . .238
Atterbury Chieftain . . . . . . . . . . . . . . .124
Atterbury Combined Chimney and
  Shade . . . . . . . . . . . . . . . . . . . . . .245
Atterbury Composite Stand Lamps . . . . .79
Atterbury Crystal . . . . . . . . . . . . . . . . .125
Atterbury/Dithridge Chimney . . . . . . . .100
Atterbury's Earliest Lamps . . . . . . . . . .120
Atterbury Eureka Base . . . . . . . .100, 121
Atterbury Filley . . . . . . . . . . . . . . . . . .123
Atterbury Figural with Vine Font . . . . .102
Atterbury Grecian . . . . . . . . . . . . . . . .125
Atterbury Hercules . . . . . . . . . . . . . . .126
Atterbury Hand Lamp No. 25 . . . . . . . .122
Atterbury, James S. . . .60, 98, 99, 124, 125

Atterbury Lamps . . . . . .102, 121-124, 126
Atterbury Maguire . . . . . . . . . . . . .121, 123
Atterbury/Merrill Clock Lamp . . . . . . .100
Atterbury's Octagon . . . . . . . . . . . . . . .121
Atterbury Ohio Lamp . . . . . . . . . . . . . .122
Atterbury O. K. . . . . . . . . . . . . . .121, 238
Atterbury Panel Bases . . . . . . . . . . . . .125
Atterbury Patented Drip-Catcher . . . . .124
Atterbury Rib and Leaf Band Lamp . . .122
Atterbury Shelley . . . . . . . . . . . . . . . .124
Atterbury's Saucer Lamp with
  Handle . . . . . . . . . . . . . . . . . . . . .121
Atterbury Scroll Lamp with
  Saucer Base . . . . . . . . . . . . . . . . .100
Atterbury Sherman Lamp . . . . . . . . . . .122
Atterbury Shoe Lamps . . . . . . . . . . . . .103
Atterbury's Squat Octagon Base . . . . . .121
Atterbury Star Lamp . . . . . . . . . . . . . .104
Atterbury's Sun . . . . . . . . . . . . . . . . . .121
Atterbury Swans . . . . . . . . . . . . . . . . . .99
Atterbury, Thomas B. . . . . . .60, 79, 98-100,
     108, 120, 124, 125, 245
Atterbury Tucker . . . . . . . . . . . . . . . . .126
Atterbury Tulip Lamp . . . . . . . . . . . . . .98
Atterbury Wave Handle with
  Diamond Foot . . . . . . . . . . . . . . . .124
Atterbury, Wm. Penn . . . . . . . . . . . . . .122
Atwood, L. J. . . . . . . . . . . . . . . . . . . . .63
Baccarat Shade . . . . . . . . . . . . . . . . . .181
Baccarat . . . . . . . . . . . . . . . . . .173, 205
Bacon Bracket . . . . . . . . . . . . . . . . . .174
Baker . . . . . . . . . . . . . . . . . . . . . . . . .18
Baker Cut . . . . . . . . . . . . . . . . . . . . . .18
Bakewell, Benjamin . . . . . . . . . . . . . . .94
Ball Shades . . . . . . . . . . . . . . . .246-247
Ball Shade Hanging Lamp . . . . . . . . . .194
Banbury . . . . . . . . . . . . . . . . . . . . . .111
Banquet and Parlour Lamps . . . . . .146-149
Banquet Lamps . . . . . . . . . . . . . . . . . .140
Banquet, Parlour, Student &
  Piano Lamps . . . . . . . . . . . . . .140-165
Baptismal Font . . . . . . . . . . . . . . . . . .83
Barnard, H. H. . . . . . . . . . . . . . . . . . .142
Bartholomew, Cassius . . . . . . . . . . . . . .74
Bartholomew, Charles L. . . . . . . . . . . . .74
Bartlett Co. Catalogue . . . . . . . . . . . . .161
Base Lamps . . . . . . . . . . . . . . . . . . . .128
Beach, E. R. . . . . . . . . . . . . . . . . . . . .23
Beaumont Glass Co. . . . . . . . . . . . . . .118
Beer Barrel Lamp . . . . . . . . . . . . . . . .106
Bellflower . . . . . . . . . . . . . . . . . . . . .109
Bertrand . . . . . . . . . . . . .51-64, 109, 120
Bertrand Accessories . . . . . . . . . . . . . .64
Bertrand Bracket Lamps . . . . . . . . . . . .61
Bertrand Burners . . . . . . . . . . . . . . . . .63
Bertrand Chimneys . . . . . . . . . . . . . . . .62
Bertrand Hanging Lamps . . . . . . . . . . . .61
Bertrand Museum . . . . . . . . . . . . .62, 64
Best Late Lamps . . . . . . . . . . . . . . . . .24
Bethesda . . . . . . . . . . . . . . . . . . . . . .55
Black Creek Pioneer Village . . .96, 97, 172
Blackman Burner . . . . . . . . . . . . . . . .244
Blake, E. S. . . . . . . . . . . . . . . . . . . . .70
Blakeslee's Patent . . . . . . . . . . . . . . . .93
Bloxam Pattern . . . . . . . . . . . . . . . . .208
Blue Glass Craze . . . . . . . . . . . . . . . .108
Bobeche . . . . . . . . . . . . . . . . . . . . . . .31
Bohemia . . . . . . . . . . . . . . . . . . .105, 157

Bohemian Glass and Lamps . . . . . . . . .104
Bohner George . . . . . . . . . . . . . . . . . .191
Bonshire, Jacob . . . . . . . . . . . . . . . . . .94
Boston and Sandwich Glass Co. . . . . .104,
     149, 250, 253
Bourne Joseph . . . . . . . . . . . . . . . . . .245
Bourne Hero Shade . . . . . . . . . . . . . . .245
Bowie . . . . . . . . . . . . . . . . . . . . . . . .19
Bowman–Heath . . . . . . . . . . . . . . . . .137
Bracket Lamps . . .166, 173, 181, 182, 184
Bracket Lamps from the Bertrand . . . . . .61
Brackets to Hold Stand Lamps . . . . . . .180
Bradford . . . . . . . . . . . . . . . . . . . . . . .90
Bradford Variant . . . . . . . . . . . . . . . . . .90
Bradley, N. L. . . . . . . . . . . . . . . . .68, 183
Bradley & Hubbard 1873
  Catalogue . . . . . . . . . . . . . .61, 254, 255
Bradley & Hubbard Parlour Lamp . . . .156
Bradley & Hubbard (B&H) . . . .21-23, 68,
     140, 141, 161, 166, 167, 182, 183,
     189, 190, 194, 197, 202, 203, 232
Bradley and Hubbard Cent. Lamp . . . . .192
Bridgeport Brass Co. . . . . . . . . . .143, 209
Bridges, John . . . . . . . . . . .94, 100, 116
Bright Line Decoration . . . . . . . . . . . . .22
Brinkerhoff, C. E. L. . . . . . . . . . . . . . .104
Bristol Brass and Clock Co. . . . . .210, 241
Brownies . . . . . . . . . . . . . . . . . .152, 153
Bryant, Edson L. . . . . . . . . . . . . . . . . .193
Bull, G. M. . . . . . . . . . . . . . . . . . . . .107
Bullseye and Comma . . . . . . . . . . . . . .18
Bullseye and Fleur-de-lis . . . . . .15, 54
Burner . . . . . . . . . . . . . . . . . . . . . . . .32
Burners & Trimmings . . . . . . . . .235-248
Burning Fluid . . . . . . . . . . . . . . . . . . .41
Butterflies and Bows . . . . . . . . . . . . . .15
Cable Base . . . . . . . . . . . . . . . . . . . .116
Cahoon, C. W. . . . . . . . . . . . . . . . . . .212
Cahoon, Charles W. . . . . . . . . . . . . . .236
Candle Lamps . . . . . . . . . . . . . . . . . .211
Candelabrum . . . . . . . . . . . . . . . . . . .211
C. A. Van Kirk & Co. . . . . . . . . . . . . . .60
Cardan Lamps . . . . . . . . . . . . . . . . . .142
Catalogue of Petroleum or Kerosene
  Oil Lamps and Chandeliers . . . . . . . .250
Centennial Exhibition, Philadelphia
  1876 . . . . . . . . . . . . . . . . . . . . . . .192
Center Medallion . . . . . . . . . . . . . . . . .24
Central Glass Co. . . . . . . . . . . . . . . . .116
Chamberlain & Smith . . . . . . . . . . . . .233
Chandelier . . . . . . . . . . . . .167, 202, 203
Charles A. Starr Catalogue . . . . . .43, 250
Chevron Band . . . . . . . . . . . . . . . . . .114
Chicago 1893 World's Fair . . . . . . . . . .147
Chimney Cleaning Devices . . . . . . . . . .233
Chimney Tidy . . . . . . . . . . . . . . . . . . .234
Chinnock, Charles . . . . . . . . . . . . . . . .159
Chinnock Patent . . . . . . . . . . . . .139, 212
City Manufacturing Co. . . . . . . . . . . . .236
Cleveland Non-Explosive Lamp Co. . .106
Close, Charles T. . . . . . . . . . . . . . . . .128
Coalport . . . . . . . . . . . . . . . . . . . . . .147
Coalport China . . . . . . . . . . . . . . . . . .165
Coleman . . . . . . . . . . . . . . . . . . . . . . .32
Collins Burners . . . . . . . . . . . . . . . . . .241
Collins-type Burner . . . . . . . . . . . . . . .233
Color & Decoration . . . . . . . . . . .104, 105
Coloured Glass . . . . . . . . . . .108, 188, 189

Columbian Exposition 1893 ........165
Combination Shades ..............245
Concentric Circles ...............114
Conquistador Lamp ................86
Consolidated Lamp and
 Glass Co. .....................150
Cooking with Kerosene ........222, 223
Coral ...........................118
Coral Pattern ...................180
Corbino, Sam .....................53
Cornelius, Robert .................63
Cornelius & Baker burners .........63
Corning Museum of Glass .....18, 83, 89,
 140, 151, 152, 192 , 204, 263
Cosmos ..........................150
Cottage Sewing Lamp .............109
Cox, Palmer .....................152
Crosby, Robert R. .............23, 100
Crown Shade .....................248
C. T. Ham Lantern ...............220
Curling Tong or Iron Heater ........233
Curling Tongs ...................234
Daisy ...........................150
Danforth, R. E. ..................41
Darkroom Lantern ................216
D. C. Ripley Patent ...............87
Deer, Dog and Warrior .............23
De Keravenan-Jones Patented
 Clocked Motor .................131
De Soto National Wildlife Refuge ...51
Design Patents ...................68
De Soto Visitors Center ...........52
Dew Drop .......................183
Dewdrop Lamp ...................129
Diamond Foot ...................124
Diamond Quilted Parlour Lamp .....151
Dietz, J. M. .....................217
Dietz Stoves, Heaters and
 Fireplaces .................224, 225
Dietz Tubular Parlor Heater ........225
Dietz & Co. ...............28, 36, 127,
 144, 166, 217, 236
Dietz & Co. Catalogue ...34, 43, 147, 250
Dietz No. 11 Tubular Hand Lamp .....171
Dillaway, Hiram .................124
Disasters ........................41
Dithridge & Co. ..........22, 23, 100
Dithridge Chimneys ..............179
Dodge, J. F. ......................36
Dodge ....................36, 37, 38
Dogwood Lamp ..................149
Double Bullseye ...................54
Double Crusie .....................26
Douglas, Richard ................244
Downer, Samuel ................39, 40
Downer Kerosene Oil Co. ..........39
Downer Mineral Sperm Lamp ........40
Dragons .........................156
Drake Well Museum Collection ...47-50
Drummond Burner and
 Chimney ...................178, 245
Drummond Electric Lamp ..........136
Duncan, George A. ....80, 81, 83, 85, 103
Dyott Burner ....................241
Dyott, Michael B. .........118, 131, 132
Dyott, Thomas B. ...........118, 132
E. & C. Gurney Co. ...............223
Early Banquet Lamps .........144, 145
Early Brass Bracket lamps .........179
Early Hall and Hanging Lamps ...185, 186
Early Night Lamps ...............209
Early Panelled Arches .............17
Eaton Lamp .....................127
Eaton/Onion Variations ...........127
Edward Miller & Co. ..........70, 198

Edward Miller & Co. 1881
 Catalogue .................142, 258
Edward Rorke & Co. ..............245
Egyptian Motif ..................108
Elisha Bacon 1875 Patented
 Lamp Stand ...................174
Enigma Lamps ...................112
Ephemera ........................28
E. P. Dodge ......................36
E. P. Gleason Mfg. Co. Catalogue .....173
E. P. Gleason Manufacturing Co. .....248
Eureka ..........................100
Evarts, John A. ..................192
Falls Heater .....................221
Fancy Iron ..................188, 189
Fellows, Hoffman & Co. .........37, 43
F.H. Lovell & Co. ..........113, 137,
 166, 178, 238, 245, 246
F. H. Lovell & Co. 1868-69
 Catalogue ......105, 106, 184, 204, 252
F. H. Lovell Company 1877-1878
 Catalogue ...........19, 40, 130, 167,
 180, 186, 190, 212, 238, 245, 256, 257
F. H. Lovell 1881-82 Catalogue ......135
F. H. Lovell & Co. 1888
 Export Catalogue ...............136
F. H. Lovell & Co. 1895 Catalogue ....181
F. H. Lovell & Co. Catalogue .......250
F. H. Lovell Price List ............246
F. H. Lovell & Co. Spanish Export
 Catalogue .....................148
Fifield, Henry S. .................233
Fifield's Lamp Chimney ............233
Fine Line Decoration .............22, 23
Fire-Fly Lamp ...................212
Fireside Burners ..............239, 241
Fish, W. L. ......................72
Float Lamp ......................232
Floor Lamps .................160, 161
Florence Lamp Stove .............222
Flower Holder ...................232
Flower, Rosewell P. ..............133
Folmer, William F. ...............227
Folmer & Schwing Mfg. Co. ........227
Footwarmers .................218, 219
Foster ..........................109
Fostoria Glass Co. ...........150, 162
Fostoria Parlour Lamps .........163, 164
Frink, I. P. .....................159
Fritz Heckert Studio .............157
Frosted Glass .................20, 21
Frosted Shades ...............246, 247
Fry, C. H., Jr. ...................74
Gaslighting ......................32
George Bohner & Co. .............191
George Duncan & Sons ......80-83, 103
George F. Bassett 1883 Catalogue ....193
Gesner, Abraham .................39
Giddens, Paul H. .................49
Gilbert, O. Rundle .............69, 78
Girandoles .......................35
Glass Lamps, Pressed or Blown ...14-19
Globe Shades ...................246
Glow Night Lamps ...............208
Goddess of Liberty ...............102
Gone-With-The-Wind lamp ........150
Grape and Festoon ............93, 116
Greenfield, J. A. .................74
Greenough's Patent Lamps ..........28
Gregory, Mary ..................149
Griffins ........................156
G. W. Brown & Co. ..............132
Hall Lamps ..............166, 167, 187
Hanging Lamps ..................166
Hanging Lamps from the *Bertrand* .....61

Hanna, G. V. ....................142
Hardens Hand Grenade ............108
Harvard Double Student Lamp .......159
Heart Base with Circle Band
 Blown Font ....................15
Hearts and Stars ..................56
Hearts Under Glass ................55
Heaters ........................221
Heath, Abel G. ..................137
Henry Ford Museum ...............17
Hero Shade .....................245
Handel Parlour Lamp .............154
Hero Lamp ......................194
Hinks Lamps ....................204
Hinrichs, Charles F. A. ............78
Hinrichs, F. A. ..................158
Hitchcock Lamps .........133, 135, 136
Hitchcock, Robert ................133
Hitchcock Stemwinder Lamp .......133
Hitchcock Sidewinder Lamp ........133
Hitchcock Wire Harp Lamp .........135
H. Leonard & Sons Catalogues ......173
H. Leonard & Sons 1888 Wholesale
 Catalogue .........242, 243, 260, 261
Hobbs, John H. ...................31
Hobbs, John L. ..................109
Hobbs, Brockunier & Co. .........53, 55,
 110, 114
Hobbs Clinch-connector Lamps ......110
Hobbs Diamond Cluster Melon .......114
Hobbs Frances Ware ...............118
Hobbs Fruit Medallion .............117
Hobbs Full-Rib ..................110
Hobbs Glass Co. .........117, 205, 206
Hobbs Hands ....................119
Hobbs Lamps .........109, 115-117
Hobbs Snowflake Lamps ...........109
Hobbs Optic .................118, 180
Hobbs Pillar-molded Font ..........115
Hobbs Rib and Optic Panel .........114
Hobbs Wheeling Panelled ..........116
Hobbs Wheeling Plain .............116
Hobbs X-Band and Loop ...........114
Holmes Booth and Haydens
 (H. B. & H.) .....63, 66, 209, 215, 241
Home-made Safety Cage ...........234
Hooper, H. N. ....................32
Hot-Cast Porcelain Lamp Stand .....113
Houghton & Wallace Lard Lamp .....29
Household Table Lamps .........79-139
H. R. Ives & Co. .................226
Hubbard, Spencer,
 Bartlett & Co. ...........161, 167, 259
Hughes, Seymour .................75
Humphrey, James Y. ...............64
Hutchison, Henry C. .............208
Hutchinson Burners ..............208
Iden, John F. ....................42
Illuminator Bases ................247
Iron Double Crusie ...............26
Irwin, John H. ..............171, 224
Ives, Hiram .....................244
Ives, James .....................217
Ives, Julius .....................39
Ives/Iden Spelter Figural Lamp .......106
Ives & Co. ...............147, 202, 251
Ives Patent Lamp Co. .............182
Ives' Reflector Hanging Lamp .......189
Ivy or Plant Stand ...............232
Jacobs, Timothy T. ...............64
Jacques, D. L. ...................219
Jacques 1865 Footwarmer ..........219
James Hinks & Son Limited
 Catalogue .....................204
J. B. Greene Patent Model ...........72

J. H. Hobbs, Brockunier and Co. . . . . . .117
Jones, Edward F. . . . . . . . . .63, 65, 66, 179
Jones, George A. . . . . . . . . . . . . . .131, 132
Jones Museum of Glass and
    Ceramics . . . . . . . . . . . . . . . . . . . . . . .157
J. Stouvenel & Co. . . . . . . . . . . . . . . . . .28
J. P. Smith, Son & Co. . . . . . . . . . . . . . . .94
Judson, Anson . . . . . . . . . . . . . . . . . . . .62
Julius Ives & Co. Catalogues . . . . . . . .251
Juno Center Draft Lamp . . . . . . . . . . . .156
Kerosene Heaters . . . . . . . . . . . . . . . . .226
Kerosene Lighting Catalogues . . .249-263
Kinnear Lard Lamp . . . . . . . . . . . . . . . . .29
Kintz, Joseph . . . . . . . . . . . . . . . . . . . . .68
Kittel, Joseph . . . . . . . . . . . . . . . . . . . .157
Kleeman, Carl A. . . . . . . . . . . . . . .78, 158
Kleeman Student Lamp Patent Model . .78
Kneeland, S. R. . . . . . . . . . . . . . . . . . . . .23
Kranzow Mechanical Lamp . . . . . . . . .139
La Belle Glass Co. . . . . . . . . . . . . . . . . .15
Langford, H. . . . . . . . . . . . . . . . . . . . . .107
Lantern Footwarmer . . . . . . . . . .218, 219
Lantern Patent Model . . . . . . . . . . . . . . .75
Leader Burner . . . . . . . . . . . . . . . . . . . .178
Leader Student Lamp . . . . . . . . . . . . . .143
Library Lamps . . . . . . . . . . . . . . .195-201
Library Lamp Shades . . . . . . . . . .206-207
Lighting Chart . . . . . . . . . . . . . . . . . . . .26
Lincoln, W. O. . . . . . . . . . . . . . . . . . . . .143
Lincoln Leader Lamp . . . . . . . . . . . . . .142
Lincoln Lamp . . . . . . . . . . . . . . . . . . . .143
Little Harry's Night Lamp . . . . . . . . . .212
Little Samuel Figures . . . . . . . . . . . . . .119
Lithophane . . . . . . . . . . . . . . . . . . . . . .187
Lomax, George . . .100, 118, 124, 132, 203
Lomax Utah Font . . . . . . . . . . . . . . . . .244
London Tea Company U.S.A. . . . . . . .201
Loomis Photography . . . . . . . . . . . .18, 19
Loop and Rib Band . . . . . . . . . . . . . . .109
Lovell, F. H. . . . . . . . . . . . . . . . . . . . . .104
Lovell, W. A. . . . . . . . . . . . . . . . . . . . . .137
Lovell . . . . . . . . . . . . . . . . . . . . .236, 244
Lovell Catalogue, 1868-69 . . . . . . . . . .186
Lovell & Co. Catalogue, 1877-78 . . . . .144
Lovell Drummond Radiator . . . . . . . . .245
Lovell Wholesale Price List, 1877-78 . .190
Lux-Dux Burners . . . . . . . . . . . . . . . . .235
Macbeth Co. . . . . . . . . . . . . . . . . . . . . .233
Mackenzie House Museum . . . . . . . . .236
Magnifying Lens . . . . . . . . . . . . . . . . .234
Maize Lamps . . . . . . . . . . . . . . . . . . . .129
Make-dos . . . . . . . . . . . . . . . . . . .228-229
Marks Samuels Patent Model . . . . . . . . .77
Manhattan Brass Co. . . . . . . . . . .214, 215
Matches and Match Holders . . . . .230-232
Mather, John A. . . . . . . . . . . . . . . . .47-50
May, S. Elwood . . . . . . . . . . . . . . .133-135
Mayflower . . . . . . . . . . . . . . . . . . . . . .150
May Lamp . . . . . . . . . . . . . . . . . . . . . .138
Mechanical Lamps . . . . . . . . . . . .130, 139
Mechanical Lamp Patents . . . . . . .266, 267
Melville, David . . . . . . . . . . . . . . . . . . .32
Meriden Britannia Co. . . . . . . . .157, 161
*Meriden Britannia Silver Plate*
    *Treasury* . . . . . . . . . . . . . . . . . . . . . .161
Meriden Flint Glass Co. . . . . . . . . . . . .245
Merrill, R.S. . . . . . . . . . . . . . . . . . . . . .100
Merrill, Rufus Spaulding . . . . . . . . . . . .40
Metal Finishes . . . . . . . . . .106, 169, 170
Mica Chimney . . . . . . . . . . . . . . . . . . .107
Miller, Edward . . . . . . . . . . . . . . .141, 198
Minerva Goblet . . . . . . . . . . . . . . . . . . .91
Minerva Lamp . . . . . . . . . . . . . . . . . . . .91
M. H. Collins Patent Model
    Chimney and Burner . . . . . . . . . . . .71

Miniature & Night Lamps . . . . . .208-212
Moehring Mineral Sperm Lamp . . . . . . .40
Morse, Edward F. . . . . . . . . . . . . . . . . . .76
Mrs. Potts Sad Iron . . . . . . . . . . . . . . . .226
Mt. Washington . . . . . . . . . . . .18, 23, 100,
                      152, 247, 248
Mt. Washington #209 Font . . . . . . . . . .19
Mt. Washington Blown Fonts . . . . . . . . .19
Mt. Washington Brownie Lamp . . . . . .153
Mt. Washington Cameo Glass Shade . .205
Mt. Washington Fonts . . . . . . . . . . . . .112
Mount Washington Glass
    Company . . . . . . . .18, 22, 113, 152, 153
Mt. Washington Howe . . . . . . . . . . . . . .18
Mt. Washington Pressed Fonts . . . . . . . .18
Mt. Washington Shades . . . . . . . . .185, 202
Munn & Co. . . . . . . . . . . . . . . . . . . . . . .65
Museum of the Visitation de
    Mount de Chantal . . . . . . . . . . . . . .119
Myrtle . . . . . . . . . . . . . . . . . . . . . . . . . .93
National Burner . . . . . . . . . . . . . . . . . .209
National Museum of American
    History . . . . . . . . . . . . . . . . . . . . . . .30
Neilson, George . . . . . . . . . . . . . . . . . . .63
Ne Plus Ultra Burners . . . .62, 63, 209, 241
Neverout Safety Lantern . . . . . . . . . . . .220
New Calcium Light Burner 1870
New England Glass Co. . . . . . . . . .105, 194
New England Peach Blow
    Hobnail Shade . . . . . . . . . . . . . . . .198
New Ideal Lamp . . . . . . . . . . . . . . . . . .134
Nickel-Plate Glass Co. . . . . . . . . . . . . .111
Night Lamps and Miniatures . . . . . . . .208
Night Lamps . . . . . . . . . . . . . . . . .29, 212
No-Chimney Eagle Burner . . . . . . . . . .209
Non-explosive . . . . . . . . . . . . . . . . . . . .41
Oglebay Institute Mansion House
    School . . . . . . . . . . . . . . . . . . . . . . .119
Olmstead, L. H. . . . . . . . . . . . . . . . . . .212
Onion Lamp . . . . . . . . . . . . . . . . . . . . .127
Optic Screw Socket Lamps . . . . . . . . .109
Oregon Shades . . . . . . . . . . . . . . .246-247
Orpen Patent . . . . . . . . . . . . . . . . . . . .172
Owl Lamp . . . . . . . . . . . . . . . . . . . . . . .20
Pairpoint Orchid Parlour Lamp . . . . . .154
Paper Lamps . . . . . . . . . . . . . . . . . . . .107
Papier Mache Lamp . . . . . . . . . . . . . . .107
Parker & Whipple . . . . . . . . . . . . . . . .100
Parker Hanging Lamps . . . . . . . . . . . . .197
Parker Lamp . . . . . . . . . . . . . . . . . . . .198
Parlour Lamps . . . . . . . . . . .140, 141, 150,
                 151, 154, 156, 157
Pashley, George . . . . . . . . . . . . . . . . . .244
*Patent Gazettes* . . . . . . . . . . . . . . . . . . .65
Patented Lighting . . . . . . . . . . . . . . .65-78
Patent Lamps . . . . . . . . . . . . . . . . . . . . .27
Patent Models . . . . . . . . . . .69-78, 80
Patent Office Reports . . . . . . . . . . . . . . .65
Pennsylvania Historical &
    Museum Commission . . . . . .47, 49, 50
Perfect Lamp Chimney Stove . . . . . . . .213
Perkins, John M. . . . . . . . . . . . . . . . . . . .70
Perkins, Orson N. . . . . . . . . . . . . . . . . . .70
Perkins & House Argand Table Lamp . .106
Perkins and House Patent Models . . . . . .70
Petroleum . . . . . . . . . . . . . . . . . . . . .39, 40
Phoenix Glass Co. . . . . . . . . . . . . . . . .154
Photography . . . . . . . . . . . . . . . . . . . . . .7
Piano Lamps . . . . . . . . . . . . . . . . .160, 161
Pillar-molded . . . . . . . . . . . . . . . . . . . . .31
Pillar-mold Font . . . . . . . . . . . . . . . . . .115
Pithole Creek . . . . . . . . . . . . . . . . . . . . .49
Platt, Dr. A. H. . . . . . . . . . . . . . . . . . . . .69
Plume & Atwood Manufacturing
    Co. . . . . . . . . . . . . . . . . . . . . . .159, 238

Plume & Atwood Prong Burners . . . . . .239
Plume & Atwood Prong Burners
    Basic Construction . . . . . . . . . . . . . .240
Porter, J. . . . . . . . . . . . . . . . . . . . . . . . .28
Pre-kerosene Glass Lamps . . . . . . . . . . .30
Princess Lamp . . . . . . . . . . . . . . . . . . .129
Prisms and Diamond Point . . . . . . . . . .18
Prong Burners . . . . . . . . . . . . . . . . . . .239
Pucca Lamp . . . . . . . . . . . . . . . . . . . . .139
Punkah Top . . . . . . . . . . . . . . . . . . . . .139
Pursell, Jesse . . . . . . . . . . . . . . . . . . . . .52
Putnam & Co. . . . . . . . . . . . . . . . . . . .209
Queen Victoria . . . . . . . . . . . . . . . .10, 25
Rakow Library (Corning Museum) . . . . .18
Reach, Robert . . . . . . . . . . . . . . . . . . . .41
Reddick, James . . . . . . . . . . . . . . . . . . .98
Reichman, Christian . . . . . . . . . . . . . . .60
Reighard, Jacob . . . . . . . . . . . . . . . . . .126
Reversible Drummond Radiator . . . . . .245
Ridge, Joseph . . . . . . . . . . . . . . . . . . . .62
Ripple and Swirl . . . . . . . . . . . . . . . . . .15
Ripley, Daniel C. . . . . . . . . .80, 83-85, 89
Ripley, Daniel C. Sr. . . . . . . . . . . . . . . .80
Ripley & Co. . . . . . . . . .80, 82, 84-88, 103
Ripley's Fancy Lamp . . . . . . . . . . . . . . .87
Ripley Metal-band Lamp . . . . . . . . . . . .81
Ripley Patented Glass Font . . . . . . . . . .182
Ripley Patent Hand Lamp . . . . . .81, 103
Ripley Patent Model . . . . . . . . . . . . . . .87
Ripley Patent Pending . . . . . . . . . . . . . .81
Ripley's Two-handled Tableware Set . . .82
Ripley's Warrior Lamp . . . . . . . . . . . . .86
Ripley Wedding Lamp . . . . . . . . .82, 100
Rival Library Lamp . . . . . . . . . . . . . . .194
Robertson, R. J. . . . . . . . . . . . . . . . . . .208
Rochester Lamp Frame . . . . . . . . . . . . .198
Rochester Spring Fixture Library
    Lamp . . . . . . . . . . . . . . . . . . . . . . .201
Roelofs, Anthony . . . . . . . . . . . . . . . . .175
Roelofs Smith Patent Bracket . . . . . . .175
Rogers Smith & Co. . . . . . . . . . . . . . . .157
Rogers Brothers . . . . . . . . . . . . . . . . . .157
Rorke Combination Globe . . . . . . . . . .245
Rosecrans, General William S. . . . . . . . .69
Royal Flemish . . . . . . . . . . . . . . . . . . .152
Royal Ontario Museum . . . . . . . . . . . . .17
Russell & Erwin 1865
    Catalogue . . . . . . . . .43, 61, 66, 181, 185
Russell & Erwin Manufacturing Co. . .166
Rust, Samuel . . . . . . . . . . . . . . . . . . . . .30
Sandblasted Glass . . . . . . . . . . . . . . . . .21
Samuel Rust Lard Lamp . . . . . . . . . . . .29
Sandwich Glass Co. . . . . . . . . . . .23, 149
Sandwich Historical Society Glass
    Museum . . . . . . . .19, 82, 131, 135, 136,
            141, 144, 149, 167, 212, 238
Sangster, J. . . . . . . . . . . . . . . . . . . . . . .209
Sargent, R.W. . . . . . . . . . . . . . . . . . . . .30
Savage, J. B. . . . . . . . . . . . . . . . . . . . . .76
Savage & Hawley Burner . . . . . . . . . . .212
Savage & Morse . . . . . . . . . . . . . . . . . .76
Schneider, B.B. . . . . . . . . . . . . . . . . . .244
*Scientific American* . . . . . . . . . . . . .65, 66
Scoville Burners . . . . . . . . . . . . . . . . . .239
Scroll and Rib . . . . . . . . . . . . . . . .99, 120
Seidensticker, Frederick R. . . . . . . . . .182
Selleck, D. . . . . . . . . . . . . . . . . . . . . . .209
Shades . . . . . . . . . . . . . . . . . . . .205, 244
Shaffer, Henry E. . . . . . . . . . . . . . . . . .142
Shanks, Thomas . . . . . . . . . . . . . . . . . .23
Shaw, W. F. . . . . . . . . . . . . . . . . . . . . .60
Sherwoods Special Service Outfit . . . . .139
Shield and Star Make-Do lamp . . . . . .228
Shirley, F. S. . . . . . . . . . . . . . . . .23, 100
Shirley, Frederick S. . . . . . . . . . . . . . . .22

Slocomb, Samuel .................37
Smith, L. C. ....................236
Smith, Roland H. .................99
Smith, W. H. ...............179, 236
Smithsonian Institution ..........78
Solar Lamps ................34, 144
Spalding, R. H. ..................28
Spencer, C. F. ..............142, 159
Squat Shades ...................248
S. R. Bowie & Co. ...............141
Southland Catalogue, 1859 ........43
Spencer Lamp ...................142
Student Lamps ....140, 142, 143, 158, 159
Star and Punty ..............30, 112
Star in Circle ...................21
Star Tumbler Lantern ............216
Starr, Wm. H. ...................27
Starr 1861 Catalogue ............166
Stevens, G. M. ..................107
Stevens, John ..................217
Stevens/Dietz Lantern ...........217
Summer Girl Kerosene Heater .....226
Surprise Burner ................193
Syphon Study Lamp .............142
Textured Gold and Polychrome
   Vase Lamp ..................154
The City Mfg. Co. ..............179
The Florence Machine Co. .......222
The Harden Hand Fire
   Extinguisher Co. ............108
The Hubbard Spencer, Bartlett & Co.
   Catalogue circa 1900 ........259
The Kerosene Lamp Heater Co. ....72
The Little Light Increaser .......234
The National Archives ...........30
The New Dyott Burner ...........241
The New England Glass Co. ...68, 113
The New York Kerosene Oil Co. ....39

The Patent Mechanical Lamp Co. ...131
The Strong Museum .........138, 153
The Taylor & Boggs Fdy Co. .......226
The Union Glass Co. Catalogue ....254
The Yale Clock Co. ..............100
The Wanzer Lamp Co. .......137, 138
Thos. Evans Co. .................129
Thomas, L. H. ..................107
Thomas, Seth ...................100
Thousand Eye with Diamond and Dot ..92
Thousand Eye Pattern (Sensation) ....93
Tiffany Lamp ...................155
Time-Indicating Night Lamps ......210
Tisdel & Nash Burner ...........209
Trimmings ..................241, 242
Triple Dolphin Base ..............43
Triple Diamond Medallion .........43
Triple Flue and Bar ..............97
Triple Peg and Loop ..............16
Tucker Mfg. Co. Vase Lamp .......106
Tucker .........................186
Tucker, Hiram ..........184, 202, 204
Tucker Mfg. Co. ................202
U.S. Fish and Wildlife Service .....51
Union Attachment ...............213
Union Glass Co. ......30, 40, 118, 159
Union Night Lamp ..............212
United States Glass Co. .....31, 80, 117
U.S. Glass Company
   Catalogue ........111, 119, 262, 263
Van Kirk & Fulton ...............60
Van Kirk Burners ................63
Vase Lamps ....................141
Venetian Glass Parlour Lamp .....154
Veronica .......................55
Vogeley, Samuel G. ............88, 89
Vogeley-Adams Patent ...........88
Votti, Carl .....................244

Waffle Cube ...................183
Waisted-Loop ...................29
Wallace & Sons Extension Lamp ...193
Wall Lamps ................166, 178
Wanzer, E. M. .................138
Wanzer Patent Portable Cooker ...138
Wanzer Sidewinder lamp ........137
Waterman, Chas. ................42
Wanzer, Richard Mott ..........137
Wanzer Lamps .........137, 138, 139
Wanzer Lamp and Cooker Co. ....138
Washington Beck ............22, 230
Watch Pocket Lamp .............227
Web Vase Lamp .................92
Wedding Lamp ..................83
Wedekind, Gustav ...............60
Wellington County Museum ......139
Welsbach .......................32
Westmoreland ...................24
Wheeler Reflector Co. ..........176
Wheeler Stand, Wall or
   Hand Lamp ..............176, 177
White Base Lamps ..............125
Whitney, Henry .............68, 113
W. L. Libbey & Son Co. .........129
Wilmot, S.R. ..................143
Willson, Thomas ................32
Wire Frame Extension Lamp ......194
Withmar, Arnold ................75
Wm. Carlton Co. ................32
Wooden Patterns ................16
Wood Lamps ...................107
Wright, M. B. ..................60
Wrought iron ..............188, 189
Yarmouth County Museum ........96
Zouave ........................18

# ☩ Value Guide

It should be stressed that this is a guide, not a price list. In the past, some values have climbed dramatically while others have changed little. There are too many unpredictable factors that affect change and while over a hundred years of experience have been averaged here, it is possible that an individuals "best guess" could be more accurate in some instances.

When a book is first prepared and a selection of examples that have heretofore never been pictured or described is presented, it is almost impossible to gauge the response of collectors and dealers. So many factors are to be considered and they are measured in different ways. Beauty, utility, craftmanship, historical significance, novelty, and rarity are all assessed and are all subject to personal preferences.

The items are noted with a low end value. A collector may feel quite secure in assuming that price is reasonable. The base price on the other hand may prove to be a real bargain if the lamp becomes popular and a demand is created.

The collectors and dealers who have contributed their considerable expertise and time to prepare this Value Guide are: Joanne and Gerry Bloxam, Larry DeCan, Drs. Lawrence B. and Susan Everett, Dr. Richard Miller, Lela and Darrel Sago, Jack Washka, and Eileen White. Collectively, their experience covers all of the United States and Canada.

Lamps in public collections and some in private collections are not priced, nor are those in advertisements and catalogue illustrations.

The value of trimmings (all parts other than the basic lamp itself) have risen significantly and may exceed the value of the lamp itself. *The lamps in this guide are valued for the most part without trimmings.* The exceptions are lamps with matching shades or chimneys, or pre-kerosene ones with original or appropriate burners. Most of these are noted WT (with trimmings) or complete. All lamps valued are considered to be in good condition regardless of evident or possible flaws.

Current value ranges for some trimmings are given where pictured to give the reader some indication of how much it may cost to complete a lamp or how much should be factored into an appropriately completed lamp.

It is important to read, to understand, and to carefully review the factors involved in a value guide. A few oft repeated maxims are worth repeating: A little knowledge is a dangerous thing and buyer beware!

Rely upon your own knowledge and seek reliable dealers who will provide a written money-back guarantee. Shop with confidence and *enjoy your collecting!*

Common generic abbreviations are:

| | |
|---|---|
| Ala. | Alabaster |
| Att. | Atterbury |
| B&H | Bradley & Hubbard |
| B&S | Boston & Sandwich |
| MTW | Mt. Washington |
| NEG | New England Glass |
| PM. | Patent Model |
| Rip. | Ripley |

Page

| | | |
|---|---|---|
| 14 | Small early glass lamps | $75.00+ |
| | miniature fluid lamp WT | 225.00+ |
| 15a. | Butterflies and Bows | 150.00+ |
| b. | Heart base with Circle Band font | 75.00+ |
| c. | Bullseye and Fleur-de-Lis | 150.00+ |
| d. | Ripple & Swirl | 150.00+ |
| 16a. | Wooden pattern | 175.00+ |
| b. | Triple Peg and Loop lamp | 150.00+ |
| 17a. | Wooden Pattern | 175.00+ |
| 18a. | MTW Howe WT | 450.00+ |
| 19b. & c. | MTW fonts only | 50.00+ |
| d. | MTW #209 WT | 500.00+ |

| | | |
|---|---|---|
| 20a. | Owl lamp | $900.00+ |
| b. | Quad Loop lamp WT | 500.00+ |
| c. | Etched crown shade | 150.00+ |
| d. | Squat shade — decorated | 75.00+ |
| 21 | Star in Circle font | 50.00+ |
| | Chimney only | 150.00+ |
| 22 | Deer, Dog and Warrior lamp | 250.00+ |
| | Fine line decoration shade | 300.00+ |
| 23 | Deer, Dog and Warrior lamp with patented match holder base | 350.00+ |
| | Fine line decoration chimney | 400.00+ |
| 24a. | Westmoreland | 150.00+ |
| | Chimneyless burner | 30.00+ |
| b. | Center Medallion | 135.00+ |
| 26b. | Double Crusie | 125.00+ |
| 29a. | Free-blown night lamp with burner | 225.00+ |
| b. | Pressed Ala. hand lamp | 350.00+ |
| c. | Waisted Loop hand lamp with burner | 325.00+ |
| d. | Houghton & Wallace lard lamp | 200.00+ |
| f. | Kinnear lard lamp | 250.00+ |
| g. | Rust lard lamp | 275.00+ |
| 30 | Pre-kerosene lamps WT, if in good condition | |
| a. | | 450.00+ |

b. . . . . . . . . . . . . . . . . . . . . . . . . . . . . 400.00+

c. . . . . . . . . . . . . . . . . . . . . . . . . . . . . 375.00+

d. . . . . . . . . . . . . . . . . . . . . . . . . . . . . 450.00+

31 Pillar-molded lamp with fluid burner . . . . . . . . 100+0.00+

34 Solar lamp . . . . . . . . . . . . . . . . . . . . . 1200.00+

35a, b, c. Girandole set . . . . . . . . . . . . . . . . . . . 800.00+

d. Peg lamp . . . . . . . . . . . . . . . . . . . . . 75.00+

e. Girandole as shown . . . . . . . . . . . . . 6500.00+

36a. Dodge-type lamp . . . . . . . . . . . . . . . 350.00+

b. J. F. Dodge lamp . . . . . . . . . . . . . . . . 300.00+

c. J. F. Dodge Font . . . . . . . . . . . . . . . 175.00+

37d. Dodge-type lamp only . . . . . . . . . . . . 250.00+

Dodge-type lamp WT . . . . . . . . . . . 450.00+

e. Dodge-type lamp . . . . . . . . . . . . . . . 250.00+

f. E. P. Dodge lamp only . . . . . . . . . . . 325.00+

Dodge-type lamp WT . . . . . . . . . . . 750.00+

38 Dodge-type lamp only . . . . . . . . . . . 1200.00+

Dodge-type lamp WT . . . . . . . . . . . 1650.00+

40 Downer lamp incomplete . . . . . . . . . . 250.00+

65 Atterbury Pressed Boss lamp . . . . . . . 125.00+

69 PM Platt & Rosecrans . . . . . . . . . . . . 650.00+

70a. PM Blake's lamp chimney . . . . . . . . . 350.00+

b. PM Perkins shade holder . . . . . . . . . . . 75.00+

c. PM House shadeholder . . . . . . . . . . . . 75.00+

71 PM Collins burner and chimney . . . . . 300.00+

72 PM Greene chimney-top heater . . . . . . 125.00+

PM Fish lamp chimney heater . . . . . . . 200.00+

74a. PM Greenfield & Fry chimney &

extra part . . . . . . . . . . . . . . . . . . . . . 200.00+

c. PM Bartholomew chimney . . . . . . . . . 150.00+

75 PM Hughes lantern . . . . . . . . . . . . . . 300.00+

76 PM Savage & Morse Wick Raiser . . . . 125.00+

77 PM Samuels lamp . . . . . . . . . . . . . . . 400.00+

79 Atterbury composite lamp only . . . . . . 175.00+

Atterbury composite lamp WT . . . . . . 400.00+

80 PM Ripley lamp with iron handle . . . . 400.00+

81 Ripley iron handle lamps:

a. . . . . . . . . . . . . . . . . . . . . . . . . . . . . 250.00+

b. . . . . . . . . . . . . . . . . . . . . . . . . . . . . 275.00+

c. . . . . . . . . . . . . . . . . . . . . . . . . . . . . 275.00+

d. . . . . . . . . . . . . . . . . . . . . . . . . . . . . 300.00+

82 Ripley tableware set: . . . . . . . . . . . . . 325.00+

Individual pieces @ . . . . . . . . . . . . . . 125.00+

Ripley Wedding lamp with match

cover and trimmings . . . . . . . . . . . . 5000.00+

84 Ripley & Duncan double handle lamps:

b. . . . . . . . . . . . . . . . . . . . . . . . . . . . . 150.00+

c. . . . . . . . . . . . . . . . . . . . . . . . . . . . . 150.00+

d. . . . . . . . . . . . . . . . . . . . . . . . . . . . . 125.00+

e. . . . . . . . . . . . . . . . . . . . . . . . . . . . . 150.00+

single handle lamps:

f. . . . . . . . . . . . . . . . . . . . . . . . . . . . . 275.00+

g. . . . . . . . . . . . . . . . . . . . . . . . . . . . . 325.00+

85 Ripley & Duncan double handle lamps:

h. . . . . . . . . . . . . . . . . . . . . . . . . . . . . 300.00+

i. . . . . . . . . . . . . . . . . . . . . . . . . . . . . 200.00+

j. . . . . . . . . . . . . . . . . . . . . . . . . . . . . 175.00+

unusual double handle:

k. . . . . . . . . . . . . . . . . . . . . . . . . . . . . 350.00+

l. . . . . . . . . . . . . . . . . . . . . . . . . . . . . 250.00+

m. . . . . . . . . . . . . . . . . . . . . . . . . . . . . 200.00+

86a. Ripley Warrior lamp . . . . . . . . . . . . . . 600.00+

d. Ripley patented font . . . . . . . . . . . . . 125.00+

87a. Ripley patent lamp only: . . . . . . . . . . 175.00+

b. Ripley patent lamp only . . . . . . . . . . . 200.00+

c. Ripley PM . . . . . . . . . . . . . . . . . . . . . 300.00+

88a. Adam's Bouquet lamp . . . . . . . . . . . . 200.00+

b. Adam's Vase lamp . . . . . . . . . . . . . . . 300.00+

89d. Adam's Temple or Applesauce lamp complete

clear . . . . . . . . . . . . . . . . . . . . . . . . . 1000.00+

color . . . . . . . . . . . . . . . . . . . . . . . . 1250.00+

e. Adam's Corner Windows complete . . 175.00+

90a. Bradford variant black base . . . . . . . . . 375.00+

b. Bradford variant complete . . . . . . . . . . 175.00+

91a. Minerva . . . . . . . . . . . . . . . . . . . . . . . 500.00+

92a. Thousand Eye pictured . . . . . . . . . . . . 275.00+

b. Web Vase lamp . . . . . . . . . . . . . . . . . 900.00+

93 Adams Ten Panel

a. . . . . . . . . . . . . . . . . . . . . . . . . . . . . 150.00+

b. . . . . . . . . . . . . . . . . . . . . . . . . . . . . 150.00+

c. . . . . . . . . . . . . . . . . . . . . . . . . . . . . 125.00+

d. Adams plain iron handle lamp . . . . . . . 300.00+

e. Grape and Festoon lamp only . . . . . . . 350.00+

94a. Adams-Bridges Reeded Handle . . . . . 150.00+

b. Adams-Bonshire white patent lamp . . 600.00+

c. Adams-Bonshire clear patent lamp . . . 125.00+

95a. Adams bracket font . . . . . . . . . . . . . . . 225.00+

b. Adams white hand lamp . . . . . . . . . . . 700.00+

97c. Triple Flute and Bar canary . . . . . . . . . 650.00+

Triple Flute and Bar canaryWT . . . . . . 800.00+

d. Triple Flute and Bar opaque white gilt 375.00+

Triple Flute and Bar opaque white gilt

WT . . . . . . . . . . . . . . . . . . . . . . . . . . 700.00+

98a. Atterbury blue and white tulip . . . . . . 1600.00+

99 Atterbury Swans:

a. Smith patent amber base . . . . . . . . . . 1500.00+

b. Transparent blue base . . . . . . . . . . . . . 1600.00+

c. All clear with Scroll font . . . . . . . . . . 2000.00+

d. Pink Alabaster base with white Alabaster

Swan font . . . . . . . . . . . . . . . . . . . . 2500.00+

e. One-piece all clear . . . . . . . . . . . . . . . 1600.00+

f. All Ala. . . . . . . . . . . . . . . . . . . . . . . 1500.00+

| | | |
|---|---|---|
| 100+a. | Atterbury Saucer base with Scroll font 250.00+ | |
| | Atterbury/Dithridge chimney . . . . . . . 350.00+ | |
| b. | Atterbury/Merrill Clock lamp . . . . . . . 800.00+ | |
| c. | Atterbury Eureka base . . . . . . . . . . . . 150.00+ | |
| d. | and page 101 Ripley/Atterbury Wedding | |
| | lamp only . . . . . . . . . . . . . . . . . . . . . 3000.00+ | |
| | Dated F. S. Shirley/ MTW chimneys, | |
| | pair . . . . . . . . . . . . . . . . . . . . . . . . . . 600.00+ | |
| 101 | Lamp only . . . . . . . . . . . . . . . . . . . . . 3000.00+ | |
| | Pair dated fine line chimneys . . . . . . . . 700.00+ | |
| 102a. | Atterbury Figural with Vine Font . . . . 600.00+ | |
| b. | Figure only . . . . . . . . . . . . . . . . . . . . . 125.00+ | |
| e. | Spelter Figural lamp . . . . . . . . . . . . . . 175.00+ | |
| 103 | Atterbury, Ripley & Duncan lamps in color | |
| a. | Single handle . . . . . . . . . . . . . . . . . . 1800.00+ | |
| b. | Single handle . . . . . . . . . . . . . . . . . . 1800.00+ | |
| c. | Single handle . . . . . . . . . . . . . . . . . . 2000.00+ | |
| d. | Single Handle . . . . . . . . . . . . . . . . . . 2000.00+ | |
| e. | Double handle . . . . . . . . . . . . . . . . . . 2200.00+ | |
| f. | Double Handle . . . . . . . . . . . . . . . . . . 800.00+ | |
| g. | Shoe — amber . . . . . . . . . . . . . . . . . 800.00+ | |
| h. | Shoe — blue . . . . . . . . . . . . . . . . . . . 900.00+ | |
| i. | Double-handle, amethyst and gold . . 1500.00+ | |
| 104a. | Atterbury Star lamp only . . . . . . . . . . 800.00+ | |
| b. | Atterbury Star lamp only . . . . . . . . . . 950.00+ | |
| c. | Alabaster composite lamp . . . . . . . . . 750.00+ | |
| d. | White alabaster Hearts and Stars | |
| | with lavender base . . . . . . . . . . . . . . 650.00+ | |
| e. | with black base . . . . . . . . . . . . . . . . . 700.00+ | |
| 105f. | Bohemian font with white base . . . . . 300.00+ | |
| g. | Bohemian font with streaked base . . . . 350.00+ | |
| h. | Bohemian font with NEG gilt base . . . 500.00+ | |
| i. | Late composite lamp only . . . . . . . . . 325.00+ | |
| | Late composite lamp WT . . . . . . . . . . 475.00+ | |
| 106a. | Iden figural lamp only . . . . . . . . . . . . . 650.00+ | |
| | Iden figural lamp WT . . . . . . . . . . . . . 950.00+ | |
| b. | Cast-iron vase lamp only . . . . . . . . . . 325.00+ | |
| c. | Perkins & House lamp complete . . . . . 375.00+ | |
| d. | Glass Beer Barrel lamp . . . . . . . . . . . 350.00+ | |
| e. | Metal Beer Barrel lamp . . . . . . . . . . . 300.00+ | |
| 107b. | Stevens wooden patent lamp only . . . . 450.00+ | |
| d. | Wooden lamp only . . . . . . . . . . . . . . . 350.00+ | |
| | WT . . . . . . . . . . . . . . . . . . . . . . . . . . 500.00+ | |
| e. | Wooden lamp only . . . . . . . . . . . . . . . 500.00+ | |
| | WT . . . . . . . . . . . . . . . . . . . . . . . . . . 600.00+ | |
| f. | Wooden lamp only . . . . . . . . . . . . . . . 350.00+ | |
| | WT . . . . . . . . . . . . . . . . . . . . . . . . . . 525.00+ | |
| g. | Wooden lamp only . . . . . . . . . . . . . . . 350.00+ | |
| | WT . . . . . . . . . . . . . . . . . . . . . . . . . . 575.00+ | |
| h. | Paper lamp . . . . . . . . . . . . . . . . . . . . 150.00+ | |
| | WT . . . . . . . . . . . . . . . . . . . . . . . . . . 300.00+ | |

| | | |
|---|---|---|
| i. | Papier Mache lamp . . . . . . . . . . . . . . . 225.00+ | |
| j. | Wooden match-safe . . . . . . . . . . . . . . 250.00+ | |
| 108a. | Early blue hand lamp only . . . . . . . . . . 450.00+ | |
| b. | Early looped hand lamp . . . . . . . . . . . 1800.00+ | |
| c. | Colored chimneys, from . . . . . . . . . . . 150.00+ | |
| | to . . . . . . . . . . . . . . . . . . . . . . . . . . . 300.00+ | |
| d. & e. | White and blue lamps only@ . . . . . . . . 625.00+ | |
| f. | Glass hand grenade . . . . . . . . . . . . . . 125.00+ | |
| 109b. | Hobbs ruby font stand lamp only . . . . 700.00+ | |
| c. | Hobbs ruby "COTTAGE" lamp | |
| | complete . . . . . . . . . . . . . . . . . . . . . . 3000.00+ | |
| d. | Hobbs gray base . . . . . . . . . . . . . . . . . 225.00+ | |
| e. | Hobbs chocolate base . . . . . . . . . . . . . 350.00+ | |
| 110 | Hobbs plunger-pressed patterns with clinch | |
| | connectors lamps only | |
| a. | Veronica . . . . . . . . . . . . . . . . . . . . . . 175.00+ | |
| b. | Bellflower . . . . . . . . . . . . . . . . . . . . . 325.00+ | |
| c. | Hearts Under Glass . . . . . . . . . . . . . . 225.00+ | |
| f. | Hobbs blue base . . . . . . . . . . . . . . . . . 275.00+ | |
| g. | Hobbs white base . . . . . . . . . . . . . . . . 250.00+ | |
| 111a. | Banbury blue opalescent . . . . . . . . . . . 650.00+ | |
| b. | Banbury white opalescent . . . . . . . . . . 650.00+ | |
| | WT . . . . . . . . . . . . . . . . . . . . . . . . . . 1000.00+ | |
| 112a. | Early composite lamp only . . . . . . . . 2500.00+ | |
| | WT . . . . . . . . . . . . . . . . . . . . . . . . . . 2900.00+ | |
| b. | Early composite lamp only . . . . . . . . 450.00+ | |
| c. | Early lamp only . . . . . . . . . . . . . . . . 325.00+ | |
| d. | Base only . . . . . . . . . . . . . . . . . . . . . . 75.00+ | |
| e. | . . . . . . . . . . . . . . . . . . . . . . . . . . . . 175.00+ | |
| f. | . . . . . . . . . . . . . . . . . . . . . . . . . . . . 250.00+ | |
| g. | . . . . . . . . . . . . . . . . . . . . . . . . . . . . 275.00+ | |
| 114 | Hobbs composite lamps a . . . . . . . . . . 225.00+ | |
| b. | . . . . . . . . . . . . . . . . . . . . . . . . . . . . 200.00+ | |
| c. | . . . . . . . . . . . . . . . . . . . . . . . . . . . . 175.00+ | |
| | Hobbs plunger-pressed lamps | |
| d. | . . . . . . . . . . . . . . . . . . . . . . . . . . . . 150.00+ | |
| e. | . . . . . . . . . . . . . . . . . . . . . . . . . . . . 150.00+ | |
| 115 | Hobbs pillar mold . . . . . . . . . . . . . . . . 350.00+ | |
| 116 | Hobbs composite lamps | |
| a. | . . . . . . . . . . . . . . . . . . . . . . . . . . . . 150.00+ | |
| b. | . . . . . . . . . . . . . . . . . . . . . . . . . . . . 150.00+ | |
| c. | Hobbs one-piece lamp . . . . . . . . . . . . 100.00+ | |
| d. | Adams one-piece lamp . . . . . . . . . . . . 100.00+ | |
| 117 | Hobbs Fruit Medallion | |
| f. | all-glass . . . . . . . . . . . . . . . . . . . . . . 150.00+ | |
| g. | composite lamp . . . . . . . . . . . . . . . . . 225.00+ | |
| 118 | Hobbs stand lamps | |
| a. | . . . . . . . . . . . . . . . . . . . . . . . . . . . . 300.00+ | |
| b. | . . . . . . . . . . . . . . . . . . . . . . . . . . . . 150.00+ | |
| c. | . . . . . . . . . . . . . . . . . . . . . . . . . . . . 150.00+ | |

119 Hobbs Hand lamps
   d. ............................. 275.00+
   e. ............................. 275.00+
   f. ............................. 300.00+
120 Atterbury stand lamp
   a. ............................. 325.00+
   Atterbury hand lamp
   b. ............................. 175.00+
121 Atterbury lamps
   a. ............................. 125.00+
   b. ............................. 140.00+
   c. ............................. 850.00+
   d. ............................. 125.00+
   e. ............................. 125.00+
122 Atterbury hand lamps
   a. ............................. 900.00+
   c. ............................. 150.00+
   d. ............................. 100.00+
   e. ............................. 175.00+
123 Atterbury hand lamps
   a. ............................. 350.00+
   b. ............................. 350.00+
   c. ............................. 350.00+
   d. ............................. 300.00+
124 Atterbury stand lamps
   a. ............................. 225.00+
   b. ............................. 150.00+
   c. ............................. 175.00+
   d. ............................. 125.00+
   e. ............................. 125.00+
125 Atterbury stand lamps
   f. ............................. 225.00+
   g. ............................. 225.00+
   h. ............................. 200.00+
   WT ............................. 375.00+
126 Atterbury Hercules
   a. ............................. 1000.00+
   Atterbury Tucker font
   c. ............................. 120.00+
127 Eaton/Onion variations
   a. ............................. 5000.00+
   b. ............................. 2000.00+
   c. ............................. 2000.00+
   d. ............................. 250.00+
   WT ............................. 400.00+
128 Iron base lamps
   a. ............................. 400.00+
   WT ............................. 575.00+
   b. ............................. 250.00+
   WT ............................. 400.00+

131 Mechanical lamps
   b. ............................. 950.00+
   c. ............................. 1300.00+
132 Mechanical lamps
   a. ............................. 750.00+
   c. ............................. 750.00+
133 Mechanical lamp
   b. ............................. 600.00+
   c. ............................. 450.00+
134 Mechanical lamp ................. 600.00+
   WT ............................. 750.00+
135 Mechanical hanging lamp .......... 750.00+
137 Mechanical lamp
   b. ............................. 500.00+
138 Mechanical lamp
   b. ............................. 500.00+
139 Mechanical lamp kit complete ...... 750.00+
140 Banquet lamp. See p 146 d.
142b. Spencer lamp complete ............ 300.00+
143 Leader lamp complete ............. 750.00+
145 Early banquet lamps all WT
   a. ............................. 2800.00+
   b. ............................. 3000.00+
   c. ............................. 3000.00+
   d. ............................. 3000.00+
   A reminder: Trimmings include the burner,
   chimney, shade holder, shade and prisms.
   Chimneys and shades have been reproduced.
146 Banquet and parlour lamps with trimmings.
   a. ............................. 825.00+
   b. ............................. 2800.00+
   c. ............................. 825.00+
   d. ............................. 825.00+
   e. ............................. 1000.00+
   f. ............................. 2200.00+
147 Banquet lamp complete ........... 1500.00+
148 Banquet & parlour lamps complete as shown
   a. ............................. 650.00+
   b. ............................. 700.00+
   c. ............................. 650.00+
   d. ............................. 550.00+
149 Parlour and vase lamps complete as shown
   a. ............................. 450.00+
   c. ............................. 600.00+
150 Parlour and vase lamps complete as shown
   a. ............................. 300.00+
   b. ............................. 300.00+
   c. ............................. 350.00+
   d. ............................. 350.00+
   e. ............................. 375.00+

151  Parlour lamps as shown
   a. . . . . . . . . . . . . . . . . . . . . . . . . . . . . . .350.00+
   c. . . . . . . . . . . . . . . . . . . . . . . . . . . .3500.00+

154  Parlour lamps as shown
   a. . . . . . . . . . . . . . . . . . . . . . . . . . . . .950.00+
   b. . . . . . . . . . . . . . . . . . . . . . . . . . . .6500.00+
   c. . . . . . . . . . . . . . . . . . . . . . . . . . . .7500.00+
   d. . . . . . . . . . . . . . . . . . . . . . . . . . . . .550.00+
   e. . . . . . . . . . . . . . . . . . . . . . . . . . . .5500.00+

155  Tiffany lamps
   a. . . . . . . . . . . . . . . . . . . . . . . . . . .15000.00+
   b. . . . . . . . . . . . . . . . . . . . . . . . . . .22000.00+

156b. Vase lamp only . . . . . . . . . . . . . . . .550.00+
   c. Composite lamp only . . . . . . . . . . . . .750.00+
   d. Griffon shade . . . . . . . . . . . . . . . . . .450.00+
     B&H lamp complete . . . . . . . . . . . . . .1500.00+

157  Meriden vase lamps with original burners
   a. . . . . . . . . . . . . . . . . . . . . . . . . . . . .450.00+
     Shade only . . . . . . . . . . . . . . . . . . . .950.00+
   b. . . . . . . . . . . . . . . . . . . . . . . . . . . . .450.00+
     Shade only . . . . . . . . . . . . . . . . . . . .650.00+

158  Student lamps complete as shown
   a. . . . . . . . . . . . . . . . . . . . . . . . . . . .2500.00+
   b. . . . . . . . . . . . . . . . . . . . . . . . . . . .1800.00+
   c. . . . . . . . . . . . . . . . . . . . . . . . . . . . .600.00+
   d. . . . . . . . . . . . . . . . . . . . . . . . . . . .2000.00+
   e. . . . . . . . . . . . . . . . . . . . . . . . . . . .1200.00+

159  Student lamps complete as shown
   a. . . . . . . . . . . . . . . . . . . . . . . . . . . .1500.00+
   b. . . . . . . . . . . . . . . . . . . . . . . . . . . .6000.00+
   c. . . . . . . . . . . . . . . . . . . . . . . . . . . .8000.00+
   d. . . . . . . . . . . . . . . . . . . . . . . . . . . . .650.00+
   e. . . . . . . . . . . . . . . . . . . . . . . . . . . .1400.00+

160  Piano lamp complete
   a. . . . . . . . . . . . . . . . . . . . . . . . . . . .2500.00+
   b. Piano lamp complete . . . . . . . . . . . . .900.00+

168  Hanging Angle lamp . . . . . . . . . . . . .900.00+
     WT . . . . . . . . . . . . . . . . . . . . . . . . . .300.00+

171  Tubular hand lamp complete . . . . . . . .150.00+

173  Baccarat squat shade . . . . . . . . . . . . .175.00+

174  Bracket, Bacon patent . . . . . . . . . . . .250.00+

175  Bracket lamp, Roelofs patent
     with font . . . . . . . . . . . . . . . . . . . . .475.00+

177  Wheeler Reflector lamp . . . . . . . . . . .350.00+

178  Wall lamps as shown
   a. . . . . . . . . . . . . . . . . . . . . . . . . . . . .100.00+
   b. . . . . . . . . . . . . . . . . . . . . . . . . . . . .125.00+
   c. . . . . . . . . . . . . . . . . . . . . . . . . . . . .125.00+
   d. . . . . . . . . . . . . . . . . . . . . . . . . . . . .125.00+
   f. . . . . . . . . . . . . . . . . . . . . . . . . . . . .250.00+

179  Brass bracket lamps. Fonts complete as shown
   a. . . . . . . . . . . . . . . . . . . . . . . . . . . . .250.00+

   b. . . . . . . . . . . . . . . . . . . . . . . . . . . . .250.00+
   Bracket
   c. . . . . . . . . . . . . . . . . . . . . . . . . . . . .250.00+
   d. . . . . . . . . . . . . . . . . . . . . . . . . . . . .225.00+

180  Thurber patent brackets
   a. . . . . . . . . . . . . . . . . . . . . . . . . . . . .400.00+
   b. . . . . . . . . . . . . . . . . . . . . . . . . . . . .350.00+
   c. . . . . . . . . . . . . . . . . . . . . . . . . . . . .350.00+
     reflector . . . . . . . . . . . . . . . . . . . . . . .85.00+
     lamp . . . . . . . . . . . . . . . . . . . . . . . . .700.00+
     U.S. Mail train decorated chimney . . .600.00+

181  Bracket lamps complete
   a. . . . . . . . . . . . . . . . . . . . . . . . . . . . .500.00+
   b. . . . . . . . . . . . . . . . . . . . . . . . . . . . .300.00+

182  Bracket lamps complete,
   a. . . . . . . . . . . . . . . . . . . . . . . . . . . . .700.00+
   b. . . . . . . . . . . . . . . . . . . . . . . . . . . . .750.00+

183a. Font etc., complete as shown . . . . . . . .700.00+
   b. Bracket only . . . . . . . . . . . . . . . . . . .250.00+

184a. Double bracket lamp . . . . . . . . . . . . .750.00+
     WT, Pair of Jones burners and
     4" shade holders . . . . . . . . . . . . . . . .400.00+
     pair of lip chimneys . . . . . . . . . . . . . .150.00+
     matched pair Oregon shades . . . . . . . .300.00+
     Single bracket lamps as shown
   b. . . . . . . . . . . . . . . . . . . . . . . . . . . . .350.00+
   c. . . . . . . . . . . . . . . . . . . . . . . . . . . . .250.00+
   d. . . . . . . . . . . . . . . . . . . . . . . . . . . . .200.00+
   e. . . . . . . . . . . . . . . . . . . . . . . . . . . . .325.00+
   f. . . . . . . . . . . . . . . . . . . . . . . . . . . . .250.00+
   g. . . . . . . . . . . . . . . . . . . . . . . . . . . . .200.00+

185  Early hall and hanging lamps as shown
   a. . . . . . . . . . . . . . . . . . . . . . . . . . . . .550.00+
   b. . . . . . . . . . . . . . . . . . . . . . . . . . . .1000.00+
   c. . . . . . . . . . . . . . . . . . . . . . . . . . . . .650.00+
   d. . . . . . . . . . . . . . . . . . . . . . . . . . . . .850.00+

186  Early brass harp only . . . . . . . . . . . . .250.00+
     WT, Font . . . . . . . . . . . . . . . . . . . . . .50.00+
     smoke bell . . . . . . . . . . . . . . . . . . . .125.00+
     Early Jones burner . . . . . . . . . . . . . . .200.00+
     Shade holder 5" . . . . . . . . . . . . . . . . .200.00+
     Scarce Oregon shade with 5" base . . .350.00+
     Tall frosted chimney . . . . . . . . . . . . . .125.00+
     Fitter is a description that came into
     use with electric lighting.

187  Hall lamps
   a. . . . . . . . . . . . . . . . . . . . . . . . . . . . .650.00+
   c. . . . . . . . . . . . . . . . . . . . . . . . . . . . .500.00+

188  Fancy Iron lamps
   a. . . . . . . . . . . . . . . . . . . . . . . . . . . . .325.00+
   b. . . . . . . . . . . . . . . . . . . . . . . . . . . . .225.00+
   d. . . . . . . . . . . . . . . . . . . . . . . . . . . . .200.00+

e. . . . . . . . . . . . . . . . . . . . . . . . . . . . . . . . 250.00+

189 Ives hanging lamps

a. . . . . . . . . . . . . . . . . . . . . . . . . . . . . . . . 800.00+

c. . . . . . . . . . . . . . . . . . . . . . . . . . . . . . . . 700.00+

190 B&H iron hanging lamps

a. . . . . . . . . . . . . . . . . . . . . . . . . . . . . . . . 700.00+

b. . . . . . . . . . . . . . . . . . . . . . . . . . . . . . . . 800.00+

191 Bohner hanging lamps

a. . . . . . . . . . . . . . . . . . . . . . . . . . . . . . . . 650.00+

b. . . . . . . . . . . . . . . . . . . . . . . . . . . . . . . . 950.00+

192 Centennial hanging lamp . . . . . . . . . . 750.00+

193 Wallace and Sons hanging lamp . . . . . 625.00+

194 Wire frame hanging lamp

a. . . . . . . . . . . . . . . . . . . . . . . . . . . . . . . . 725.00+

c. Ball shade hanging lamp . . . . . . . . . 2500.00+

195 Library lamps.

a. . . . . . . . . . . . . . . . . . . . . . . . . . . . . . . . 4500.00+

b. . . . . . . . . . . . . . . . . . . . . . . . . . . . . . . . 3500.00+

c. . . . . . . . . . . . . . . . . . . . . . . . . . . . . . . . 1800.00+

196 Library lamps

a. . . . . . . . . . . . . . . . . . . . . . . . . . . . . . . . 3000.00+

b. . . . . . . . . . . . . . . . . . . . . . . . . . . . . . . . 2500.00+

c. . . . . . . . . . . . . . . . . . . . . . . . . . . . . . . . 3500.00+

d. . . . . . . . . . . . . . . . . . . . . . . . . . . . . . . . 5500.00+

197 Library lamp . . . . . . . . . . . . . . . . . . . 2500.00+

198 Library lamps

a. . . . . . . . . . . . . . . . . . . . . . . . . . . . . . . . 5000.00+

b. . . . . . . . . . . . . . . . . . . . . . . . . . . . . . . . 4500.00+

199 Library lamps

a. . . . . . . . . . . . . . . . . . . . . . . . . . . . . . . . 4500.00+

b. . . . . . . . . . . . . . . . . . . . . . . . . . . . . . . . 4500.00+

c. . . . . . . . . . . . . . . . . . . . . . . . . . . . . . . . 4500.00+

d. . . . . . . . . . . . . . . . . . . . . . . . . . . . . . . . 6500.00+

e. . . . . . . . . . . . . . . . . . . . . . . . . . . . . . . . 6500.00+

f. . . . . . . . . . . . . . . . . . . . . . . . . . . . . . . . 7000.00+

200+ Library lamps

a. . . . . . . . . . . . . . . . . . . . . . . . . . . . . . . . 5000.00+

b. . . . . . . . . . . . . . . . . . . . . . . . . . . . . . . . 4000.00+

c. . . . . . . . . . . . . . . . . . . . . . . . . . . . . . . . 2200.00+

d. . . . . . . . . . . . . . . . . . . . . . . . . . . . . . . . 2800.00+

201 Library lamp . . . . . . . . . . . . . . . . . . . 6500.00+

202 Two-arm chandeliers as shown

a. . . . . . . . . . . . . . . . . . . . . . . . . . . . . . . . 1800.00+

b. . . . . . . . . . . . . . . . . . . . . . . . . . . . . . . . 1400.00+

c. . . . . . . . . . . . . . . . . . . . . . . . . . . . . . . . 1800.00+

203 Three-arm chandeliers as shown

a. . . . . . . . . . . . . . . . . . . . . . . . . . . . . . . . 1650.00+

b. . . . . . . . . . . . . . . . . . . . . . . . . . . . . . . . 2500.00+

c. . . . . . . . . . . . . . . . . . . . . . . . . . . . . . . . 2500.00+

204 Three-arm chandelier as shown

a. . . . . . . . . . . . . . . . . . . . . . . . . . . . . . . . 2200.00+

205 Art Glass shades. These have been seen priced between . . . . . . . . . . . . . . . . . . 150.00+
and . . . . . . . . . . . . . . . . . . . . . . . . . . . . . 800.00+

206 & 207 Rare art glass library lamp shades. This type of shade is found in a wide range of quality, colors, and design. Some are unique while others are relatively common. There are also reproductions available. These factors and collector preferences have produced a range in values from . . . . . . . . . . . . . . . . . . . . . 500.00+
to . . . . . . . . . . . . . . . . . . . . . . . . . . . . . 4500.00+
Purchases should be made carefully and wisely.

208a. Miniatures and night lamps. Small brass lamps in excellent original condition . . . . . . . . . . . . . . . . . . . . . . . . 75.00+
worn finish brass . . . . . . . . . . . . . . . . . . 25.00+
Hutchinson burners — mint . . . . . . . . . 95.00+
worn or used . . . . . . . . . . . . . . . . . . . . . 50.00+

b. Bloxam miniature . . . . . . . . . . . . . . . . 450.00+
large flat hand . . . . . . . . . . . . . . . . . . . 650.00+
Bloxam small stand . . . . . . . . . . . . . . . 600.00+

c. Glow lamps — clear . . . . . . . . . . . . . . 75.00+
All or part white . . . . . . . . . . . . . . . . . . 90.00+
colored . . . . . . . . . . . . . . . . . . . . . . . . . 150.00+

d. Reproduction burners . . . . . . . . . . . . . 25.00+
old burners . . . . . . . . . . . . . . . . . . . . . . 35.00+

209 Small brass lamps see 208a.
Burners

a. . . . . . . . . . . . . . . . . . . . . . . . . . . . . . . . 125.00+

b. . . . . . . . . . . . . . . . . . . . . . . . . . . . . . . . 125.00+

c. . . . . . . . . . . . . . . . . . . . . . . . . . . . . . . . 60.00+

d. . . . . . . . . . . . . . . . . . . . . . . . . . . . . . . . 125.00+

e. . . . . . . . . . . . . . . . . . . . . . . . . . . . . . . . 125.00+

Small early night lamps f and g . . . . . . . 75.00+
Burners: Tisdel . . . . . . . . . . . . . . . . . . 150.00+
Ne Plus Ultra . . . . . . . . . . . . . . . . . . . . 350.00+

210 Time-Indicating Night Lamps . . . . . . . 200.00+

211 Candelabrum with candle lamps . . . . . 450.00+

212 Miniature lamps complete as shown

a. . . . . . . . . . . . . . . . . . . . . . . . . . . . . . . . 150.00+

b. . . . . . . . . . . . . . . . . . . . . . . . . . . . . . . . 150.00+

c. . . . . . . . . . . . . . . . . . . . . . . . . . . . . . . . 250.00+

f. Savage & Hawley burner . . . . . . . . . . 125.00+
lamp . . . . . . . . . . . . . . . . . . . . . . . . . . . 175.00+

214 Hurricane patent lantern

a. . . . . . . . . . . . . . . . . . . . . . . . . . . . . . . . 550.00+

215 Small lanterns as pictured

b. . . . . . . . . . . . . . . . . . . . . . . . . . . . . . . . 550.00+

c. . . . . . . . . . . . . . . . . . . . . . . . . . . . . . . . 350.00+

d. . . . . . . . . . . . . . . . . . . . . . . . . . . . . . . . 250.00+

e. . . . . . . . . . . . . . . . . . . . . . . . . . . . . . . . 250.00+

f. . . . . . . . . . . . . . . . . . . . . . . . . . . . . 250.00+
g. . . . . . . . . . . . . . . . . . . . . . . . . . . . . 250.00+
h. . . . . . . . . . . . . . . . . . . . . . . . . . . 1000.00+
i. . . . . . . . . . . . . . . . . . . . . . . . . . . . . 275.00+
j. . . . . . . . . . . . . . . . . . . . . . . . . . . . . 400.00+
216a. Tumbler lantern . . . . . . . . . . . . . . . . . 175.00+
d. Darkroom lantern . . . . . . . . . . . . . . . . . 75.00+
217a. Archer & Pancoast lantern . . . . . . . . . 150.00+
b. Stevens /Dietz lantern . . . . . . . . . . . . . 175.00+
218 Lantern footwarmer . . . . . . . . . . . . . . 250.00+
219 Lantern footwarmer . . . . . . . . . . . . . . 850.00+
220a. C. T. Ham lantern . . . . . . . . . . . . . . . 275.00+
b. bicycle lantern . . . . . . . . . . . . . . . . . . . 150.00+
221a. Stove lantern . . . . . . . . . . . . . . . . . . . 350.00+
b. Falls Heater . . . . . . . . . . . . . . . . . . . . . 250.00+
c. Electric lamp . . . . . . . . . . . . . . . . . . . . 175.00+
222d. Union stove . . . . . . . . . . . . . . . . . . . . 125.00+
225b. Fire Place Heater dated . . . . . . . . . . . 450.00+
c. Fire Place Heater undated . . . . . . . . . 450.00+
226b. Kerosene heater . . . . . . . . . . . . . . . . . 125.00+
227a. Watch pocket lamp . . . . . . . . . . . . . . . 850.00+
c. Make-do lamp . . . . . . . . . . . . . . . . . . . 125.00+
228 & 229 Make-do's
a. . . . . . . . . . . . . . . . . . . . . . . . . . . . . 175.00+
b. . . . . . . . . . . . . . . . . . . . . . . . . . . . . . 65.00+
c. . . . . . . . . . . . . . . . . . . . . . . . . . . . . . 65.00+
d. . . . . . . . . . . . . . . . . . . . . . . . . . . . . . 85.00+
e. . . . . . . . . . . . . . . . . . . . . . . . . . . . . . 85.00+
f. . . . . . . . . . . . . . . . . . . . . . . . . . . . . . 95.00+
g. . . . . . . . . . . . . . . . . . . . . . . . . . . . . 275.00+
h. . . . . . . . . . . . . . . . . . . . . . . . . . . . . 275.00+
i. . . . . . . . . . . . . . . . . . . . . . . . . . . . . 125.00+
230a. Splints-approximately 15 . . . . . . . . . . 45.00+
b. Early matches . . . . . . . . . . . . . . . . . . . 75.00+
Glass match holders
c. . . . . . . . . . . . . . . . . . . . . . . . . . . . . 125.00+
d. . . . . . . . . . . . . . . . . . . . . . . . . . . . . 150.00+
e. . . . . . . . . . . . . . . . . . . . . . . . . . . . . . 75.00+
231 Iron match holders
f. . . . . . . . . . . . . . . . . . . . . . . . . . . . . 130.00+
g. . . . . . . . . . . . . . . . . . . . . . . . . . . . . 175.00+

h. . . . . . . . . . . . . . . . . . . . . . . . . . . . . . 95.00+
i. . . . . . . . . . . . . . . . . . . . . . . . . . . . . . 75.00+
j. . . . . . . . . . . . . . . . . . . . . . . . . . . . . 175.00+
k. . . . . . . . . . . . . . . . . . . . . . . . . . . . . . 45.00+
232a. Insects, match holders . . . . . . . . . . 125.00+
novelties . . . . . . . . . . . . . . . . . . . . . . 125.00+
b. Float lamp . . . . . . . . . . . . . . . . . . . . . 250.00+
d. flower holder . . . . . . . . . . . . . . . . . . . 225.00+
233a. Lamp chimney heater . . . . . . . . . . . . . 175.00+
b. Chimney with curling iron heater . . . . 300.00+
Lamp only . . . . . . . . . . . . . . . . . . . . . . 75.00+
c. Chimney cleaning devices . . . . . . . . . . 50.00+
Lamp only . . . . . . . . . . . . . . . . . . . . . . 75.00+
234a. Jointed,curling tongs . . . . . . . . . . . . . . 65.00+
b. Magnifying lens . . . . . . . . . . . . . . . . . 125.00+
c. Chimney tidy . . . . . . . . . . . . . . . . . . . . 90.00+
d. Home-made safety cage for lamps . . . . 65.00+
240 P&A Fireside burners . . . . . . . . . . . . . 40.00+
Later prong burners . . . . . . . . . . . . . . . 15.00+
244 Lomax lamp . . . . . . . . . . . . . . . . . . . 125.00+
WT . . . . . . . . . . . . . . . . . . . . . . . . . . . 350.00+
245a. Rorke globe . . . . . . . . . . . . . . . . . . . . 350.00+
Bourne shade . . . . . . . . . . . . . . . . . . . 450.00+
246 4" Frosted shades
a. . . . . . . . . . . . . . . . . . . . . . . . . . . . . 125.00+
b. . . . . . . . . . . . . . . . . . . . . . . . . . . . . 225.00+
c. . . . . . . . . . . . . . . . . . . . . . . . . . . . . . 75.00+
3" & 3$^1$/$_2$" shades are much less
247 4" Frosted shades
a. . . . . . . . . . . . . . . . . . . . . . . . . . . . . 125.00+
b. . . . . . . . . . . . . . . . . . . . . . . . . . . . . 175.00+
c. . . . . . . . . . . . . . . . . . . . . . . . . . . . . 150.00+
d & e. . . . . . . . . . . . . . . . . . . . . . . . . . . . . 175.00+
f. . . . . . . . . . . . . . . . . . . . . . . . . . . . . 100.00+
g. . . . . . . . . . . . . . . . . . . . . . . . . . . . . 175.00+
h. . . . . . . . . . . . . . . . . . . . . . . . . . . . . 250.00+
248 Squat shades
a. . . . . . . . . . . . . . . . . . . . . . . . . . . . . 125.00+
b. . . . . . . . . . . . . . . . . . . . . . . . . . . . . 450.00+
c. . . . . . . . . . . . . . . . . . . . . . . . . . . . . 175.00+
d. . . . . . . . . . . . . . . . . . . . . . . . . . . . . 150.00+

ROCHESTER LAMP CO. 25 WARREN ST 1201 B. WAY WONDER OF THE WORLD

# Other Titles in this series from
# *Echo Point Books*

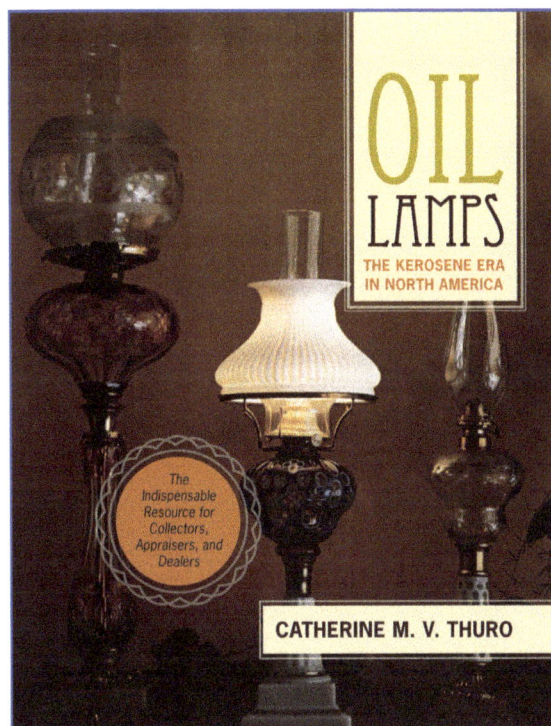

## Oil Lamps: The Kerosene Era in North America

*by Catherine M. V. Thuro*

An in-depth exploration of lamps of the Kerosene Age, this renowned work contains over 900 photographs, illustrations from catalogues and journals, and detailed descriptions of over 1000 lamp models. The definitive text on the subject, *Oil Lamps* is an invaluable resource for collectors, students, and researchers of early lighting in North America.

HARDCOVER ISBN 978-1-63561-072-7

## Oil Lamps II: Glass Kerosene Lamps

*by Catherine M. V. Thuro*

A great resource for oil lamp collectors and appreciators of fine glass antiques, part two of the *Oil Lamp* series is dedicated to the glass kerosene lamps that illuminated and decorated the spaces of yesteryear. The 200+ full color photographs and detailed descriptions artfully and accurately showcase these beautiful and rare lamps.

HARDCOVER ISBN 978-1-63561-068-0

Our books may be ordered from any bookstore or online purveyor of books, or directly through our Web site, www.echopointbooks.com. Or visit our retail store, located in Brattleboro, Vermont.